FAIRY TAIL

35

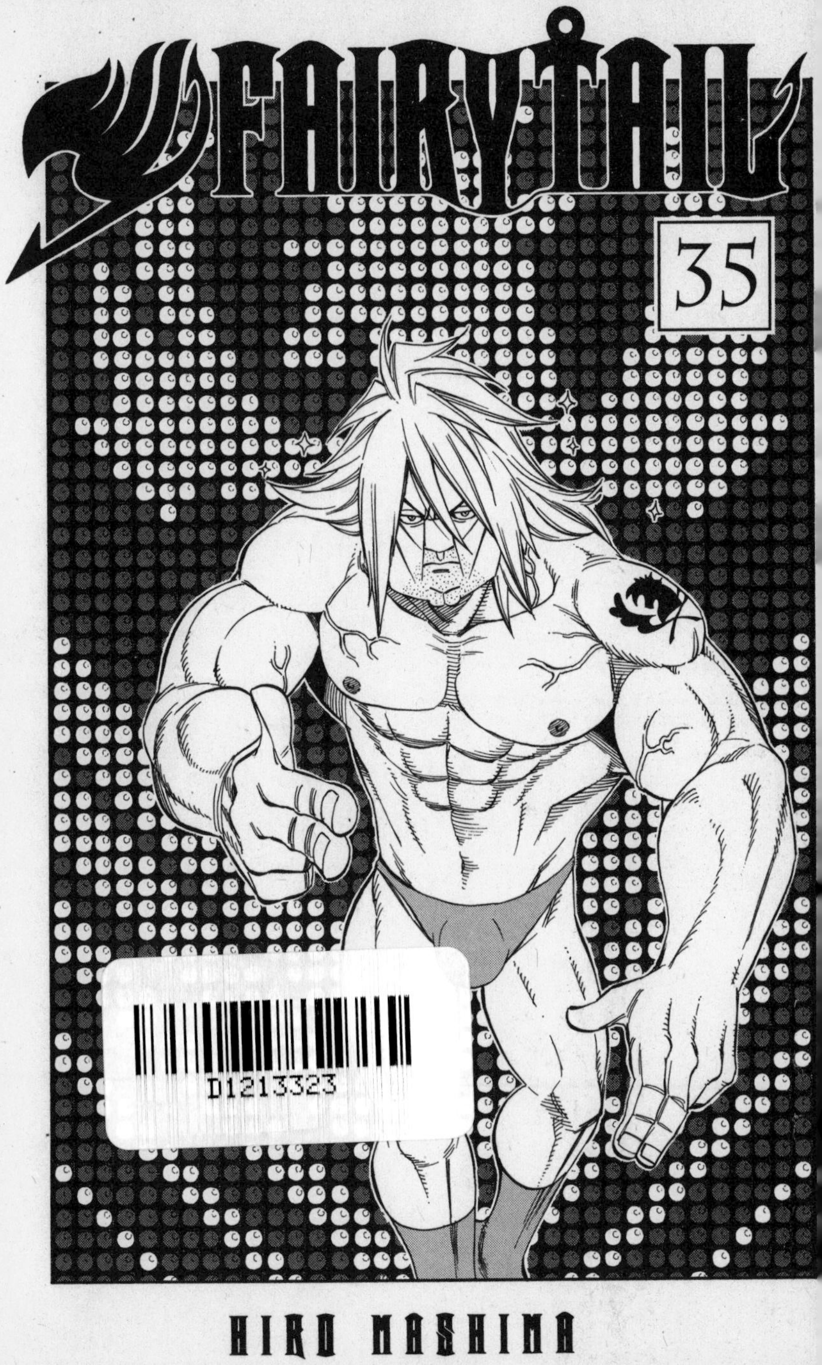

HIRO MASHIMA

FAIRY TAIL 35
CONTENTS

FAIRY TAIL
フェアリーテイル

Grand Magic Games Fourth Day Interim Results

1. Saber Tooth	34P+10	→	1. Saber Tooth	44P
2. Mermaid Heel	32P+3	→	2. Fairy Tail B	36P
3. Lamia Scale	31P+4	→	3. Mermaid Heel	35P
4. Fairy Tail B	30P+6	→	3. Lamia Scale	35P
5. Fairy Tail A	27P+8	→	3. Fairy Tail A	35P
6. Blue Pegasus	18P+2	→	6. Blue Pegasus	20P
7. Quatro Puppy	14P+1	→	7. Quatro Puppy	15P

Chapter 292: Thoughts Joined as One

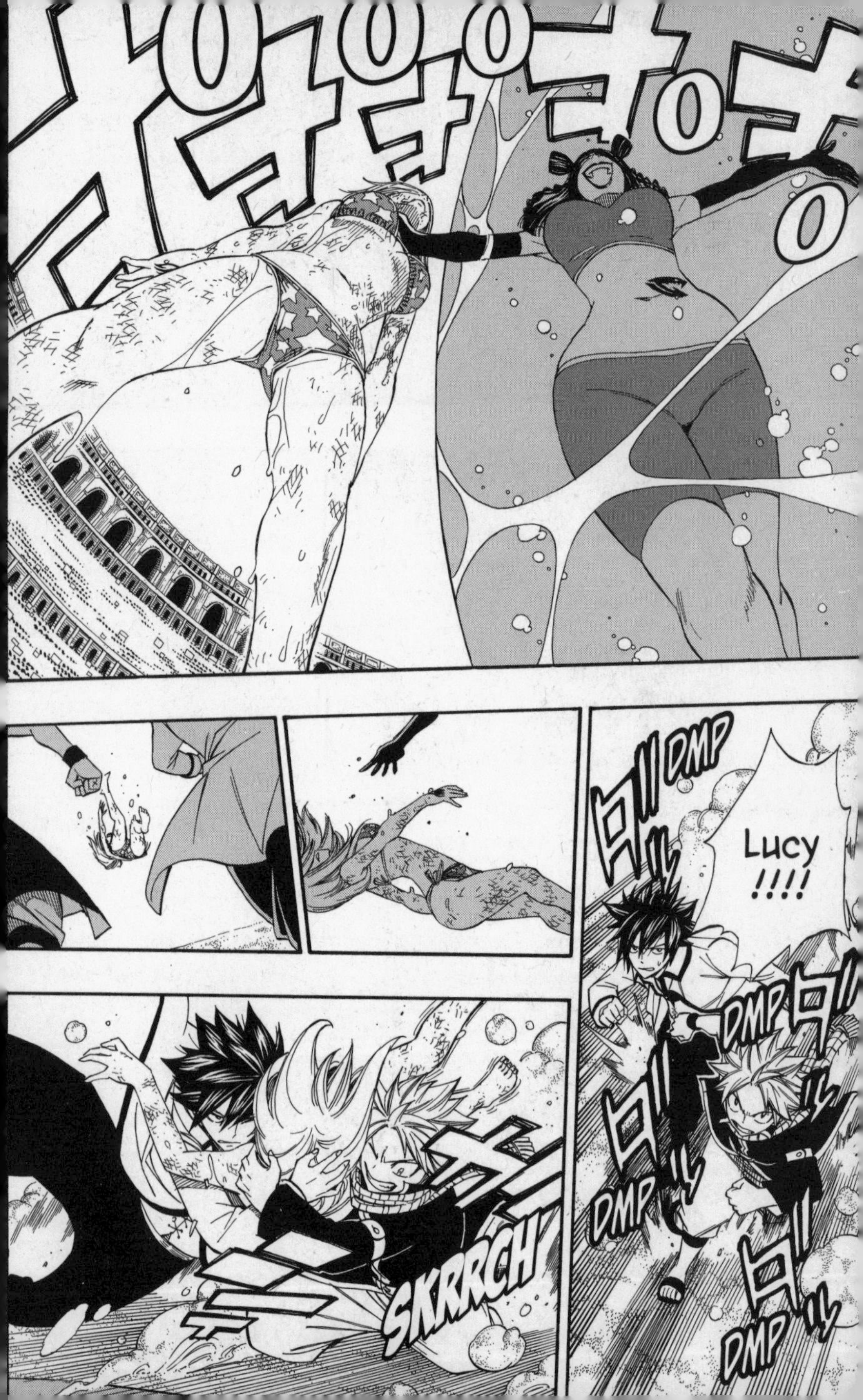
DMP
Lucy !!!!
DMP
DMP
DMP
SKRRCH

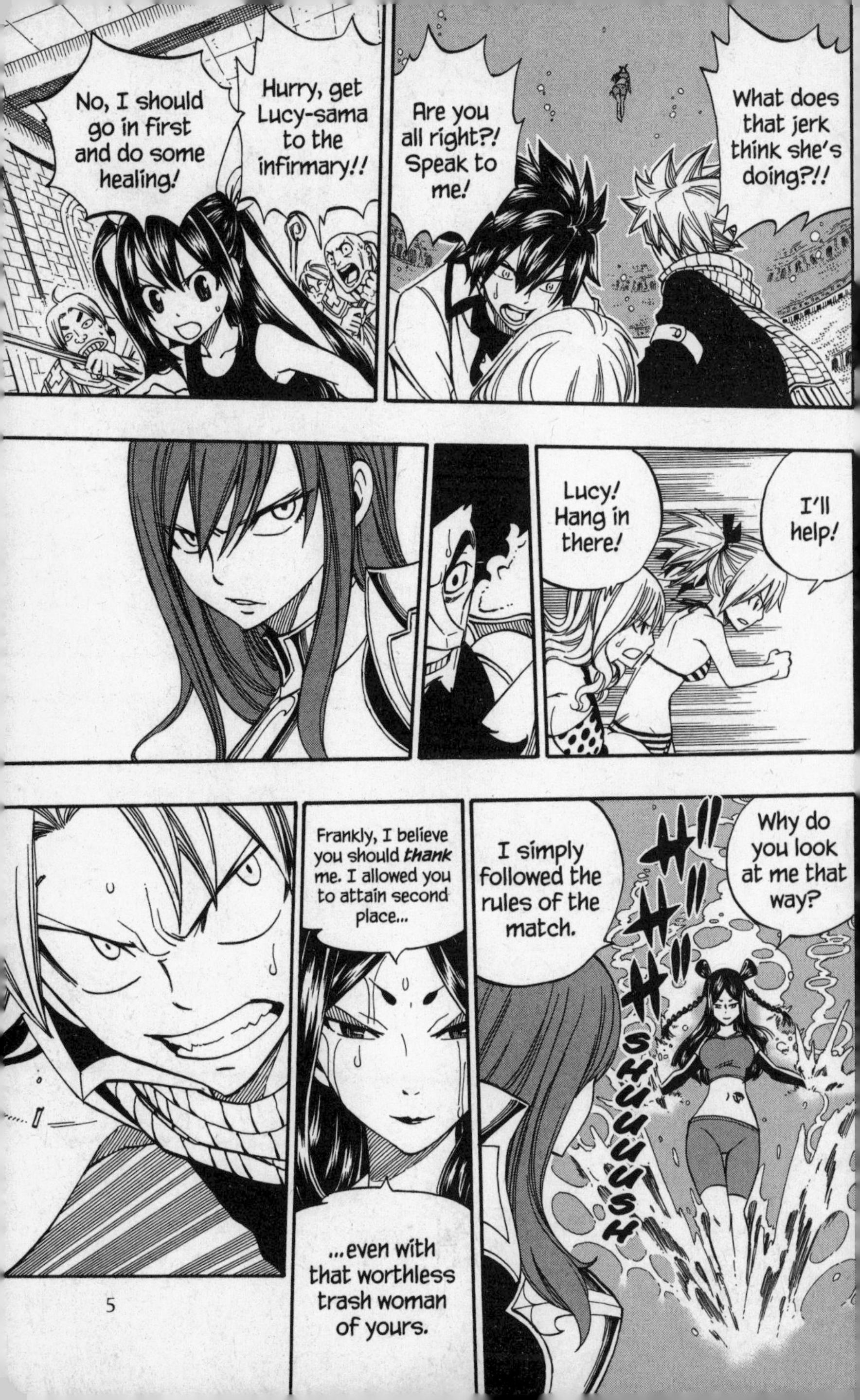
What does that jerk think she's doing?!!
Are you all right?! Speak to me!
Hurry, get Lucy-sama to the infirmary!!
No, I should go in first and do some healing!
I'll help!
Lucy! Hang in there!
Why do you look at me that way?
SHUUUUSH
I simply followed the rules of the match.
Frankly, I believe you should *thank* me. I allowed you to attain second place...
...even with that worthless trash woman of yours.

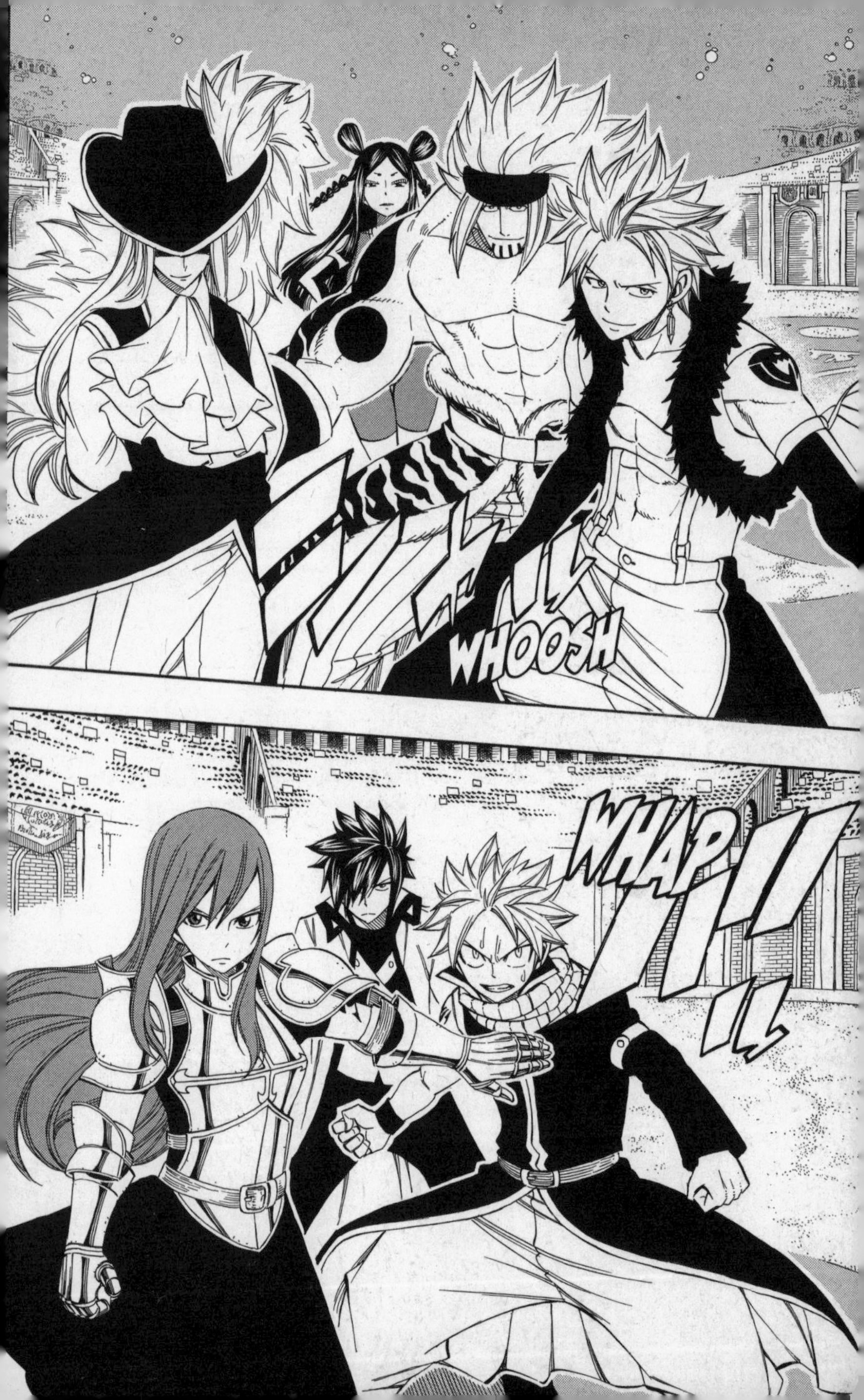
WHOOSH
WHAP!!

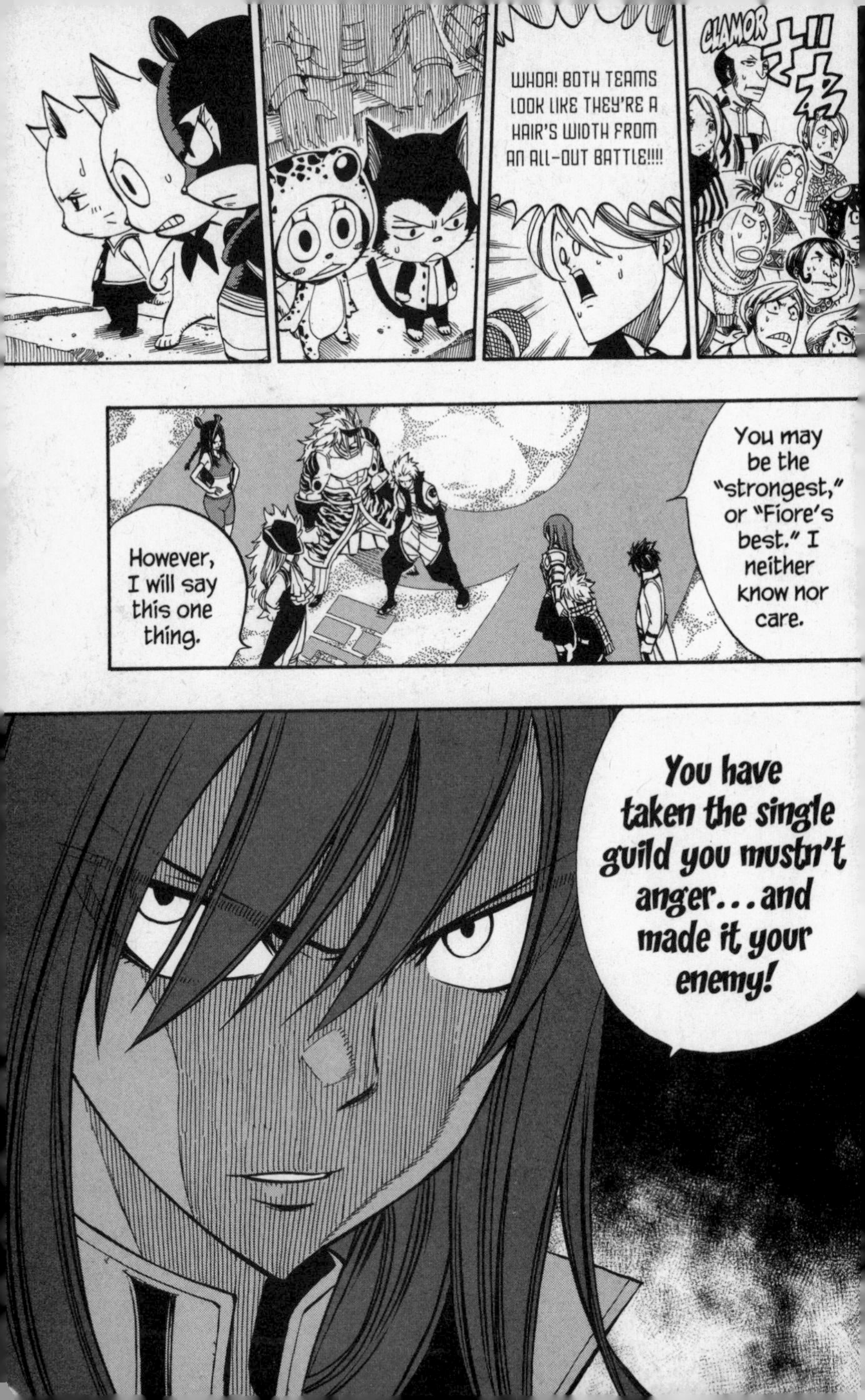
CLAMOR
WHOA! BOTH TEAMS LOOK LIKE THEY'RE A HAIR'S WIDTH FROM AN ALL-OUT BATTLE!!!!
You may be the "strongest," or "Fiore's best." I neither know nor care.
However, I will say this one thing.
You have taken the single guild you mustn't anger...and made it your enemy!

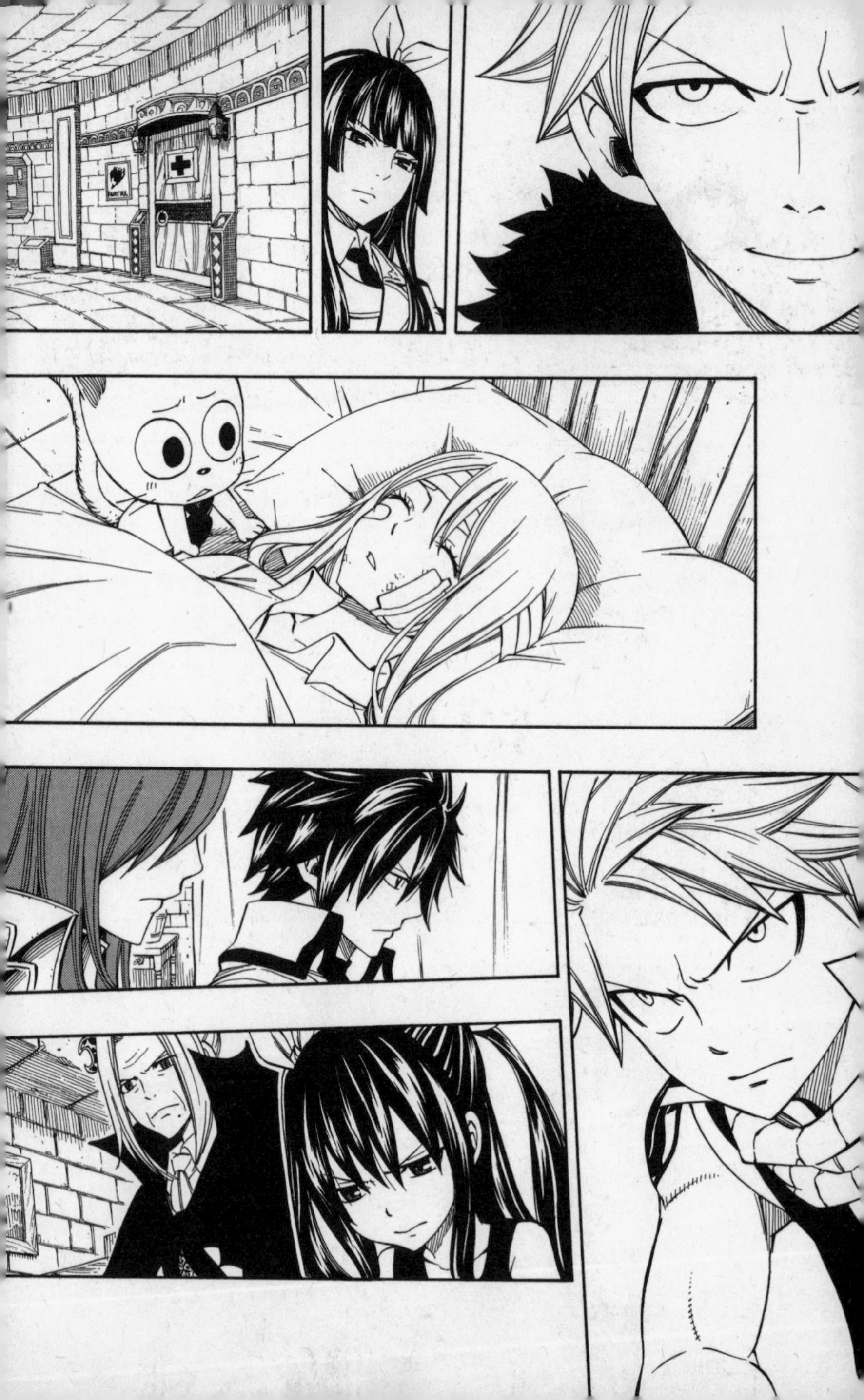

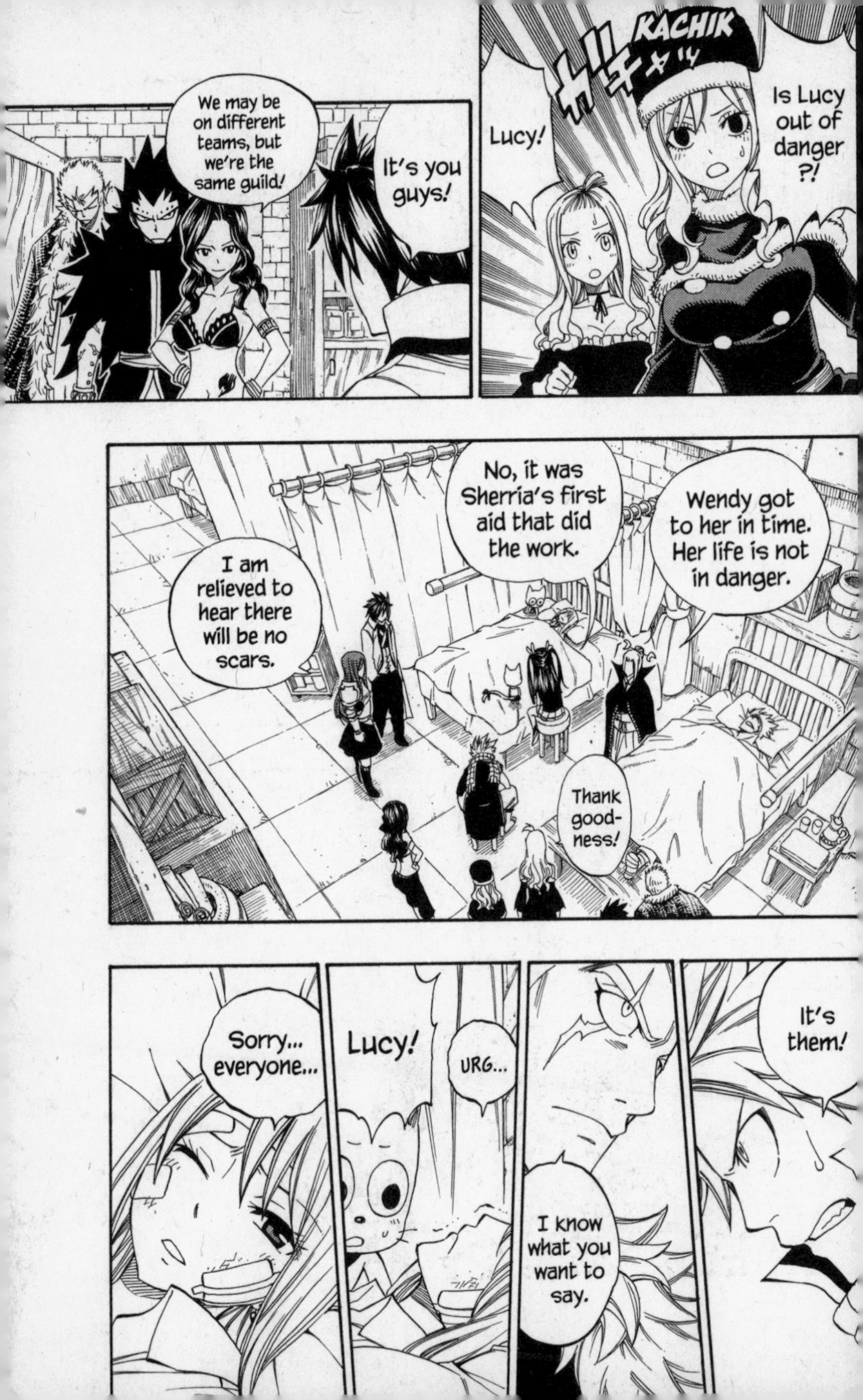
KACHIK
Is Lucy out of danger ?!
Lucy!
It's you guys!
We may be on different teams, but we're the same guild!
Wendy got to her in time. Her life is not in danger.
No, it was Sherria's first aid that did the work.
I am relieved to hear there will be no scars.
Thank good-ness!
It's them!
I know what you want to say.
URG...
Lucy!
Sorry... everyone...

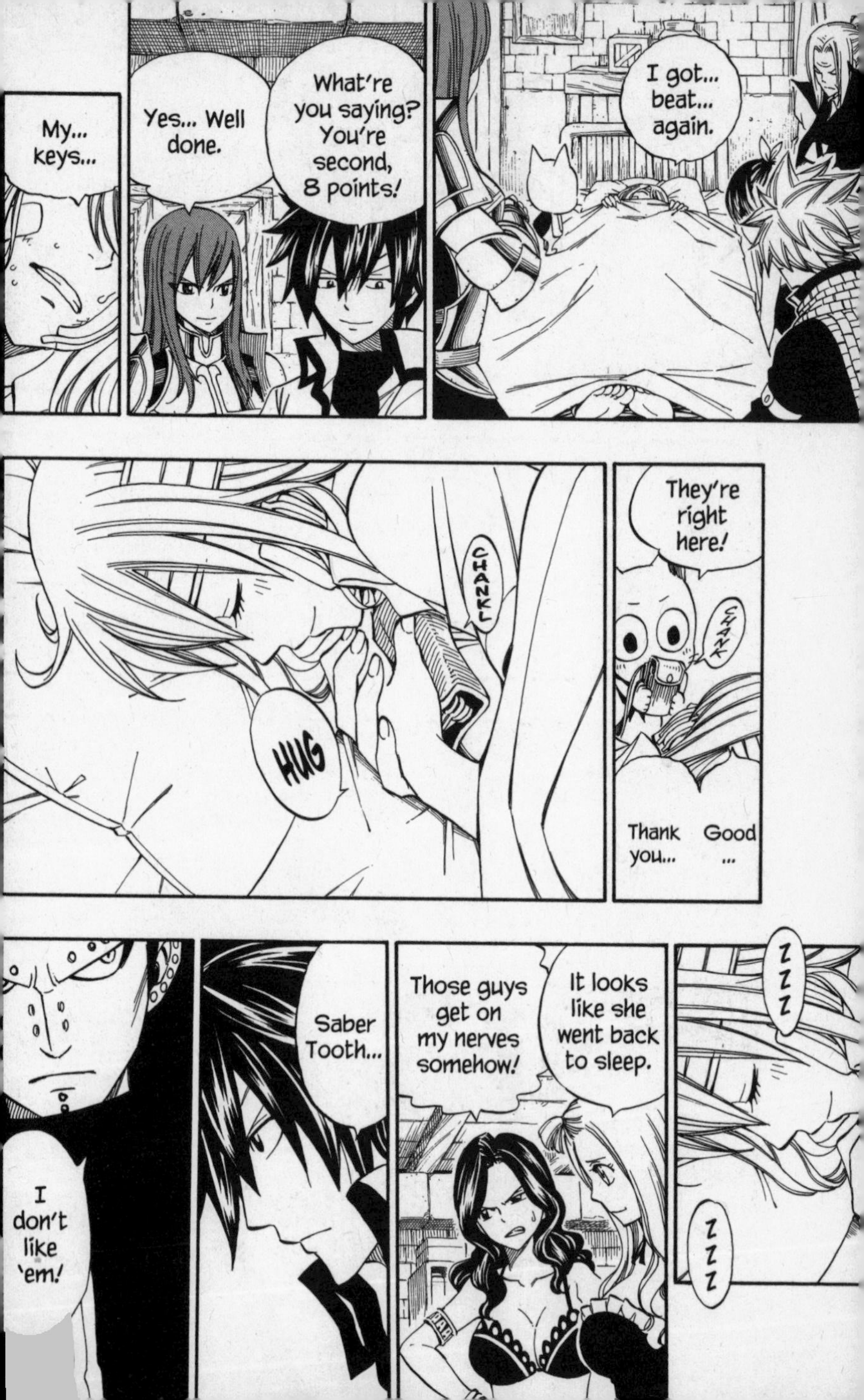
I got... beat... again.
What're you saying? You're second, 8 points!
Yes... Well done.
My... keys...
They're right here!
CHANK
Good ...
Thank you...
CHANK!
HUG
ZZZ
ZZZ
It looks like she went back to sleep.
Those guys get on my nerves somehow!
Saber Tooth...
I don't like 'em!

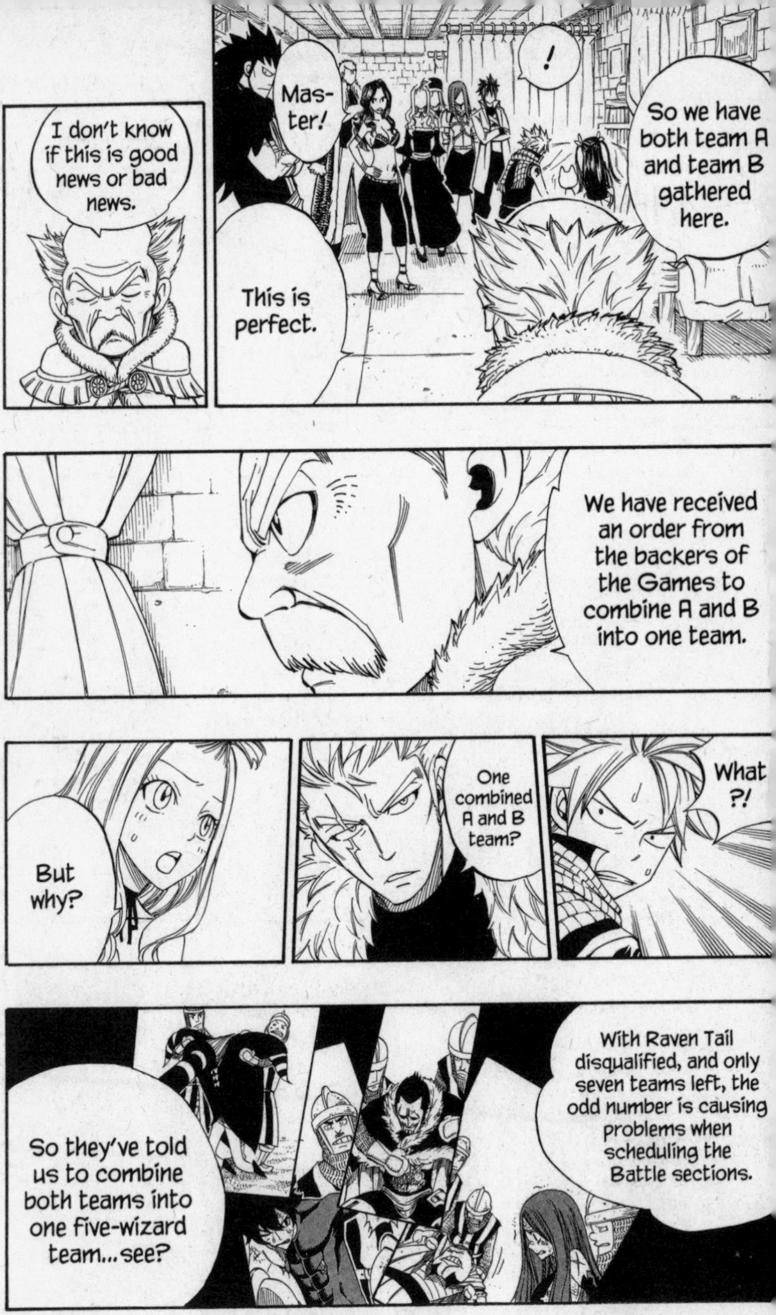

!
So we have both team A and team B gathered here.
Master!
This is perfect.
I don't know if this is good news or bad news.
We have received an order from the backers of the Games to combine A and B into one team.
What?!
One combined A and B team?
But why?
With Raven Tail disqualified, and only seven teams left, the odd number is causing problems when scheduling the Battle sections.
So they've told us to combine both teams into one five-wizard team...see?

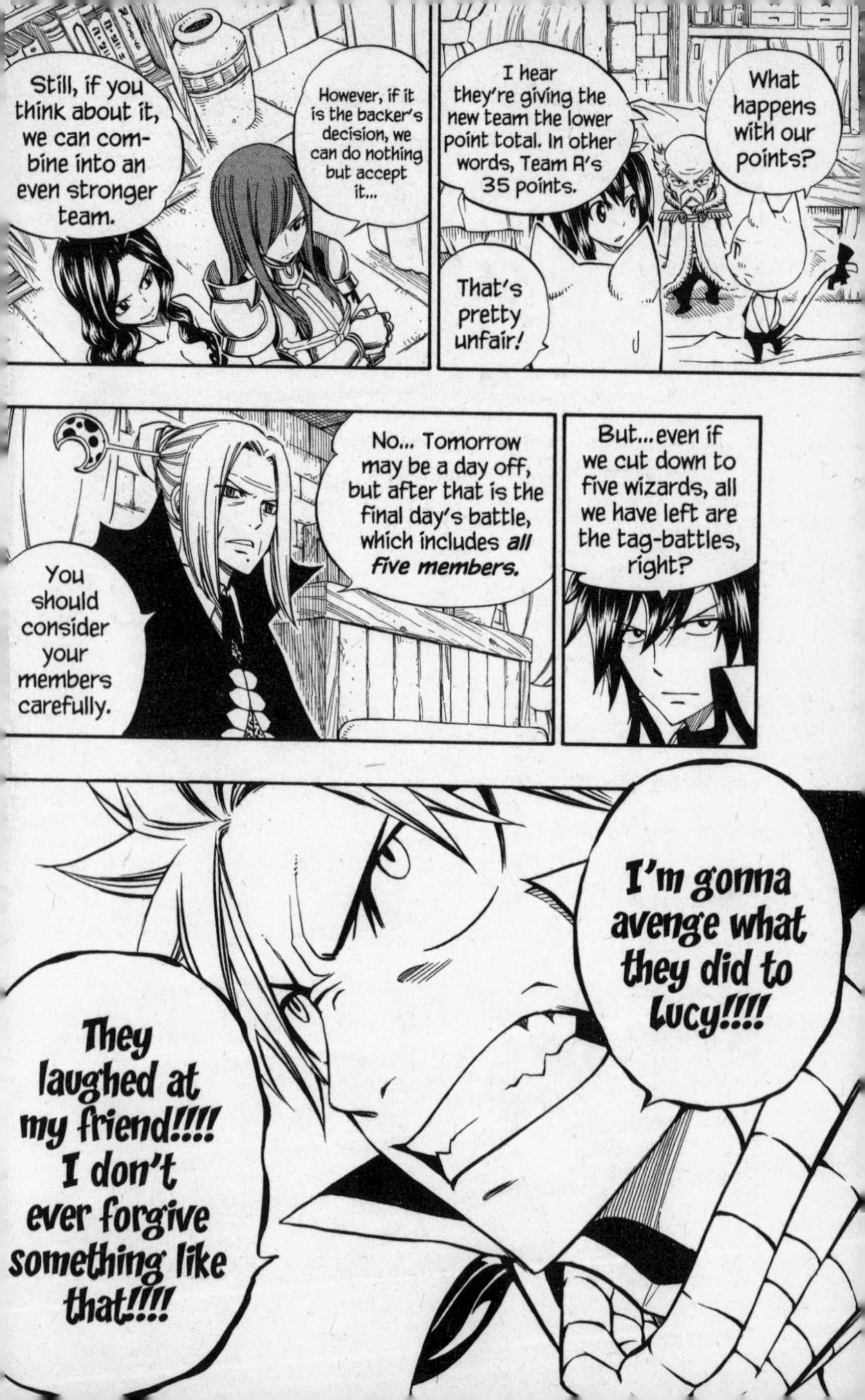
What happens with our points?
I hear they're giving the new team the lower point total. In other words, Team A's 35 points.
That's pretty unfair!
However, if it is the backer's decision, we can do nothing but accept it...
Still, if you think about it, we can combine into an even stronger team.
But...even if we cut down to five wizards, all we have left are the tag-battles, right?
No... Tomorrow may be a day off, but after that is the final day's battle, which includes *all five members.*
You should consider your members carefully.
I'm gonna avenge what they did to Lucy!!!!
They laughed at my friend!!!! I don't ever forgive something like that!!!!

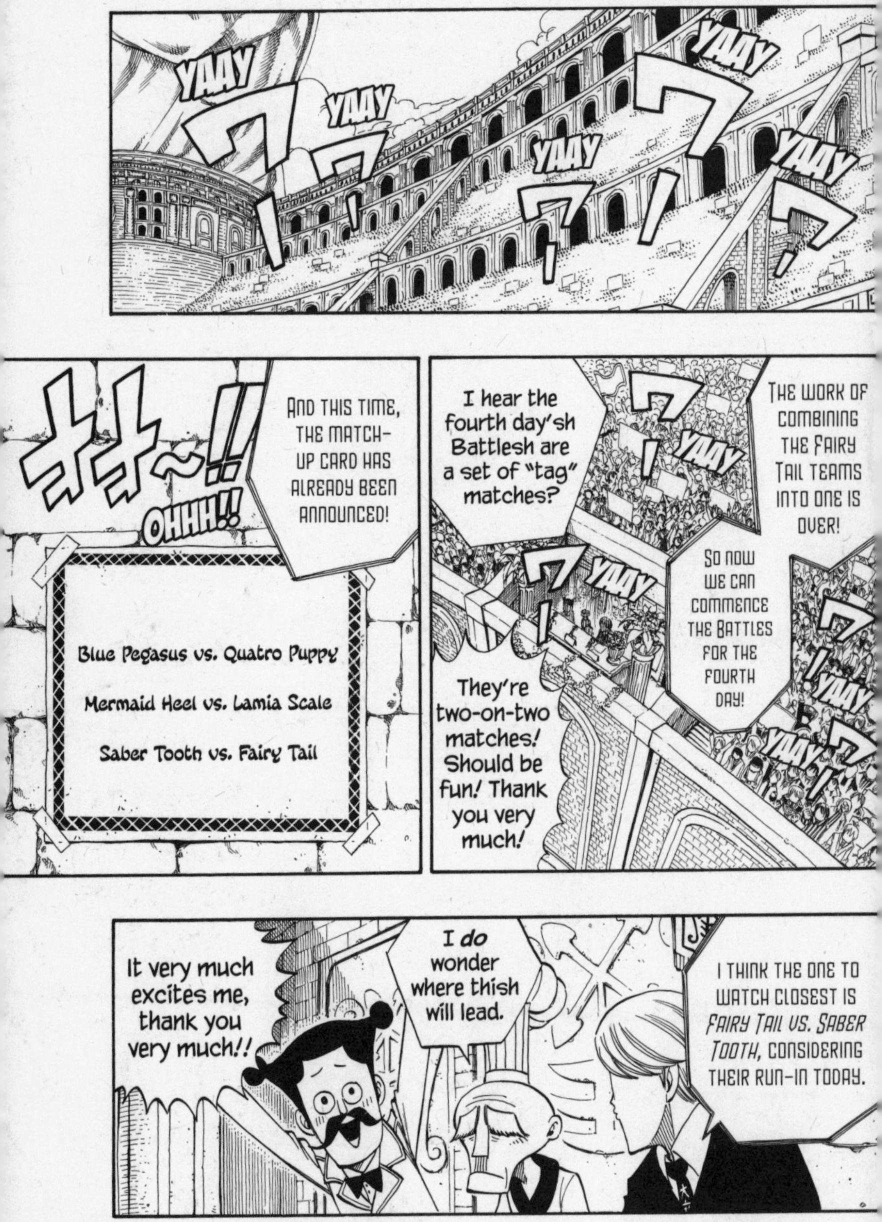
YAAY
YAAY
YAAY
YAAY
YAAY
THE WORK OF COMBINING THE FAIRY TAIL TEAMS INTO ONE IS OVER!
SO NOW WE CAN COMMENCE THE BATTLES FOR THE FOURTH DAY!
I hear the fourth day'sh Battlesh are a set of "tag" matches?
They're two-on-two matches! Should be fun! Thank you very much!
YAAY
YAAY
YAAY
YAAY
AND THIS TIME, THE MATCH-UP CARD HAS ALREADY BEEN ANNOUNCED!
OHHH!!
Blue Pegasus vs. Quatro Puppy
Mermaid Heel vs. Lamia Scale
Saber Tooth vs. Fairy Tail
I THINK THE ONE TO WATCH CLOSEST IS *FAIRY TAIL VS. SABER TOOTH*, CONSIDERING THEIR RUN-IN TODAY.
I *do* wonder where thish will lead.
It very much excites me, thank you very much!!

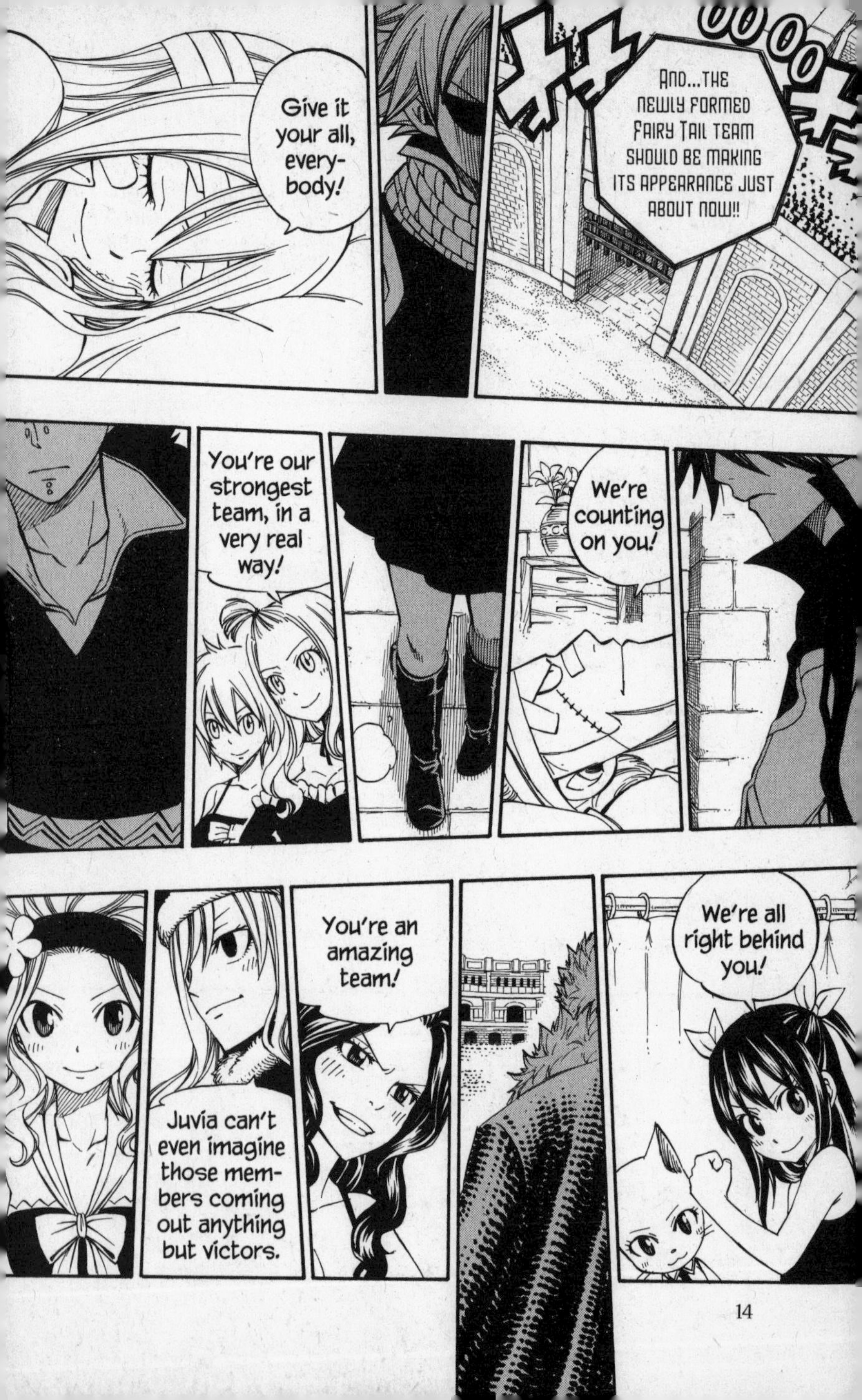
AND...THE NEWLY FORMED FAIRY TAIL TEAM SHOULD BE MAKING ITS APPEARANCE JUST ABOUT NOW!!
Give it your all, everybody!
We're counting on you!
You're our strongest team, in a very real way!
We're all right behind you!
You're an amazing team!
Juvia can't even imagine those members coming out anything but victors.

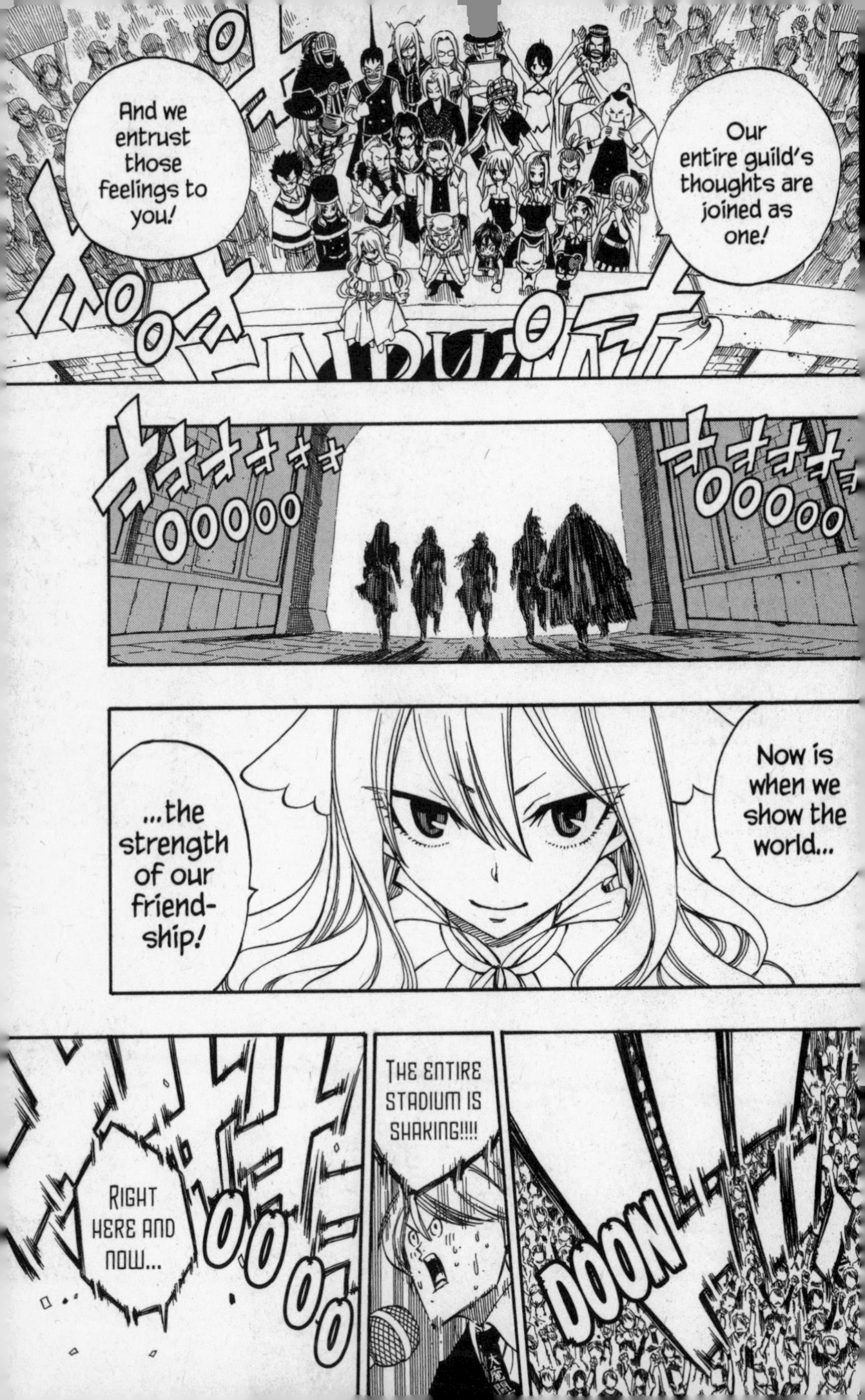
Our entire guild's thoughts are joined as one!
And we entrust those feelings to you!
OOOOO
OOOOO
Now is when we show the world...
...the strength of our friendship!
DOON
THE ENTIRE STADIUM IS SHAKING!!!!
RIGHT HERE AND NOW...
OOOO

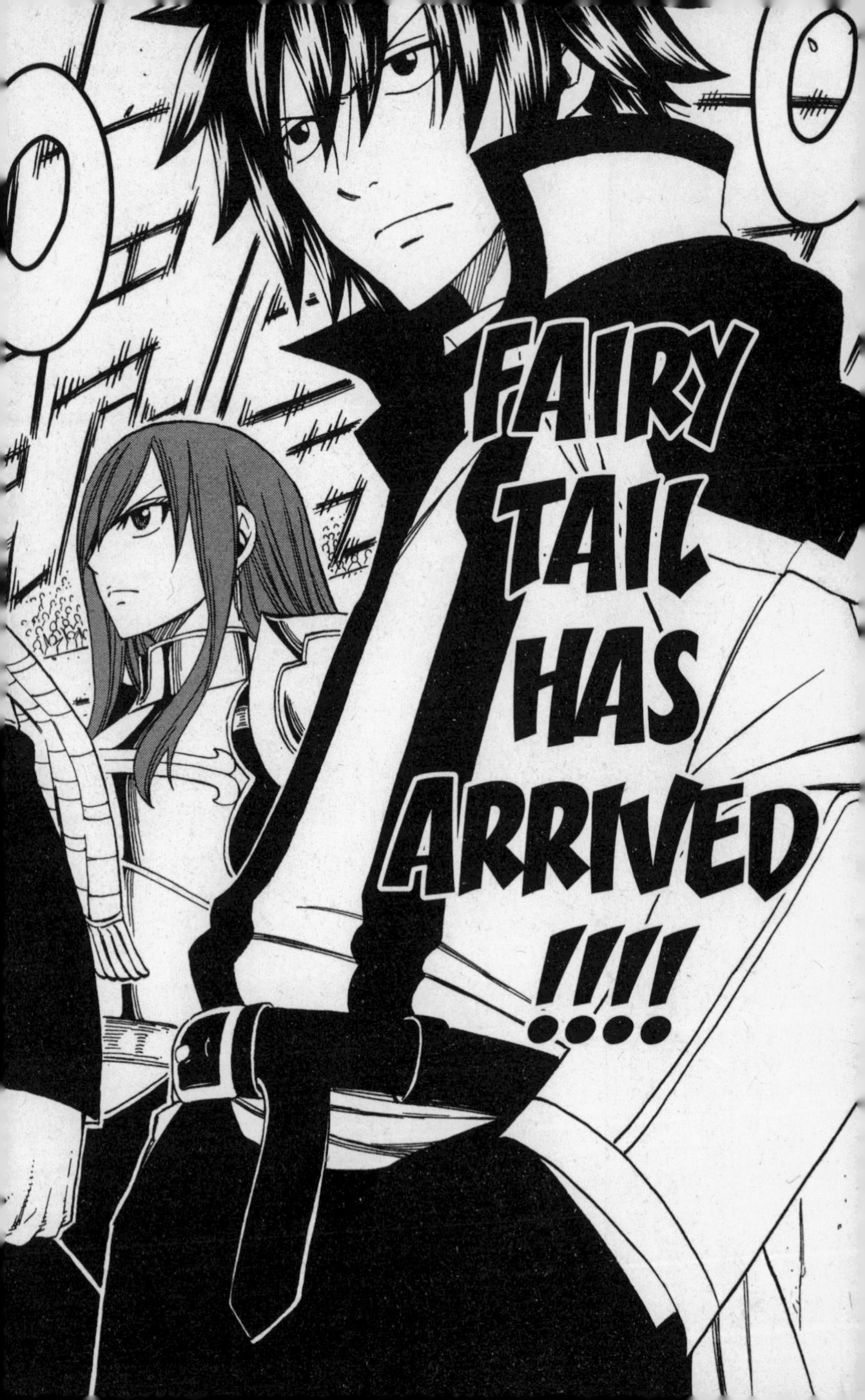
FAIRY TAIL HAS ARRIVED!!!!

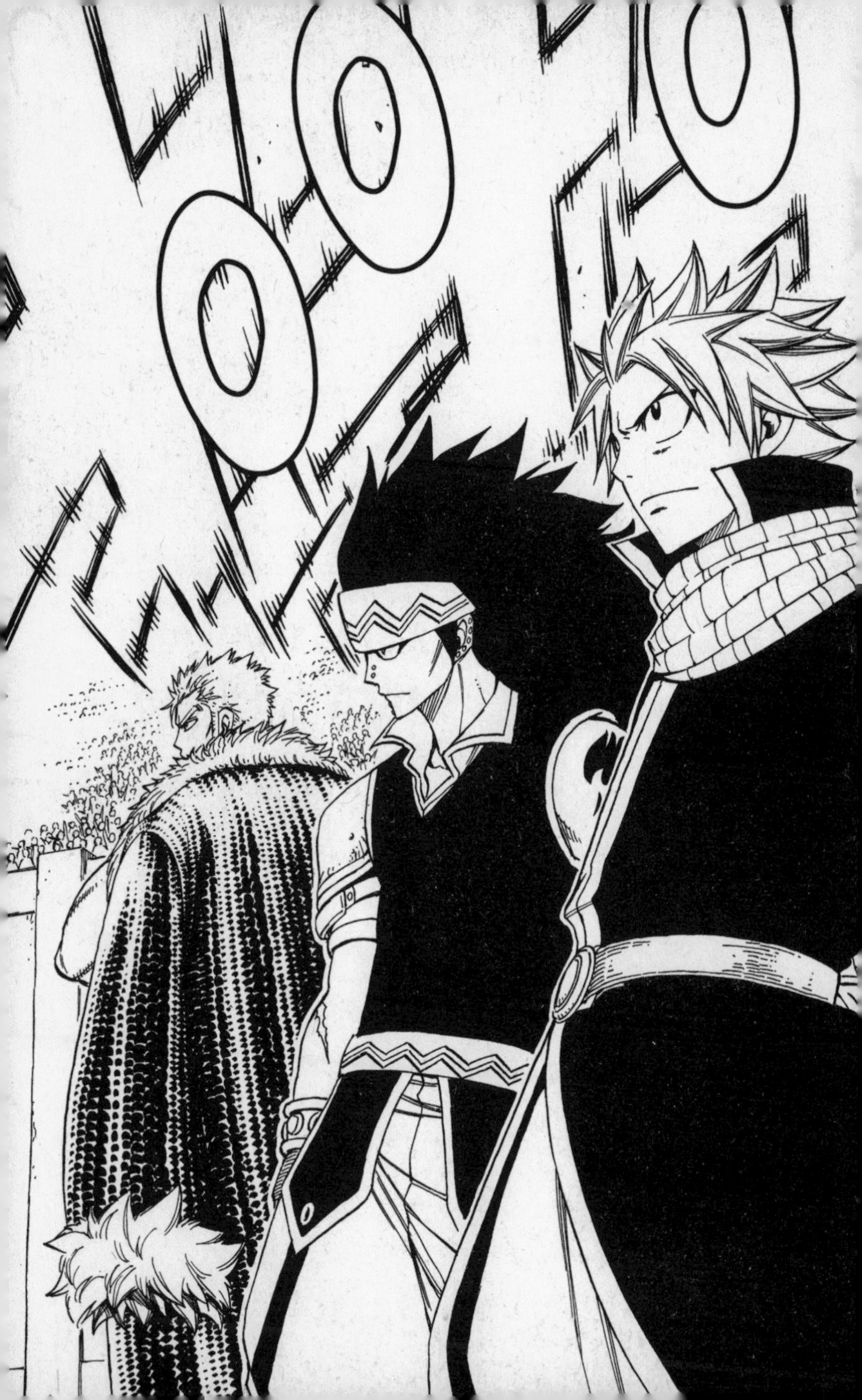

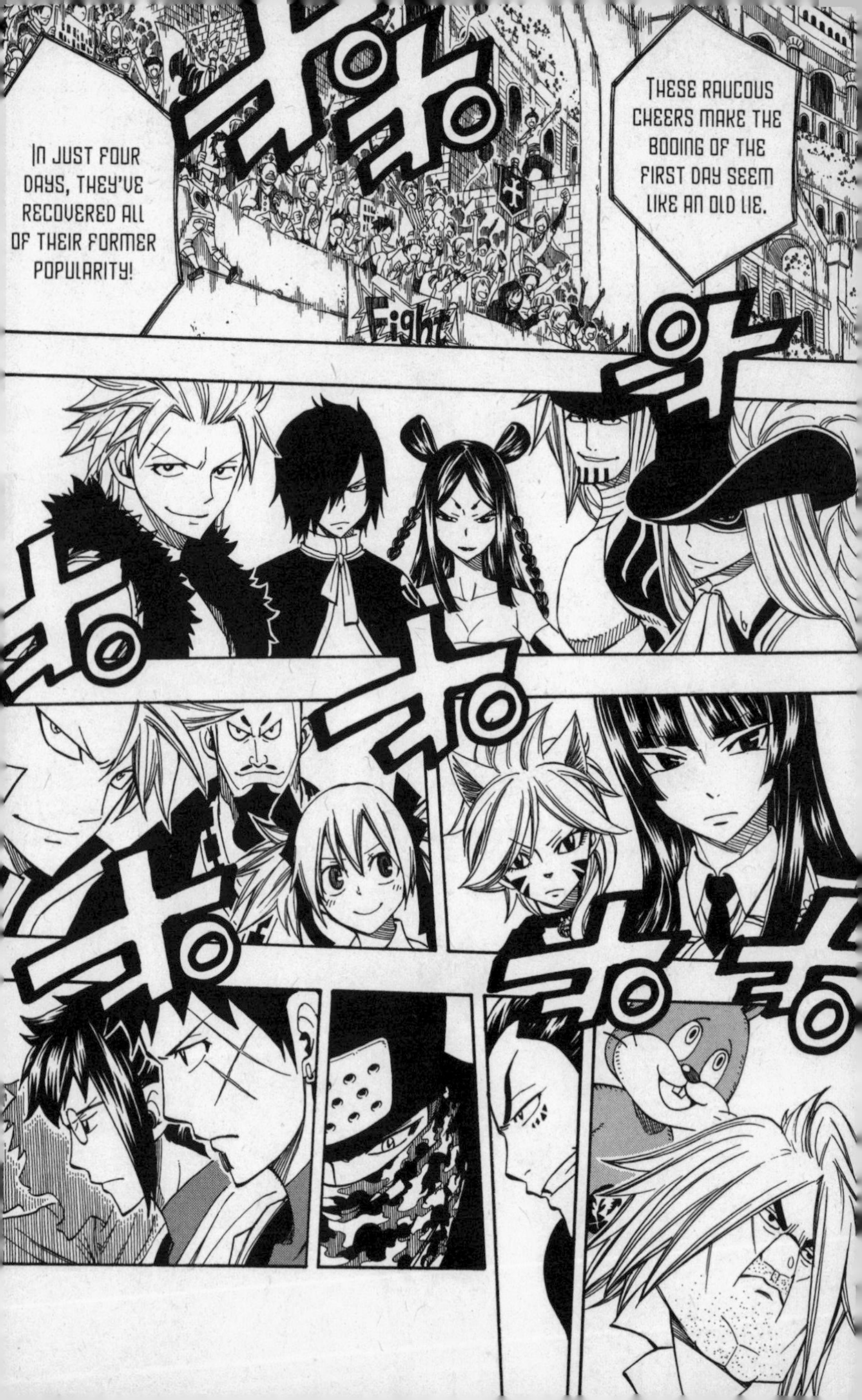
THESE RAUCOUS CHEERS MAKE THE BOOING OF THE FIRST DAY SEEM LIKE AN OLD LIE.
IN JUST FOUR DAYS, THEY'VE RECOVERED ALL OF THEIR FORMER POPULARITY!
Fight

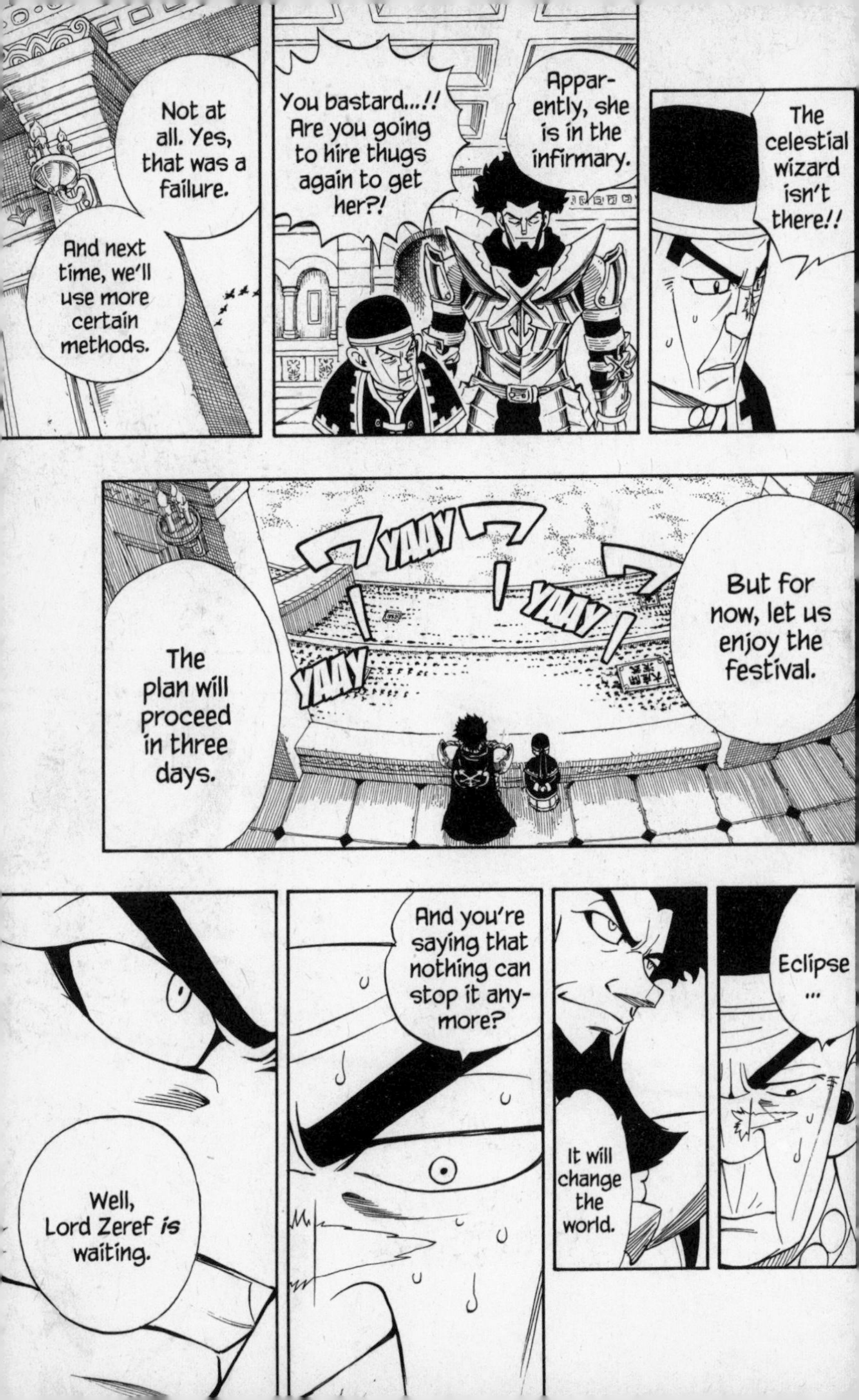
The celestial wizard isn't there!!
Apparently, she is in the infirmary.
You bastard...!! Are you going to hire thugs again to get her?!
Not at all. Yes, that was a failure.
And next time, we'll use more certain methods.
But for now, let us enjoy the festival.
YAAY
YAAY
YAAY
The plan will proceed in three days.
Eclipse ...
It will change the world.
And you're saying that nothing can stop it anymore?
Well, Lord Zeref *is* waiting.

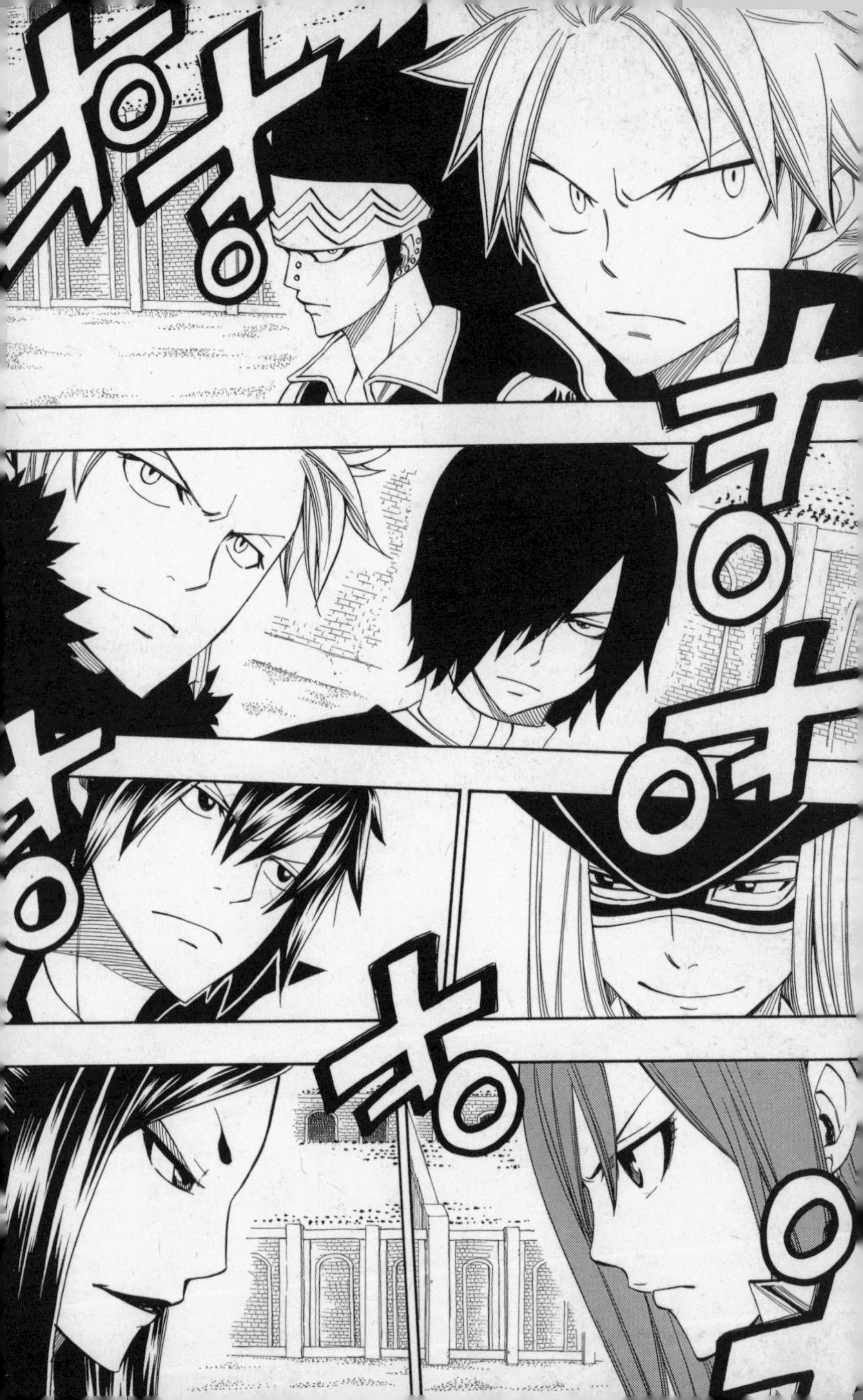

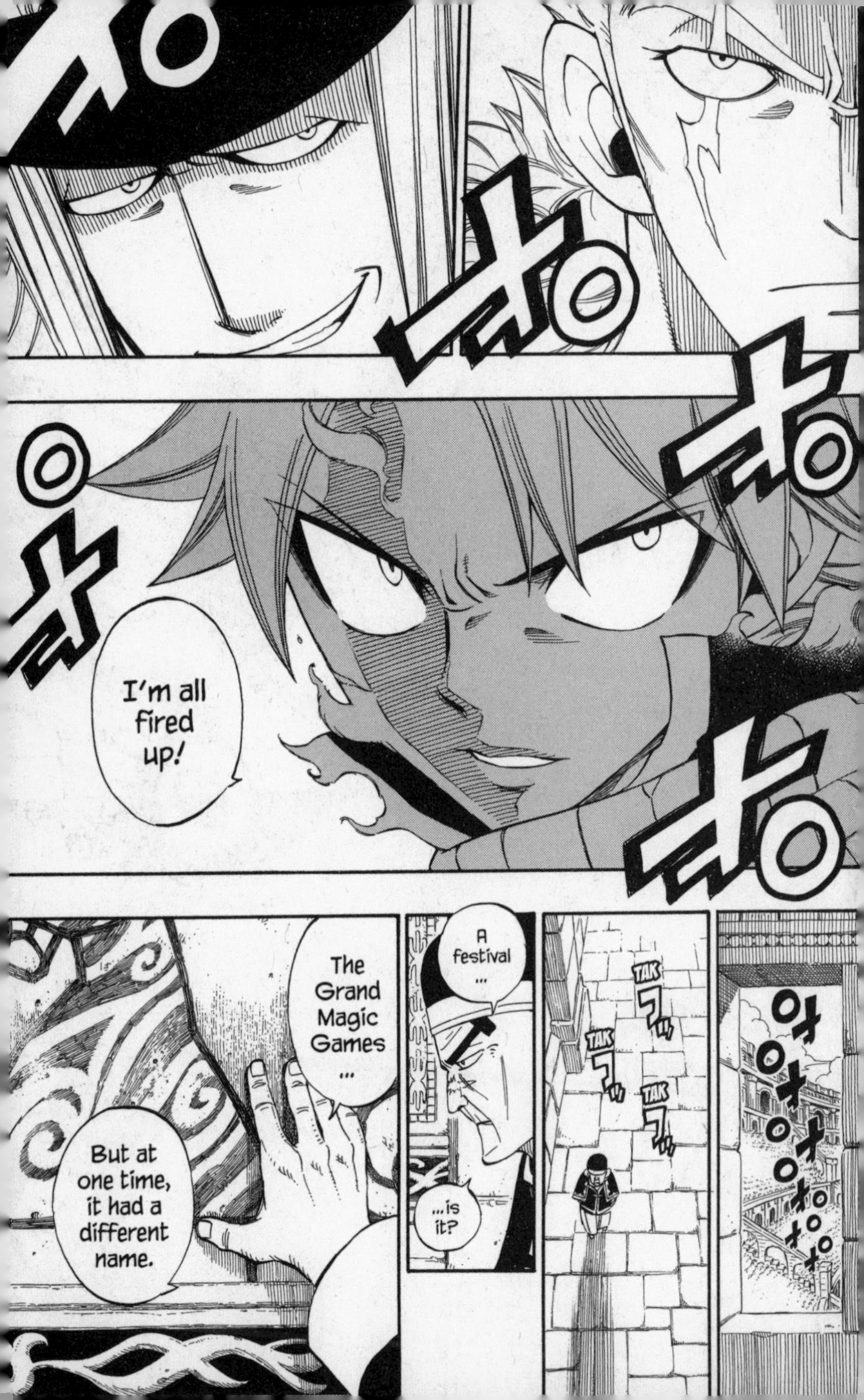
I'm all fired up!
TAK
TAK
TAK
A festival ...
...is it?
The Grand Magic Games ...
But at one time, it had a different name.

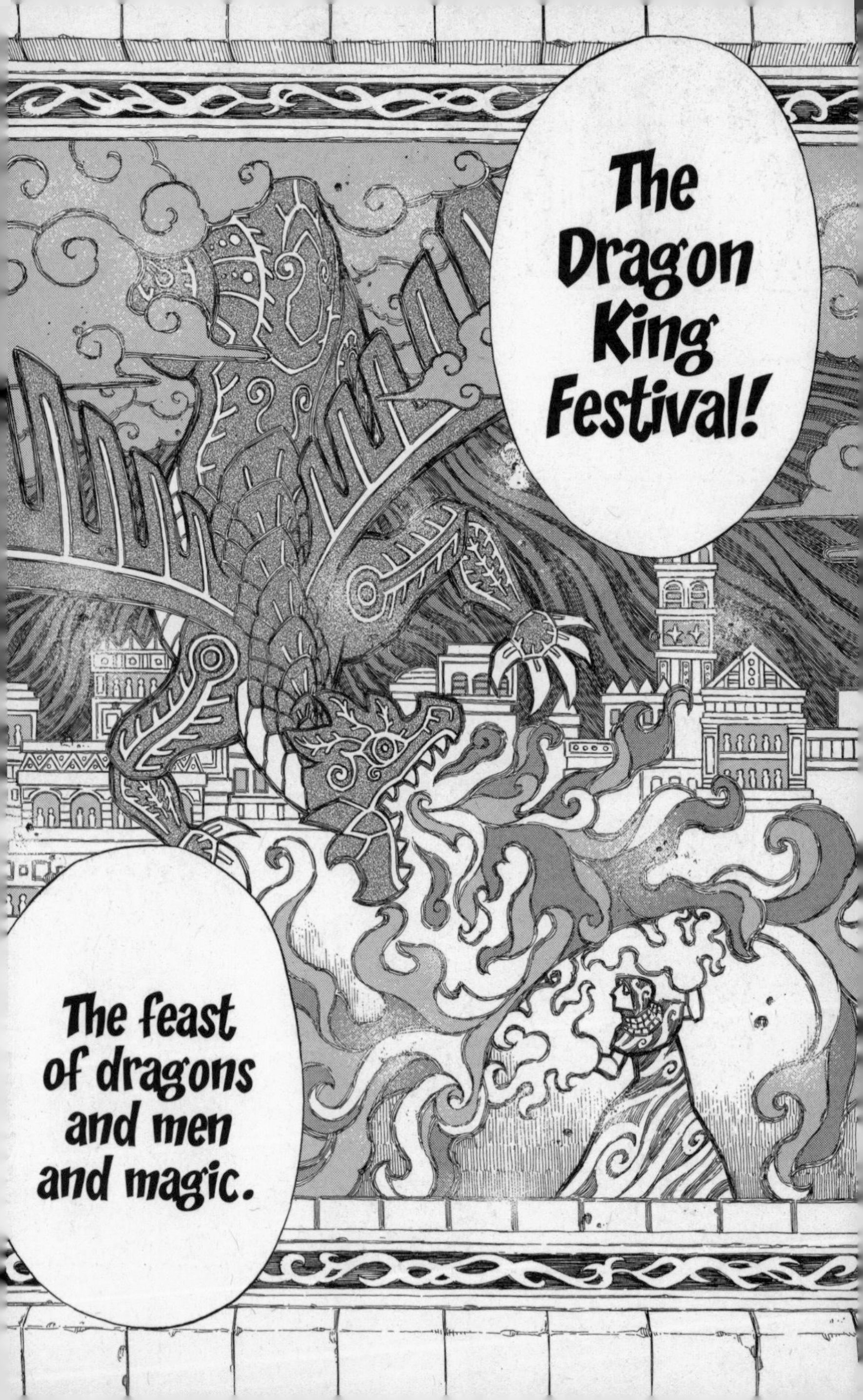
The Dragon King Festival!
The feast of dragons and men and magic.

FAIRY TAIL

フェアリーテイル

Chapter 293: A Gift for You of Perfum

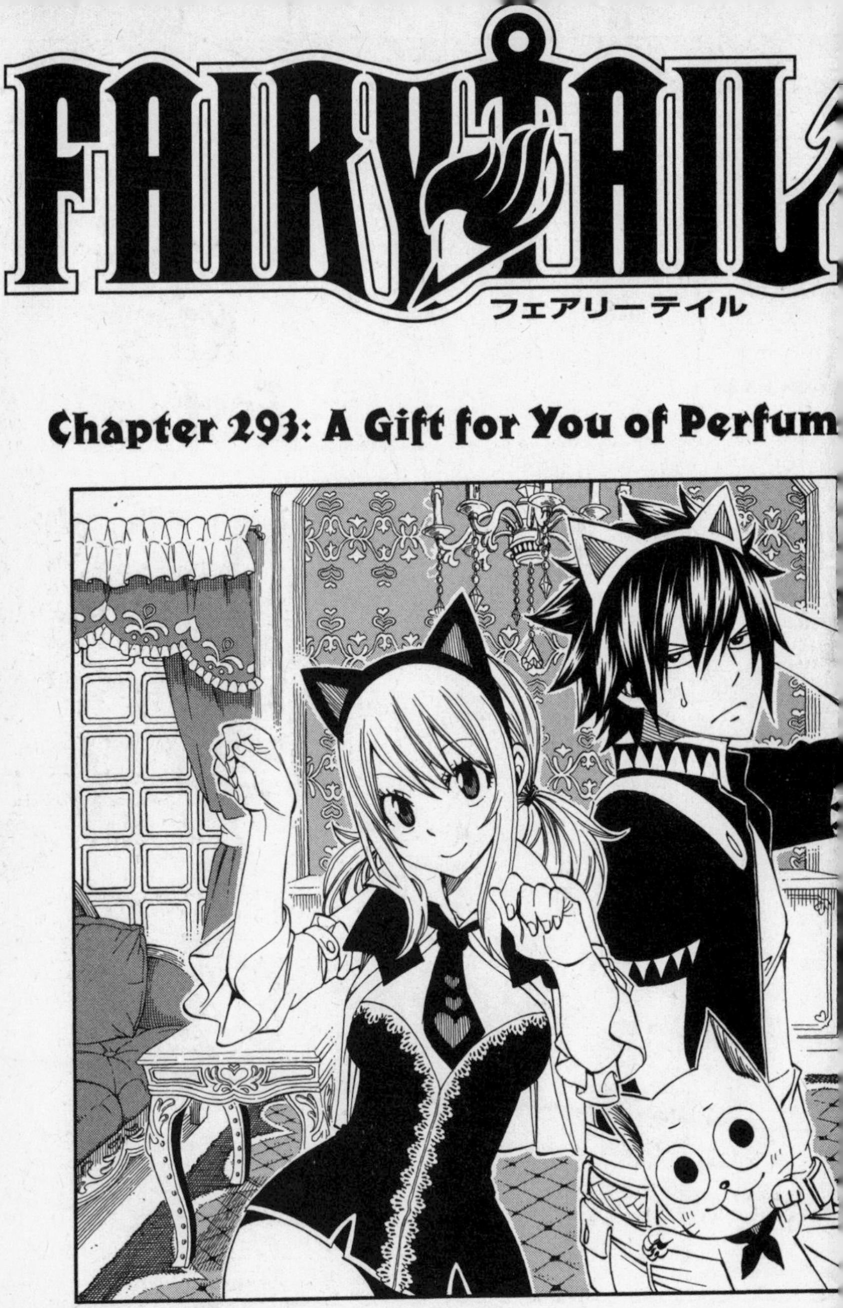

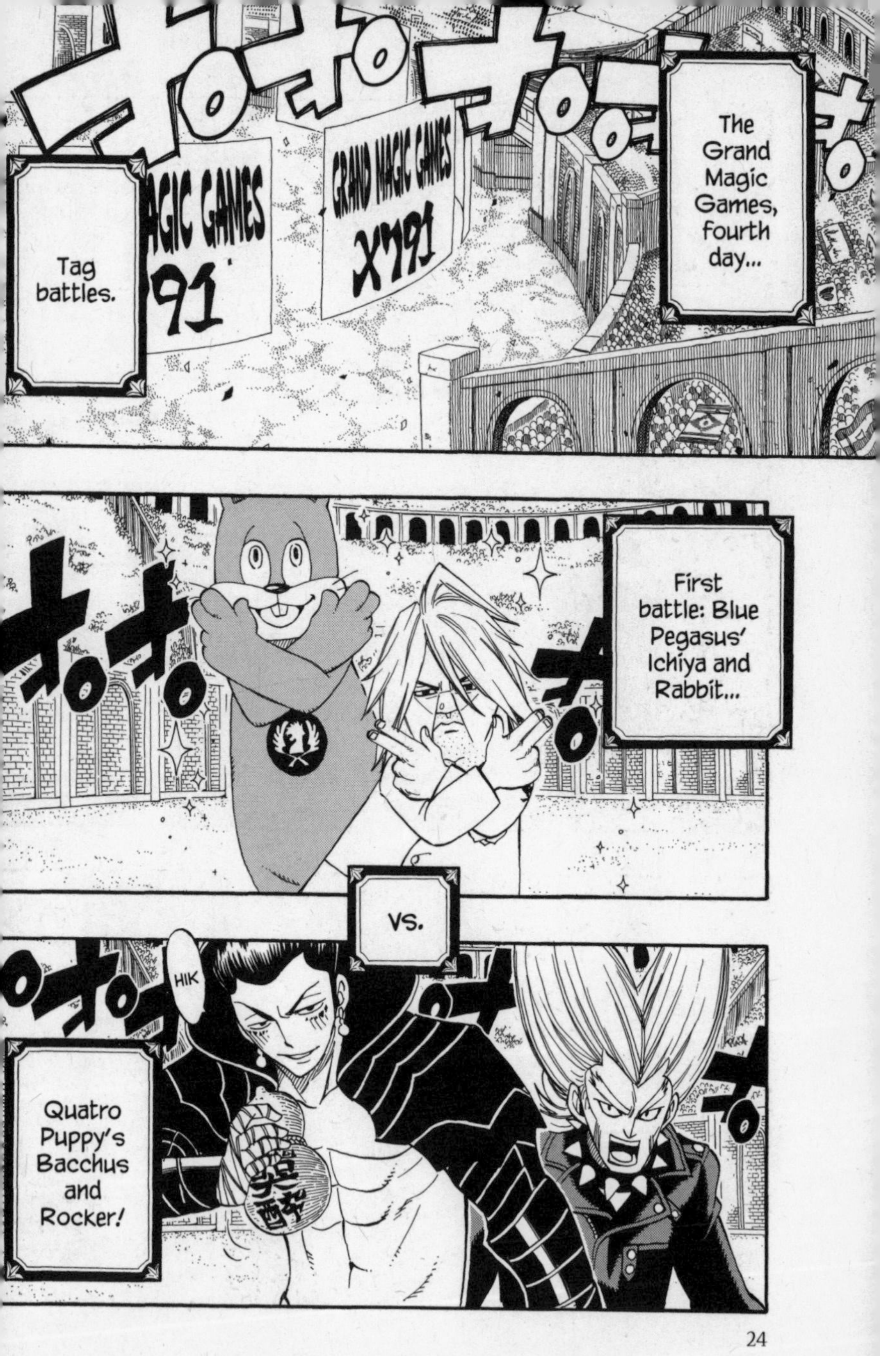
The Grand Magic Games, fourth day...
GRAND MAGIC GAMES
X791
Tag battles.
First battle: Blue Pegasus' Ichiya and Rabbit...
VS.
HIK
Quatro Puppy's Bacchus and Rocker!

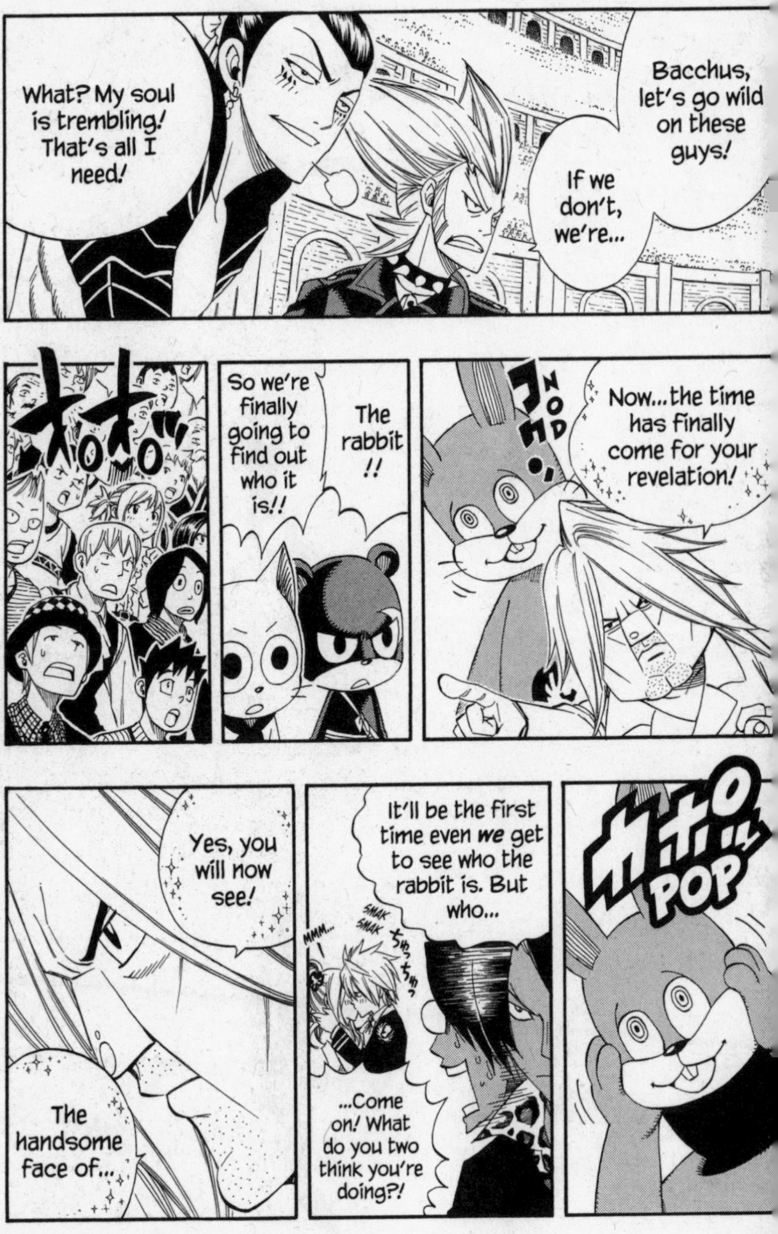
Bacchus, let's go wild on these guys!
If we don't, we're...
What? My soul is trembling! That's all I need!
NOD
Now...the time has finally come for your revelation!
The rabbit!!
So we're finally going to find out who it is!!
POP
It'll be the first time even *we* get to see who the rabbit is. But who...
SMAK SMAK
MMM...
...Come on! What do you two think you're doing?!
Yes, you will now see!
The handsome face of...

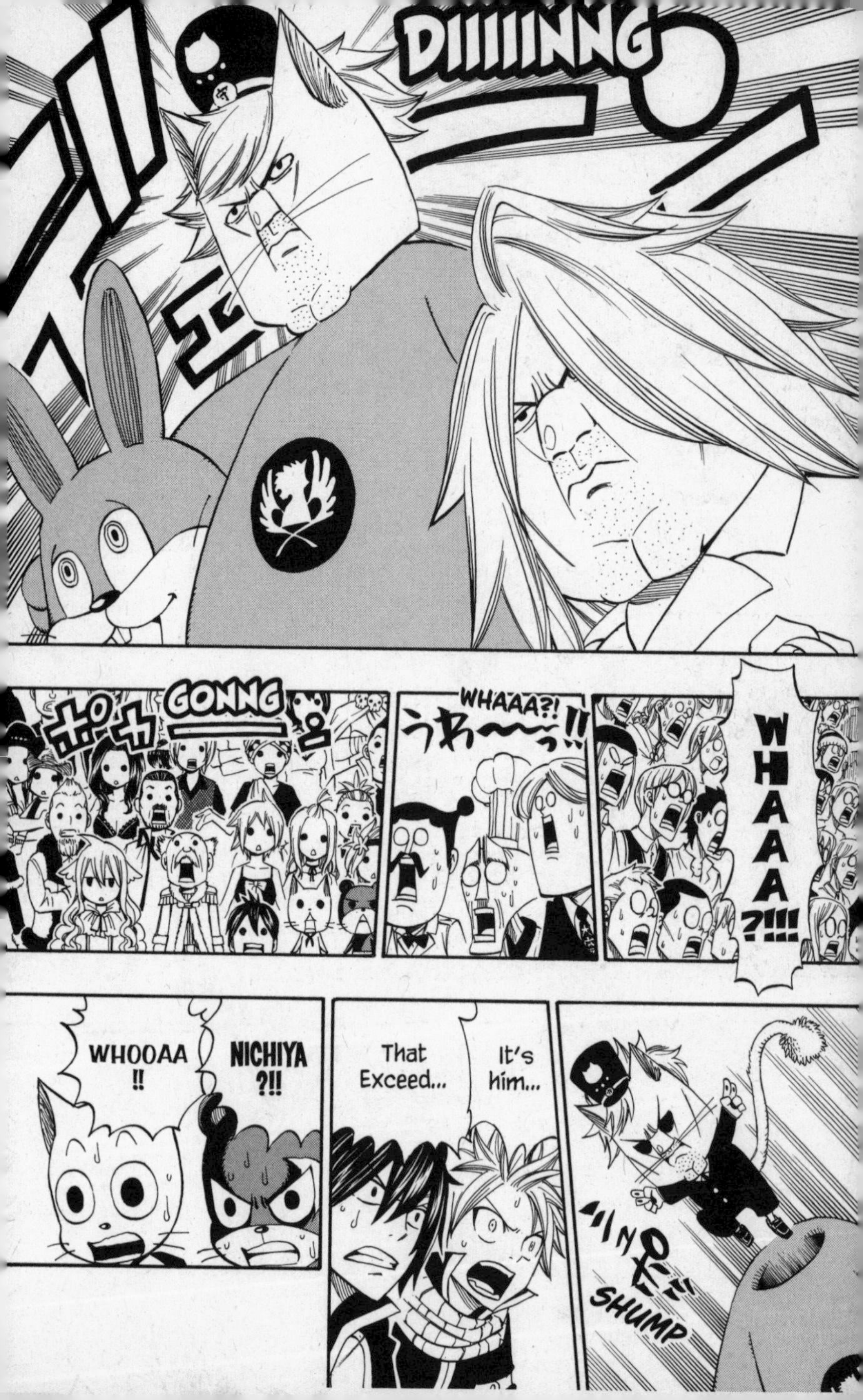
DIIIINNG
WHAAAA?!!!
WHAAA?!
うわ〜〜っ!!
GONNG
SHUMP
It's him...
That Exceed...
NICHIYA ?!!
WHOOAA !!

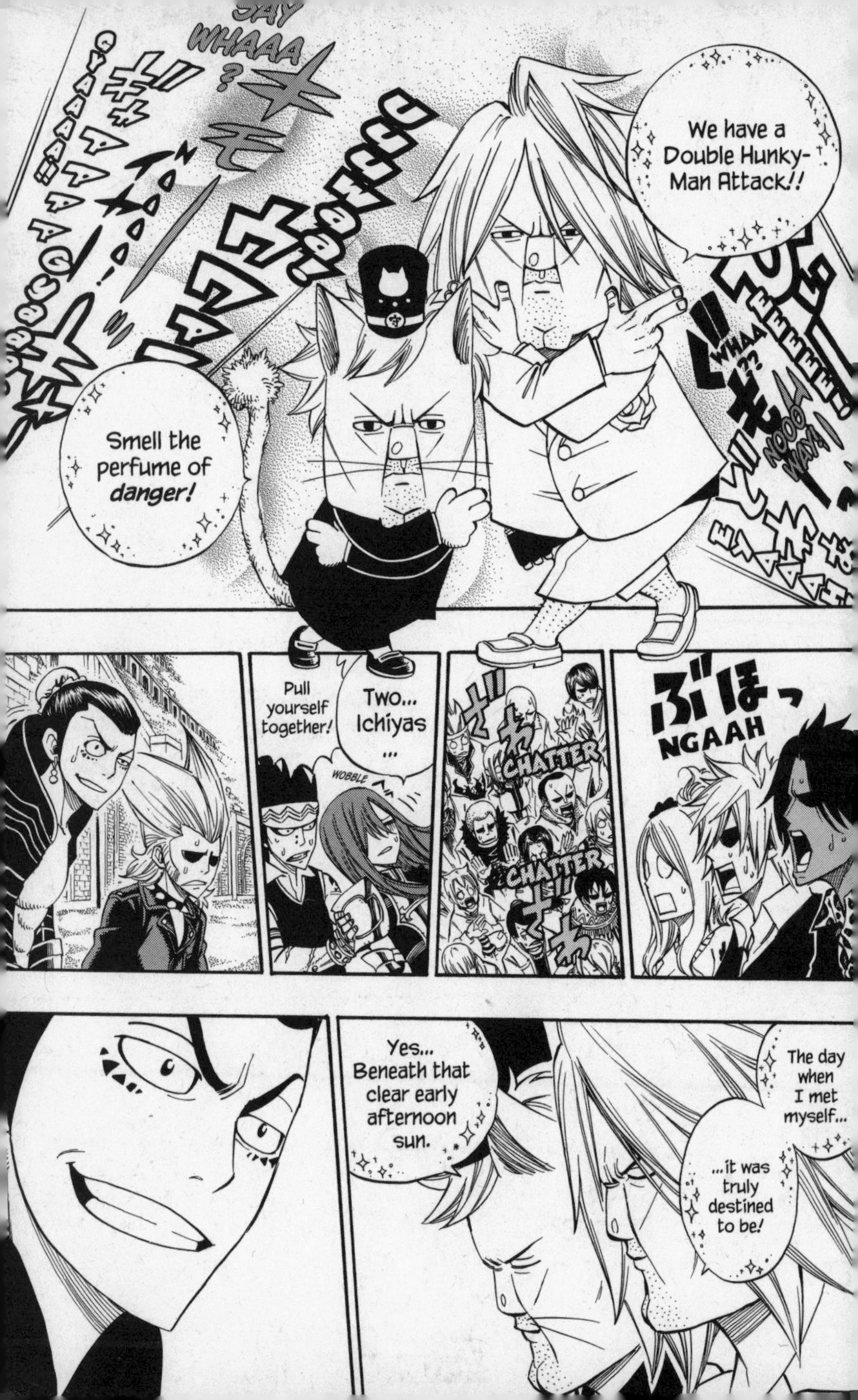
We have a Double Hunky-Man Attack!!
WHAA ??
NOOO WAY!
Smell the perfume of danger!
UWAAAA!
SAY WHAAA ?
GYAAAAAA!!
ぶほっ
NGAAH
CHATTER
CHATTER
Two... Ichiyas ...
WOBBLE
Pull yourself together!
Yes... Beneath that clear early afternoon sun.
The day when I met myself...
...it was truly destined to be!

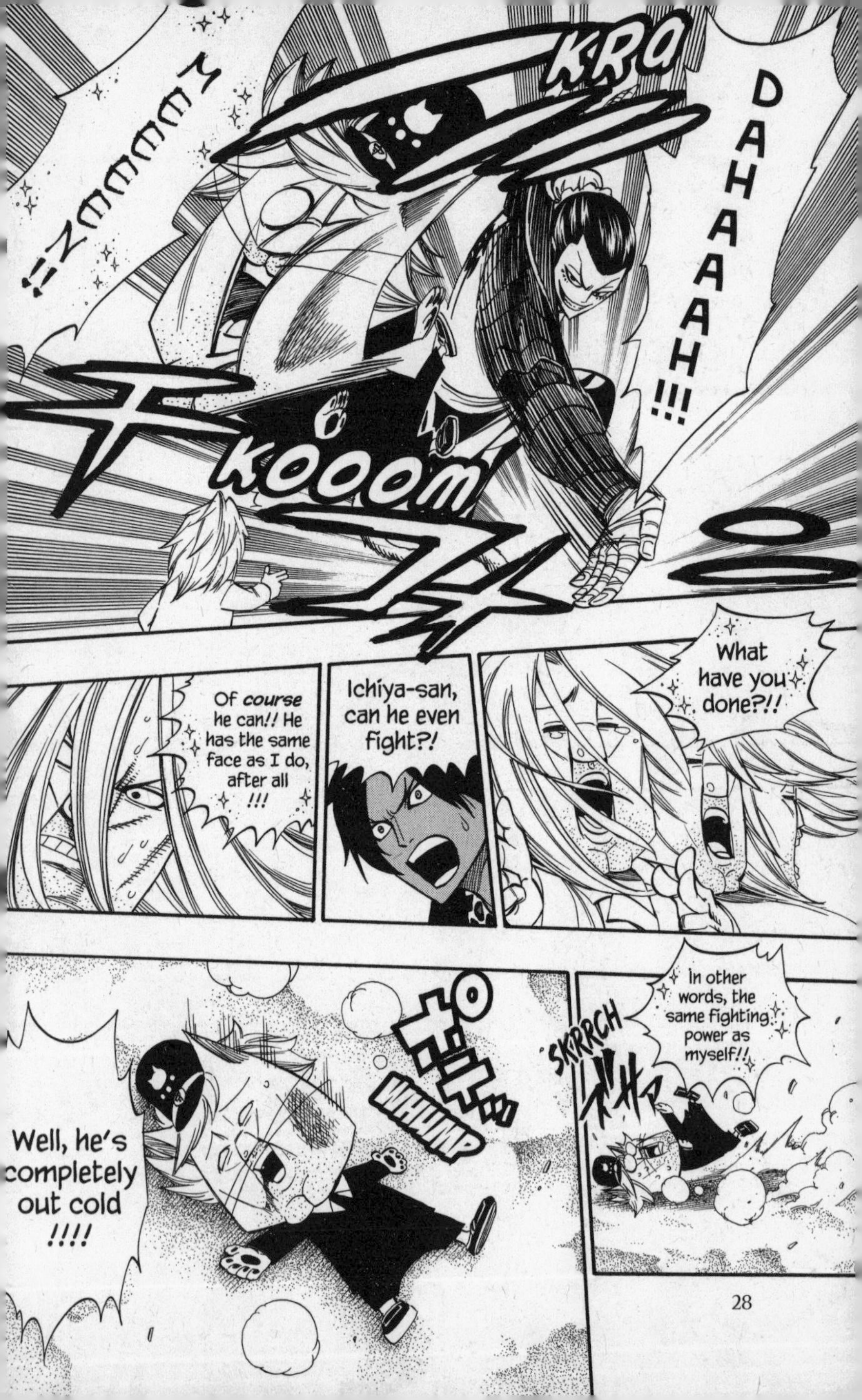

DAHAAAAAH!!!
KRA
KOOOM
What have you done?!!
Ichiya-san, can he even fight?!
Of *course* he can!! He has the same face as I do, after all !!!
SKRRCH
In other words, the same fighting power as myself!!
WHUMP
Well, he's completely out cold !!!!

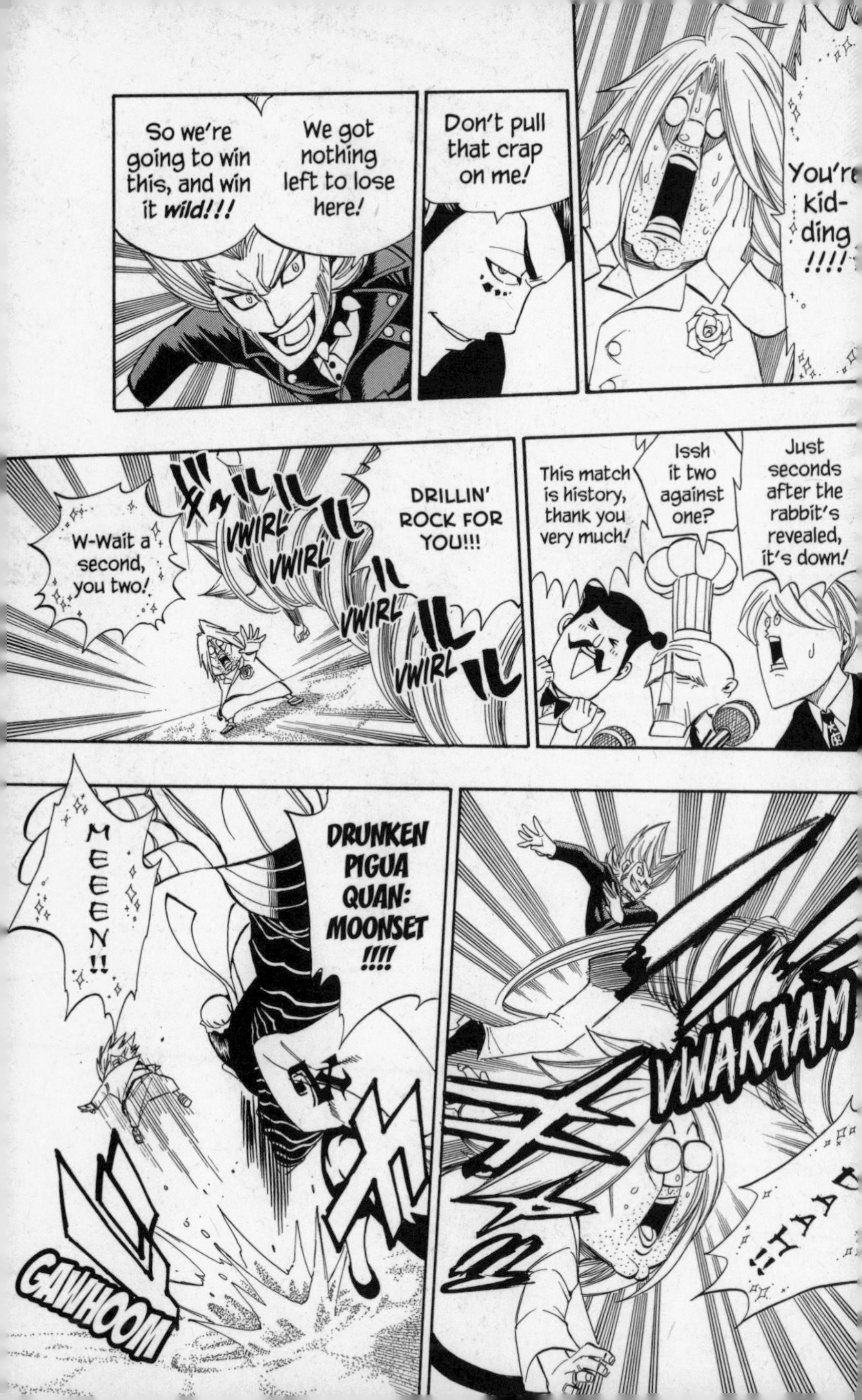
You're kid-ding!!!!
Don't pull that crap on me!
We got nothing left to lose here!
So we're going to win this, and win it wild!!!
Just seconds after the rabbit's revealed, it's down!
Issh it two against one?
This match is history, thank you very much!
DRILLIN' ROCK FOR YOU!!!
VWIRL
VWIRL
VWIRL
VWIRL
W-Wait a second, you two!
VWAKAAM
AAH!!
DRUNKEN PIGUA QUAN: MOONSET!!!!
MEEEEN!!
GAWHOOM

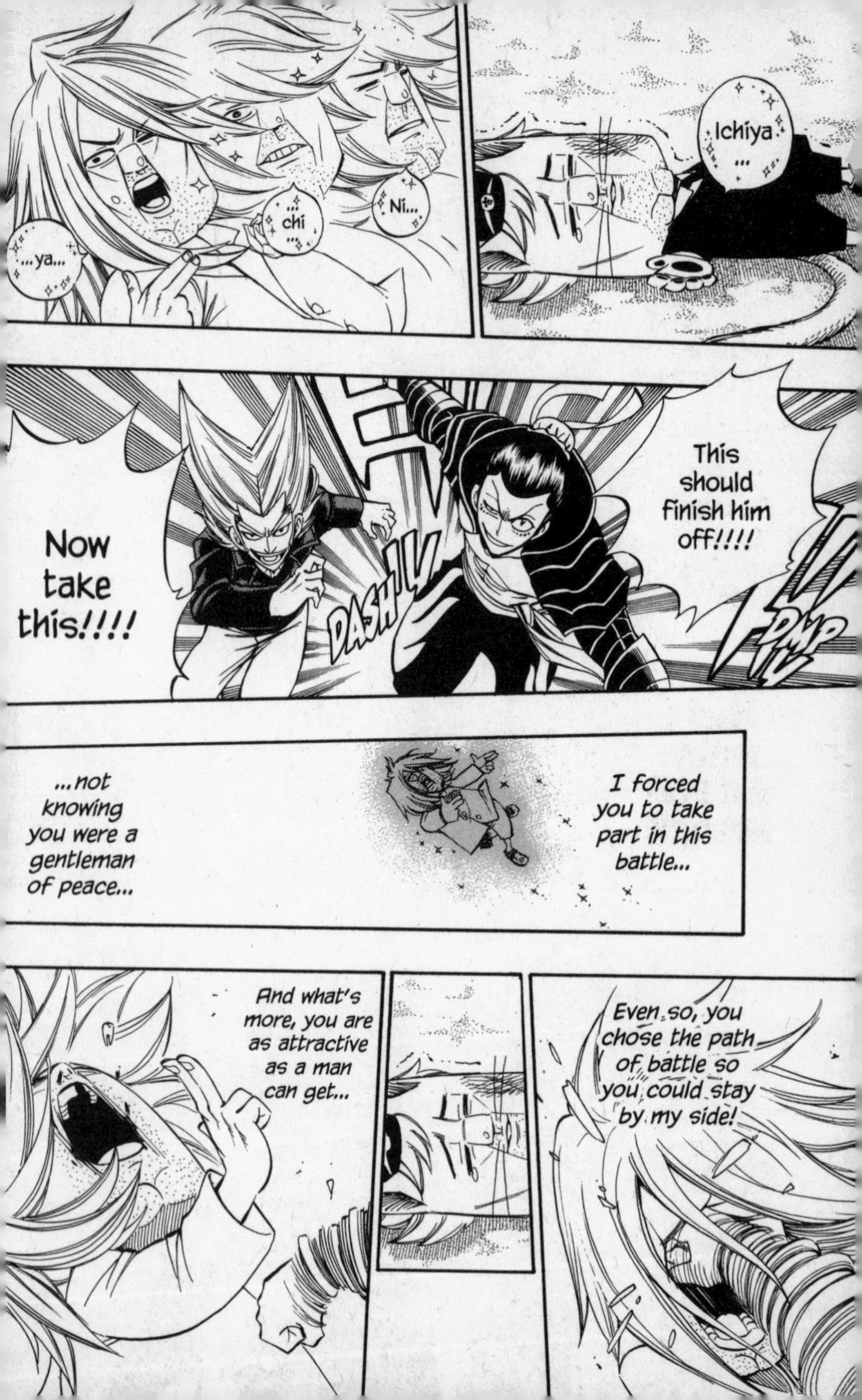
Ichiya ...
Ni...
...chi...
...ya...
This should finish him off!!!!
DMP
DASH
Now take this!!!!
I forced you to take part in this battle...
...not knowing you were a gentleman of peace...
Even so, you chose the path of battle so you could stay by my side!
And what's more, you are as attractive as a man can get...

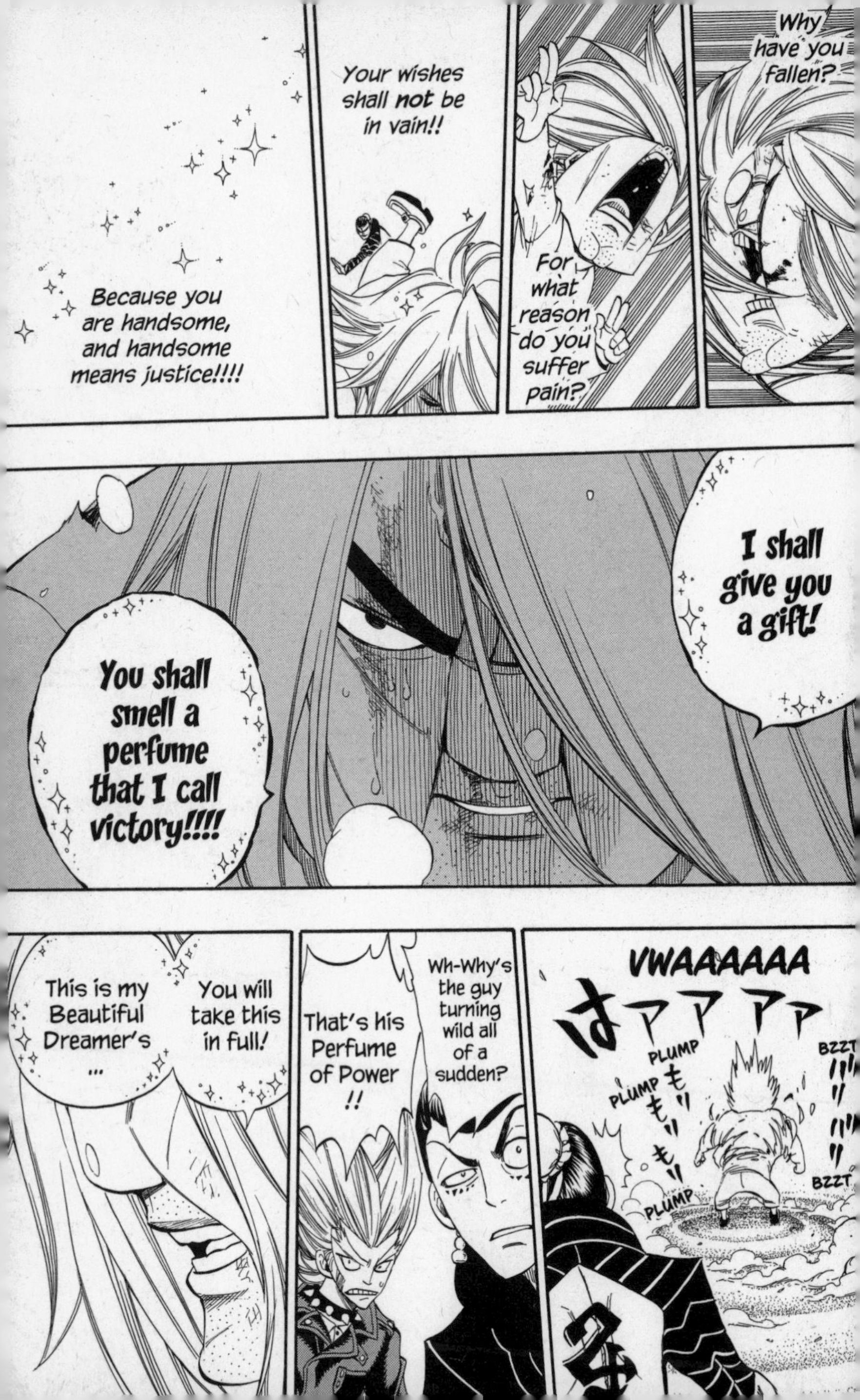
Why have you fallen?
For what reason do you suffer pain?
Your wishes shall not be in vain!!
Because you are handsome, and handsome means justice!!!!
I shall give you a gift!
You shall smell a perfume that I call victory!!!!
VWAAAAAA
はァアァ
PLUMP も
PLUMP も
PLUMP も
BZZT
BZZT
Wh-Why's the guy turning wild all of a sudden?
That's his Perfume of Power!!
You will take this in full!
This is my Beautiful Dreamer's ...

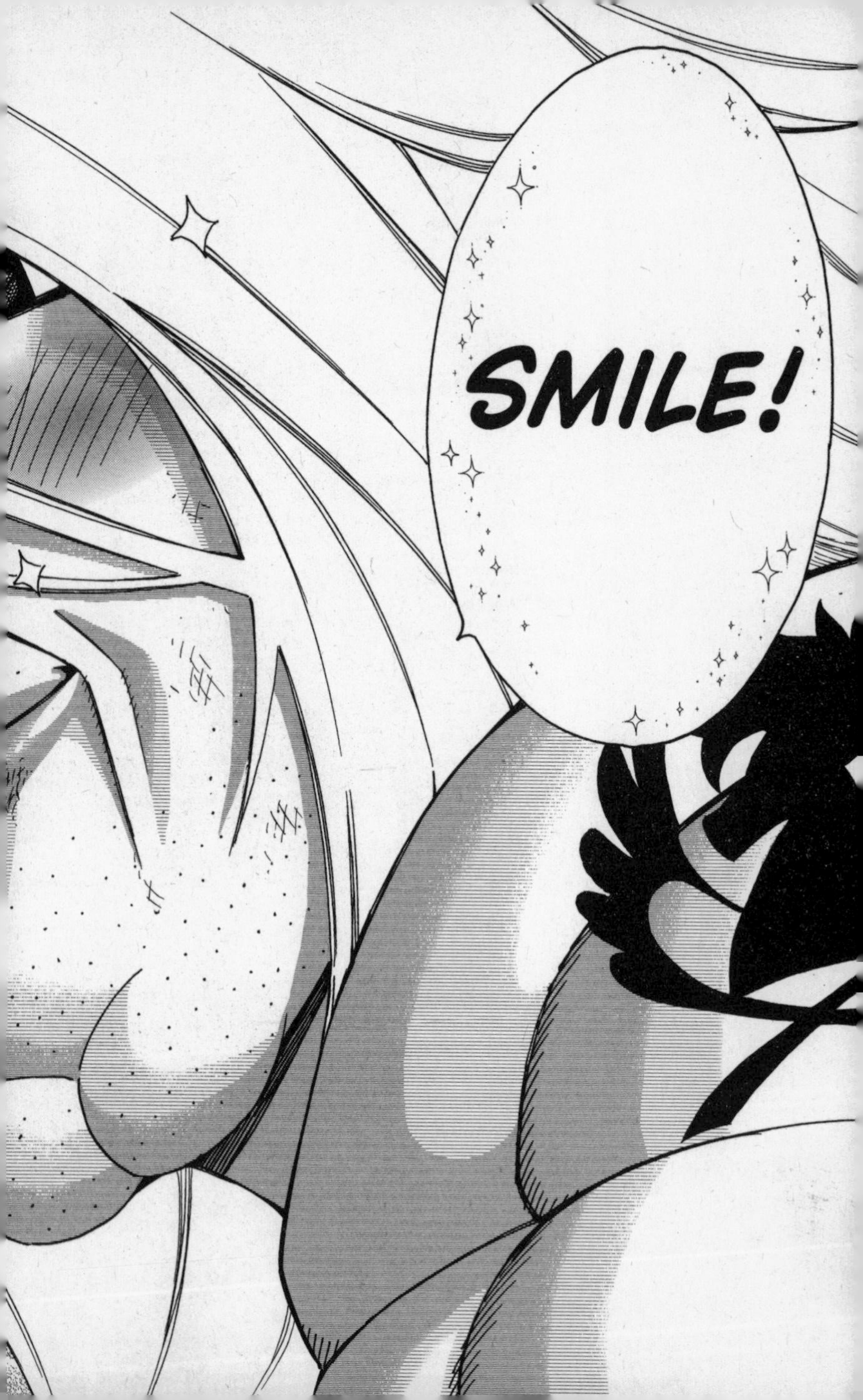
SMILE!

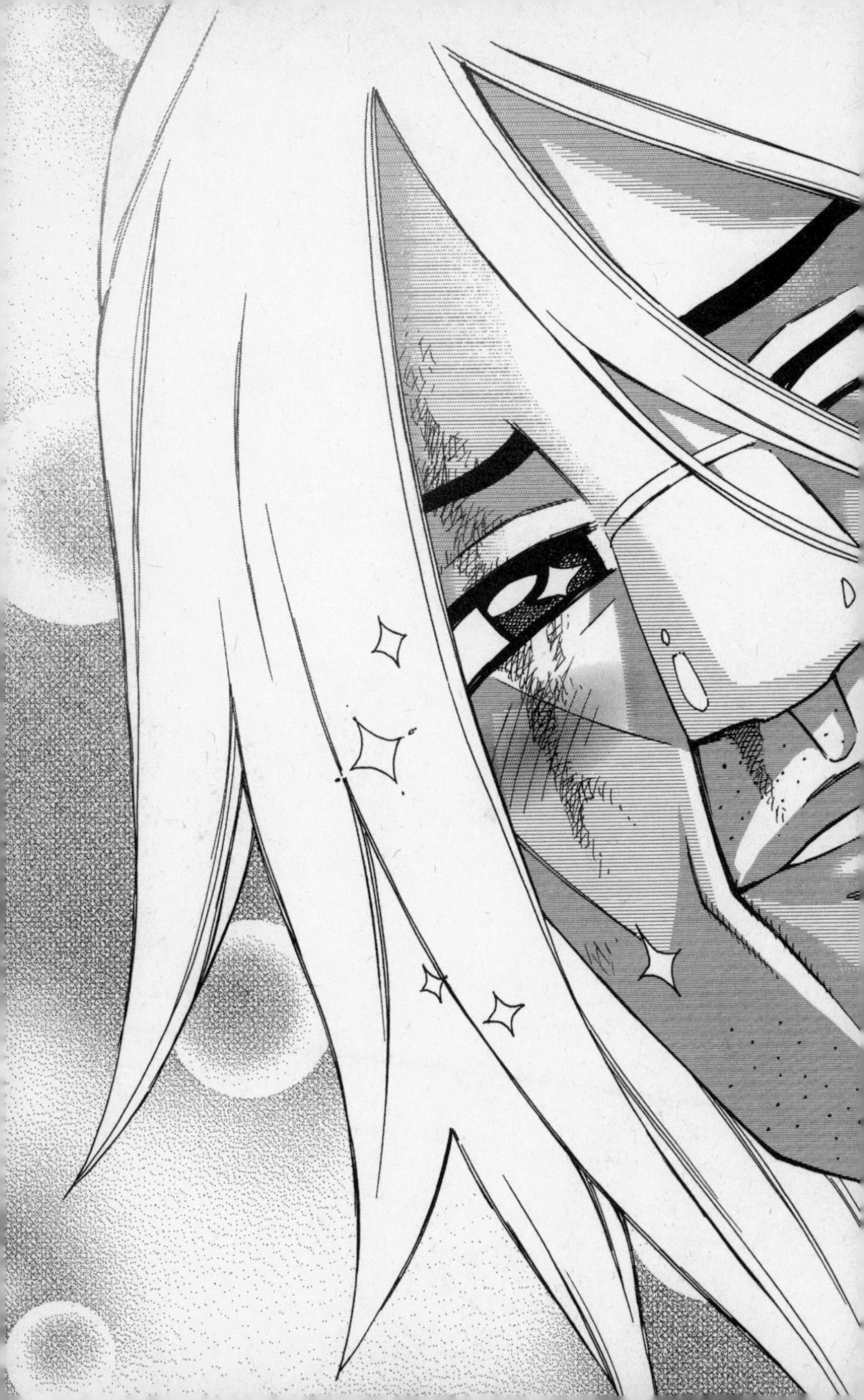

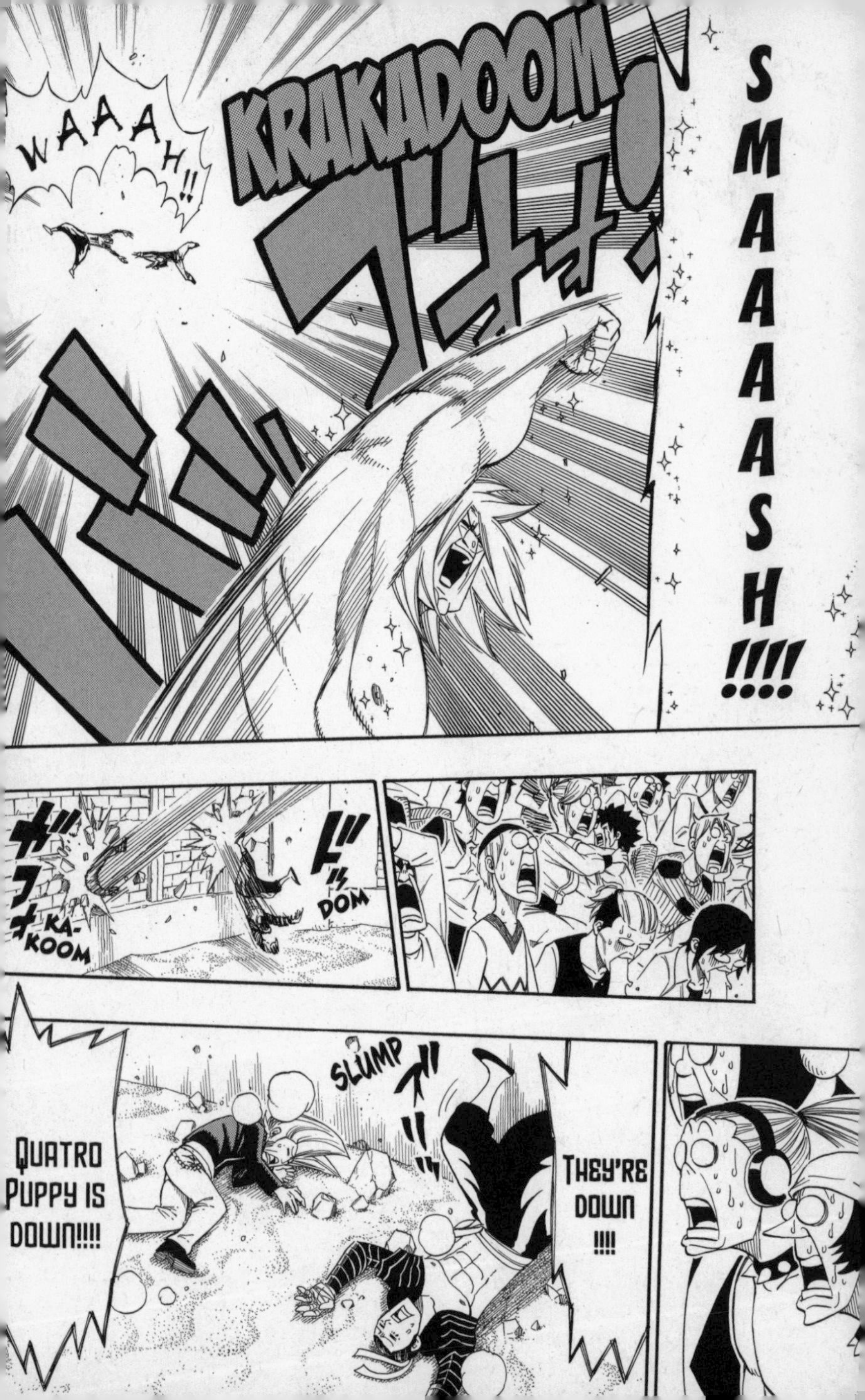
SMAAAAASH!!!!
KRAKADOOM
WAAAAH!!
DOM
KA-KOOM
They're down!!!!
SLUMP
Quatro Puppy is down!!!!

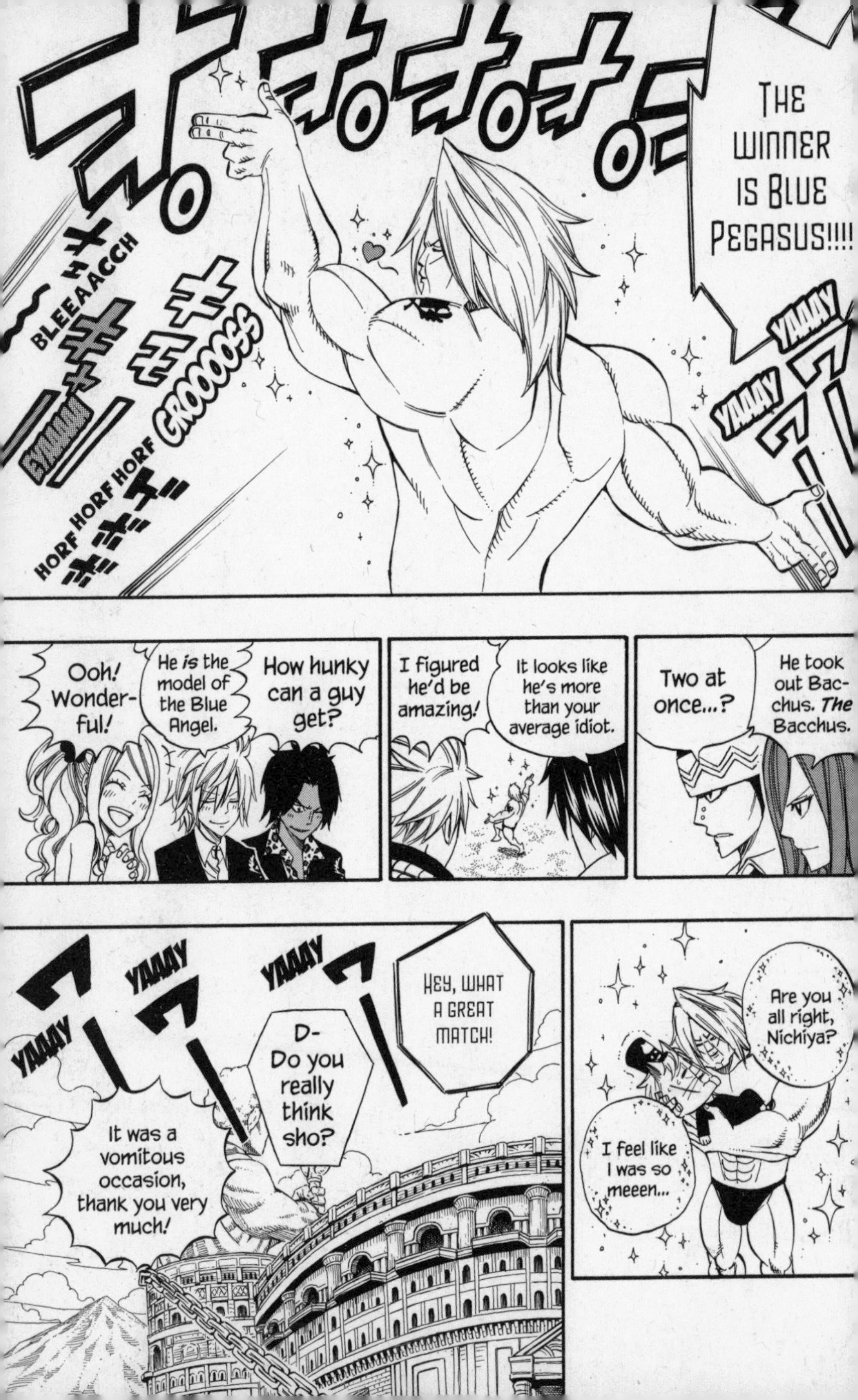
THE WINNER IS BLUE PEGASUS!!!!
YAAAY
YAAAY
BLEEAACCH
GROOOOSS
HORF HORF HORF
He took out Bacchus. *The* Bacchus.
Two at once...?
It looks like he's more than your average idiot.
I figured he'd be amazing!
How hunky can a guy get?
He *is* the model of the Blue Angel.
Ooh! Wonderful!
Are you all right, Nichiya?
I feel like I was so meeen...
HEY, WHAT A GREAT MATCH!
D- Do you really think sho?
YAAAY
YAAAY
YAAAY
It was a vomitous occasion, thank you very much!

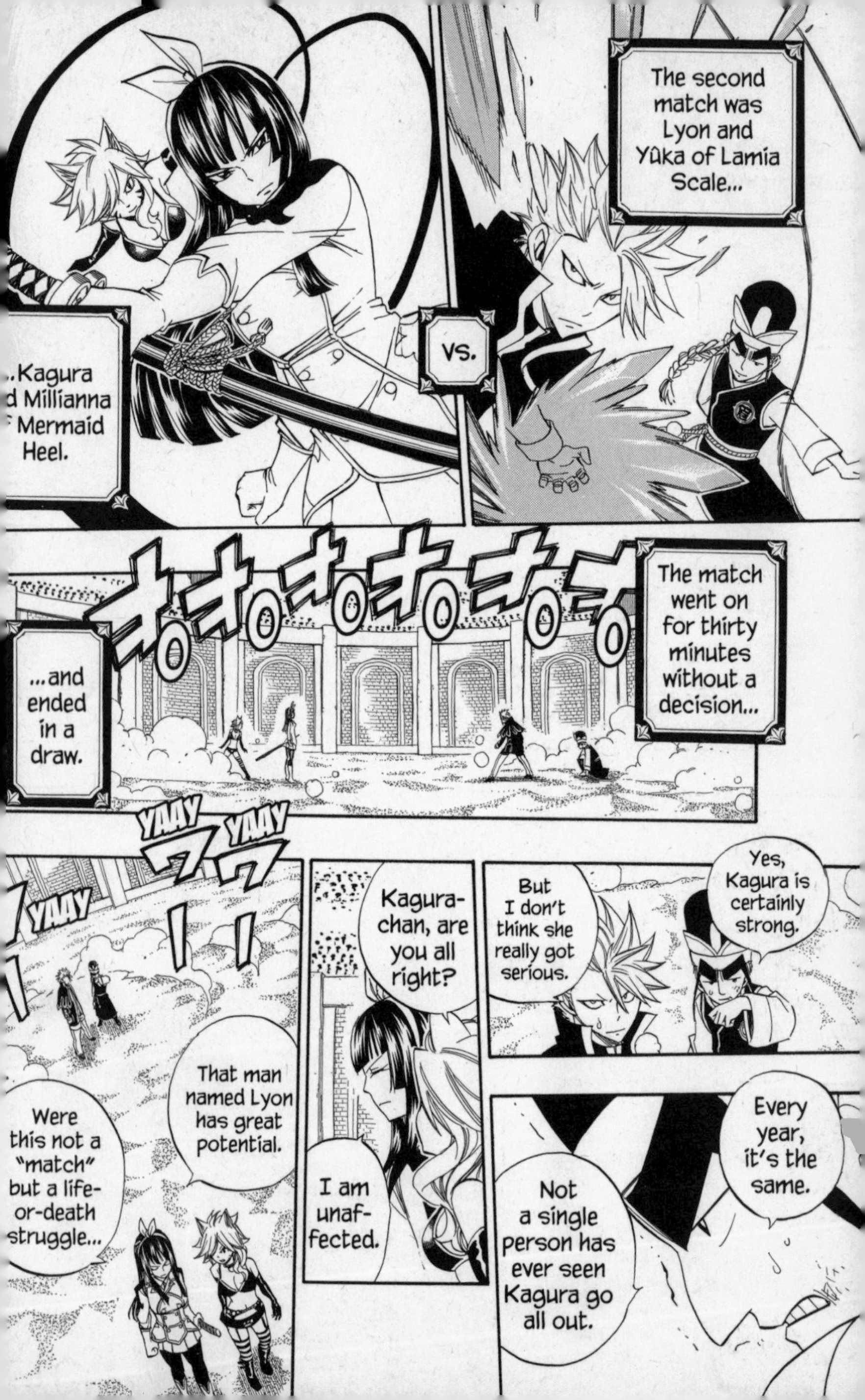
The second match was Lyon and Yûka of Lamia Scale...
vs.
..Kagura d Millianna F Mermaid Heel.
The match went on for thirty minutes without a decision...
...and ended in a draw.
Yes, Kagura is certainly strong.
But I don't think she really got serious.
Every year, it's the same.
Not a single person has ever seen Kagura go all out.
Kagura-chan, are you all right?
I am unaffected.
YAAY
YAAY
YAAY
That man named Lyon has great potential.
Were this not a "match" but a life-or-death struggle...

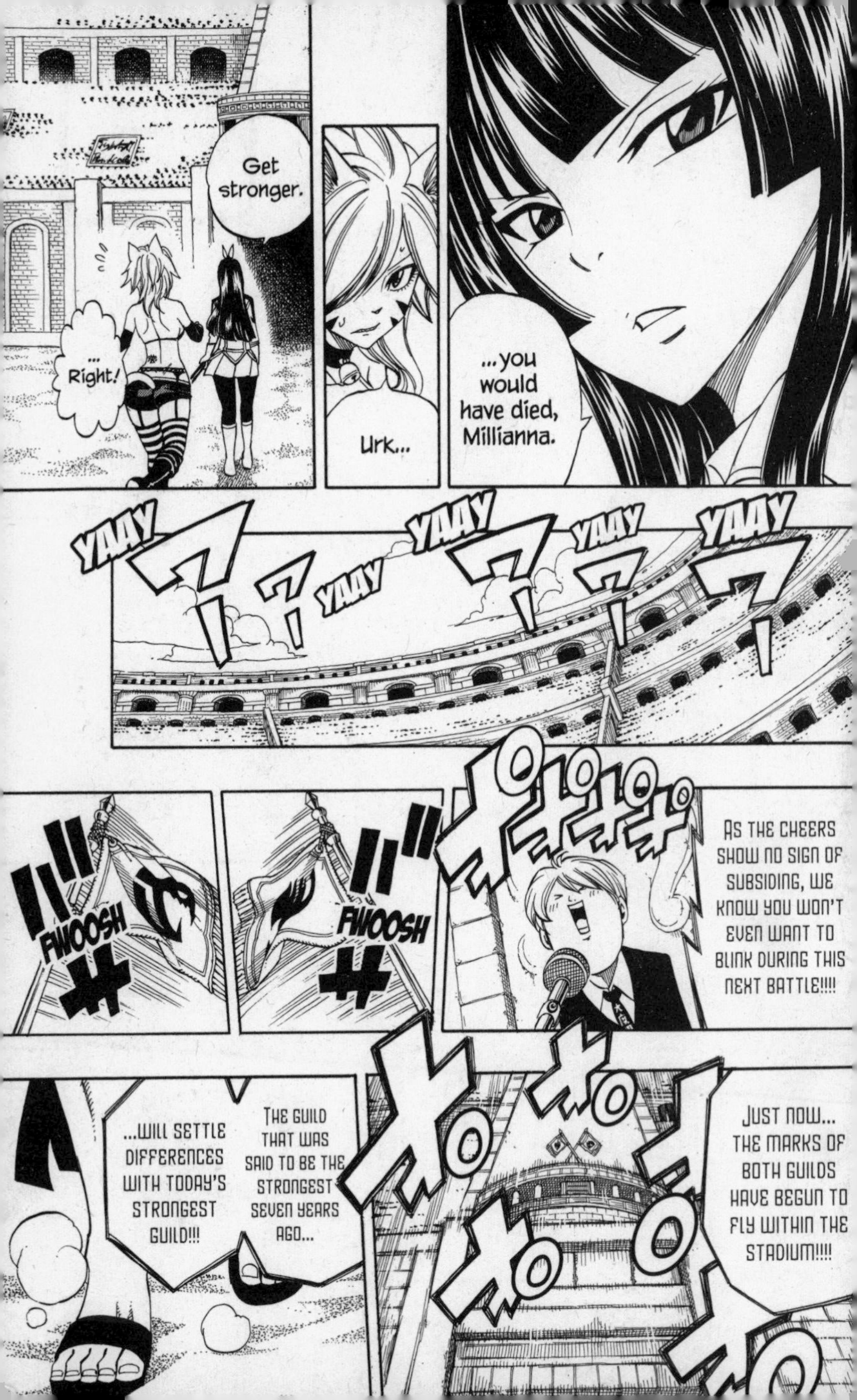
...you would have died, Millianna.
Urk...
Get stronger.
...Right!
YAAY
YAAY
YAAY
YAAY
YAAY
As the cheers show no sign of subsiding, we know you won't even want to blink during this next battle!!!!
FWOOSH
FWOOSH
Just now... the marks of both guilds have begun to fly within the stadium!!!!
The guild that was said to be the strongest seven years ago...
...will settle differences with today's strongest guild!!!

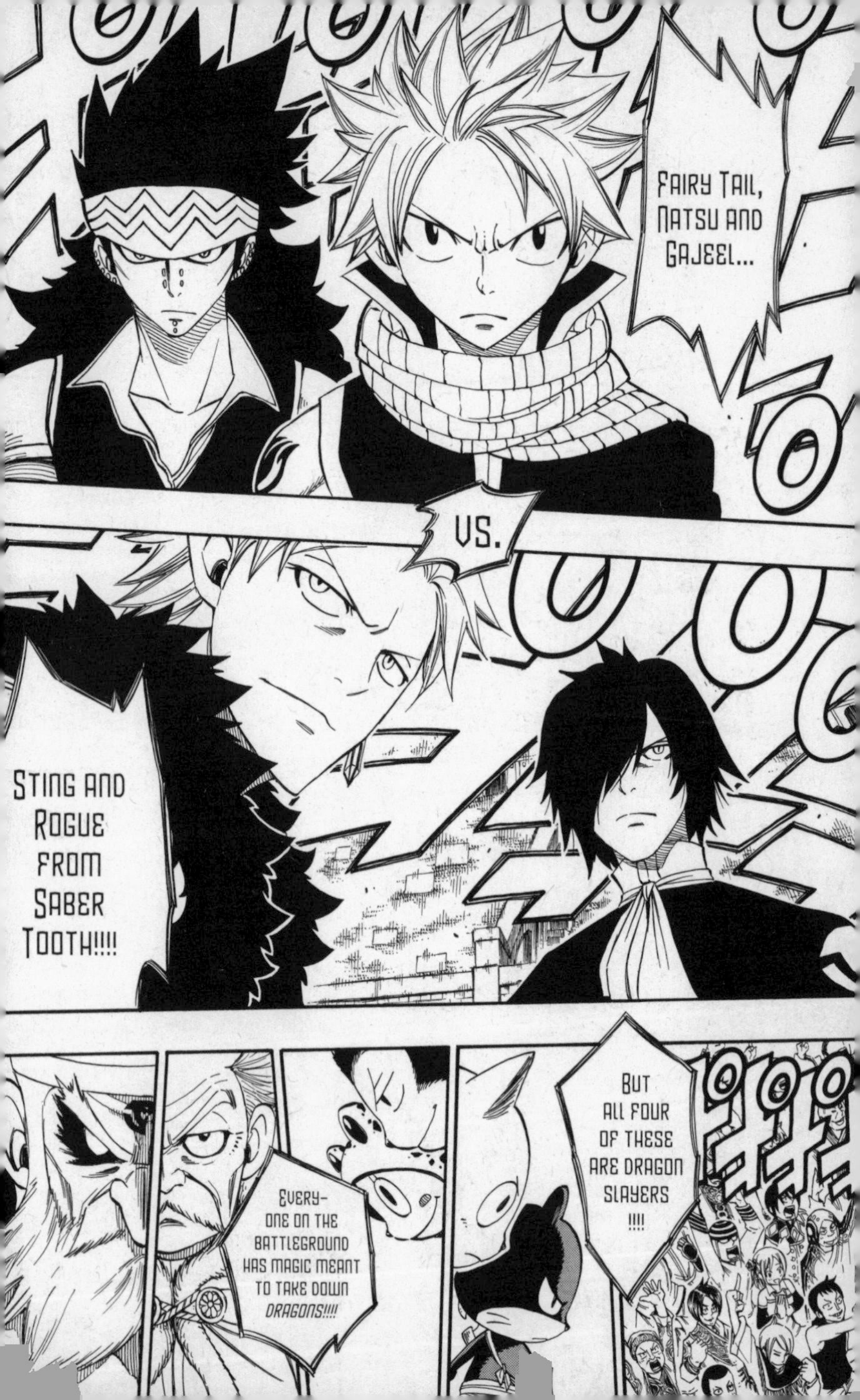
FAIRY TAIL, NATSU AND GAJEEL...
VS.
STING AND ROGUE FROM SABER TOOTH!!!!
BUT ALL FOUR OF THESE ARE DRAGON SLAYERS!!!!
EVERY-ONE ON THE BATTLEGROUND HAS MAGIC MEANT TO TAKE DOWN *DRAGONS*!!!!

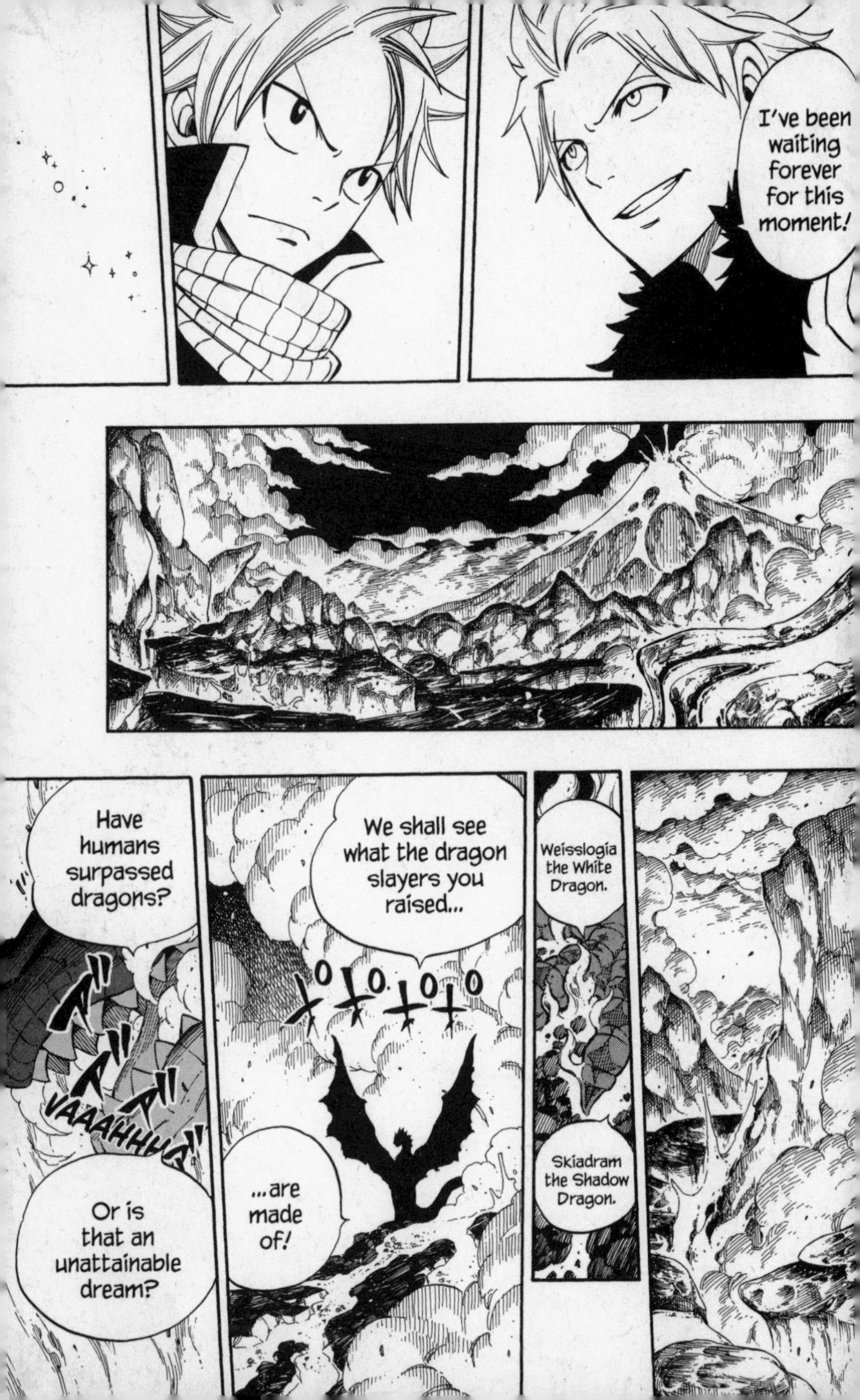

I've been waiting forever for this moment!
Weisslogia the White Dragon.
Skiadram the Shadow Dragon.
We shall see what the dragon slayers you raised...
...are made of!
Have humans surpassed dragons?
Or is that an unattainable dream?

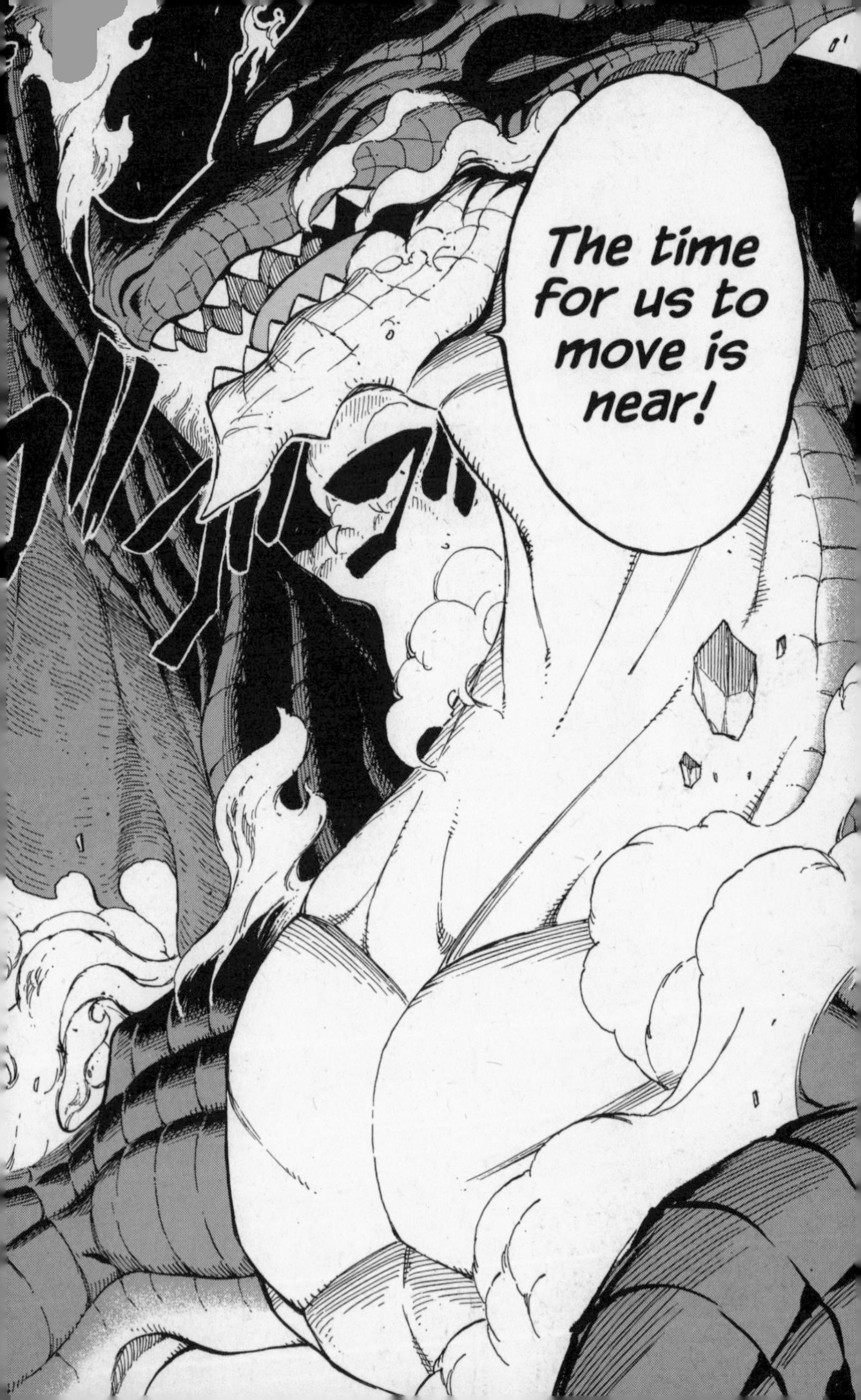
The time for us to move is near!

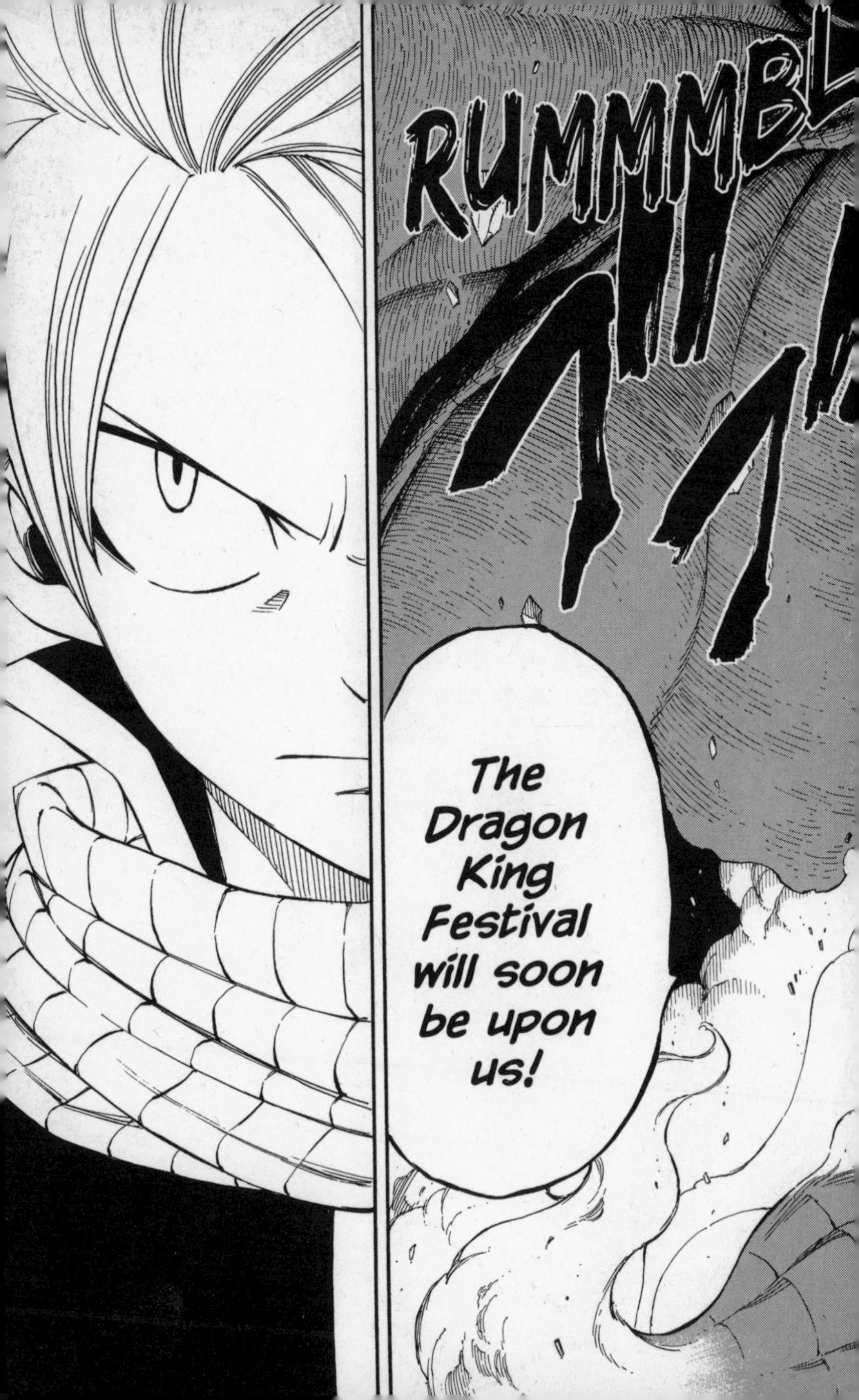
RUMMMBL
The Dragon King Festival will soon be upon us!

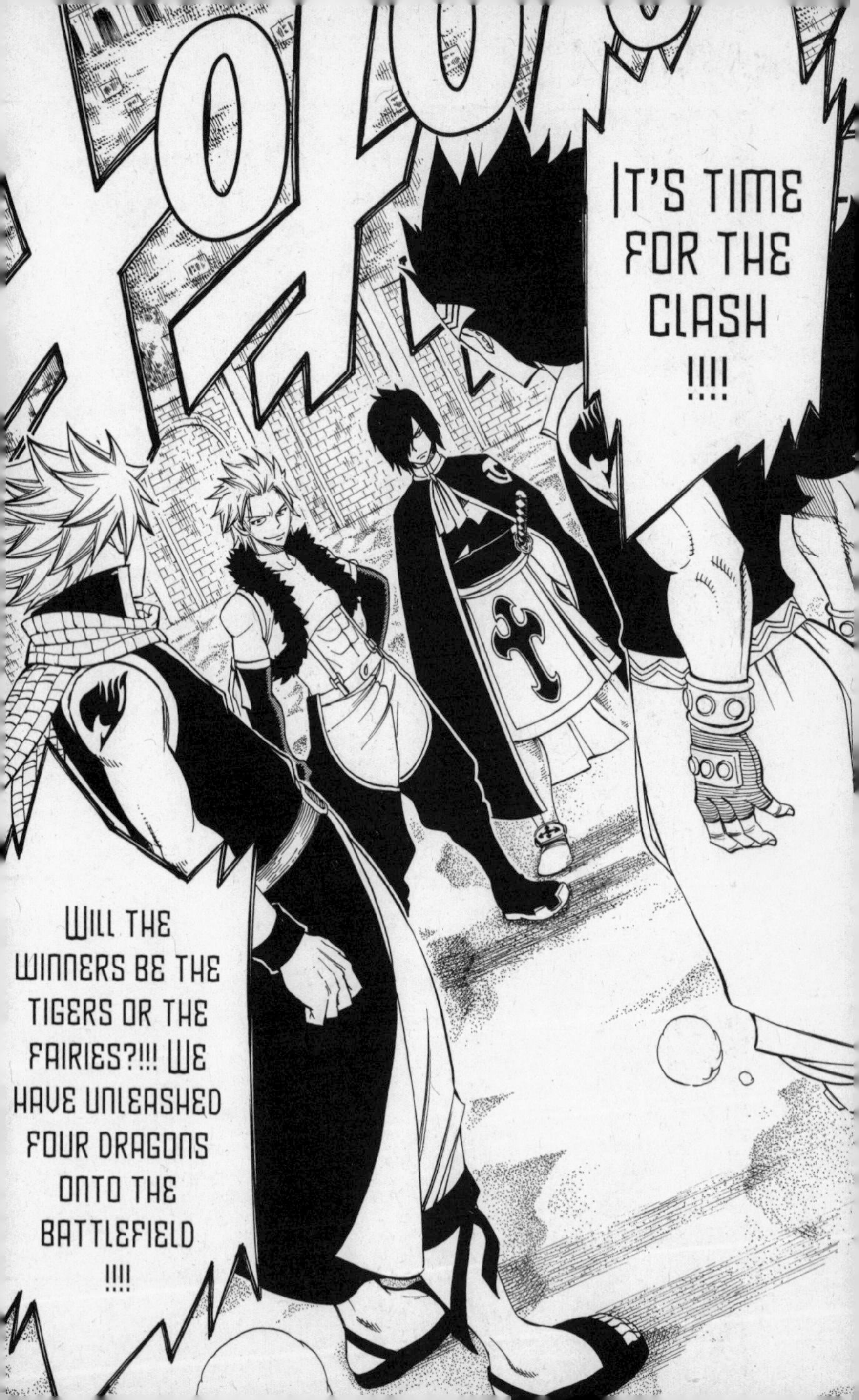

IT'S TIME FOR THE CLASH !!!!
WILL THE WINNERS BE THE TIGERS OR THE FAIRIES?!!! WE HAVE UNLEASHED FOUR DRAGONS ONTO THE BATTLEFIELD !!!!

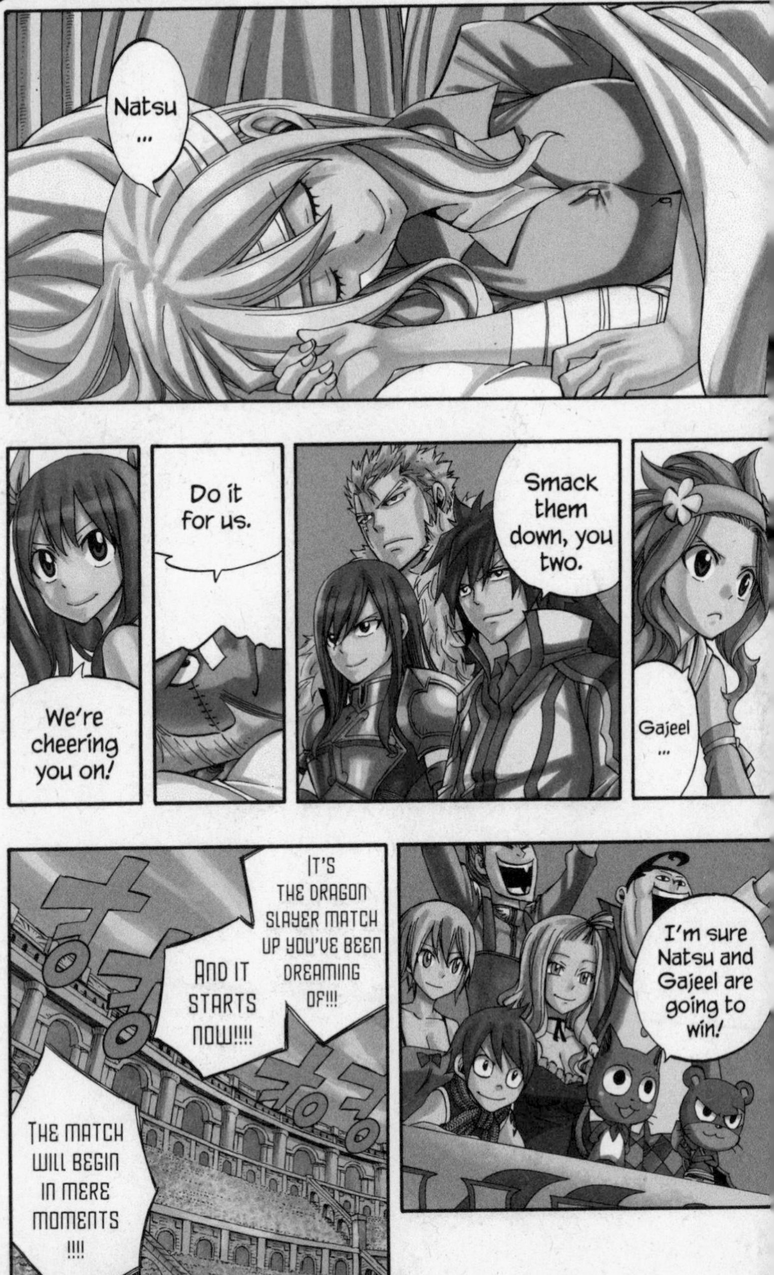
Natsu ...
Gajeel ...
Smack them down, you two.
Do it for us.
We're cheering you on!
I'm sure Natsu and Gajeel are going to win!
IT'S THE DRAGON SLAYER MATCH UP YOU'VE BEEN DREAMING OF!!!
AND IT STARTS NOW!!!!
THE MATCH WILL BEGIN IN MERE MOMENTS !!!!

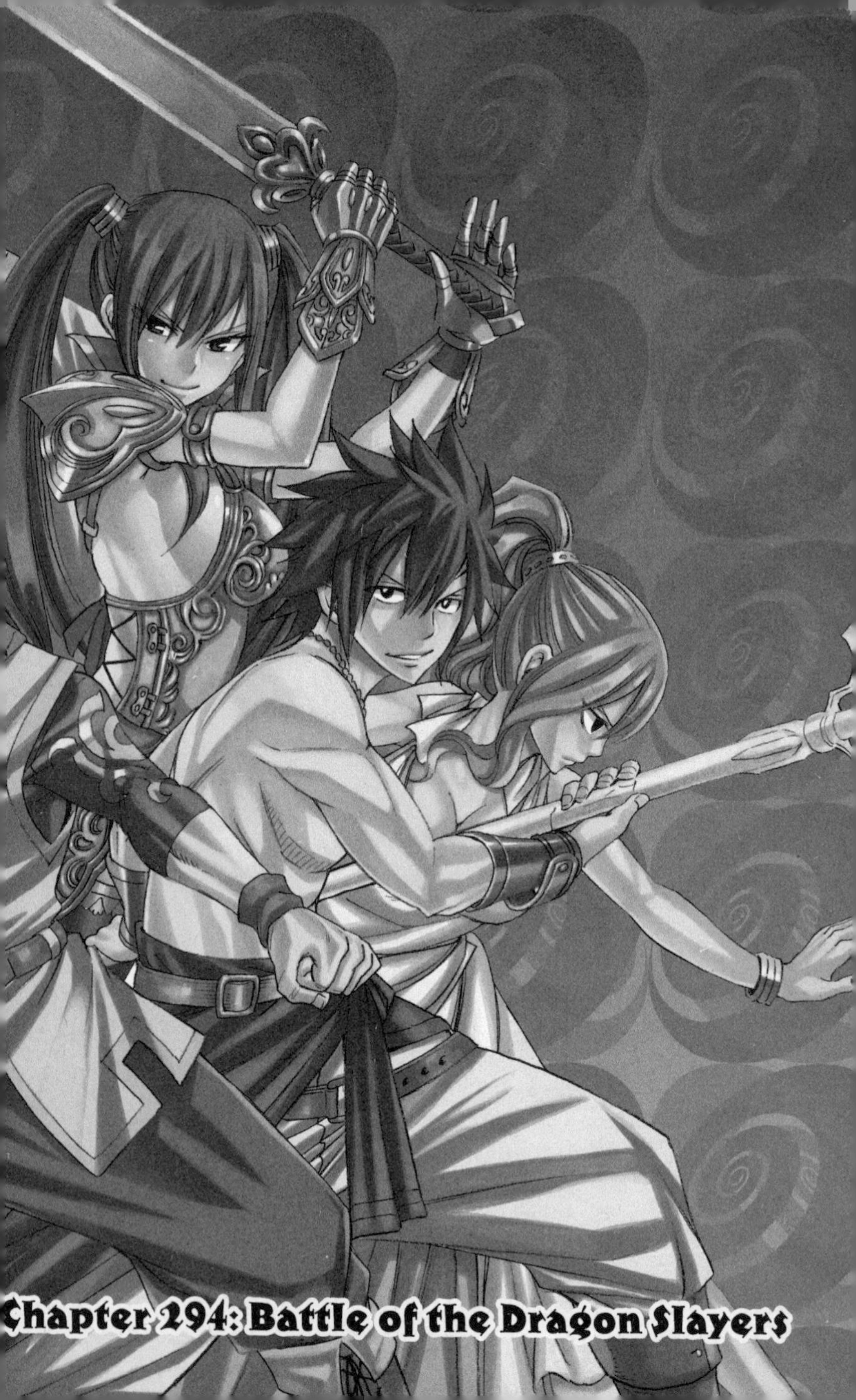

Chapter 294: Battle of the Dragon Slayers

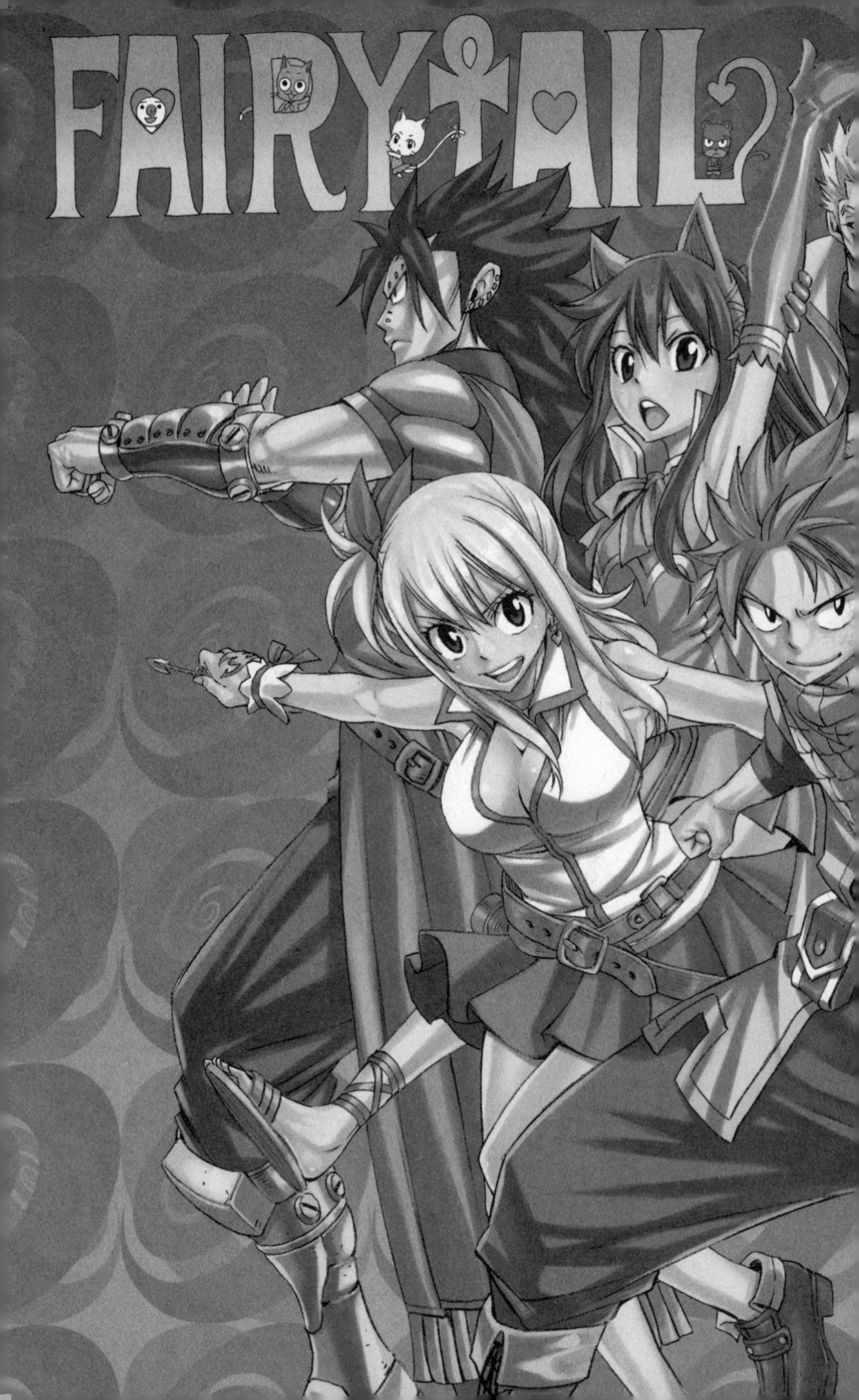
FAIRY TAIL

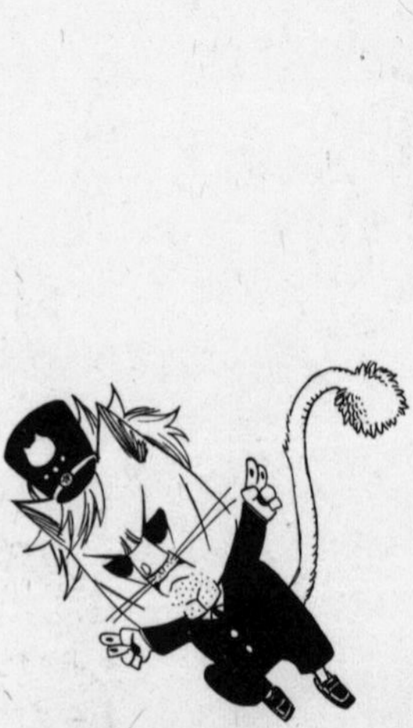

FAIRY TAIL

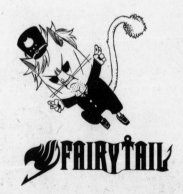

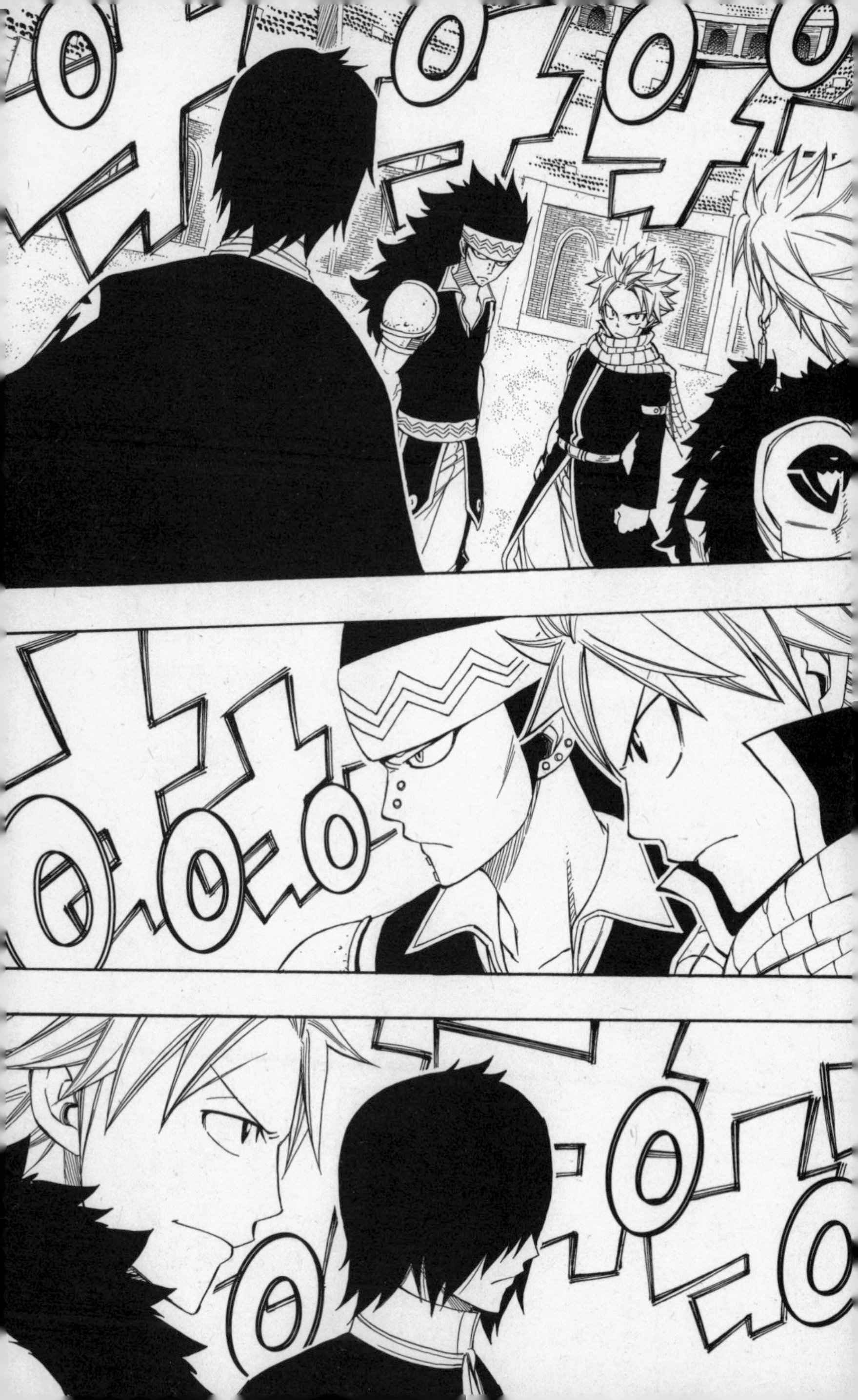

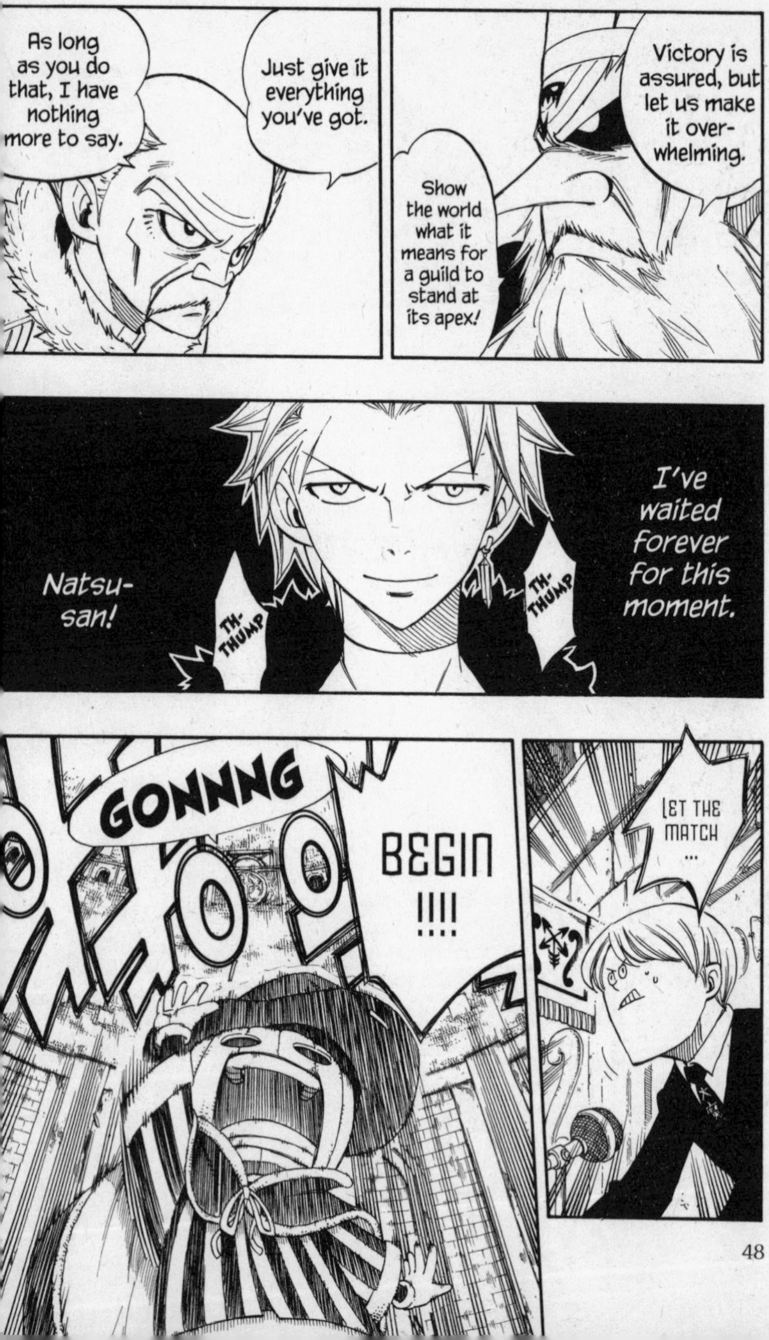

Victory is assured, but let us make it over-whelming.
Show the world what it means for a guild to stand at its apex!
Just give it everything you've got.
As long as you do that, I have nothing more to say.
I've waited forever for this moment.
TH-THUMP
TH-THUMP
Natsu-san!
LET THE MATCH ...
BEGIN !!!!
GONNNG

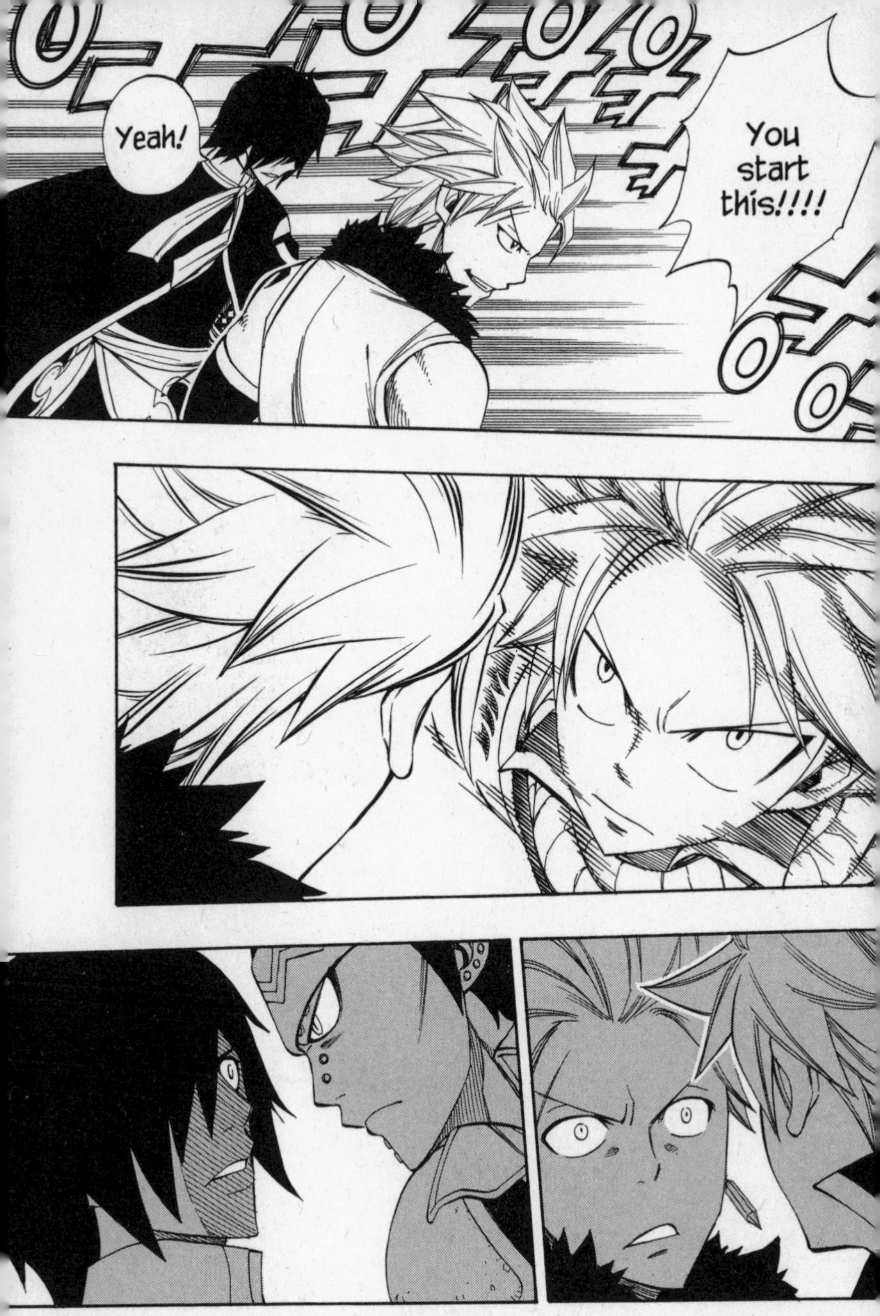
You start this!!!!
Yeah!

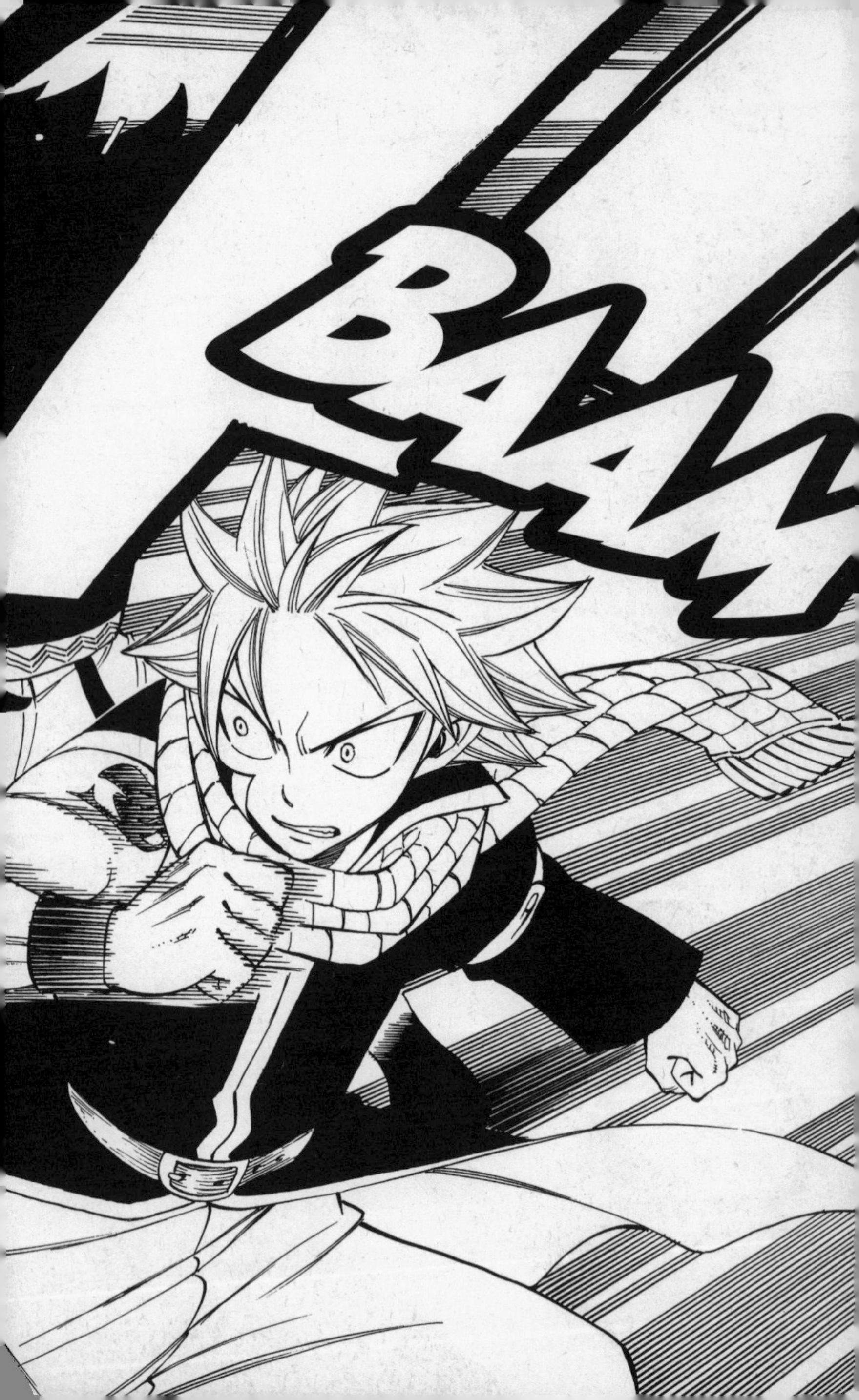
BAM

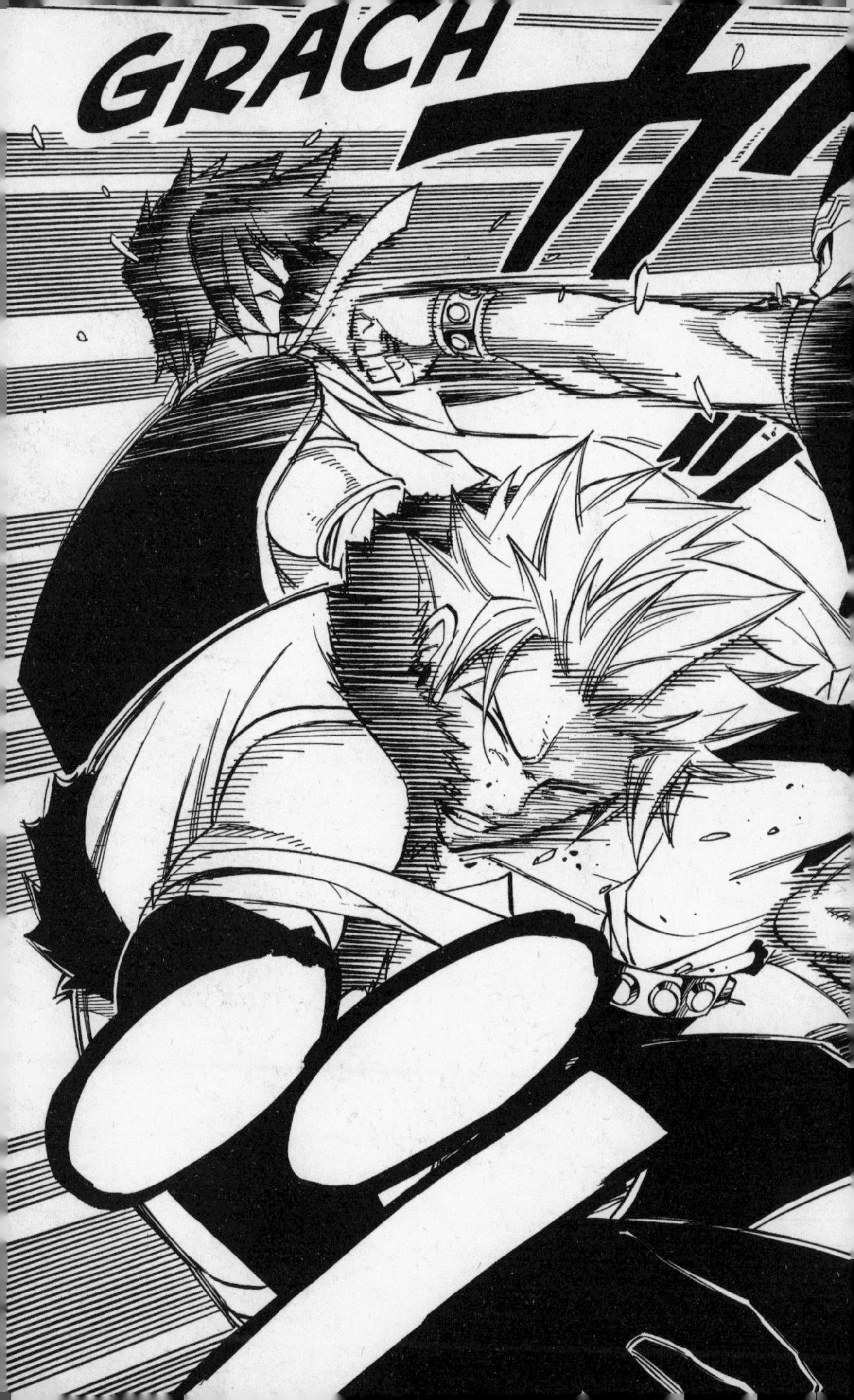
GRACH

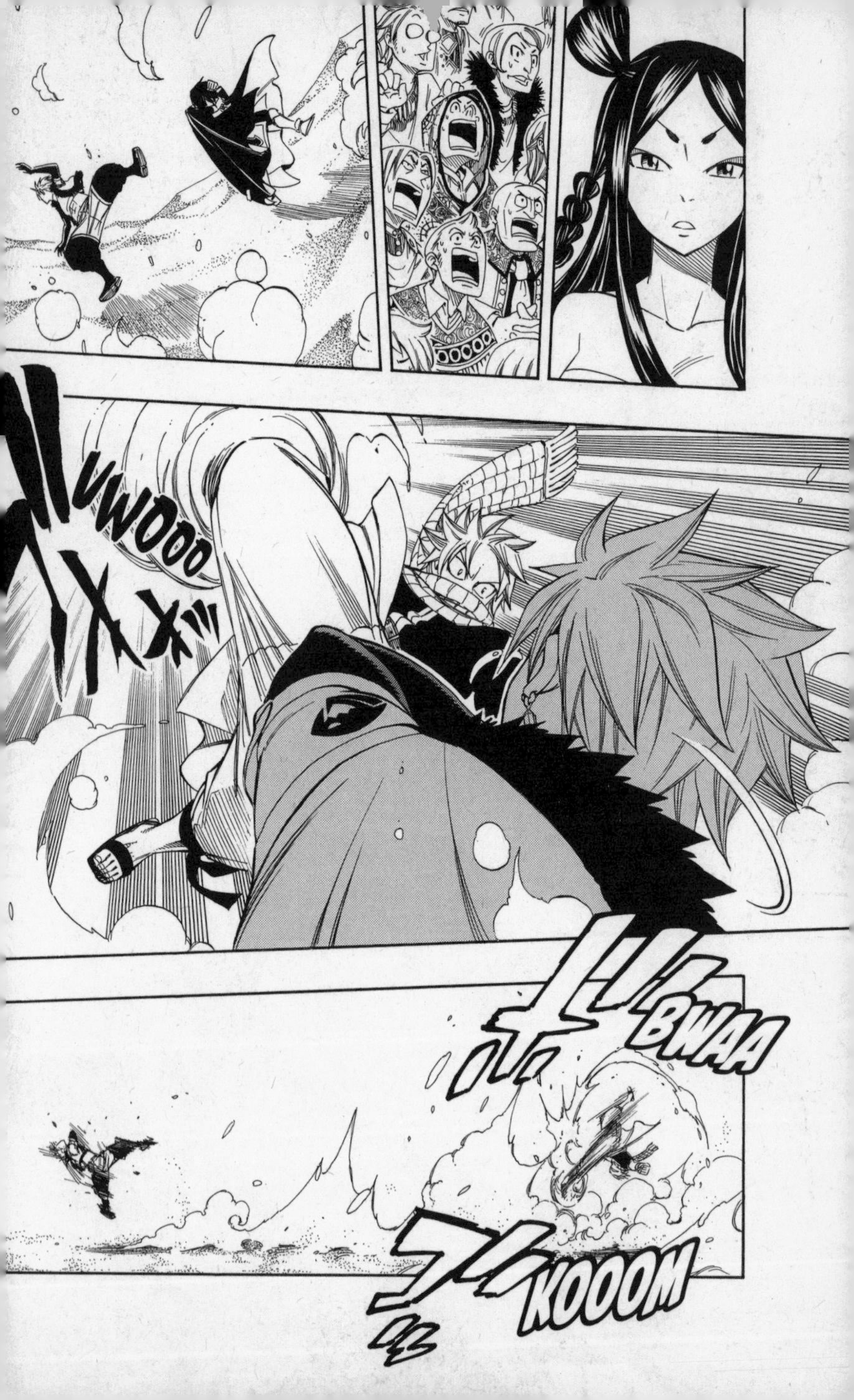
VWOOO
BWAA
KOOOM

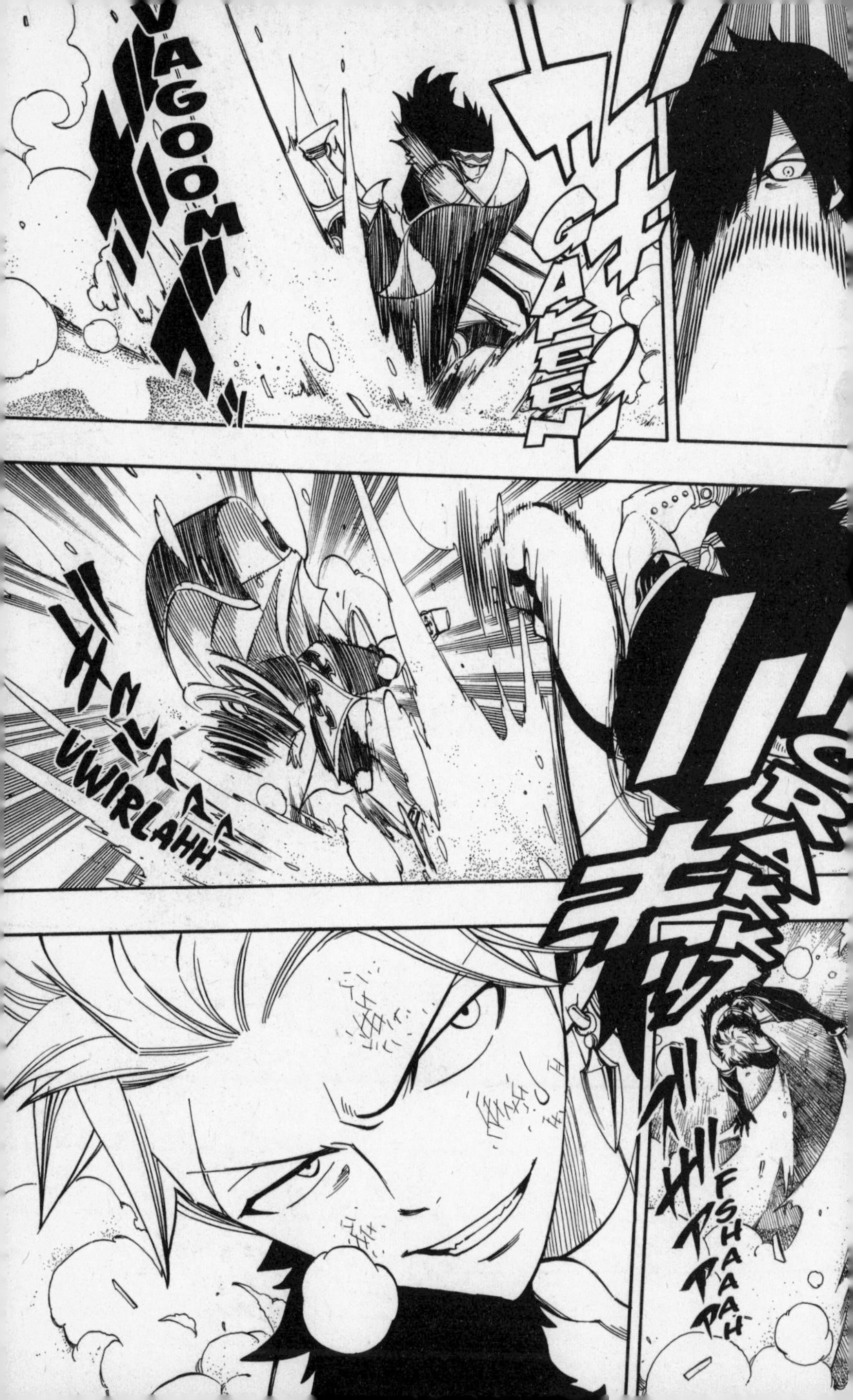
GAEEN
VAGOOM
CRAKK
UWIRLAHH
FSHAAAH

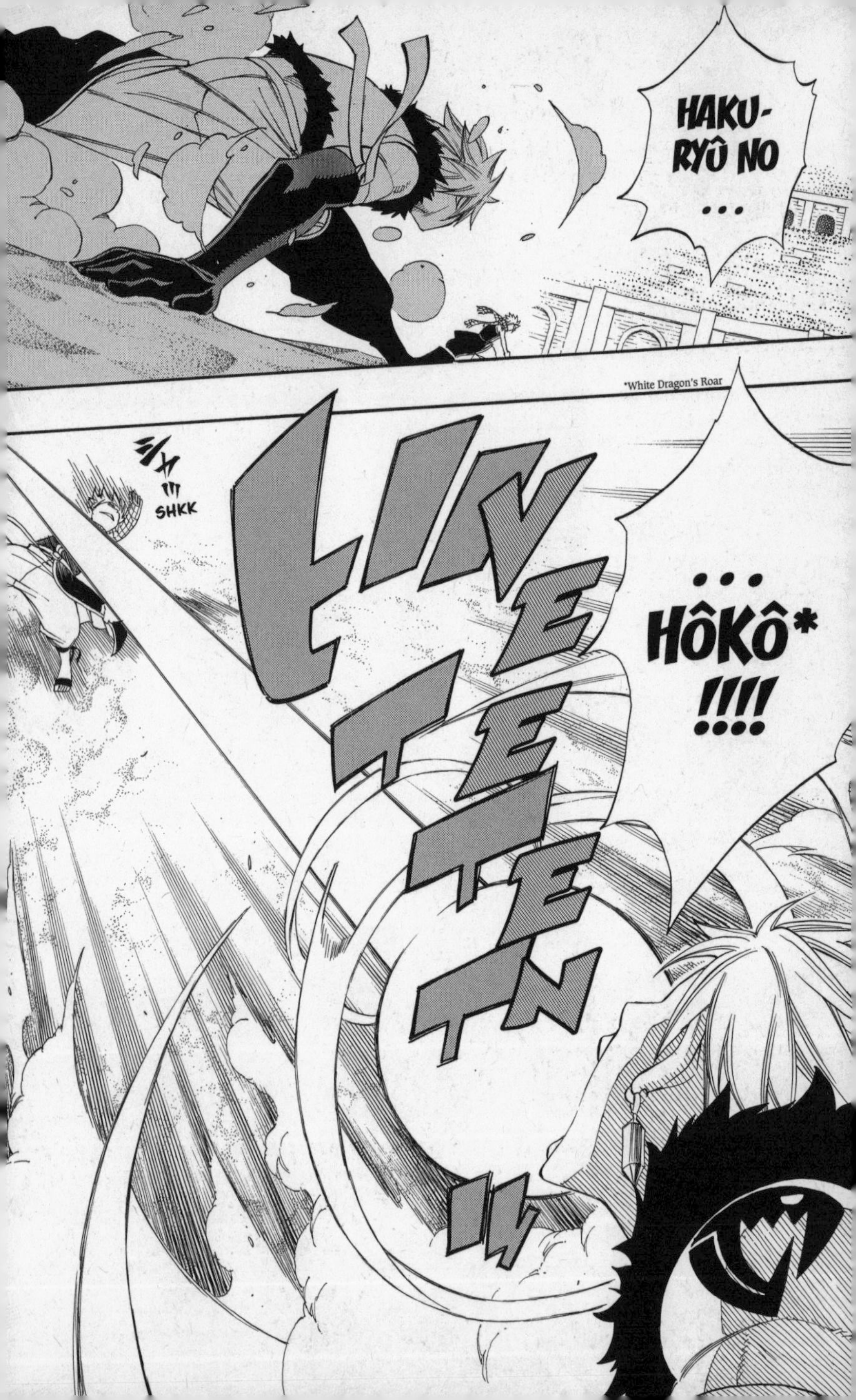
HAKU-RYÛ NO …
… HÔKÔ* !!!!
SHKK
*White Dragon's Roar

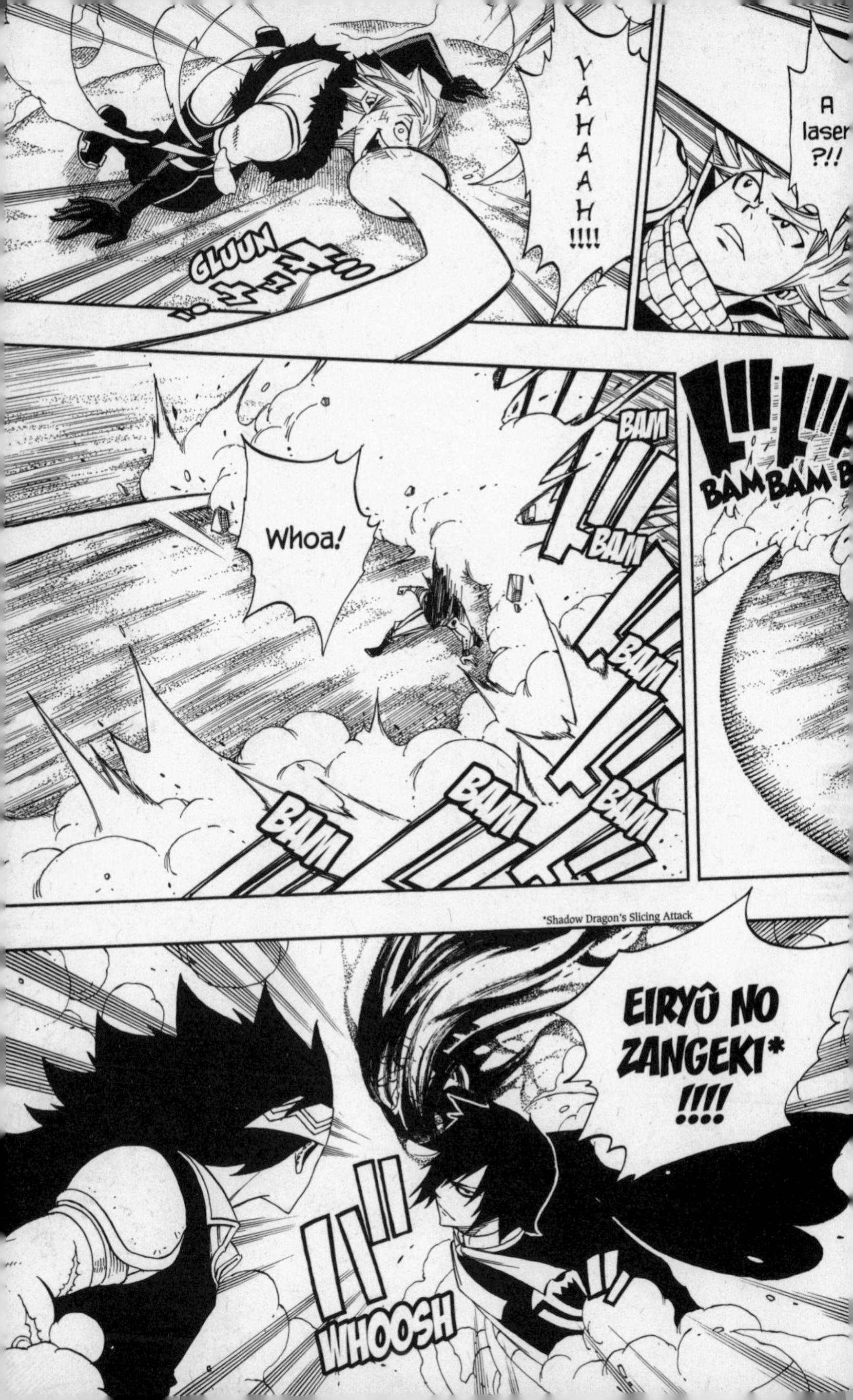
A laser?!!
YAHAAAH!!!!
GLUUN
BAM BAM B
BAM
BAM
BAM
BAM
BAM
BAM
Whoa!
EIRYÛ NO ZANGEKI* !!!!
WHOOSH
*Shadow Dragon's Slicing Attack

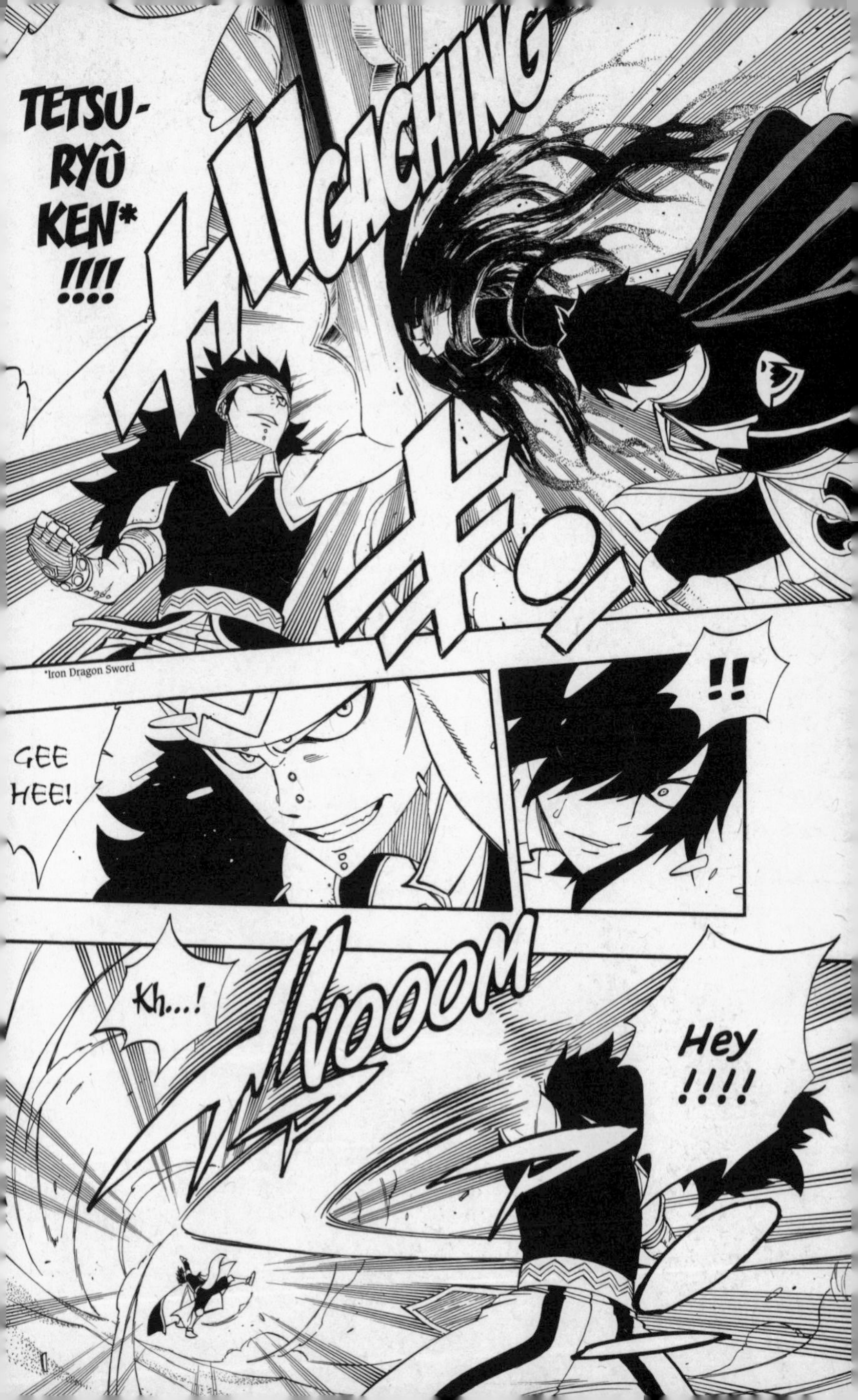
GACHING
TETSU-RYÛ KEN*!!!!
!!
GEE HEE!
Hey!!!!
VOOOM
Kh...!
*Iron Dragon Sword

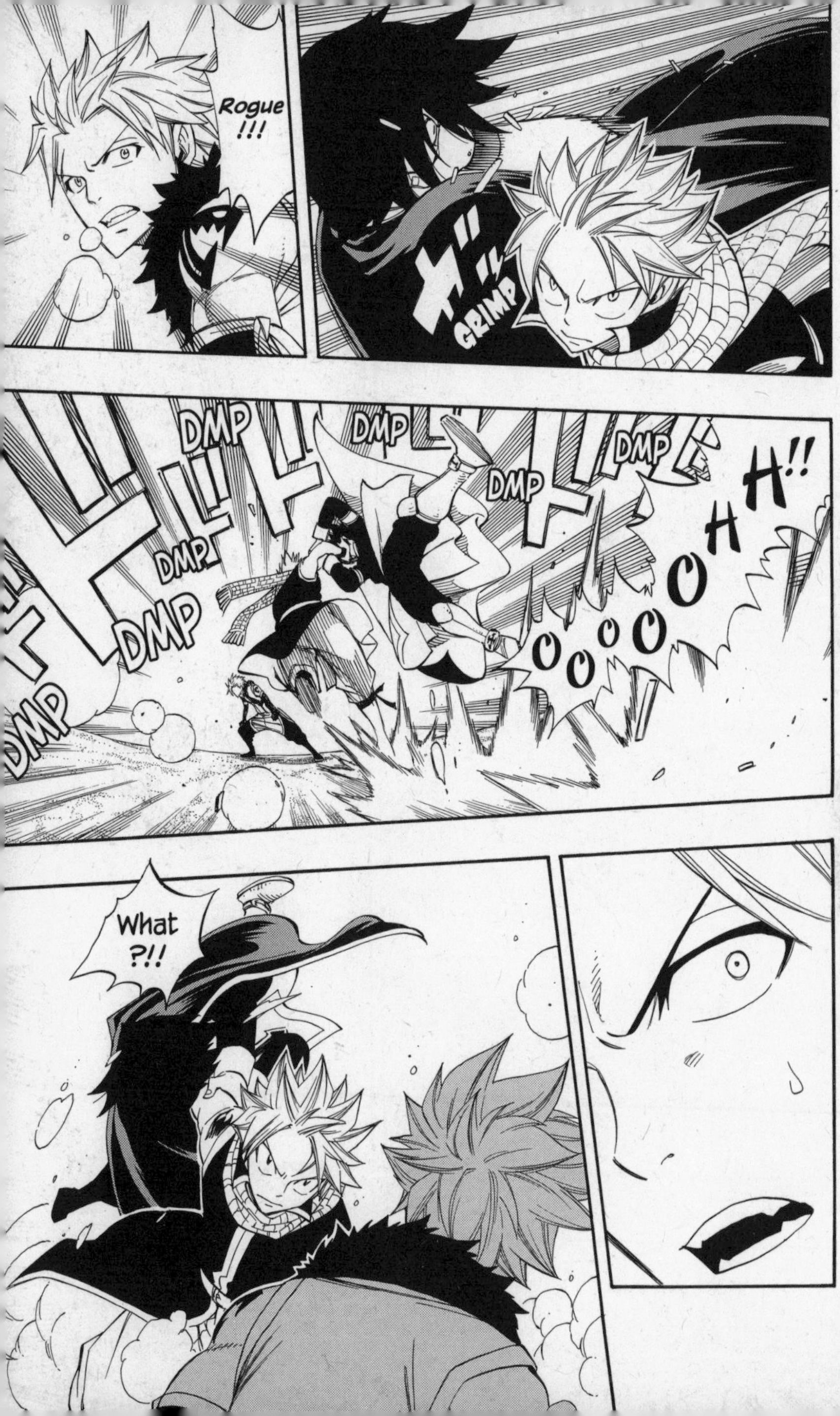
GRIMP
Rogue!!!
DMP DMP DMP DMP DMP DMP DMP DMP
OOOOOOHH!!
What?!!

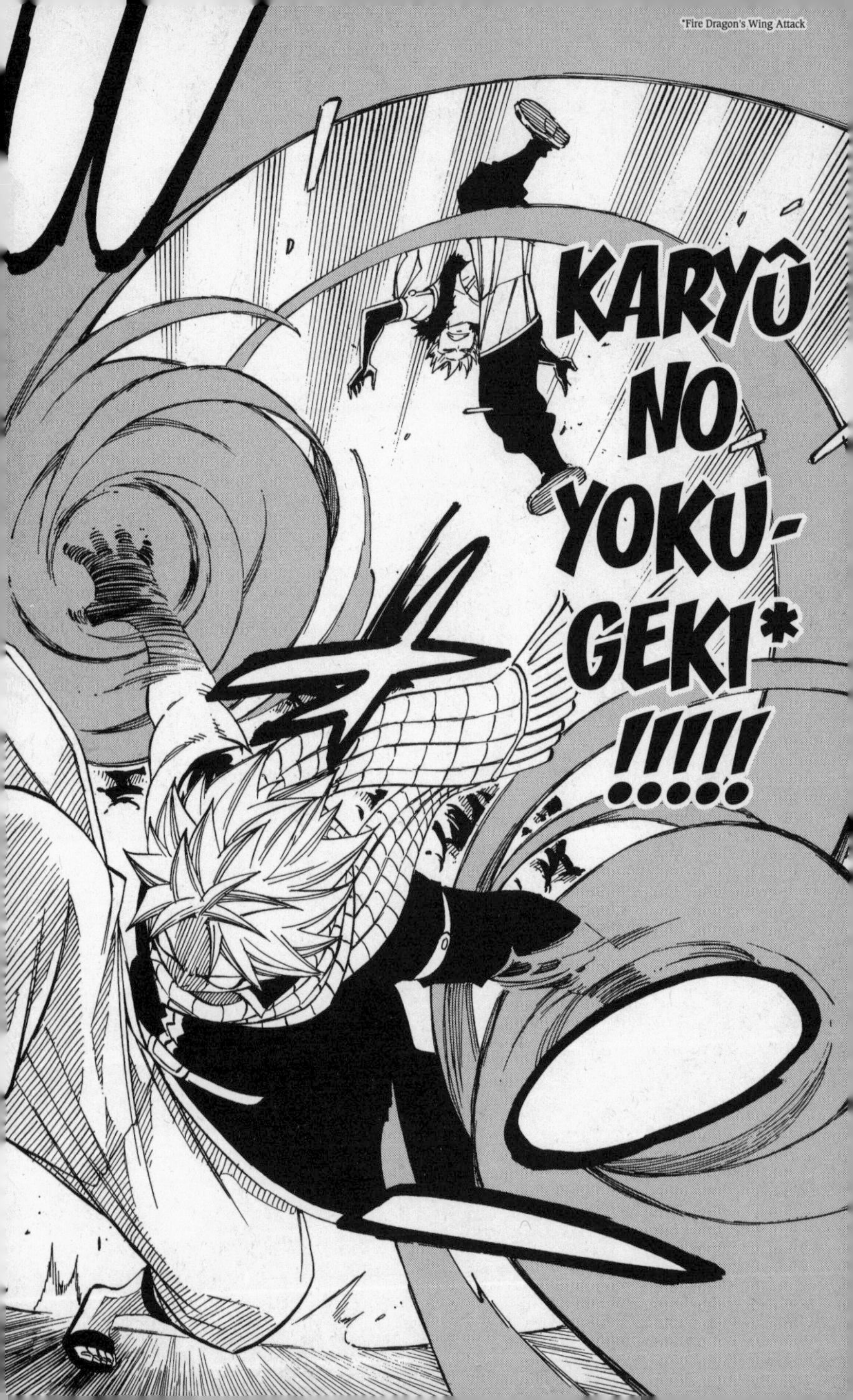
KARYÛ NO YOKU-GEKI* !!!!!
*Fire Dragon's Wing Attack

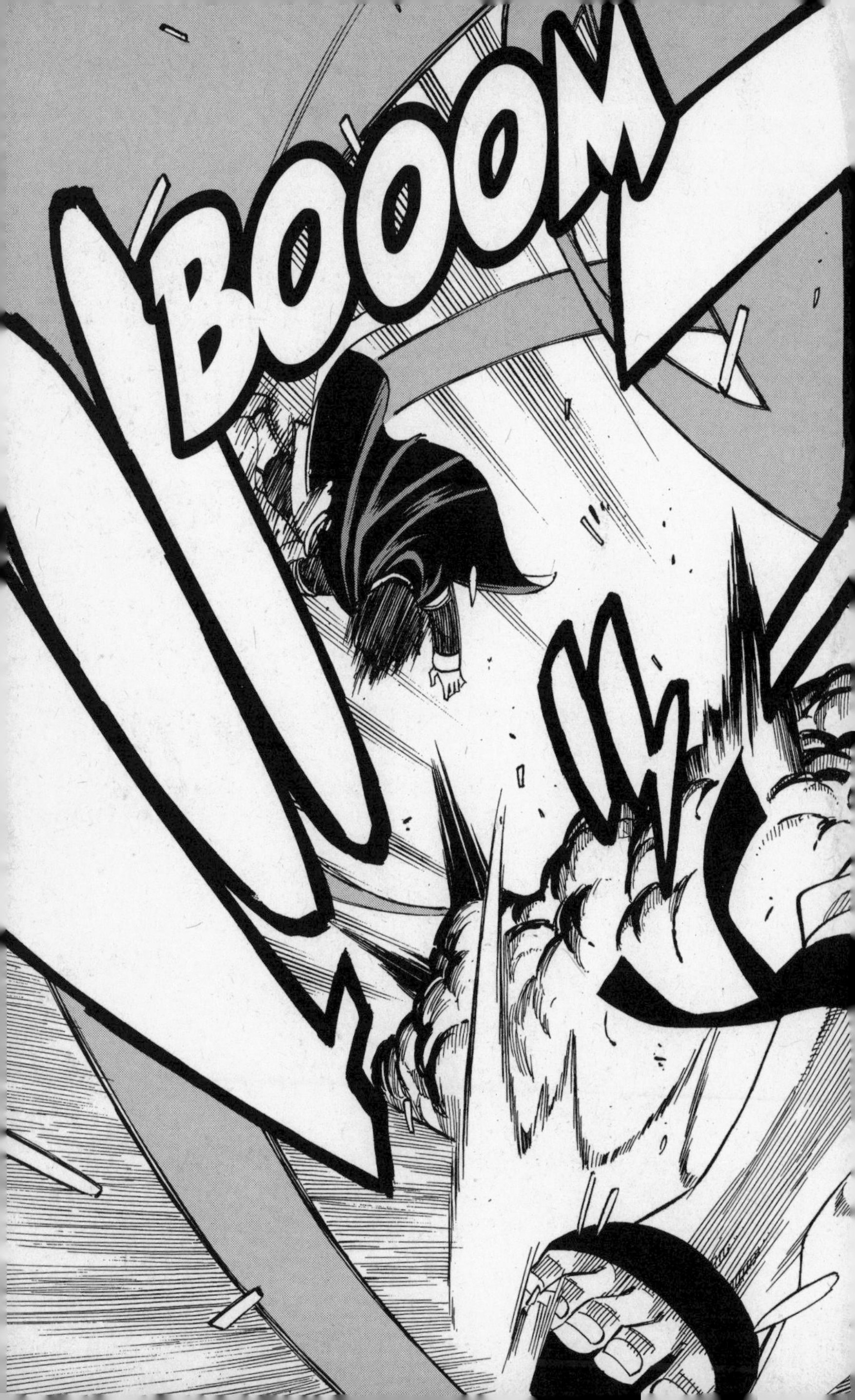
BOOOM

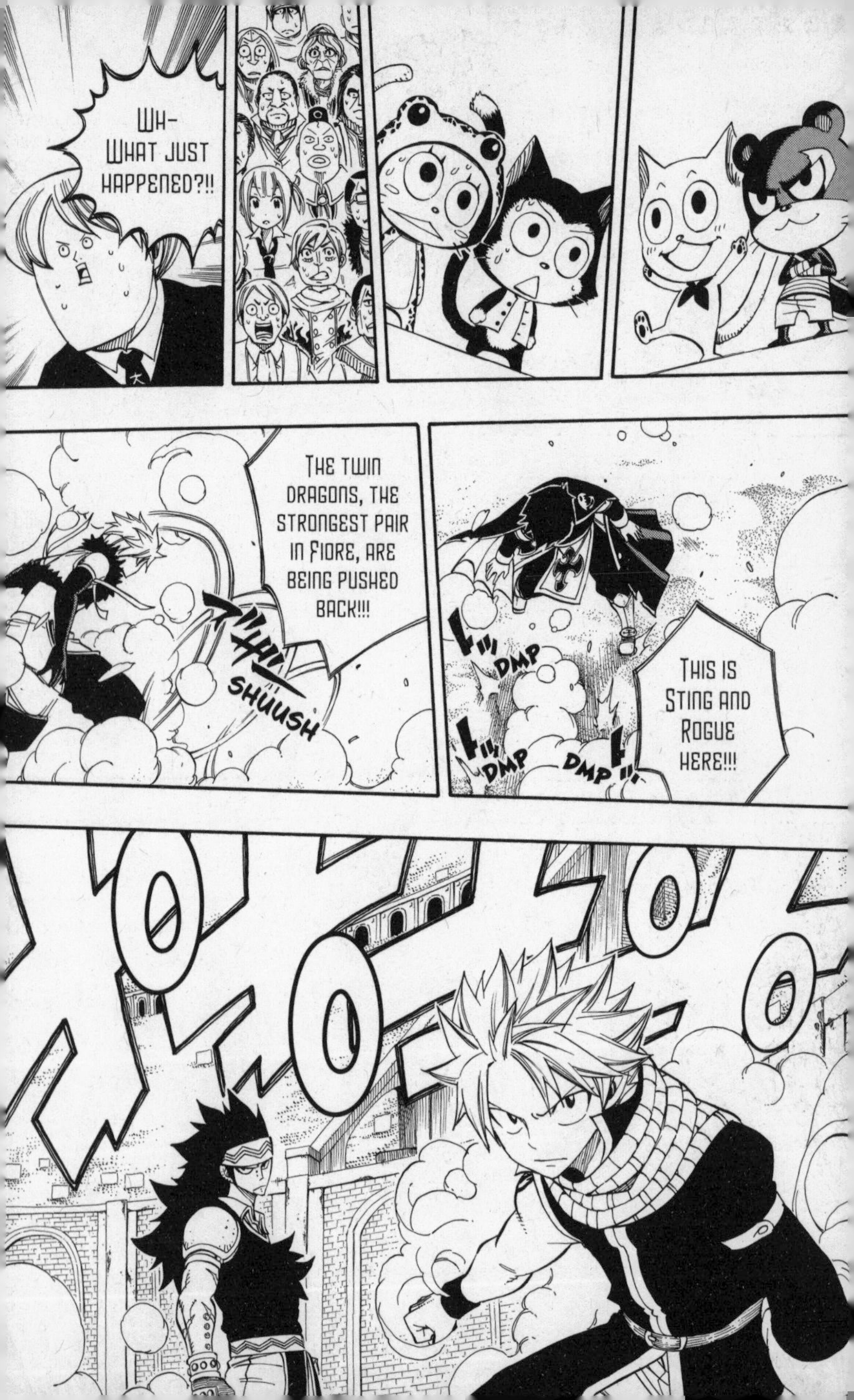

WH- WHAT JUST HAPPENED?!!
THIS IS STING AND ROGUE HERE!!!
DMP
DMP
DMP
THE TWIN DRAGONS, THE STRONGEST PAIR IN FIORE, ARE BEING PUSHED BACK!!!
SHUUSH

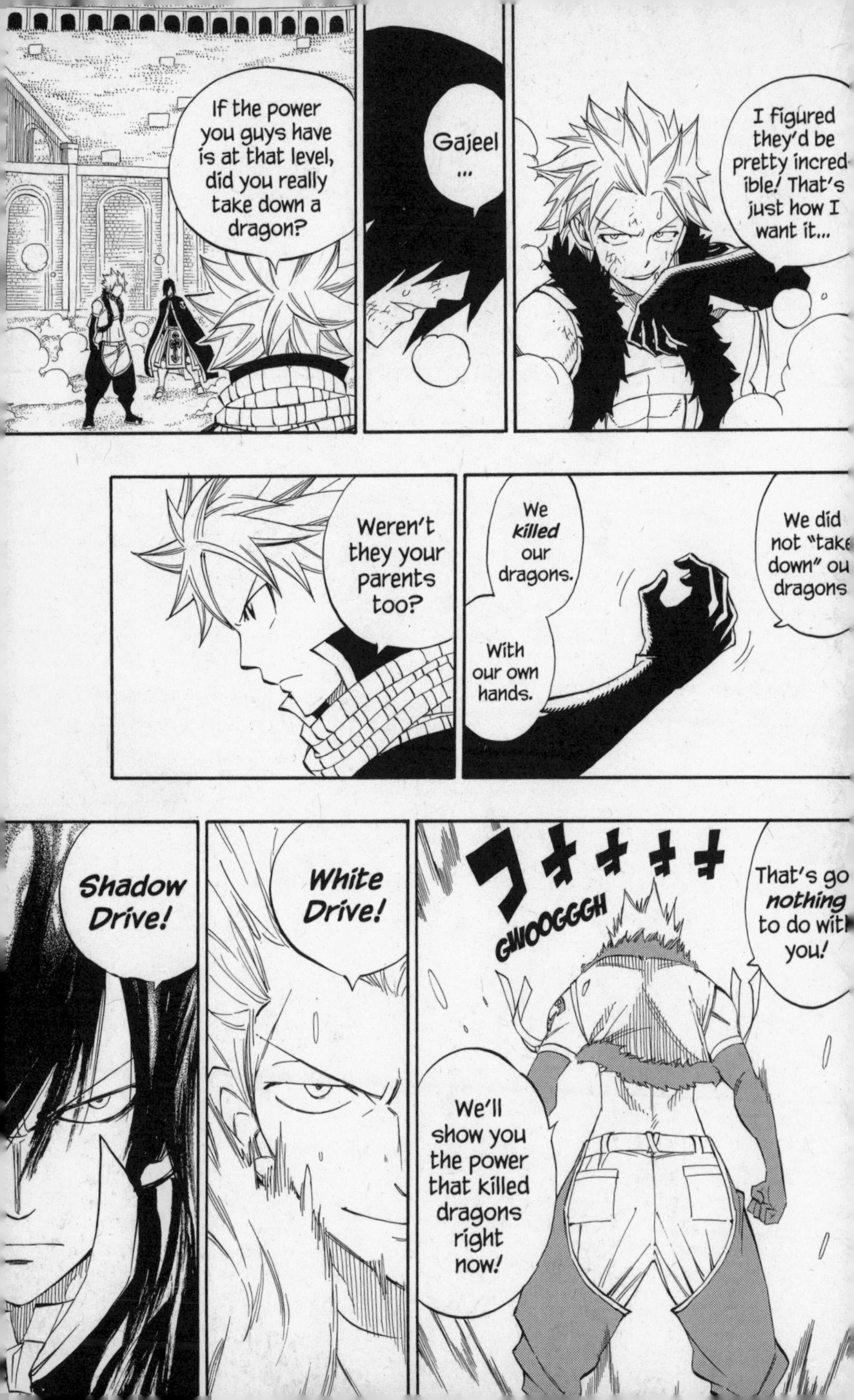

I figured they'd be pretty incred ible! That's just how I want it...
Gajeel ...
If the power you guys have is at that level, did you really take down a dragon?
We did not "take down" ou dragons
We *killed* our dragons.
With our own hands.
Weren't they your parents too?
That's go *nothing* to do wit you!
GWOOGGGH
We'll show you the power that killed dragons right now!
White Drive!
Shadow Drive!

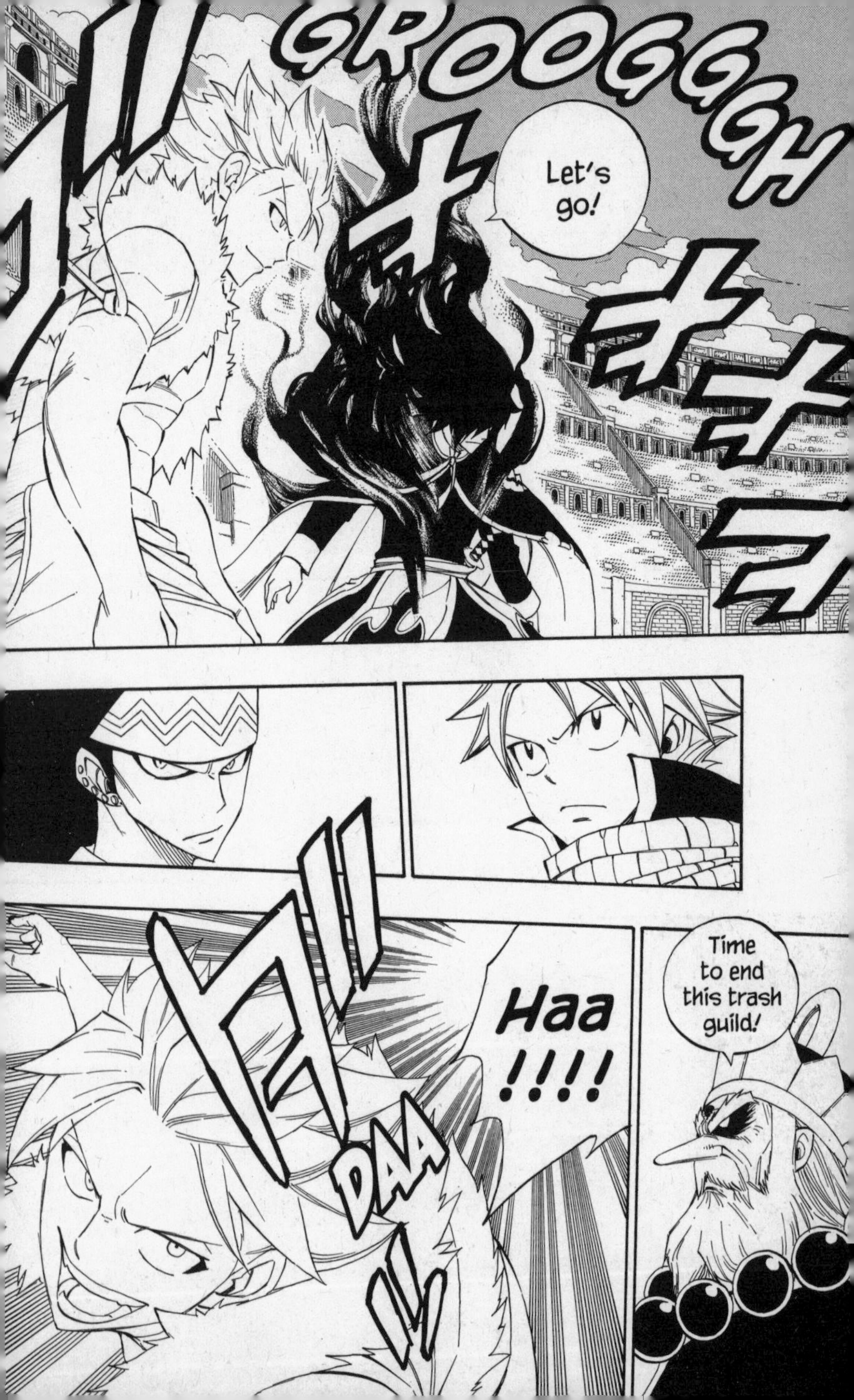
GROOGGGH
Let's go!
Time to end this trash guild!
Haa!!!!
DAA!!

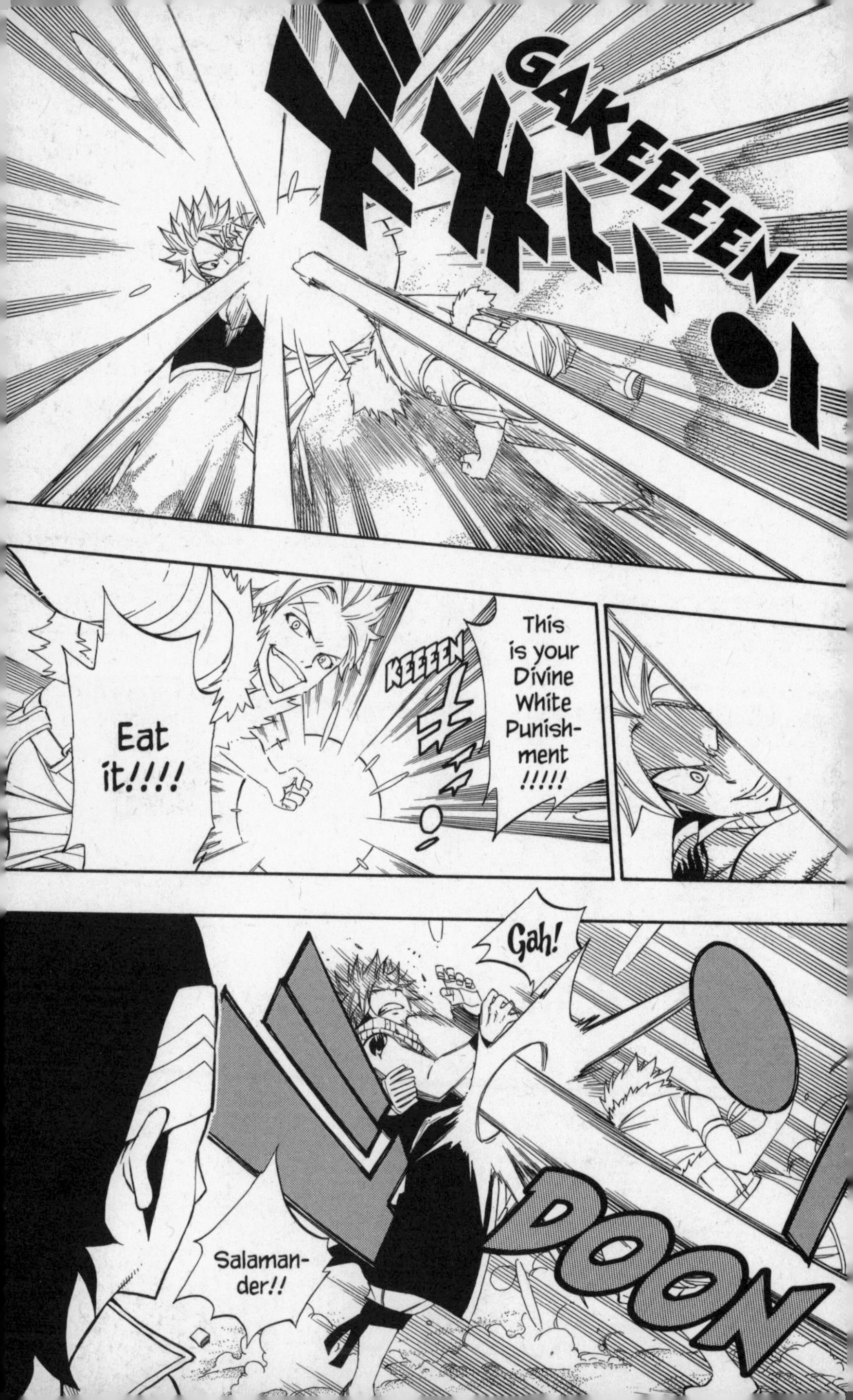

GAKEEEEN
This is your Divine White Punishment!!!!!
KEEEEN
Eat it!!!!!
Gah!
DOOON
Salamander!!

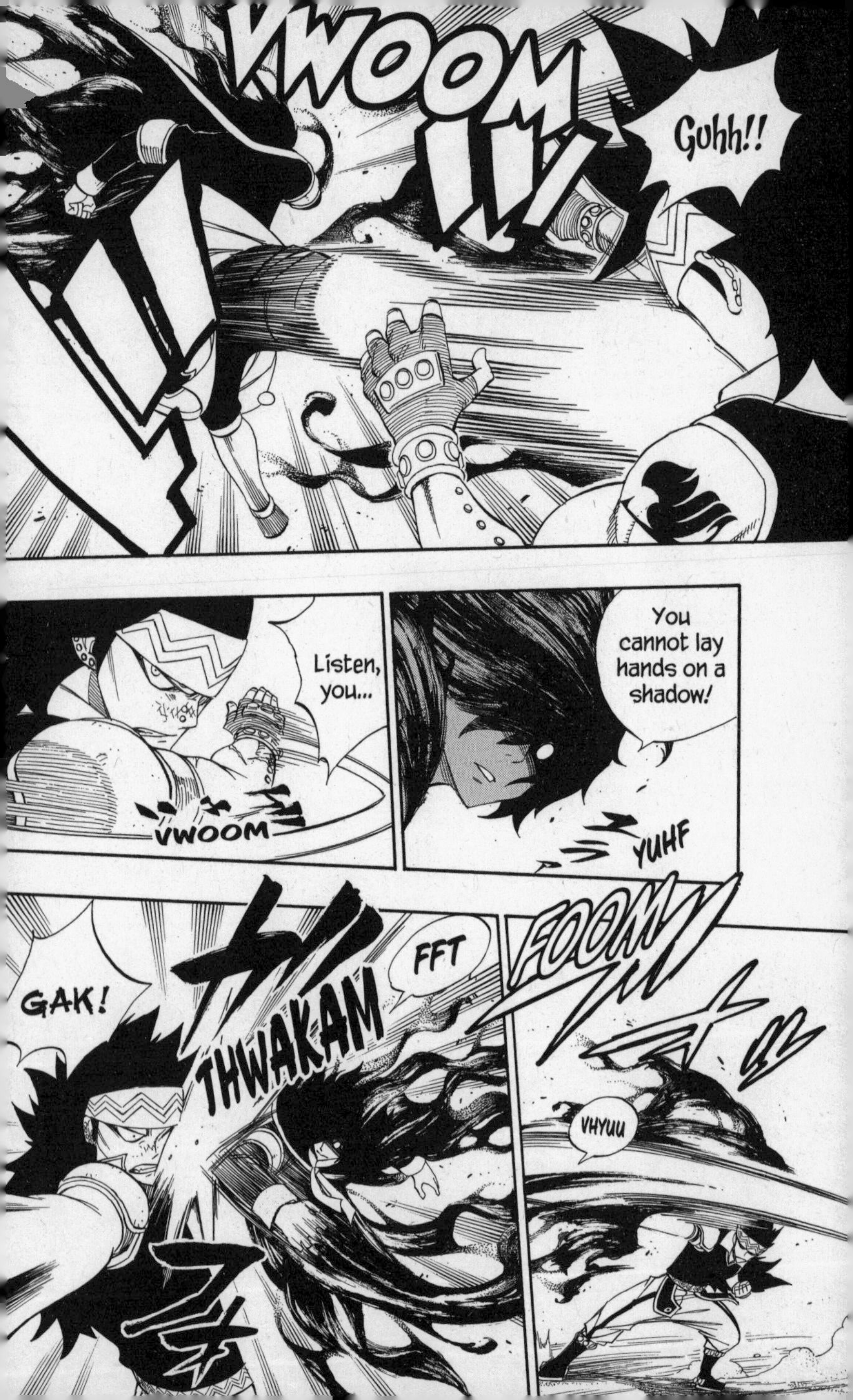
VWOOM
Guhh!!
You cannot lay hands on a shadow!
YUHF
Listen, you...
VWOOM
FOOM
VHYUU
FFT
THWAKAM
GAK!

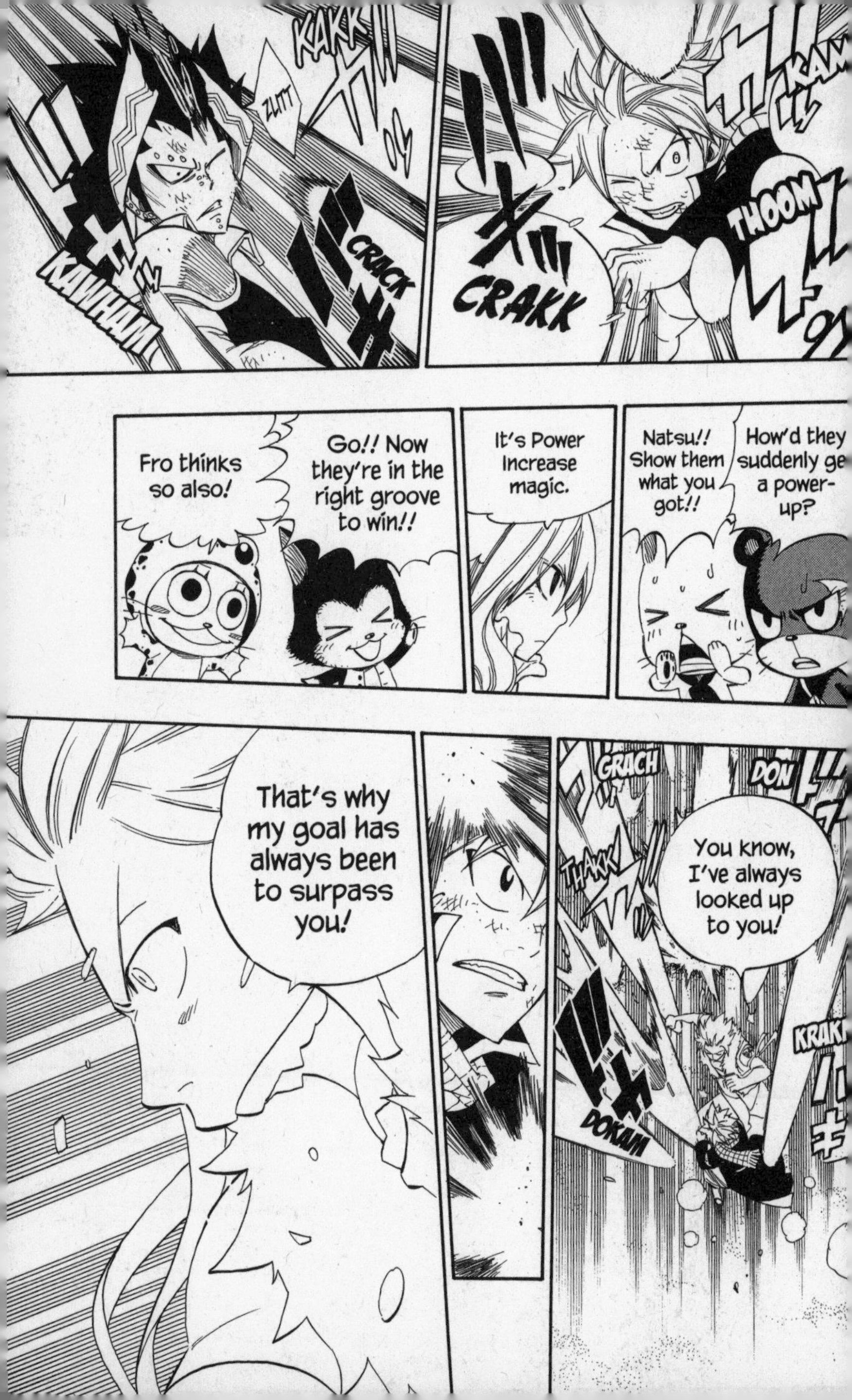
KAM
THOOM
CRAKK
KAKK
ZLITT
CRACK
KAWHAM
How'd they suddenly ge a power-up?
Natsu!! Show them what you got!!
It's Power Increase magic.
Go!! Now they're in the right groove to win!!
Fro thinks so also!
GRACH
DON
THAKK
You know, I've always looked up to you!
KRAK
DOKAM
That's why my goal has always been to surpass you!

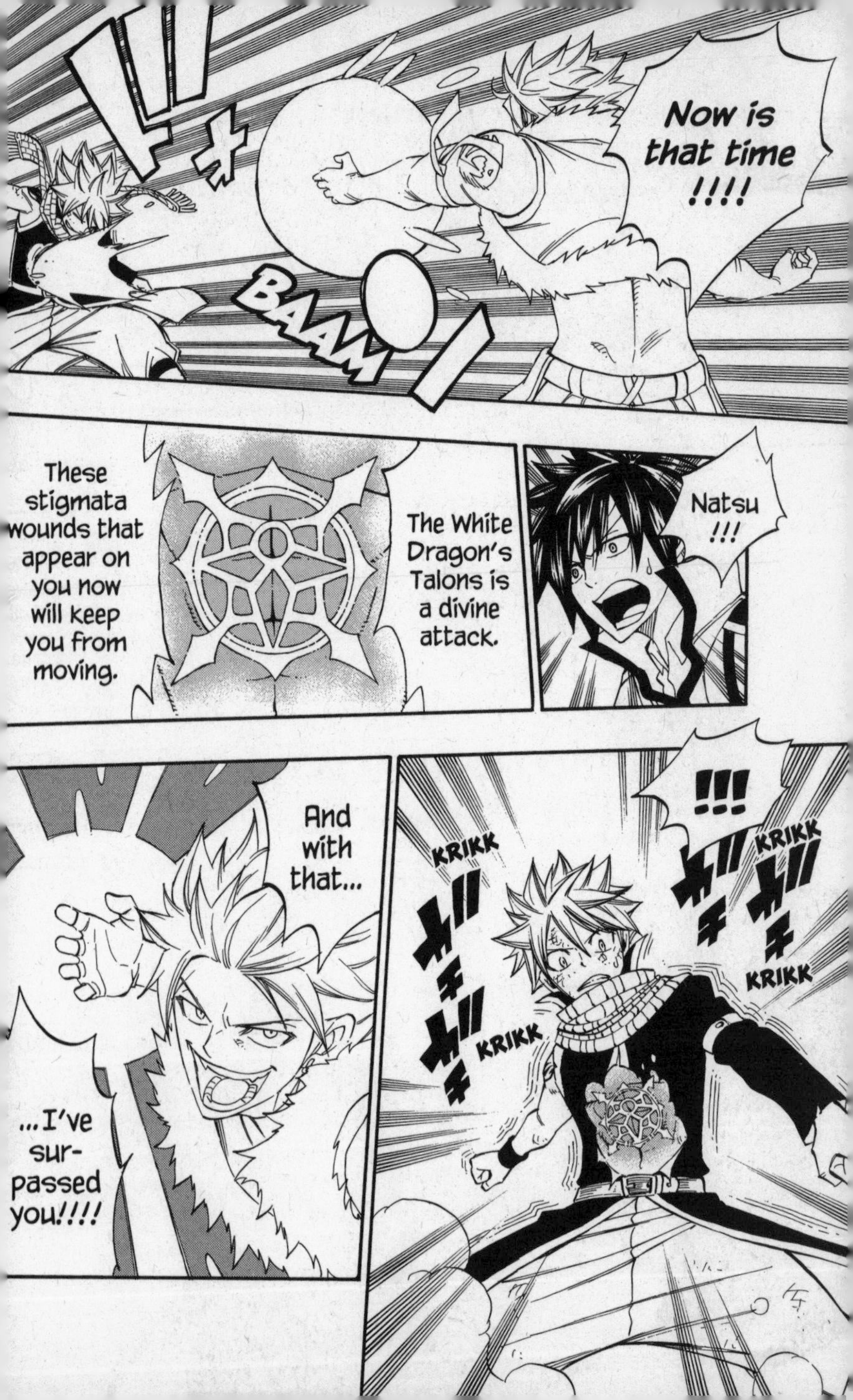
Now is that time !!!!
BAAM
Natsu !!!
The White Dragon's Talons is a divine attack.
These stigmata wounds that appear on you now will keep you from moving.
!!!
KRIKK
KRIKK
KRIKK
KRIKK
And with that...
...I've sur-passed you!!!!

SHOOM

VWOOO

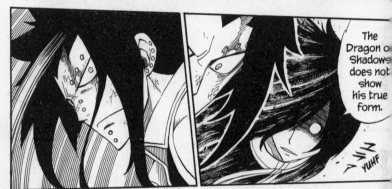

The Dragon o
Shadows
does not
show
his true
form.

YUHF

But he
hunts his
prey with
unfailing
skill!

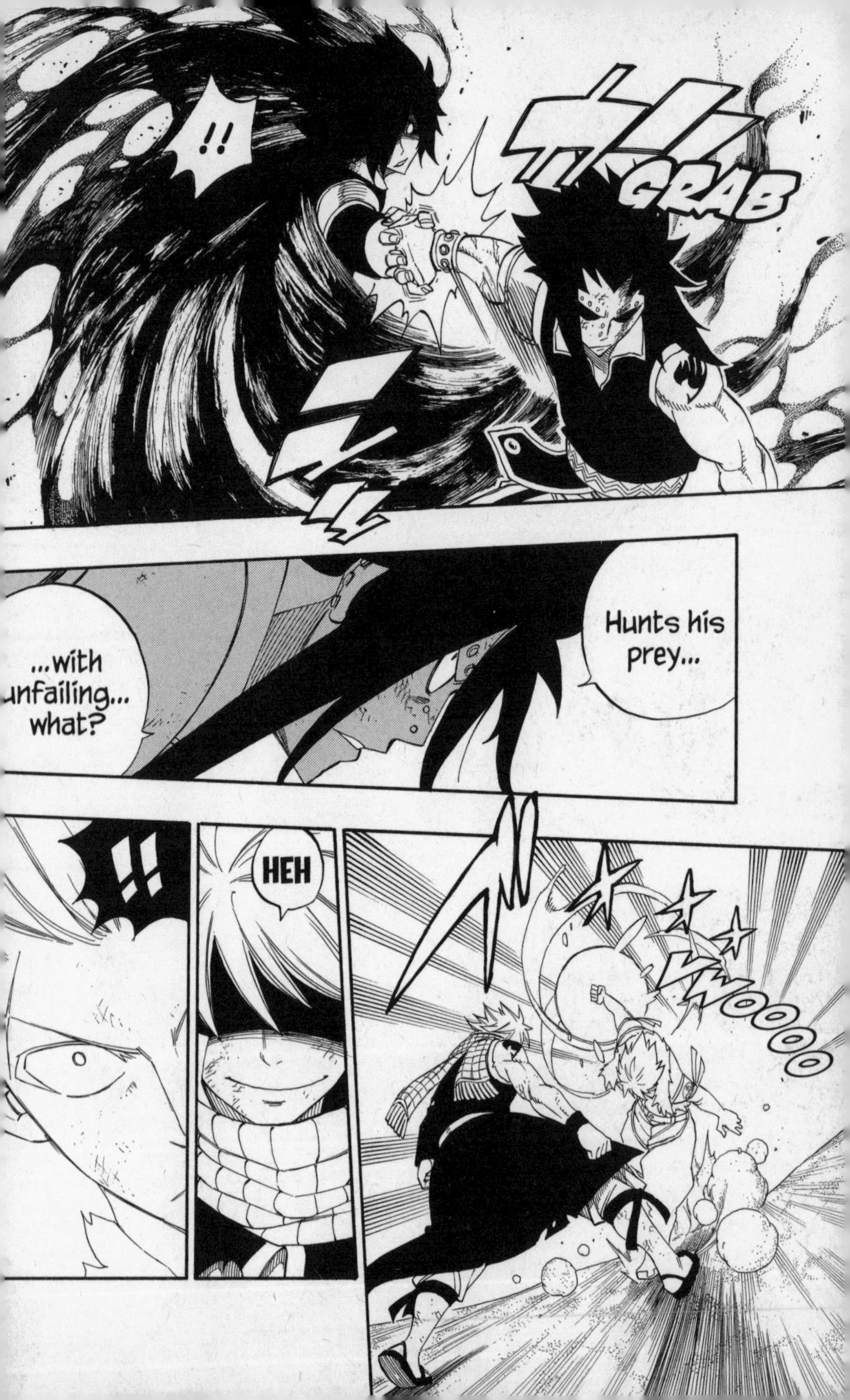

GRAB
!!
Hunts his prey...
...with unfailing... what?
VWOOOOO
HEH
!!

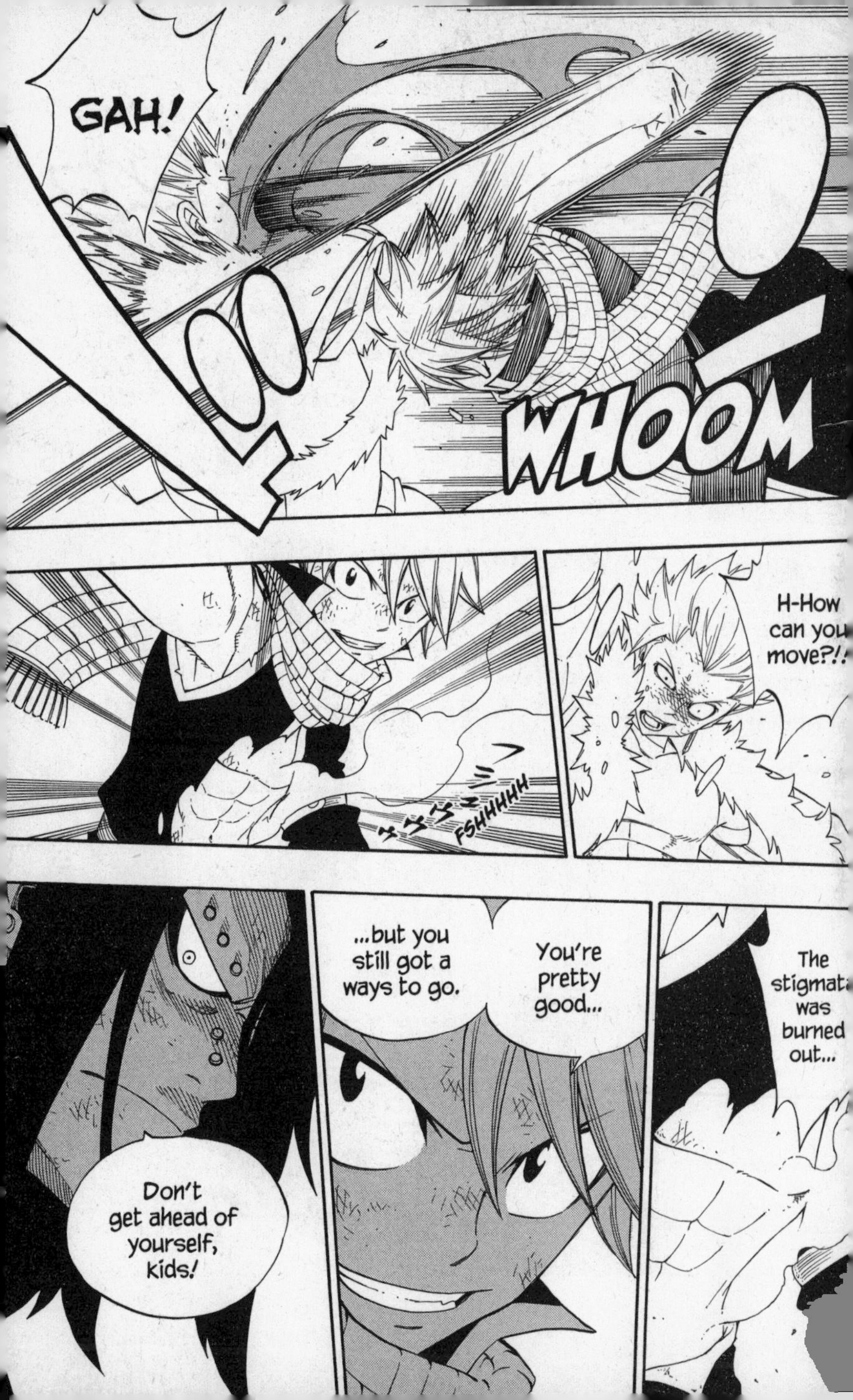
GAH!
WHOOM
H-How can you move?!
FSHHHHH
The stigmata was burned out...
You're pretty good...
...but you still got a ways to go.
Don't get ahead of yourself, kids!

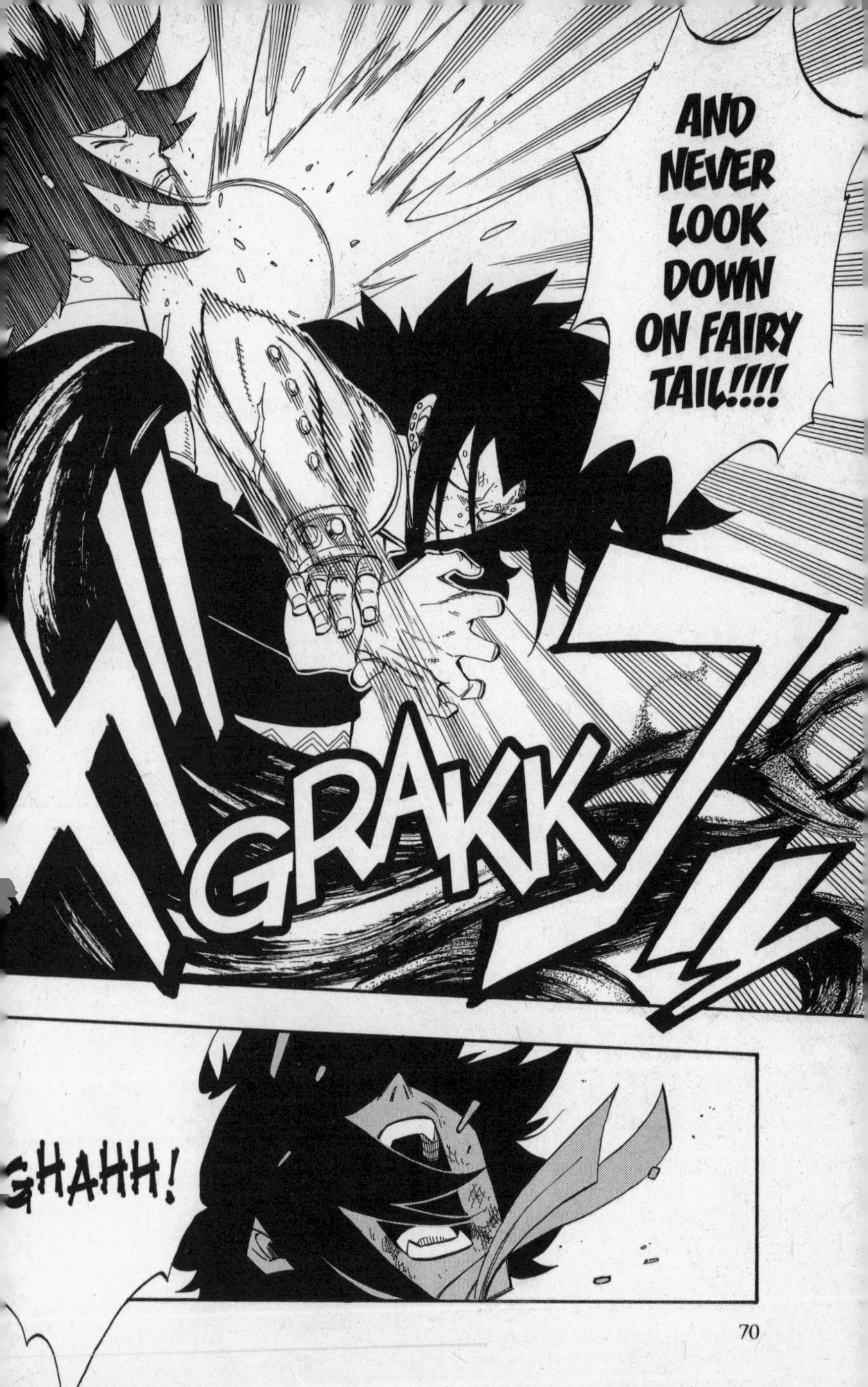
AND NEVER LOOK DOWN ON FAIRY TAIL!!!!
GRAKK
GHAHH!

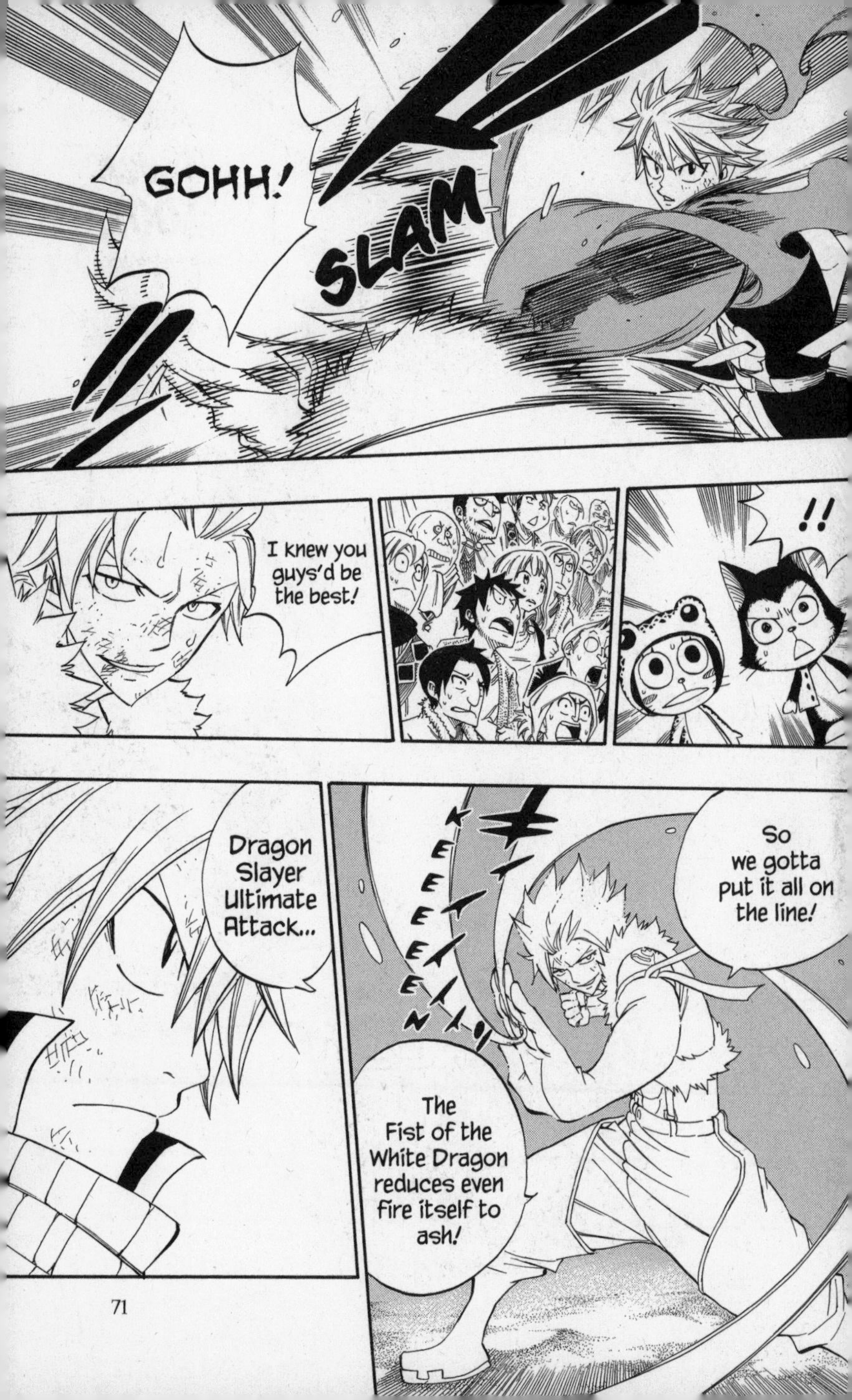
SLAM
GOHH!
!!
I knew you guys'd be the best!
So we gotta put it all on the line!
KEEEEEEEN
The Fist of the White Dragon reduces even fire itself to ash!
Dragon Slayer Ultimate Attack...

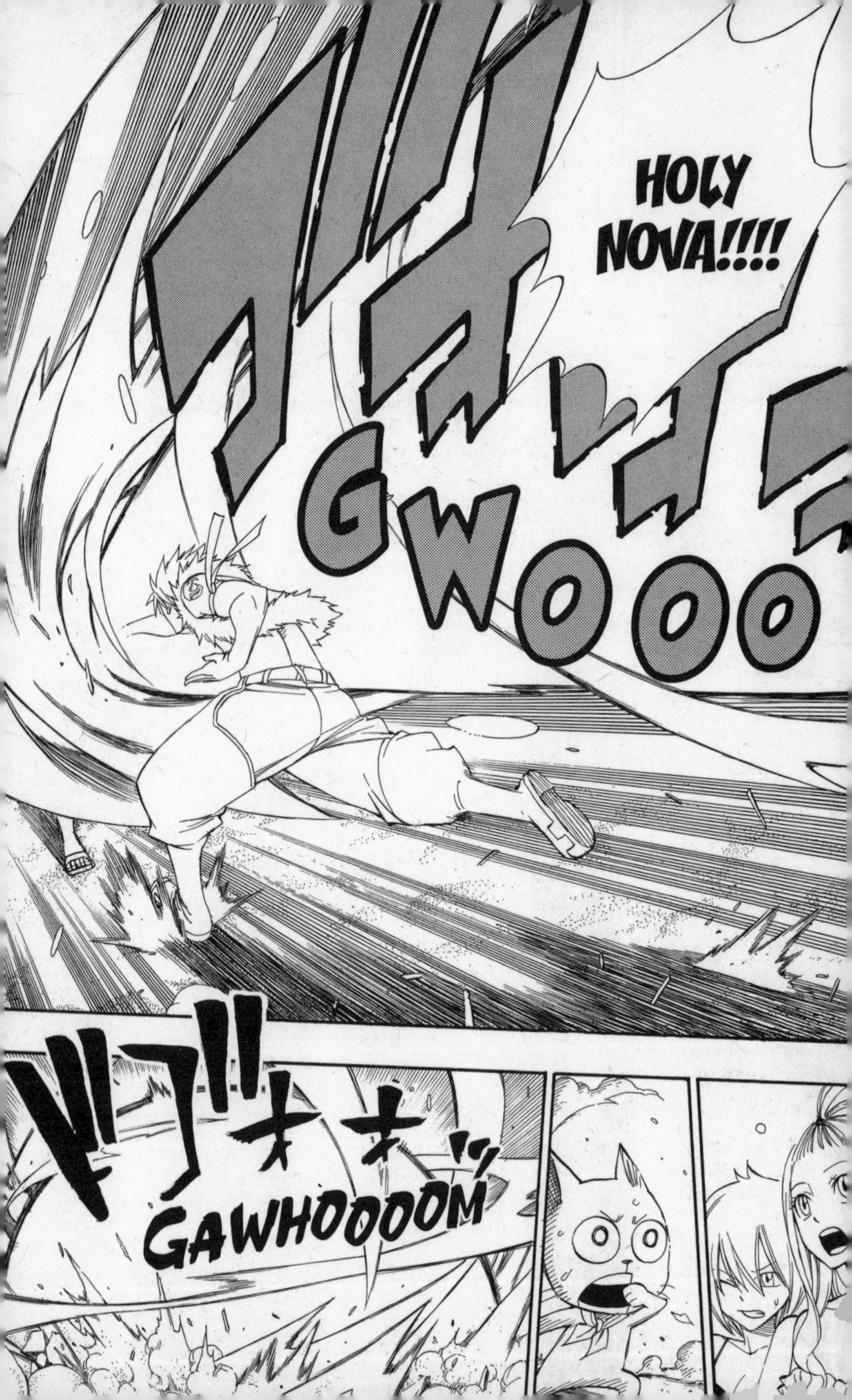
HOLY NOVA!!!!
GWOOO
GAWHOOOOOM

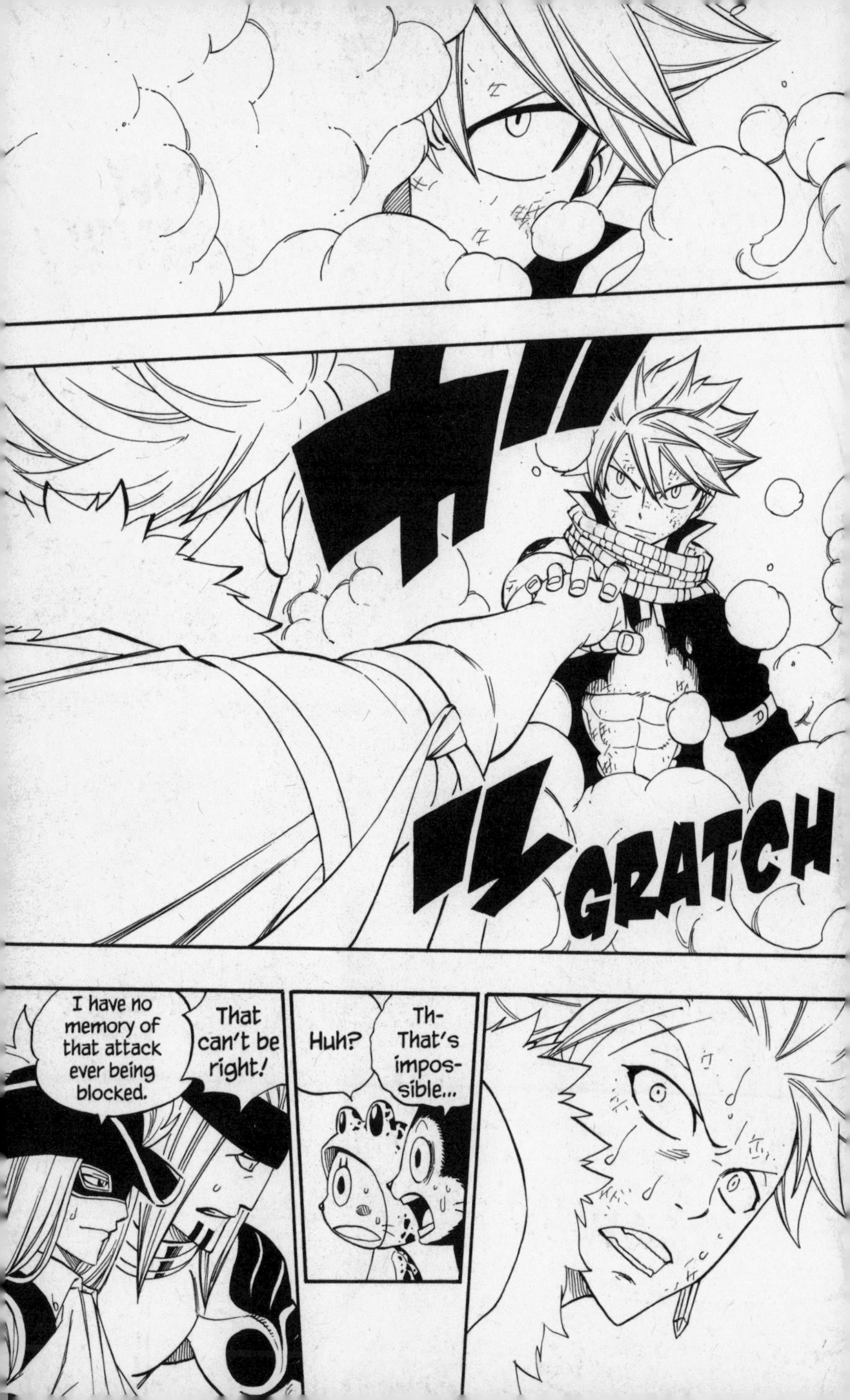
GRATCH
Th- That's impos- sible...
Huh?
That can't be right!
I have no memory of that attack ever being blocked.

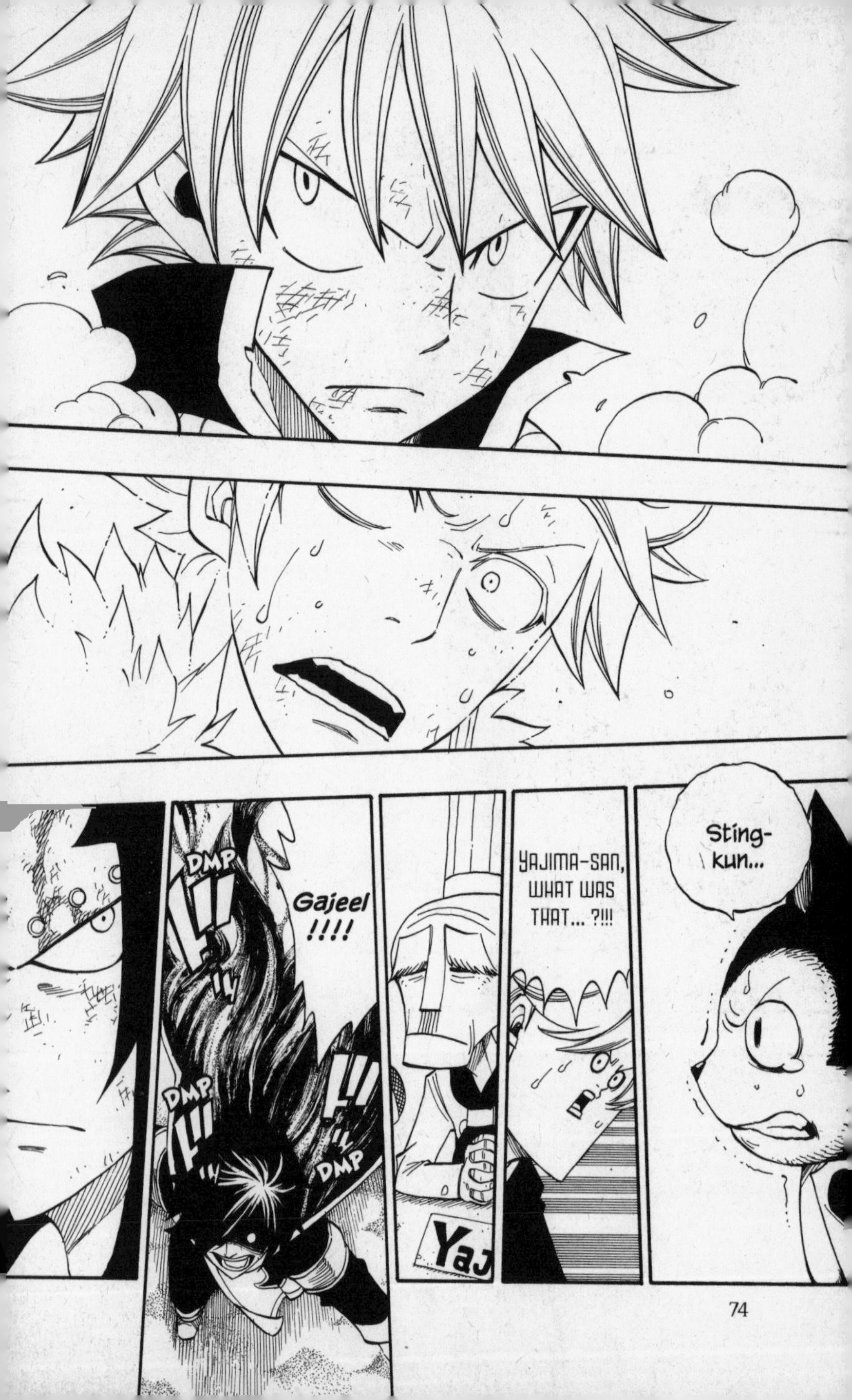
Sting-kun...
YAJIMA-SAN, WHAT WAS THAT... ?!!
Yaj
Gajeel !!!!
DMP
DMP
DMP

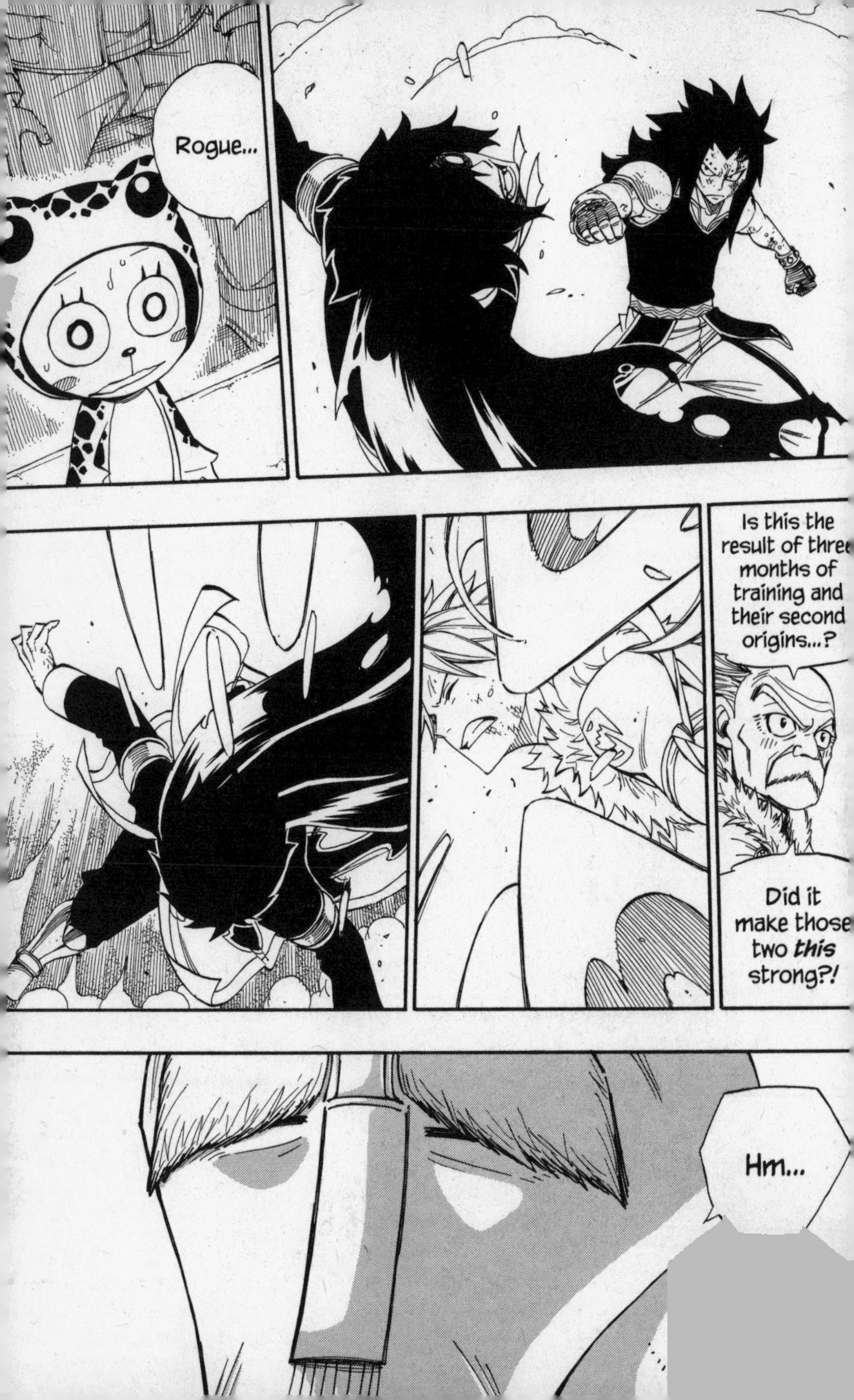
Rogue...
Is this the result of three months of training and their second origins...?
Did it make those two *this* strong?!
Hm...

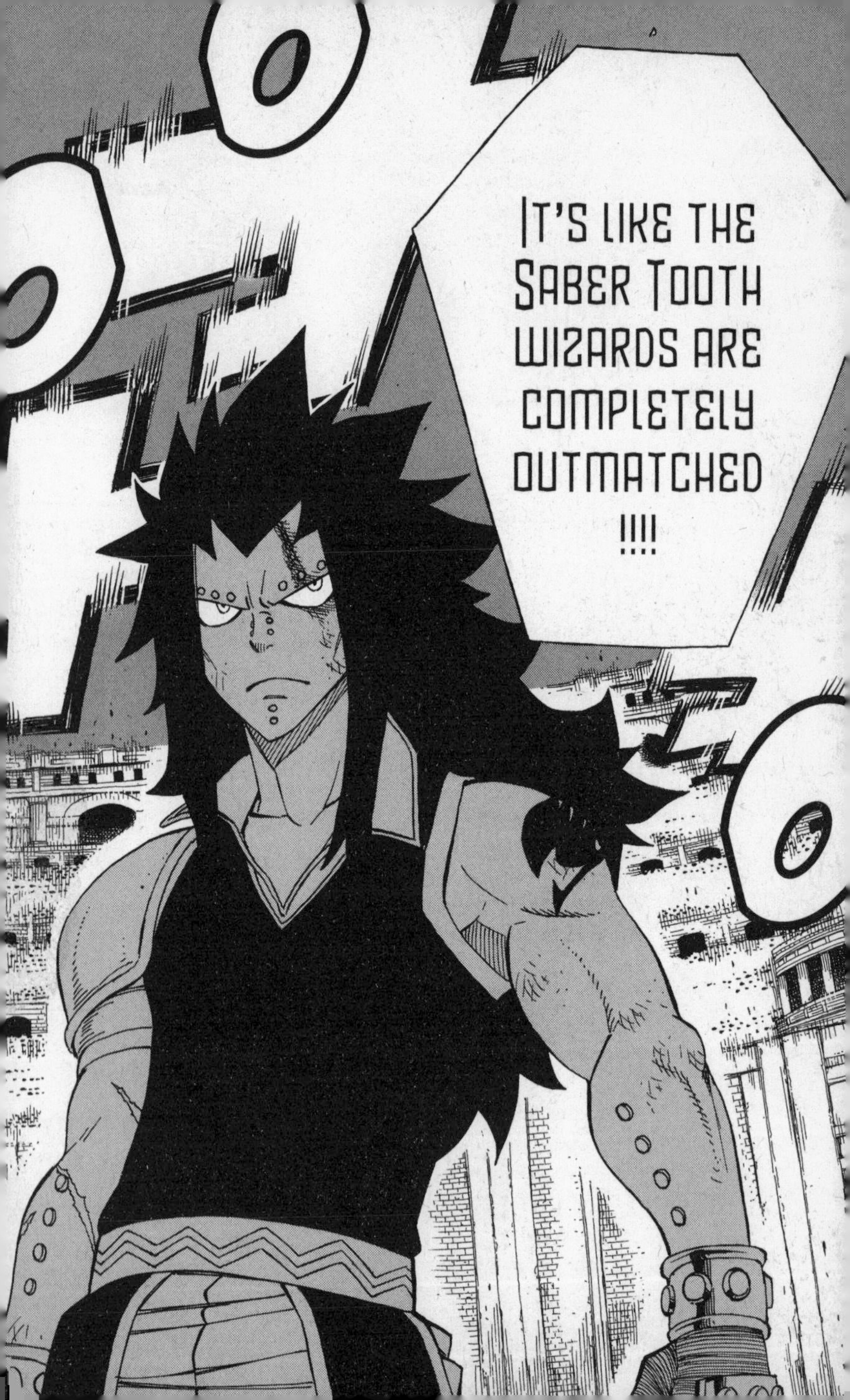
It's like the Saber Tooth wizards are completely outmatched !!!!

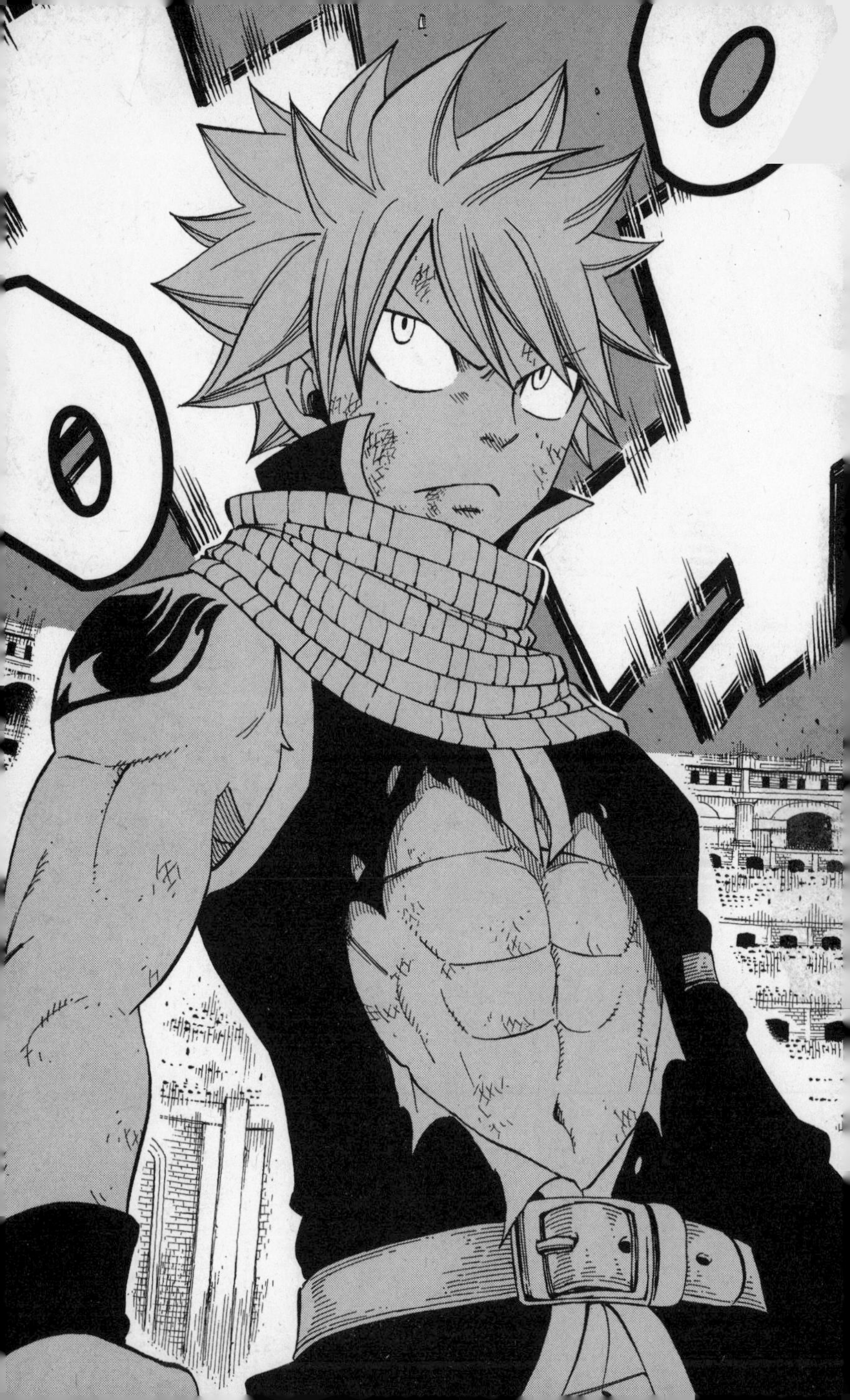

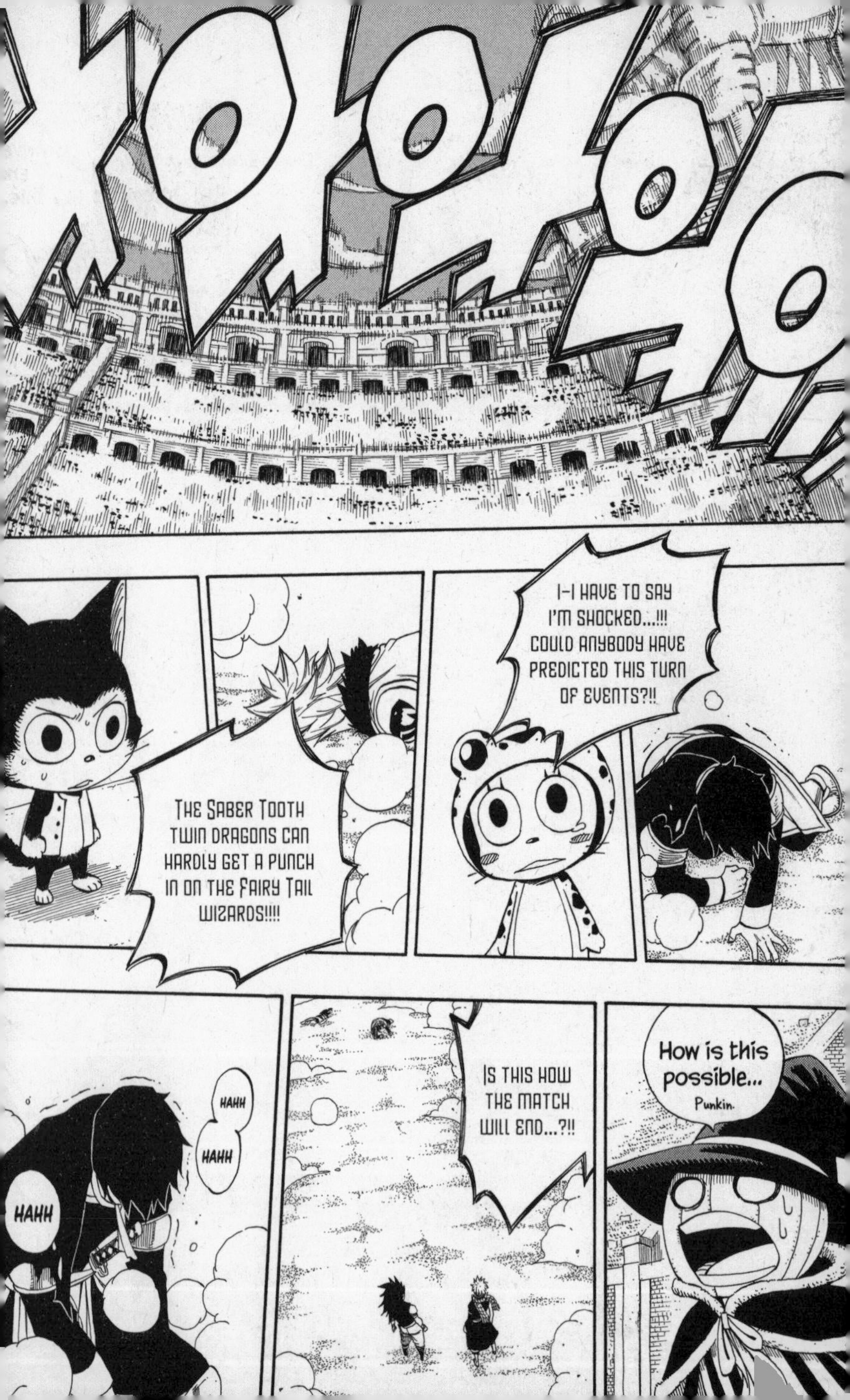
I-I HAVE TO SAY I'M SHOCKED...!!! COULD ANYBODY HAVE PREDICTED THIS TURN OF EVENTS?!!
THE SABER TOOTH TWIN DRAGONS CAN HARDLY GET A PUNCH IN ON THE FAIRY TAIL WIZARDS!!!!
How is this possible...
Punkin.
IS THIS HOW THE MATCH WILL END...?!!
HAHH
HAHH
HAHH

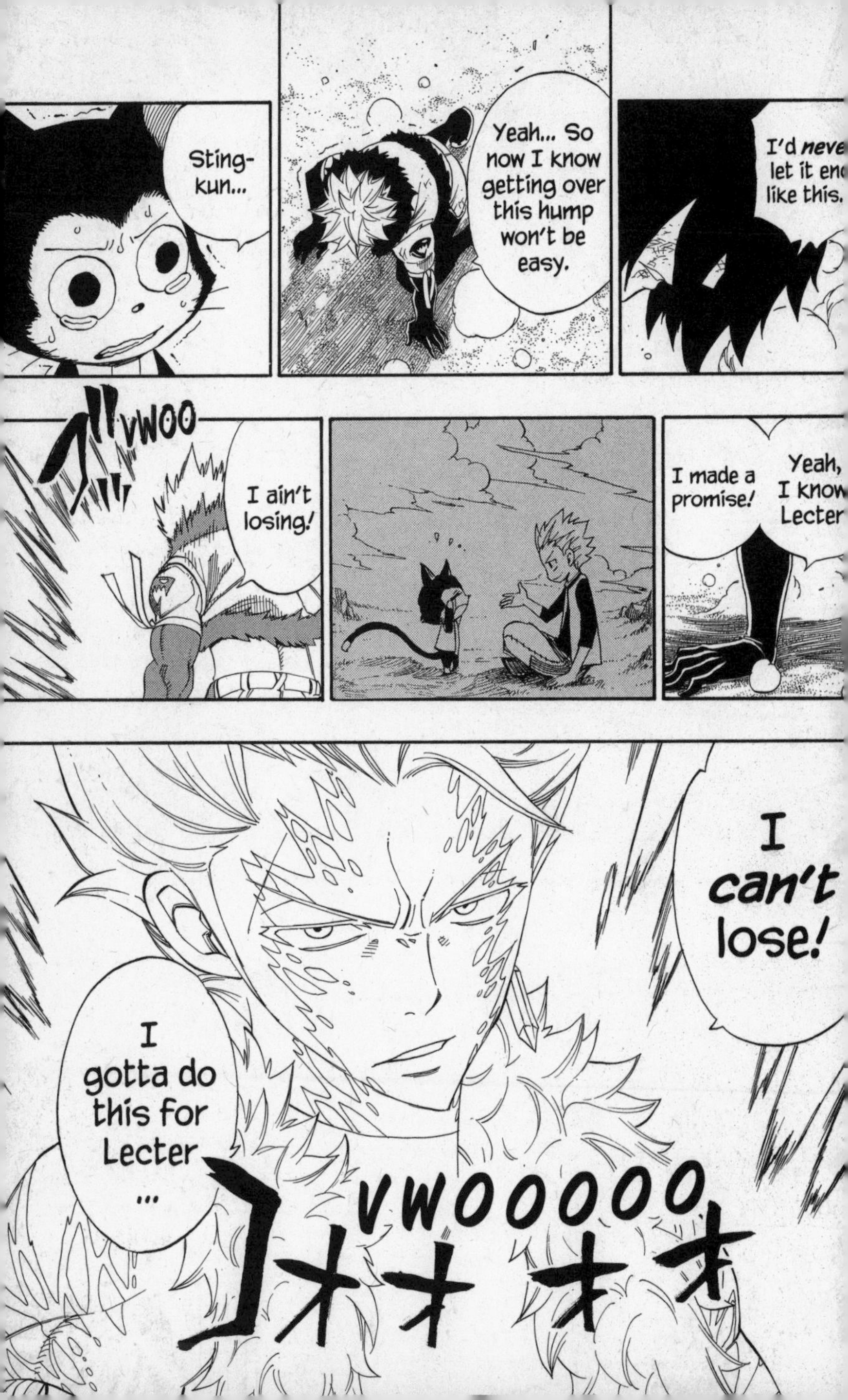
I'd neve let it en like this.
Yeah... So now I know getting over this hump won't be easy.
Sting-kun...
Yeah, I know Lecter
I made a promise!
I ain't losing!
VWOO
I can't lose!
I gotta do this for Lecter ...
VWOOOOO
コオオ オオ

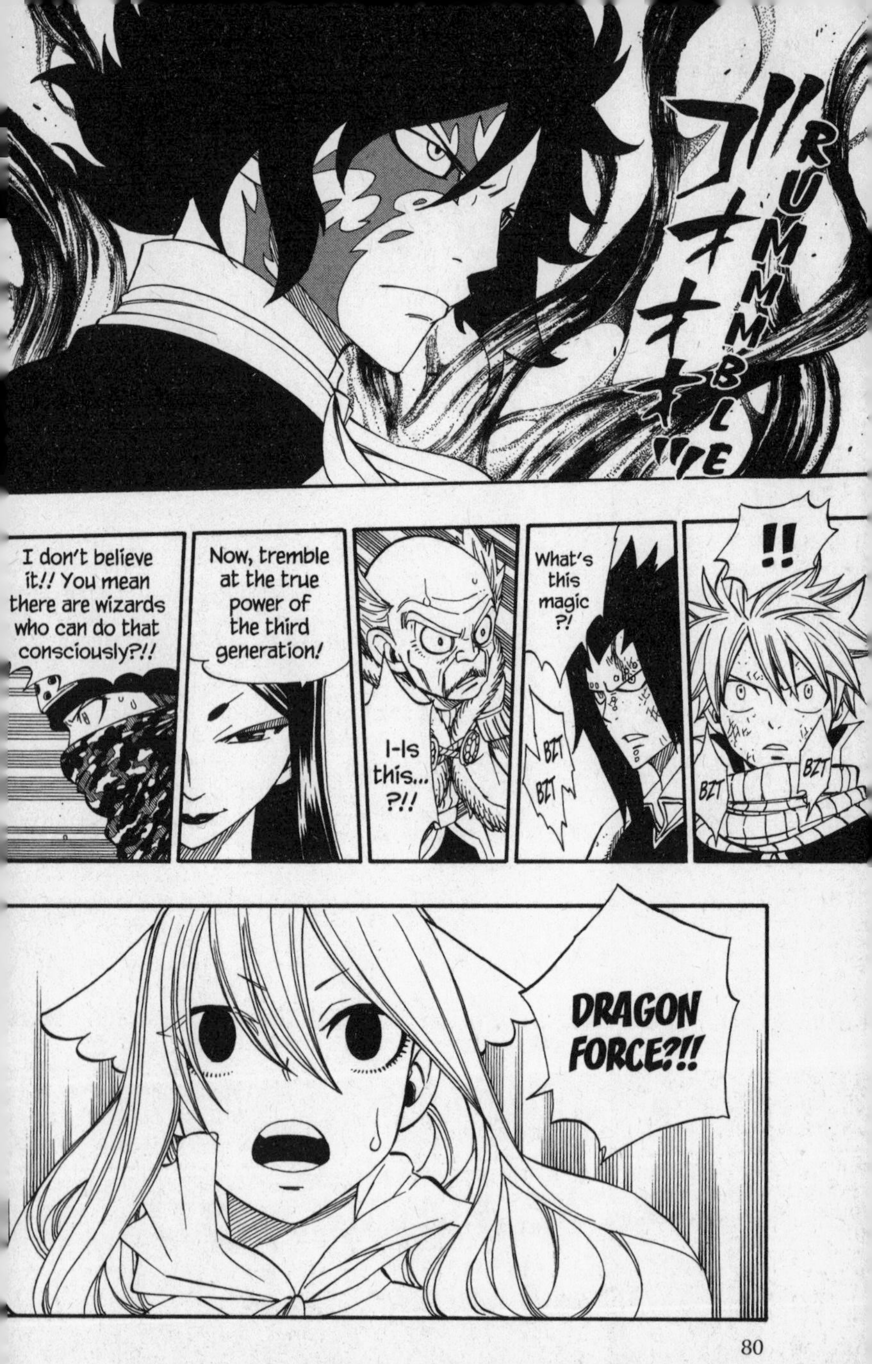
RUMMMMBLE
!!
BZT
BZT
What's this magic?!
BZT
BZT
I-Is this...?!!
Now, tremble at the true power of the third generation!
I don't believe it!! You mean there are wizards who can do that consciously?!!
DRAGON FORCE?!!

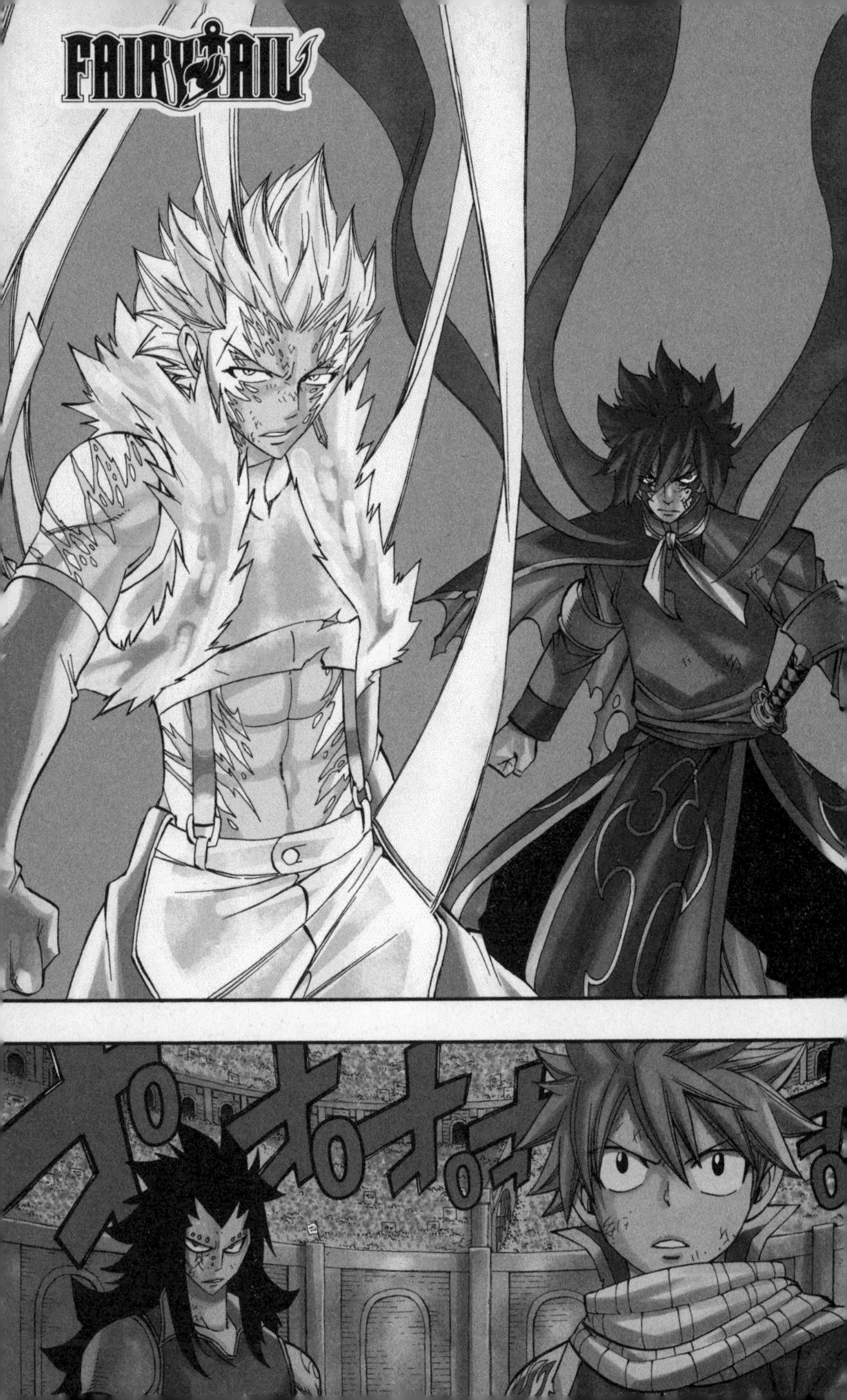
FAIRY TAIL

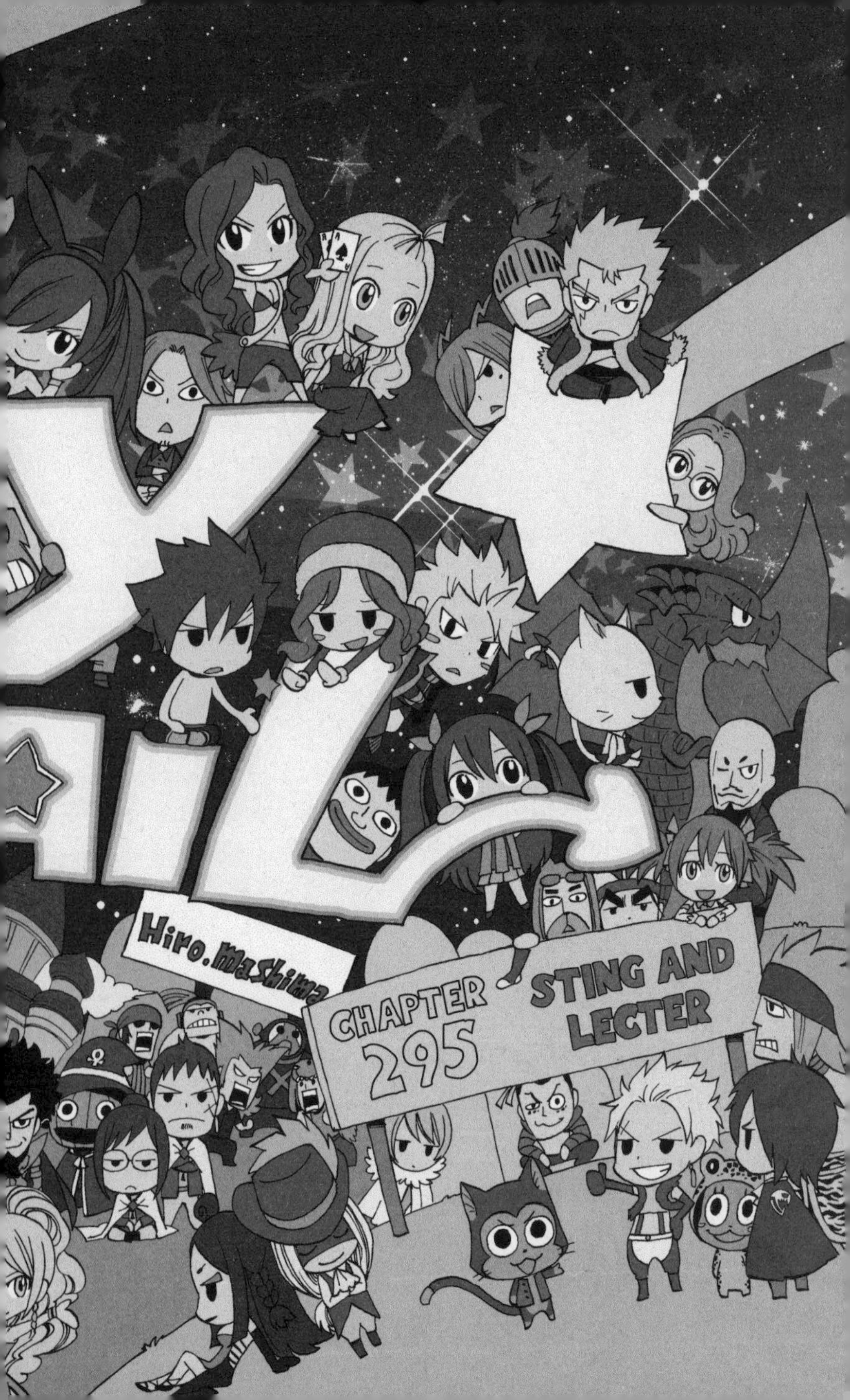
Hiro.mashima
CHAPTER 295
STING AND LECTER

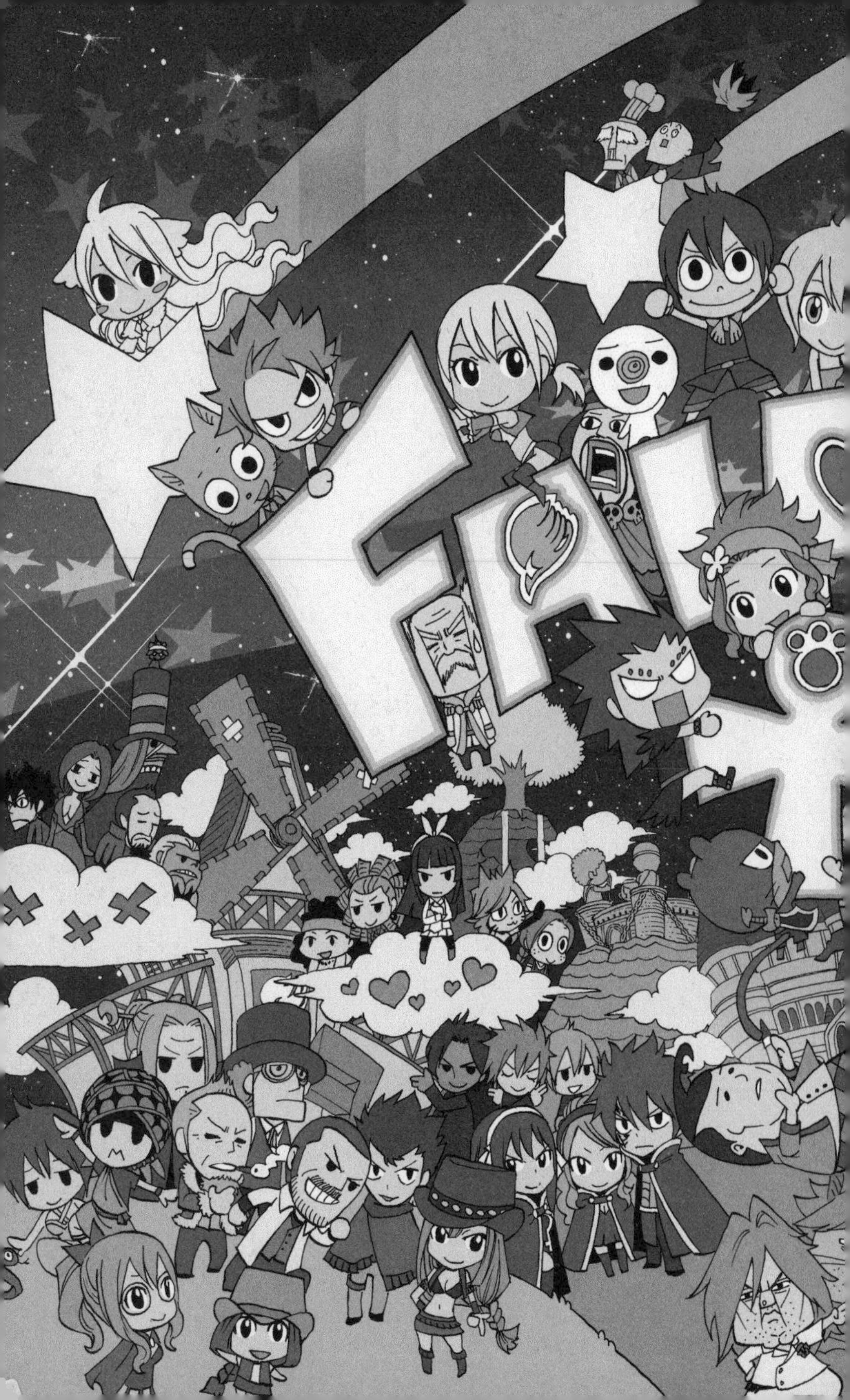

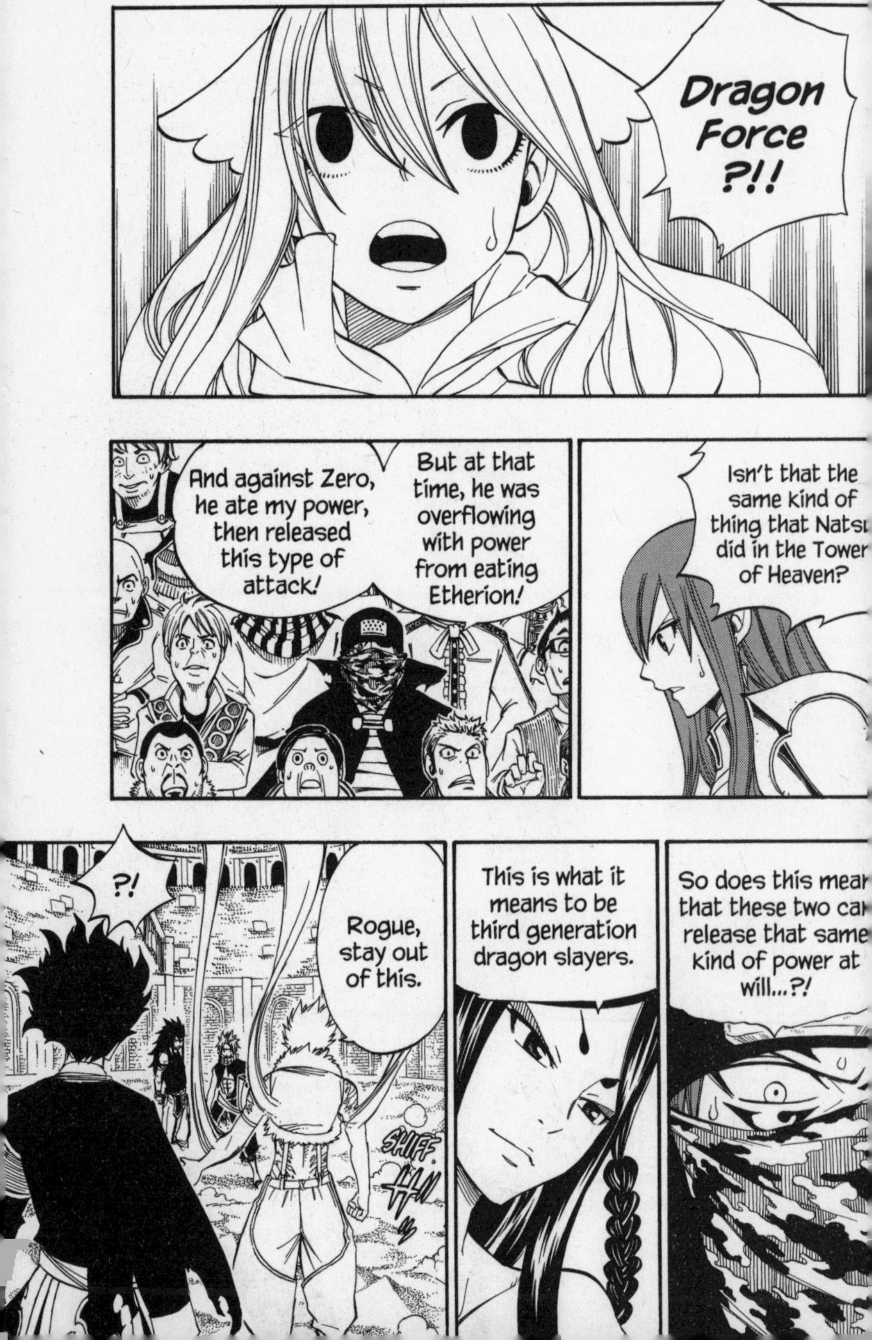
Dragon Force ?!!
Isn't that the same kind of thing that Natsu did in the Tower of Heaven?
But at that time, he was overflowing with power from eating Etherion!
And against Zero, he ate my power, then released this type of attack!
So does this mean that these two can release that same kind of power at will...?!
This is what it means to be third generation dragon slayers.
Rogue, stay out of this.
?!
SHIFF

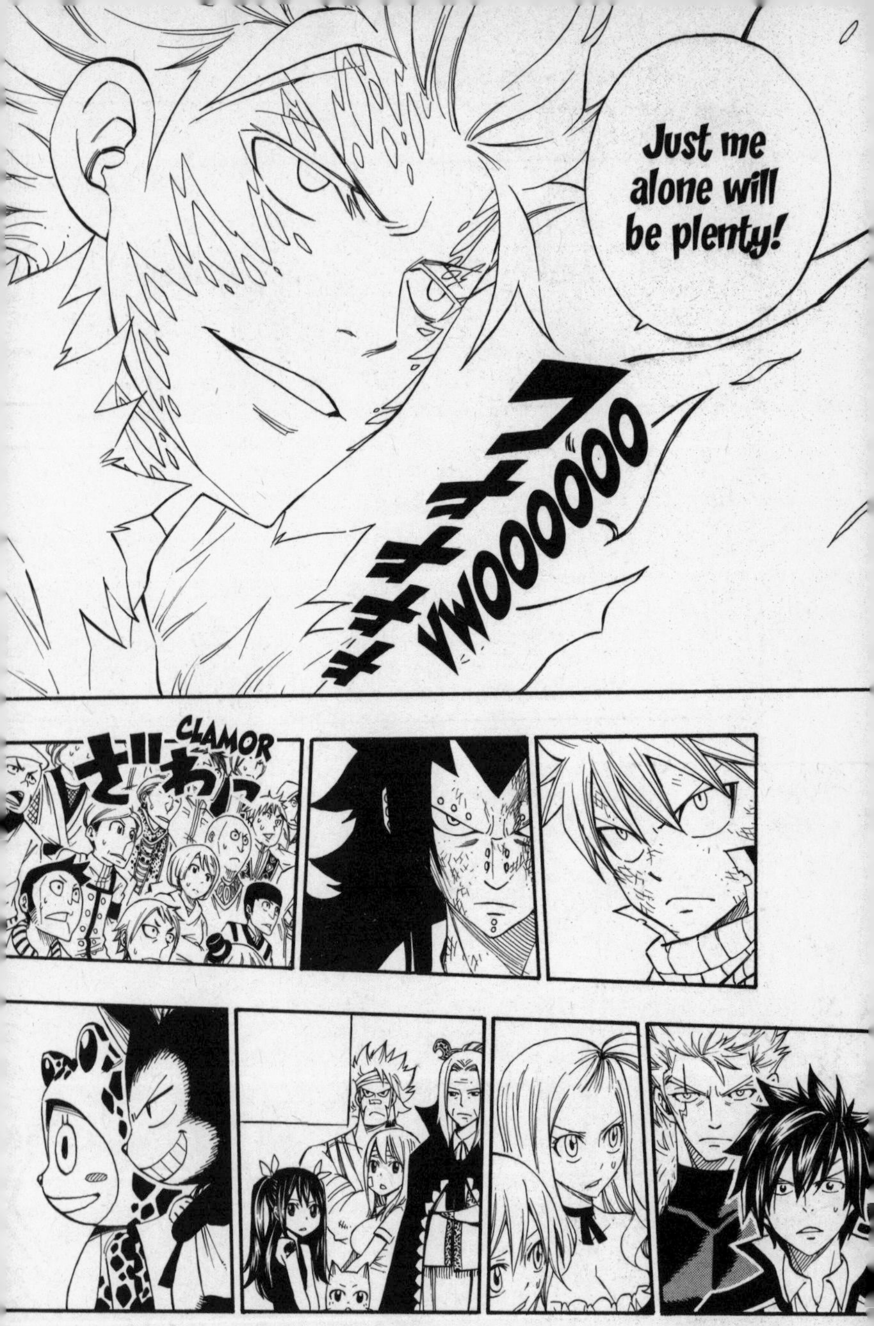
Just me alone will be plenty!
VWOOOOOO
CLAMOR
ざわっ

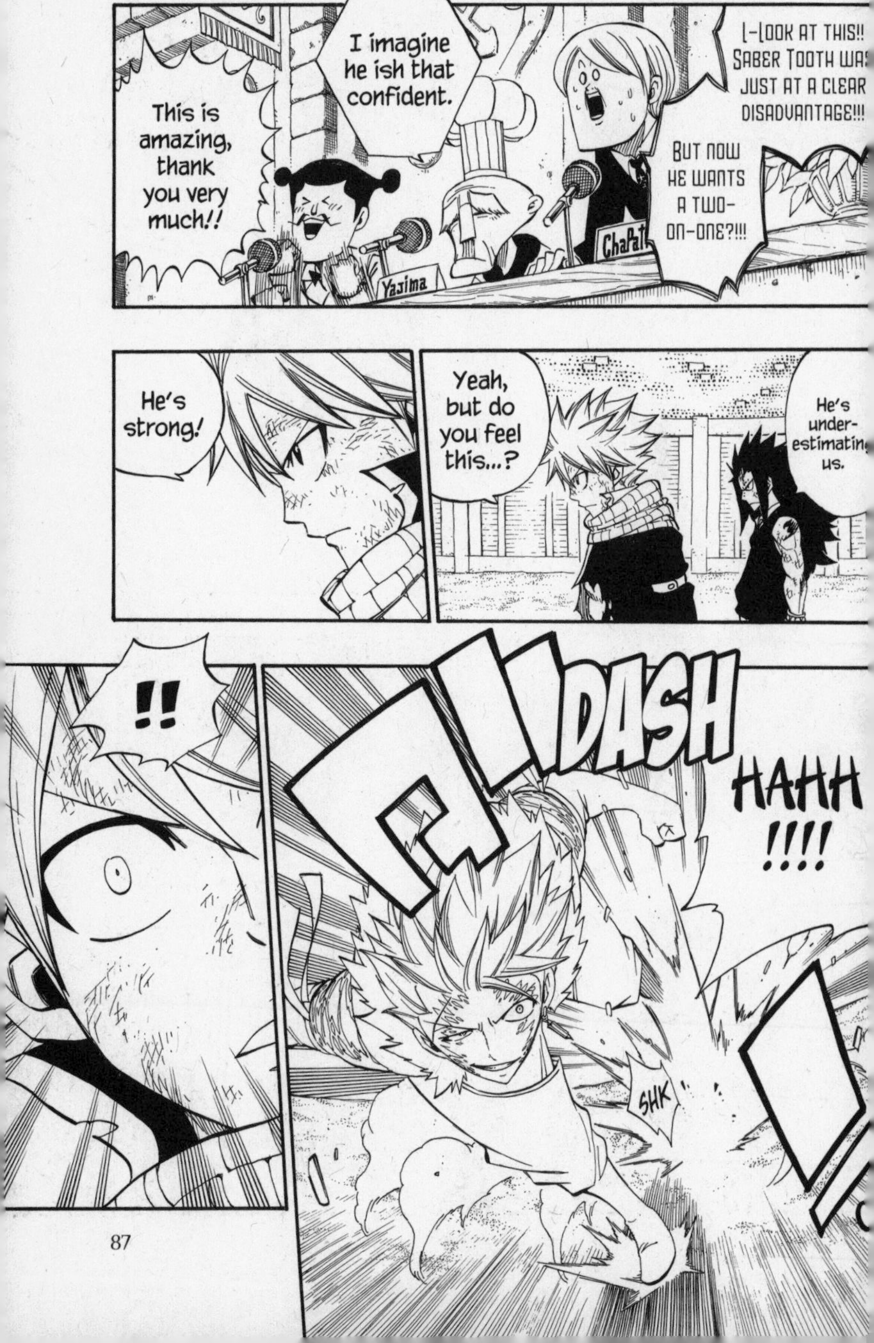
L-LOOK AT THIS!! SABER TOOTH WAS JUST AT A CLEAR DISADVANTAGE!!!
BUT NOW HE WANTS A TWO-ON-ONE?!!!
I imagine he ish that confident.
This is amazing, thank you very much!!
ChaPati
Yajima
He's under-estimating us.
Yeah, but do you feel this...?
He's strong!
DASH
HAHH!!!!
SHK
!!

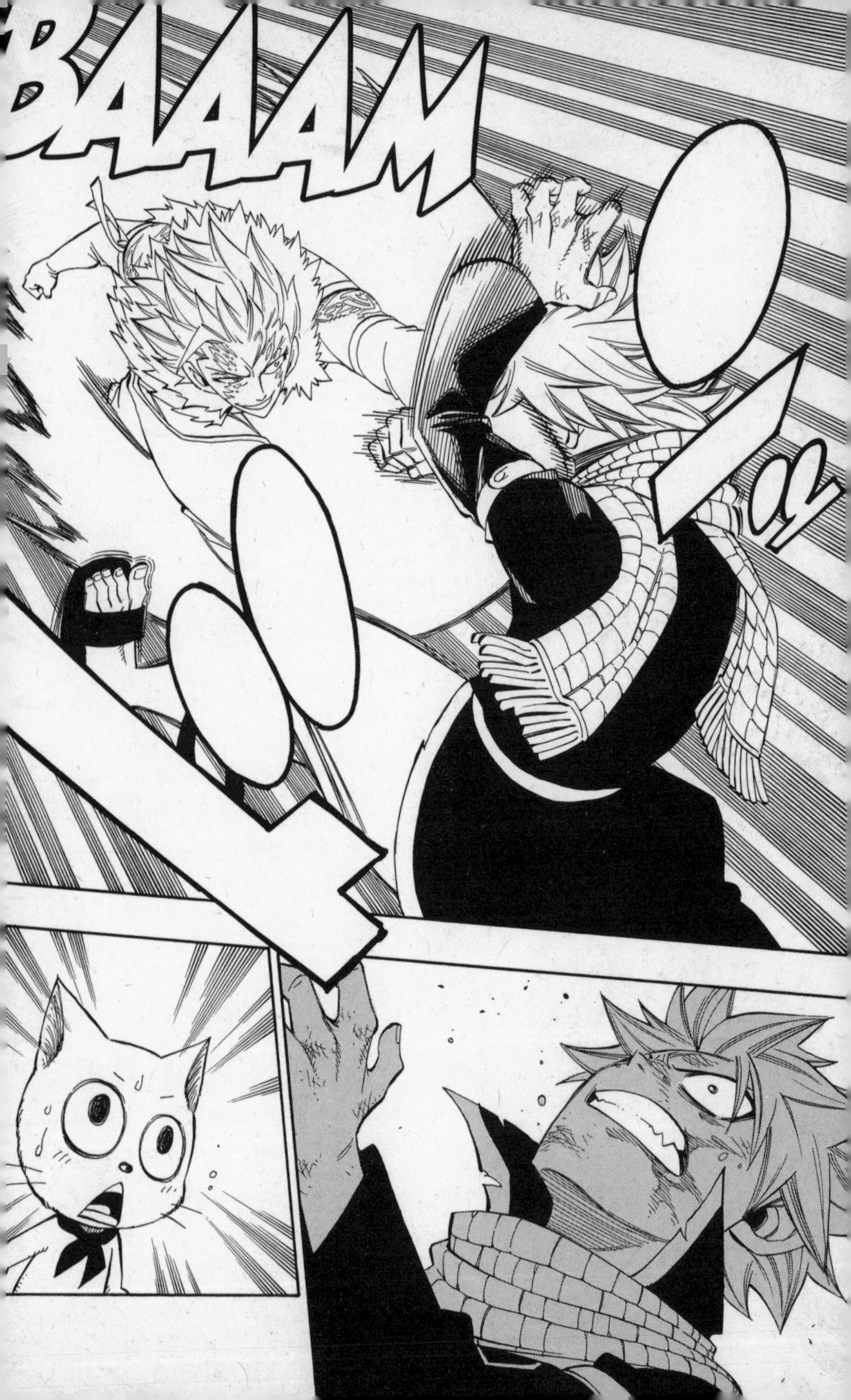
BAAM

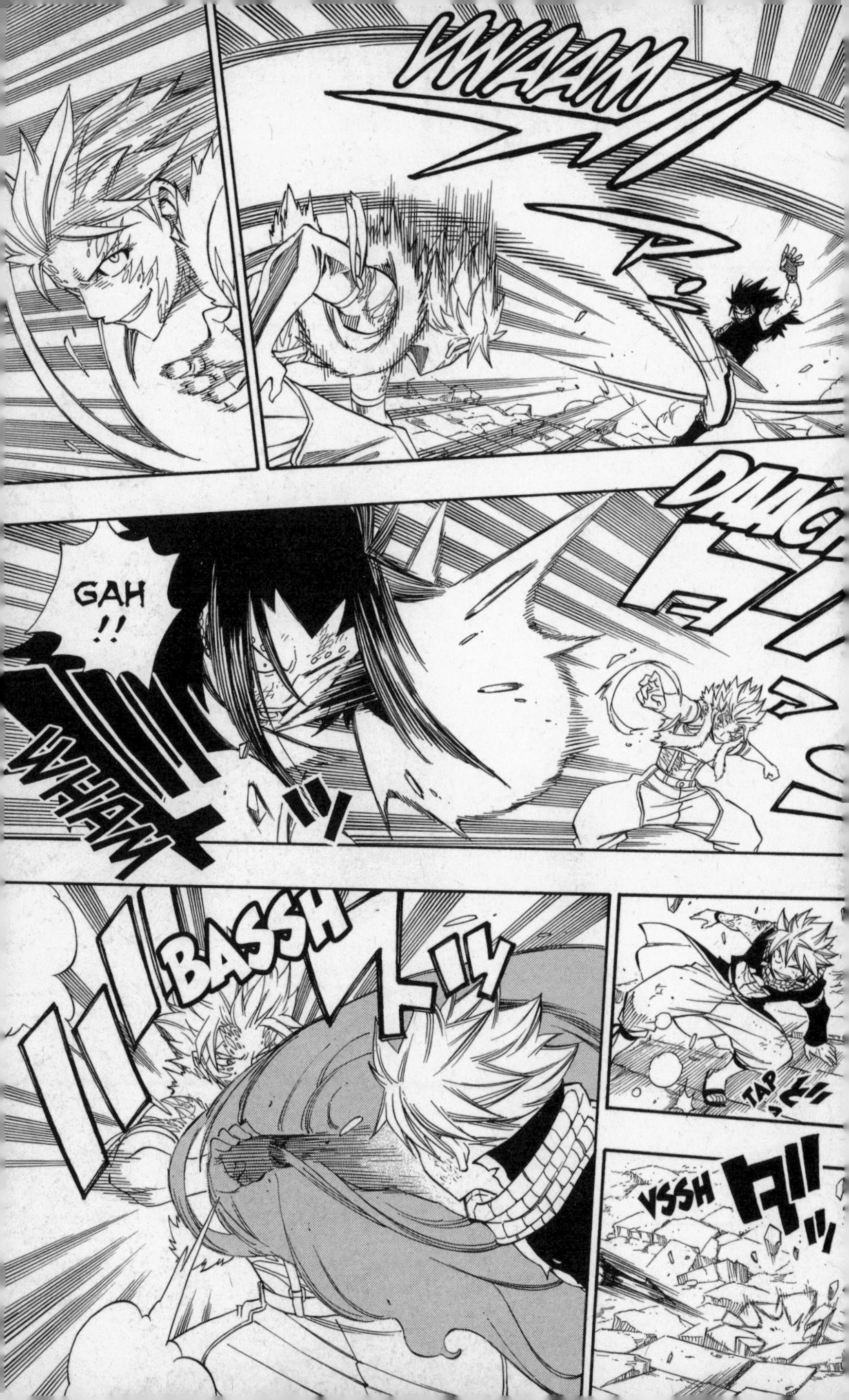
WHAAM
GAH!!
WHAM
TAP
VSSH
BASSH

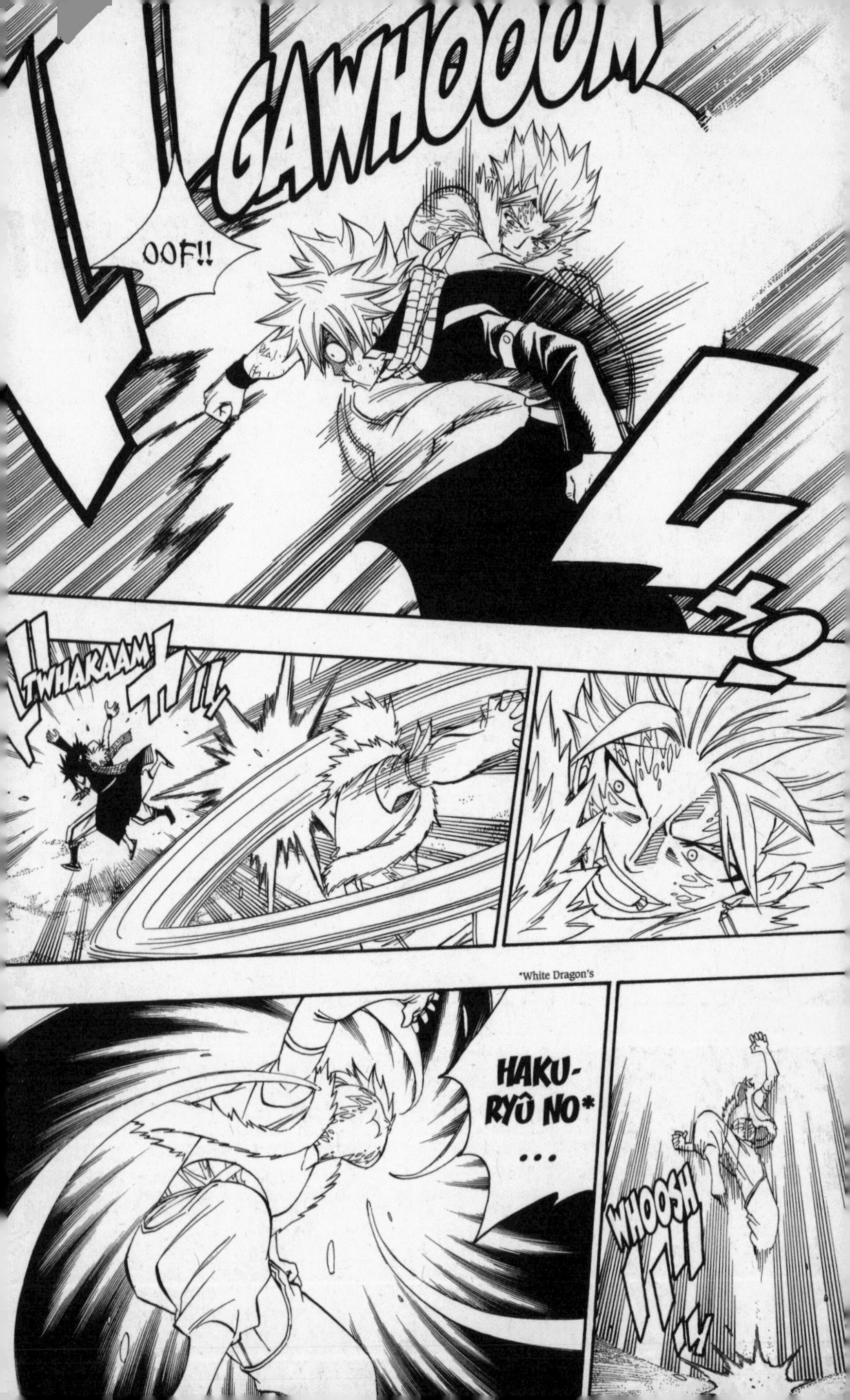
GAWHOOOM
OOF!!
TWHAKAAM
WHOOSH
HAKU-RYÛ NO* ...

*White Dragon's

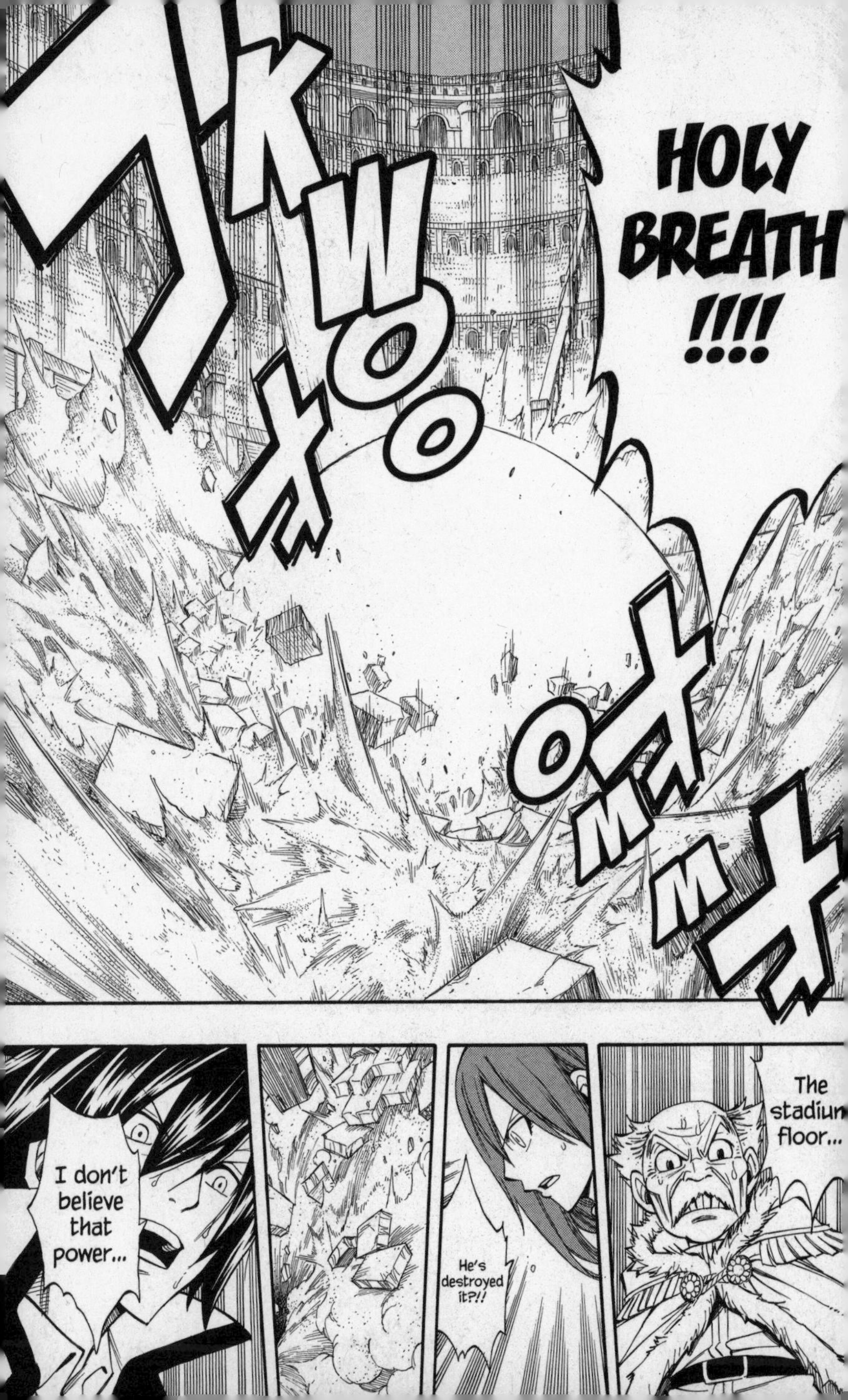
HOLY BREATH!!!!
KWOO
OMM
The stadium floor...
He's destroyed it?!!
I don't believe that power...

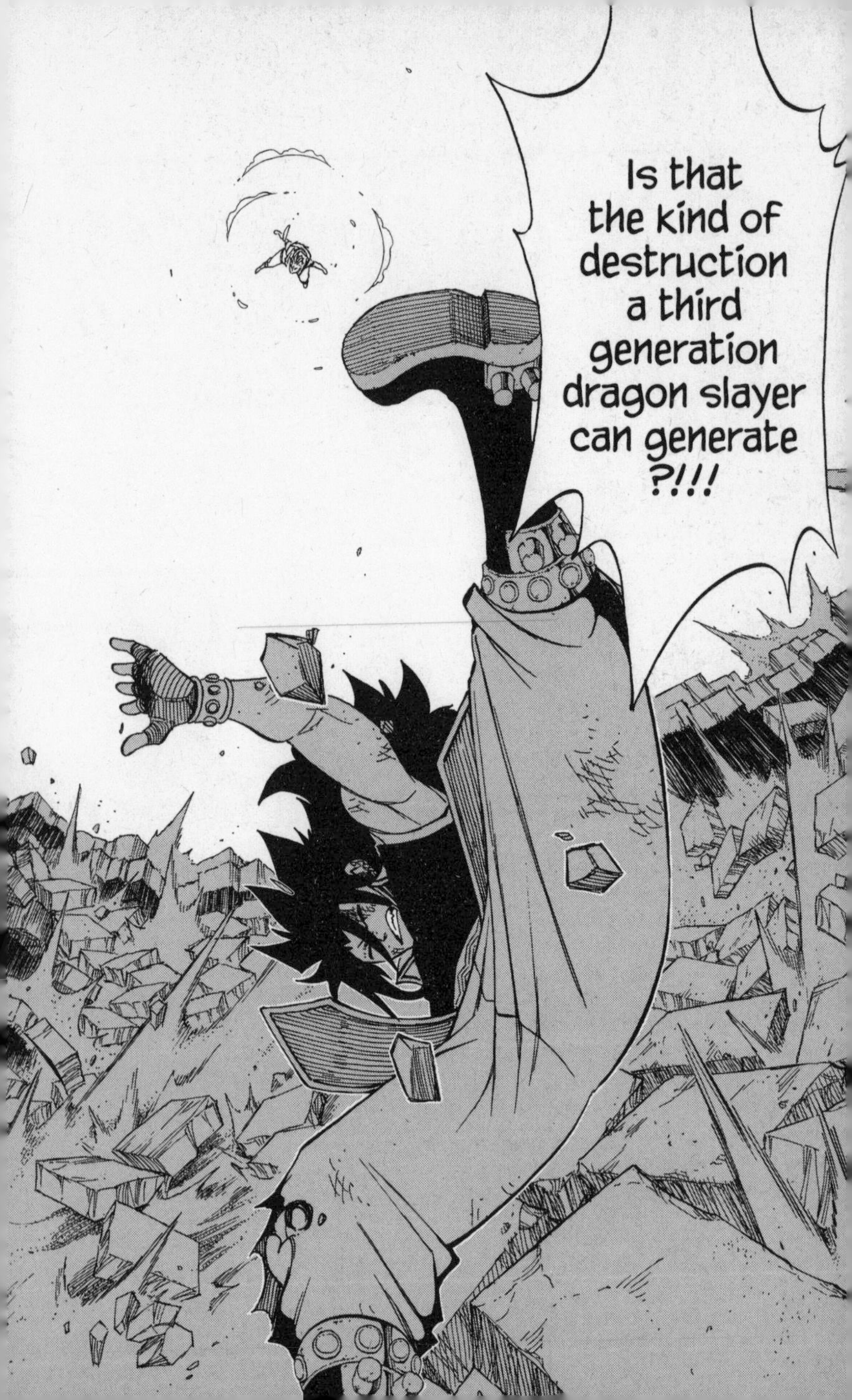
Is that the kind of destruction a third generation dragon slayer can generate ?!!!

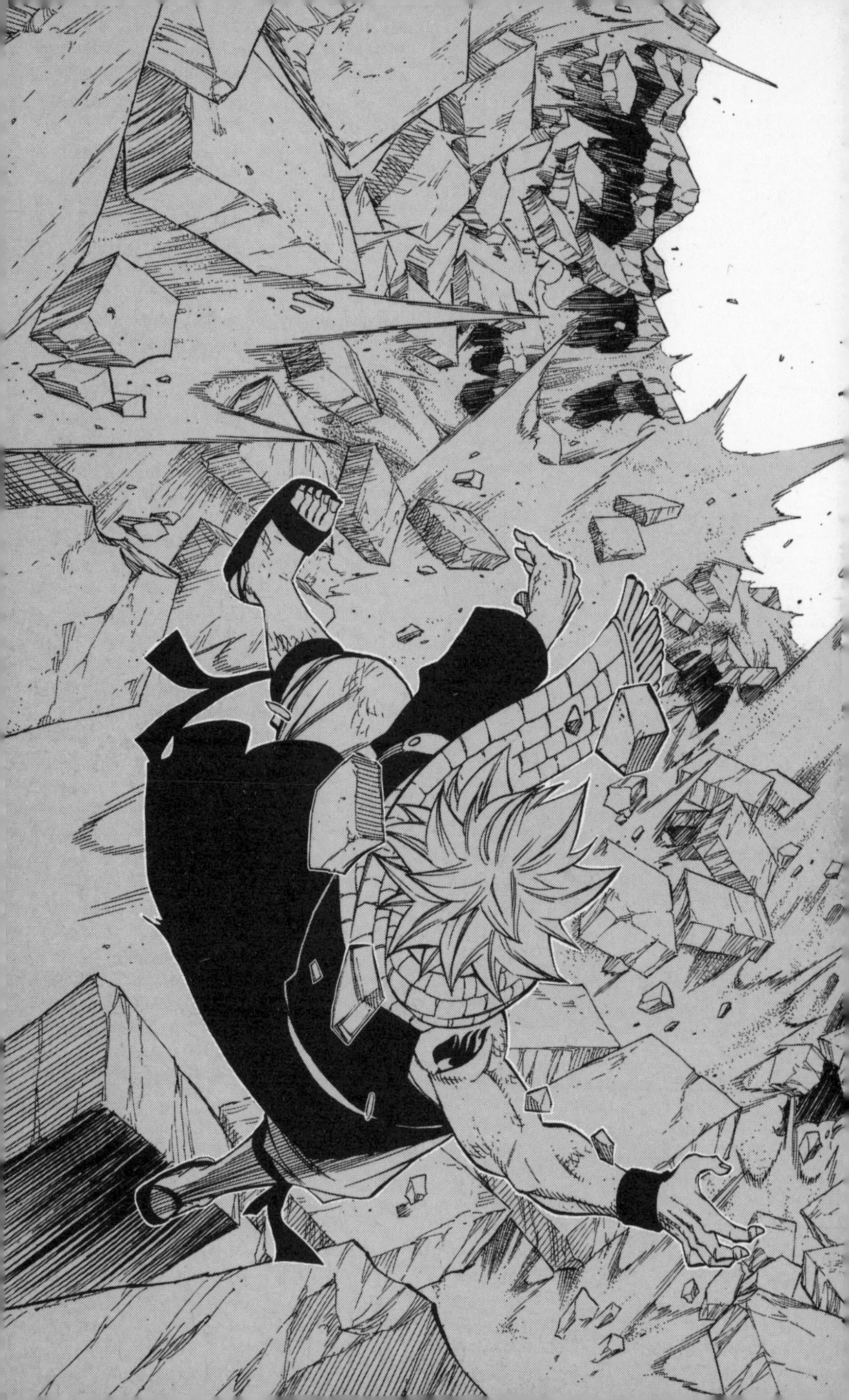

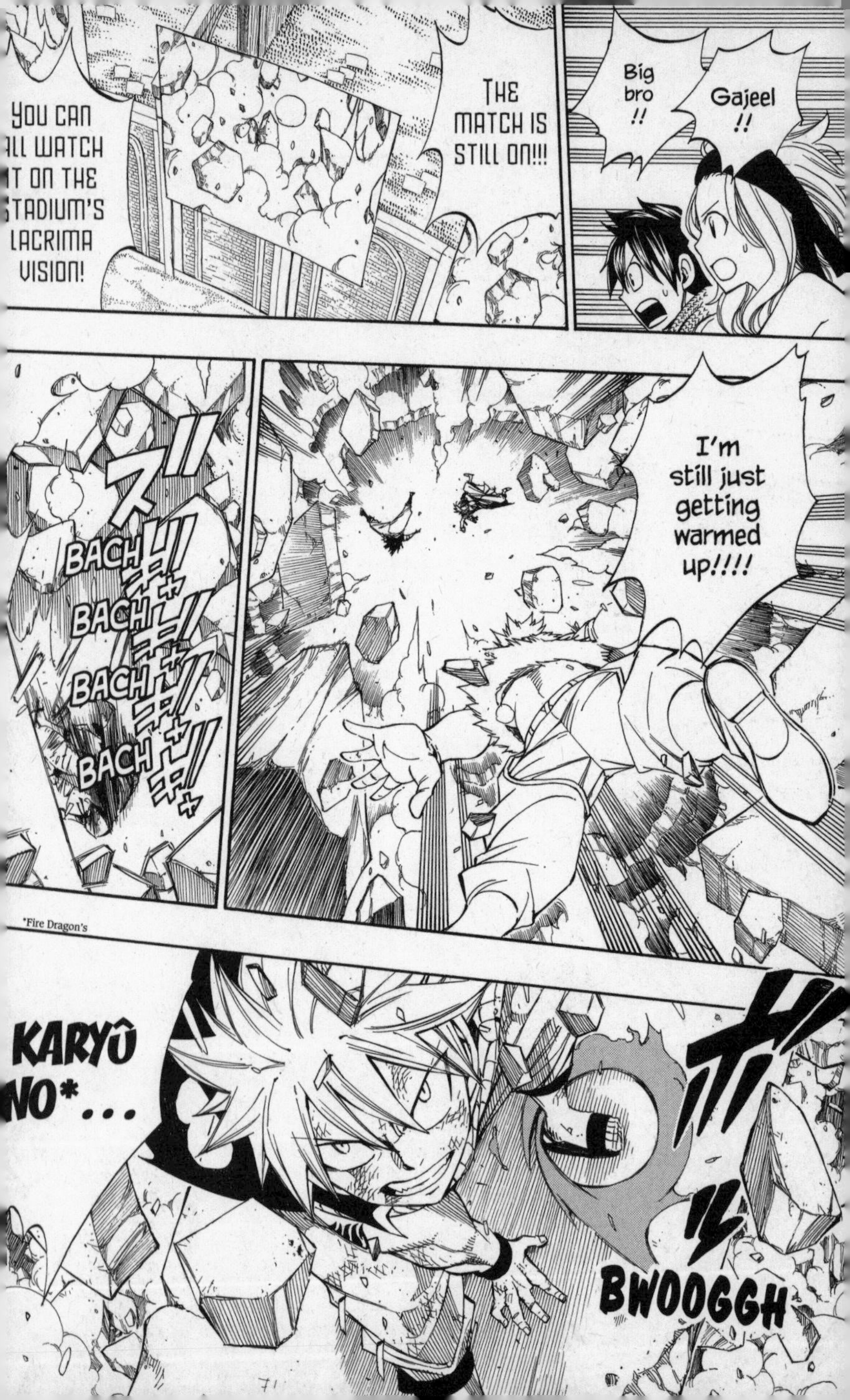
Gajeel !!
Big bro !!
THE MATCH IS STILL ON!!!
YOU CAN LL WATCH T ON THE TADIUM'S LACRIMA VISION!
I'm still just getting warmed up!!!!
BACH
BACH
BACH
BACH
KARYÛ NO*...
BWOOGGH
*Fire Dragon's

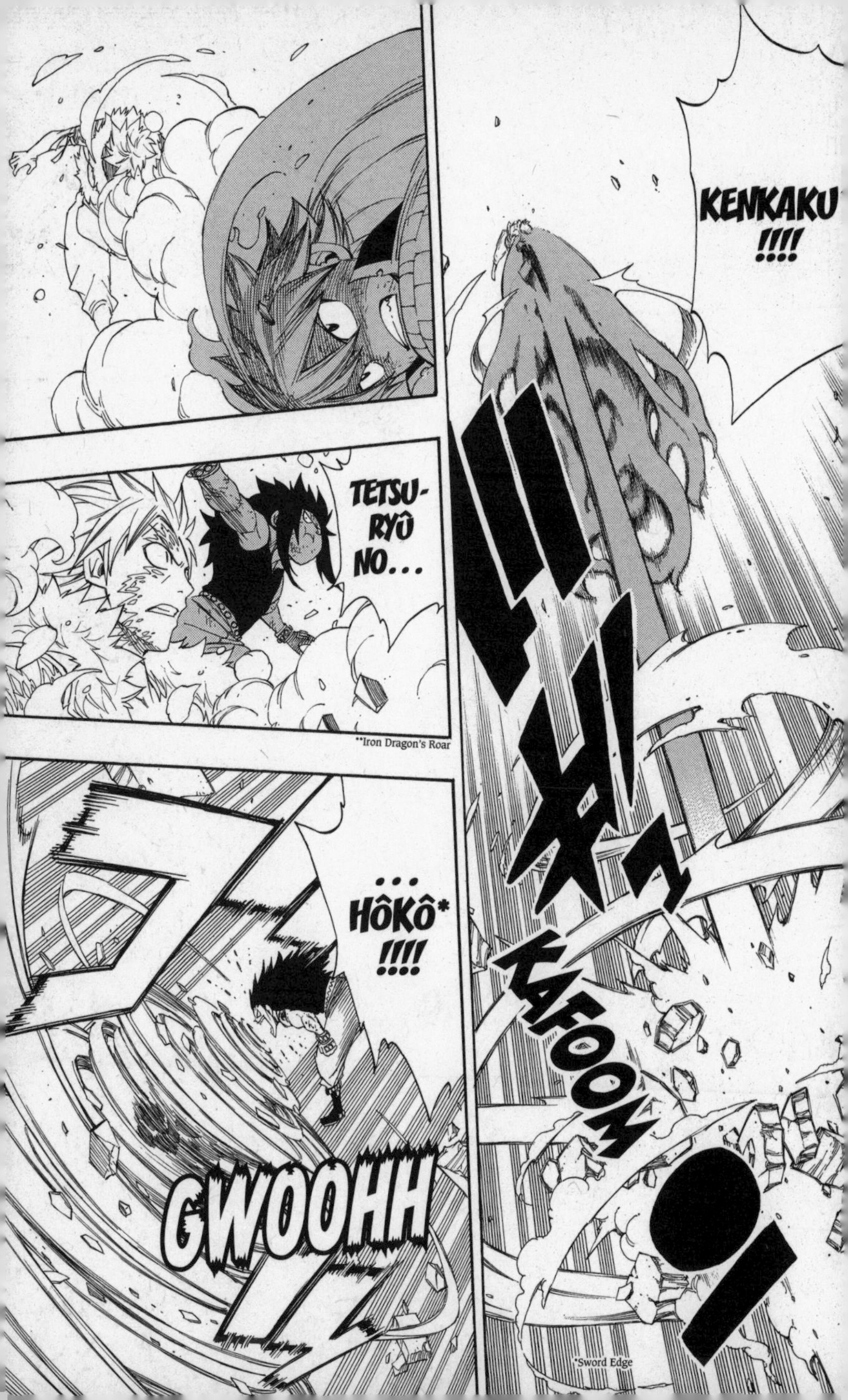
KENKAKU !!!!
KAFOOM
TETSU-RYÛ NO...
...HÔKÔ* !!!!
GWOOHH
*Sword Edge

**Iron Dragon's Roar

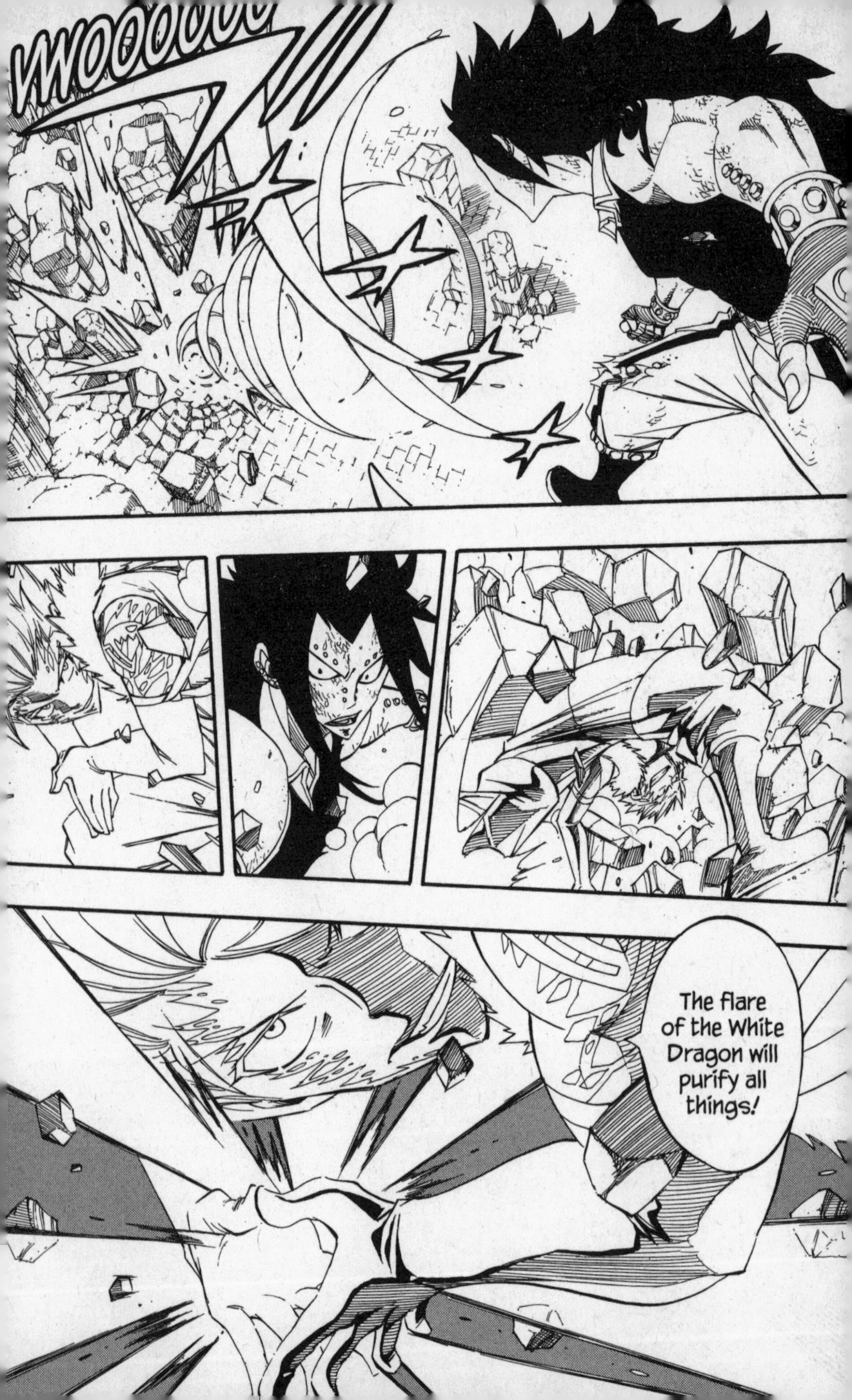
VWOOOOOO
The flare of the White Dragon will purify all things!

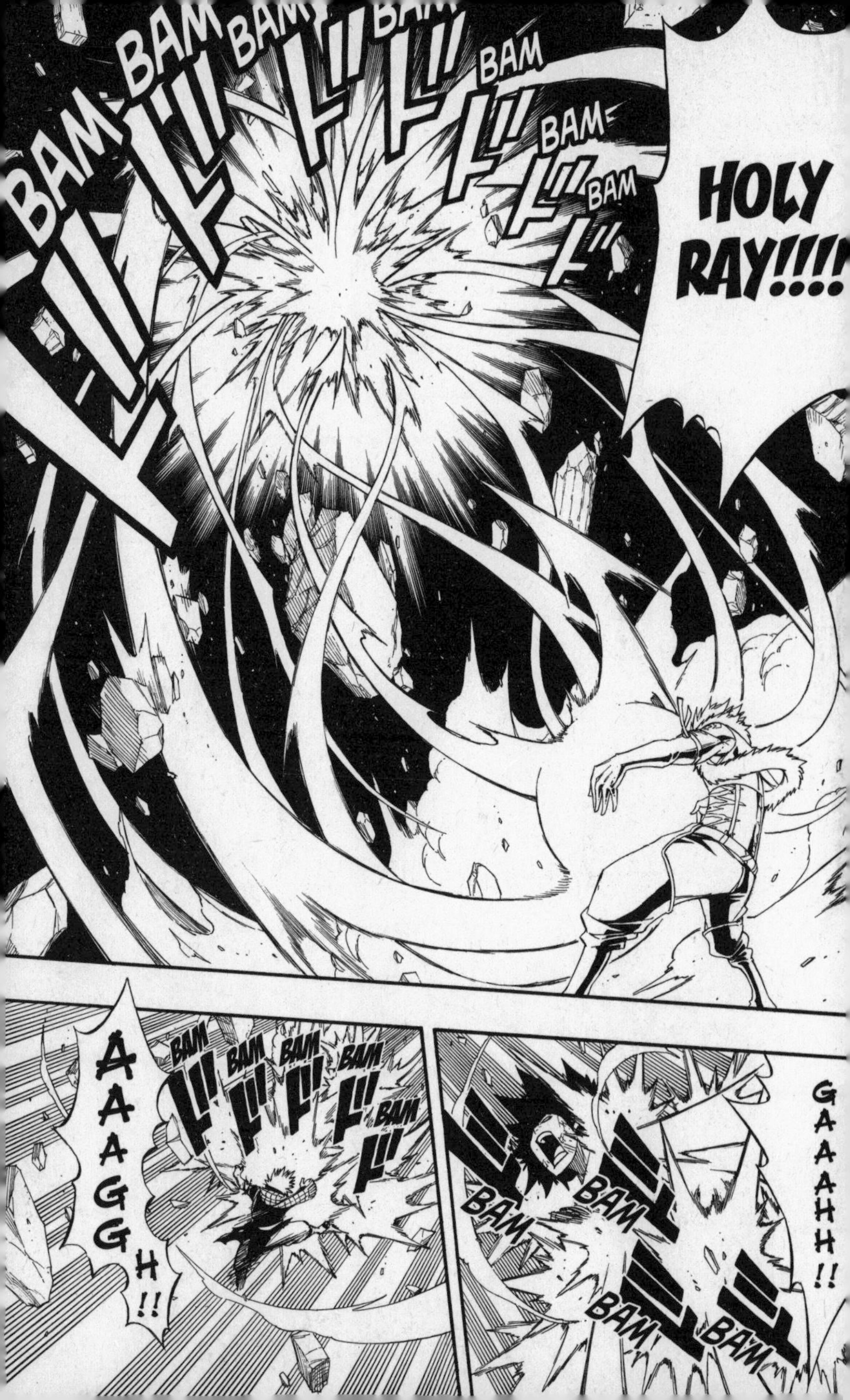
HOLY RAY!!!!
BAM BAM BAM BAM BAM BAM BAM
GAAAHH!!
BAM BAM BAM BAM
AAAGGH!!
BAM BAM BAM BAM BAM

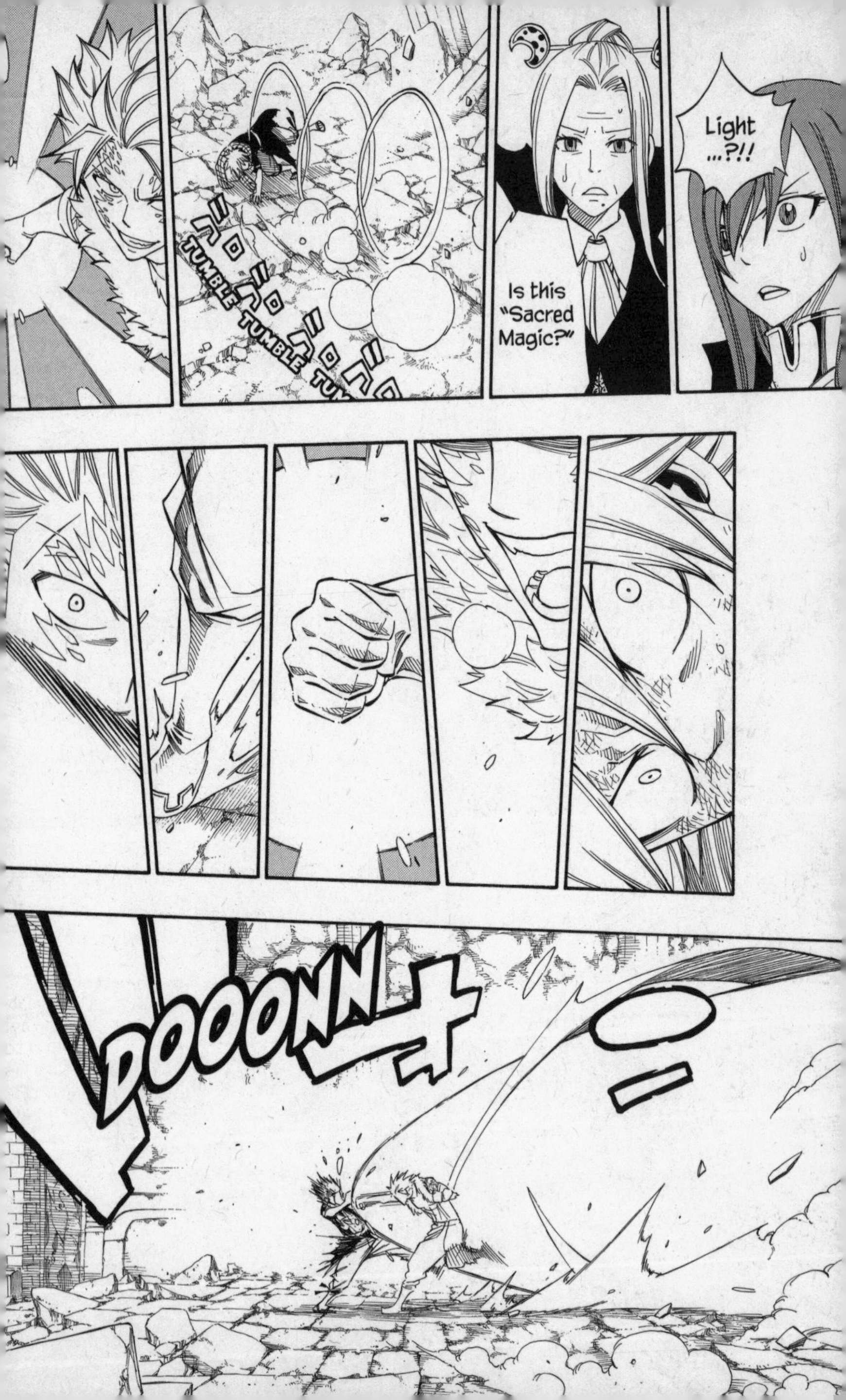
Light ...?!!
Is this "Sacred Magic?"
TUMBLE TUMBLE TU
DOOONN

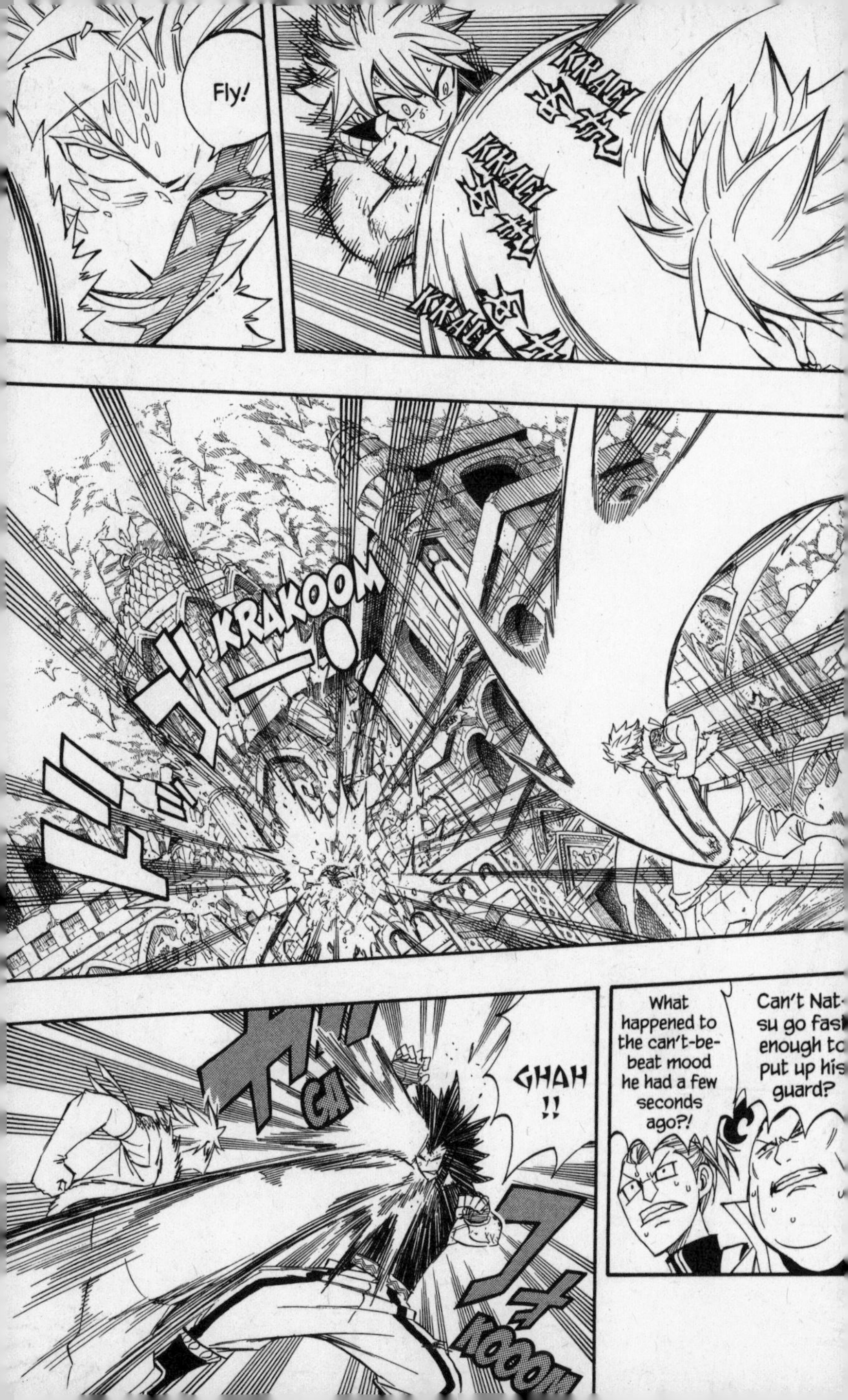
KRAG!
KRAG!
KRAG!
Fly!
KRAKOOM
Can't Nat-su go fast enough to put up his guard?
What happened to the can't-be-beat mood he had a few seconds ago?!
GHAH!!

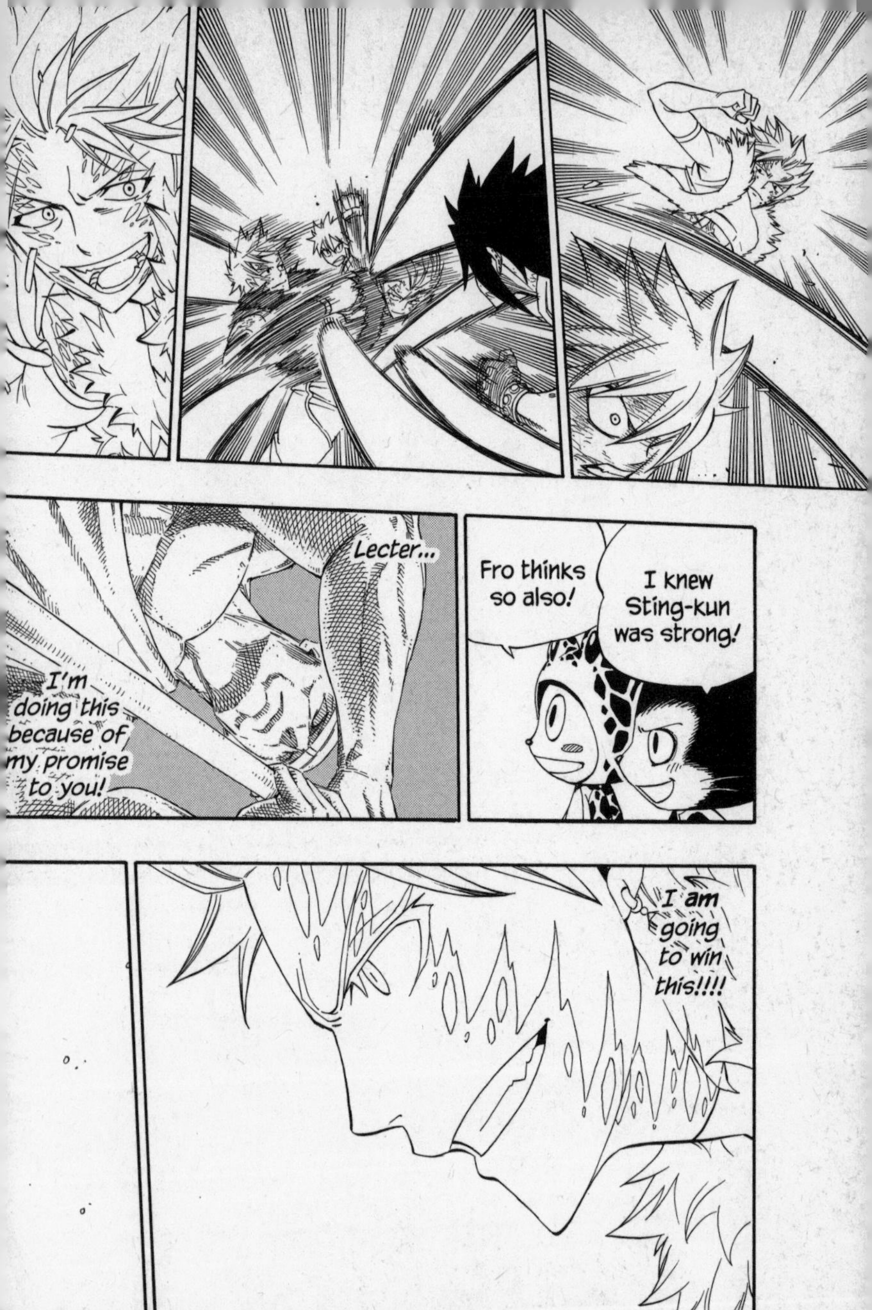
I knew Sting-kun was strong!
Fro thinks so also!
Lecter...
I'm doing this because of my promise to you!
I am going to win this!!!!

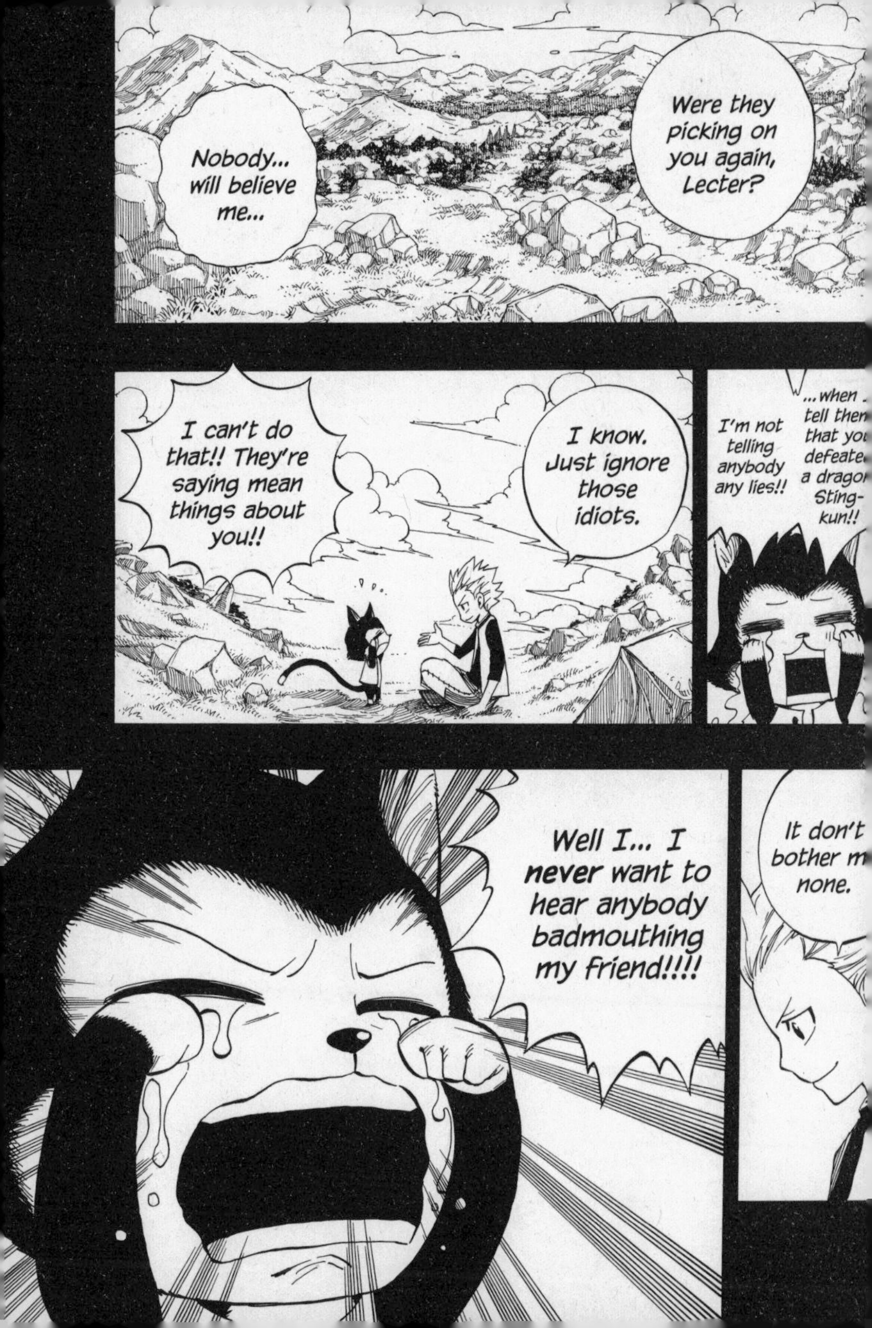
Were they picking on you again, Lecter?
Nobody... will believe me...
...when tell the that yo defeate a drago Sting-kun!!
I'm not telling anybody any lies!!
I know. Just ignore those idiots.
I can't do that!! They're saying mean things about you!!
It don't bother m none.
Well I... I **never** want to hear anybody badmouthing my friend!!!!

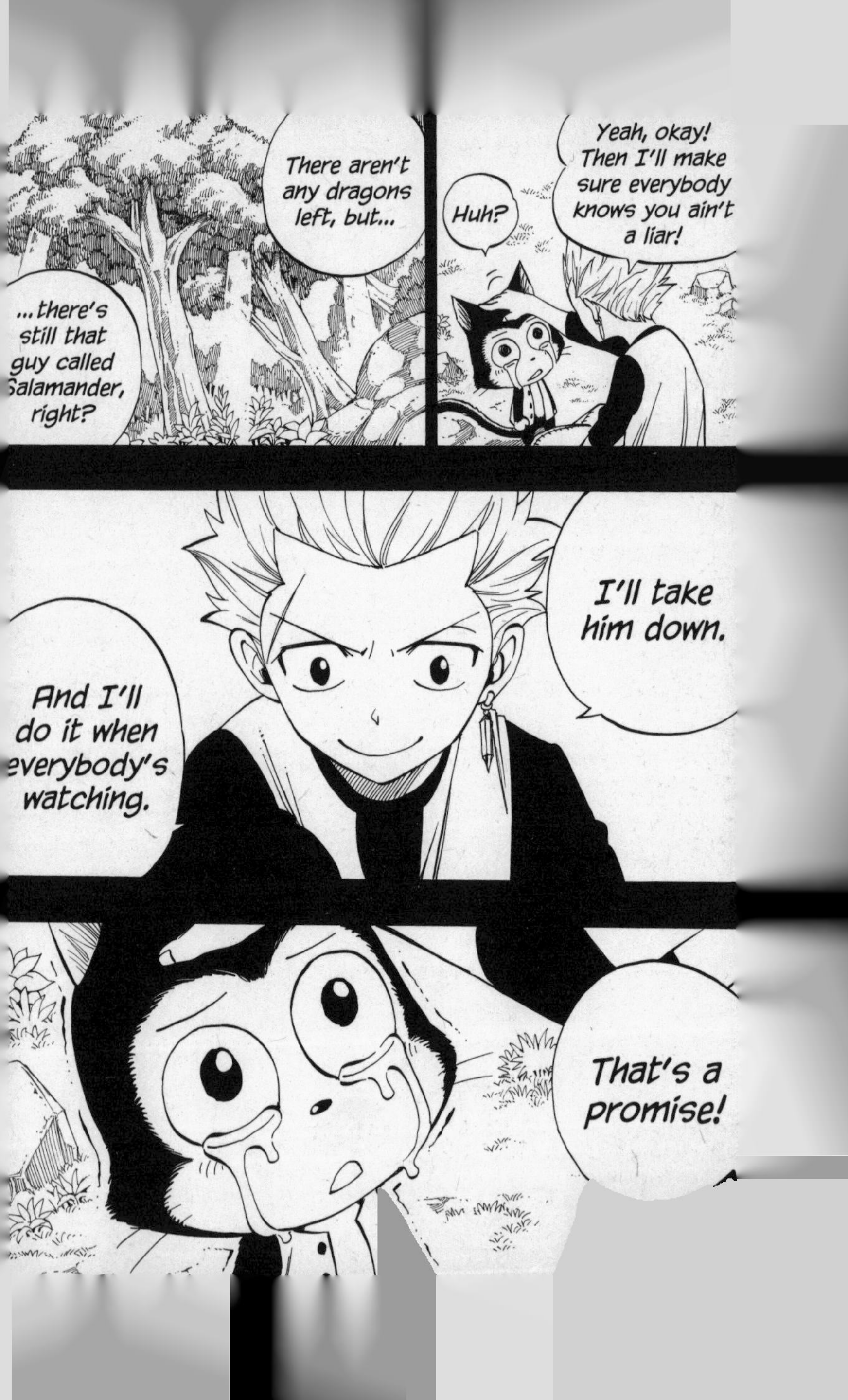
Yeah, okay! Then I'll make sure everybody knows you ain't a liar!
Huh?
There aren't any dragons left, but...
...there's still that guy called Salamander, right?
I'll take him down.
And I'll do it when everybody's watching.
That's a promise!

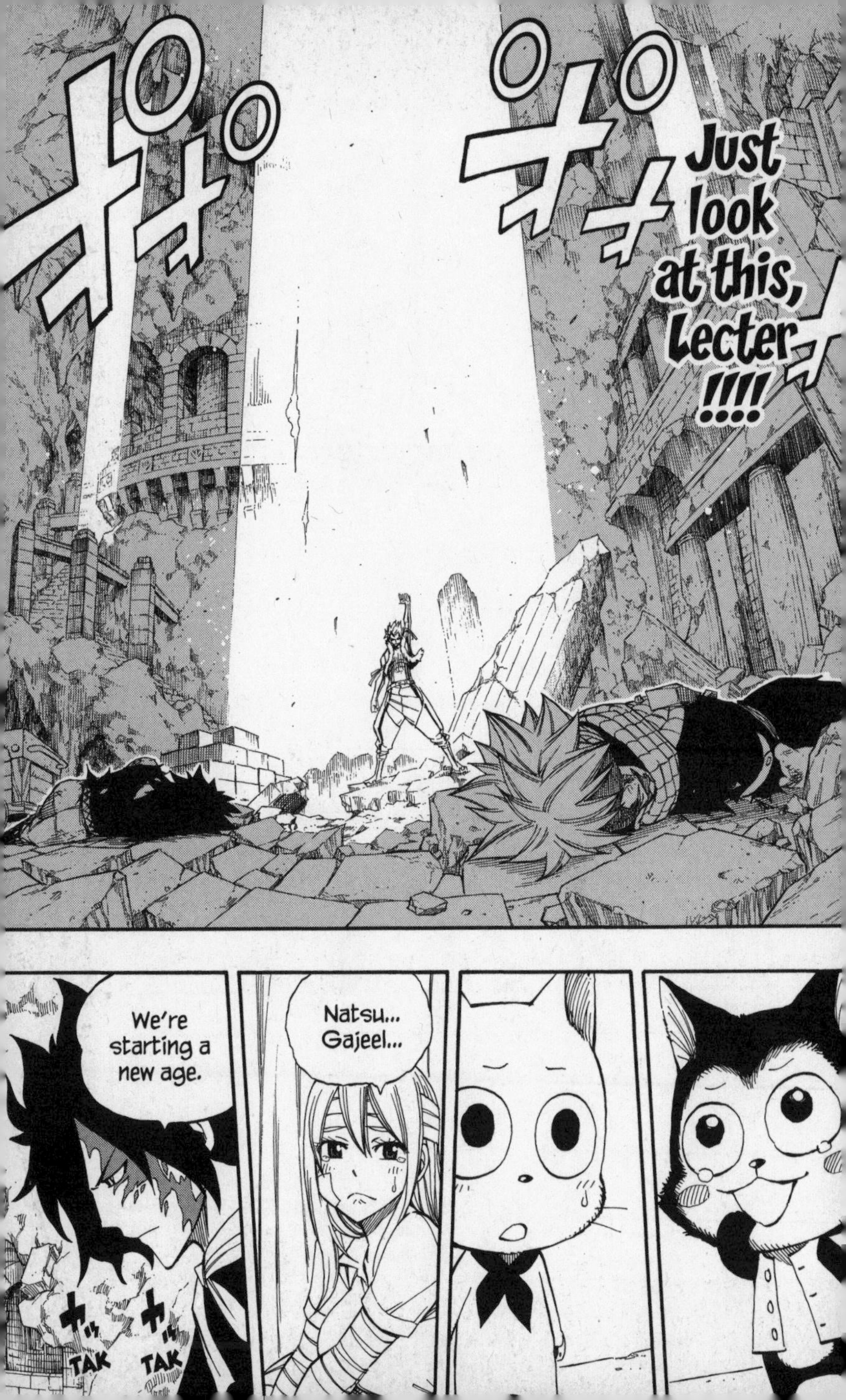
Just look at this, Lecter!!!!
Natsu... Gajeel...
We're starting a new age.
TAK
TAK

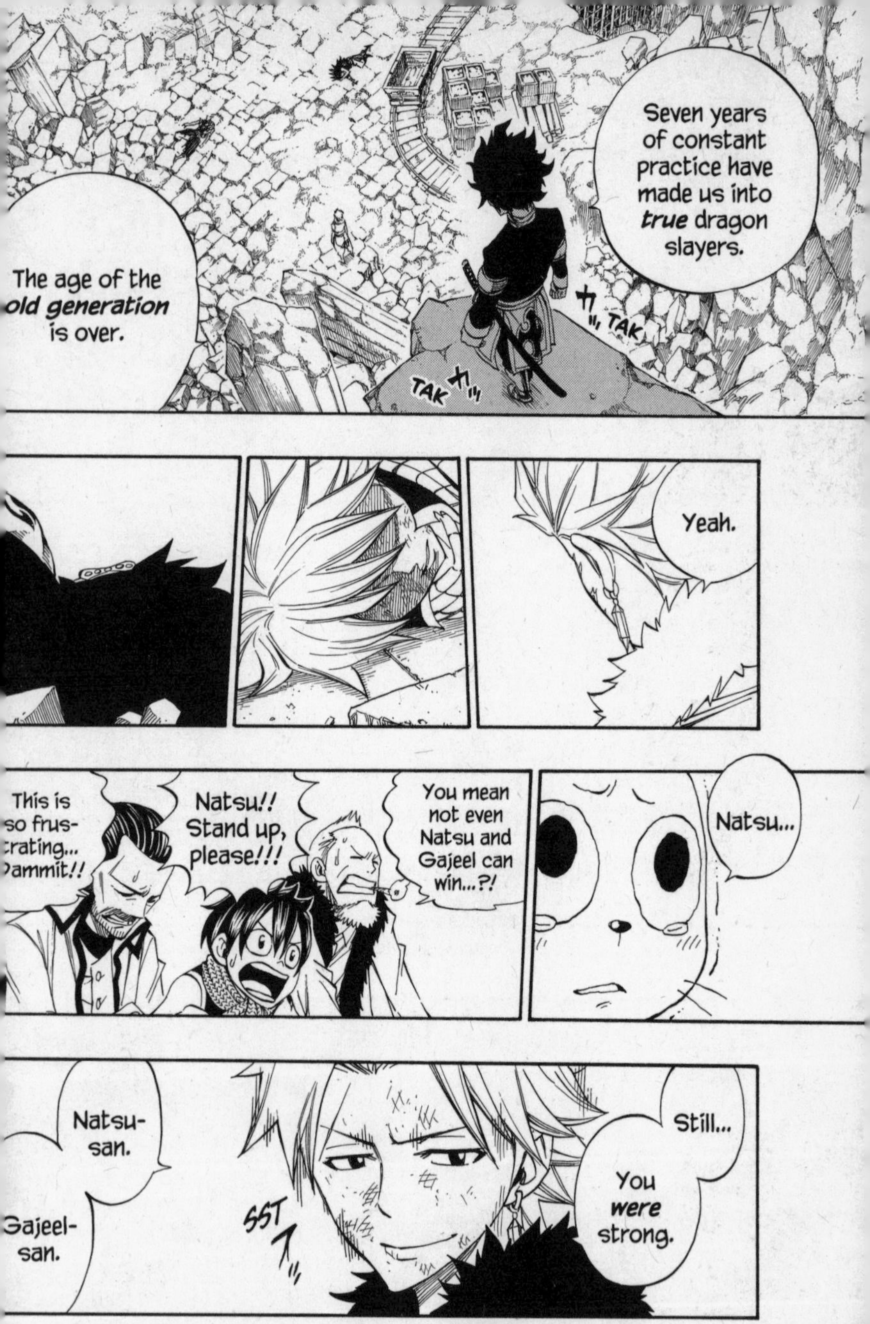
Seven years of constant practice have made us into *true* dragon slayers.
The age of the *old generation* is over.
TAK
TAK
Yeah.
Natsu...
You mean not even Natsu and Gajeel can win...?!
Natsu!! Stand up, please!!!
This is so frus-trating... Dammit!!
Still...
You *were* strong.
SST
Natsu-san.
Gajeel-san.

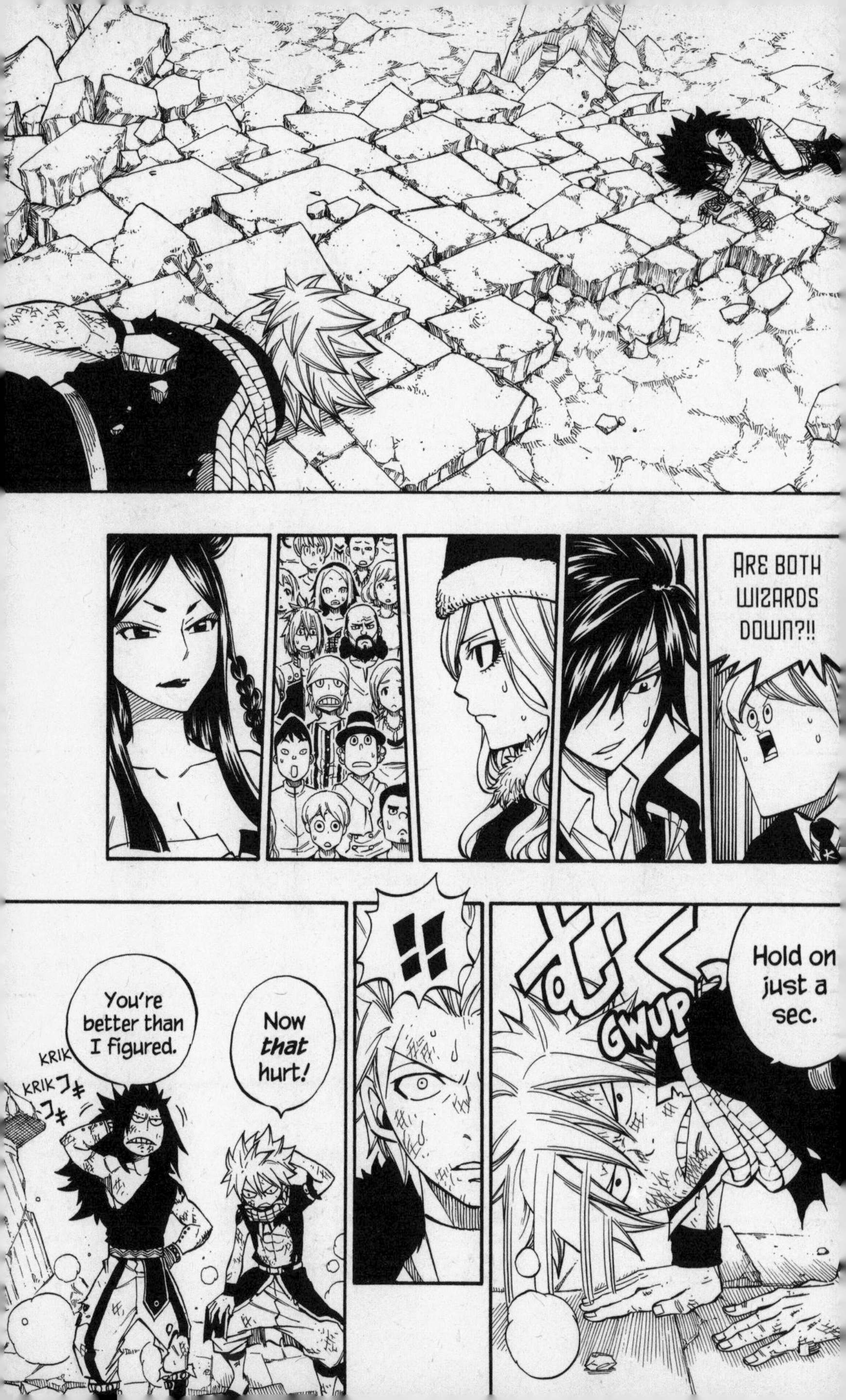
ARE BOTH WIZARDS DOWN?!!
Hold on just a sec.
GWUP
!!
Now *that* hurt!
You're better than I figured.
KRIK KRIK
コキ コキ

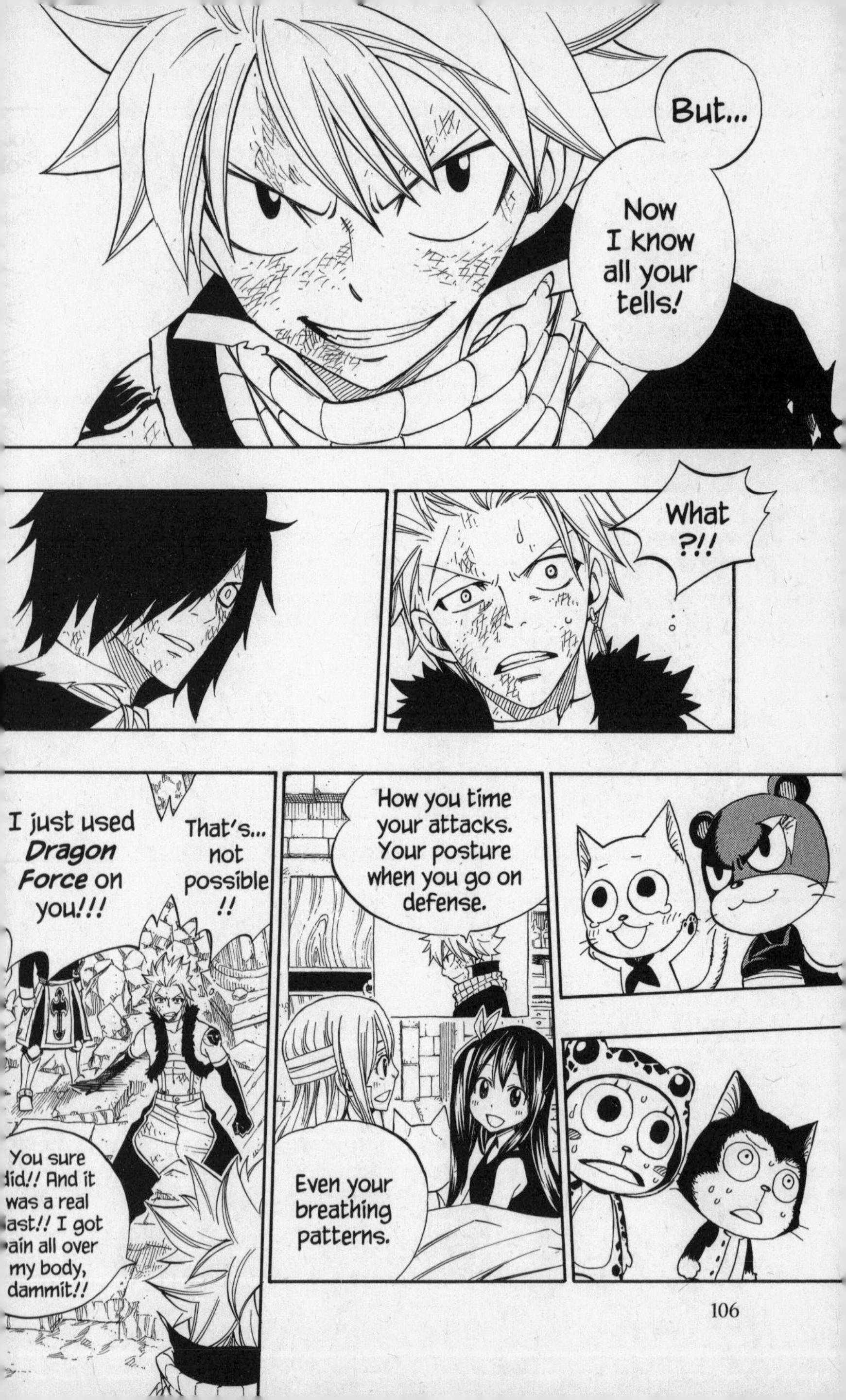
But...
Now I know all your tells!
What?!!
How you time your attacks. Your posture when you go on defense.
Even your breathing patterns.
That's... not possible!!
I just used *Dragon Force* on you!!!
You sure did!! And it was a real ast!! I got ain all over my body, dammit!!

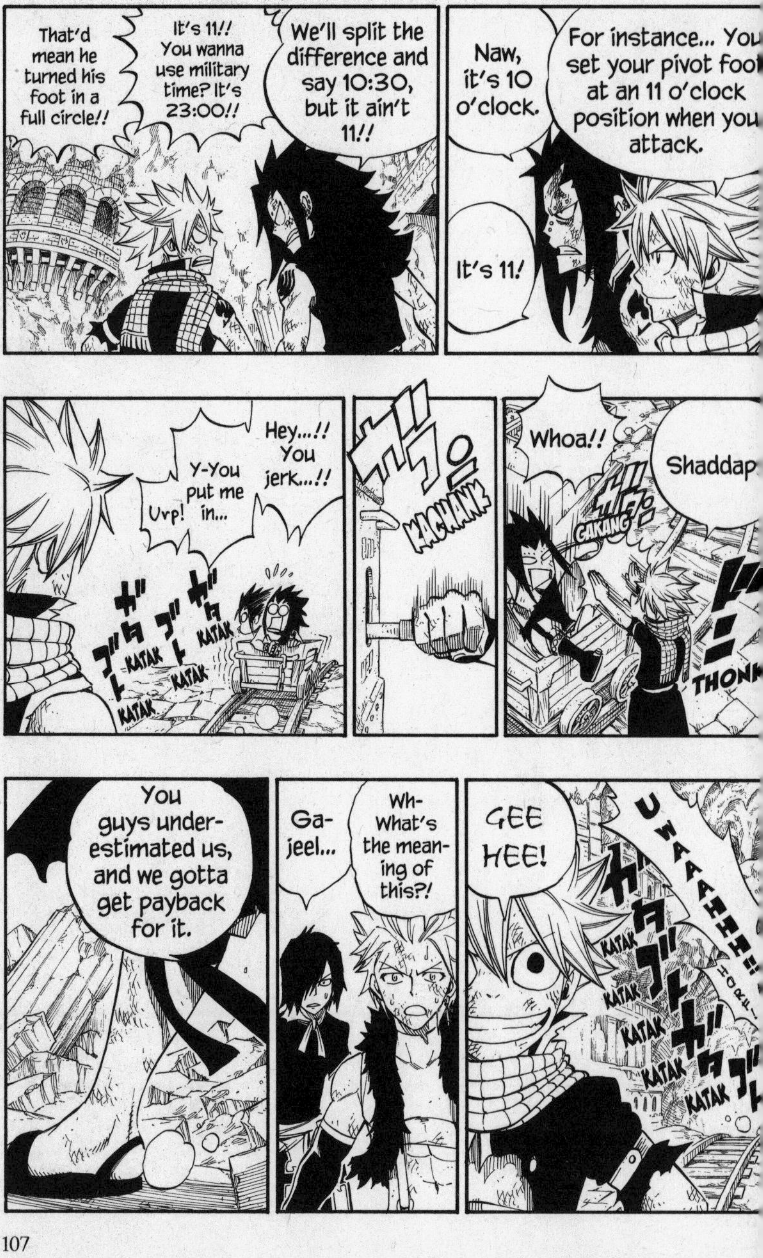
For instance... Yo set your pivot foo at an 11 o'clock position when you attack.
Naw, it's 10 o'clock.
It's 11!
We'll split the difference and say 10:30, but it ain't 11!!
It's 11!! You wanna use military time? It's 23:00!!
That'd mean he turned his foot in a full circle!!
Shaddap
Whoa!!
GAKANG
THON
KACHANK
Hey...!! You jerk...!!
Y-You put me in...
Urp!
KATAK
KATAK
KATAK
KATAK
UWAAAAHHH!!
KATAK
KATAK
KATAK
KATAK
KATAK
GEE HEE!
Wh-What's the mean-ing of this?!
Ga-jeel...
You guys under-estimated us, and we gotta get payback for it.

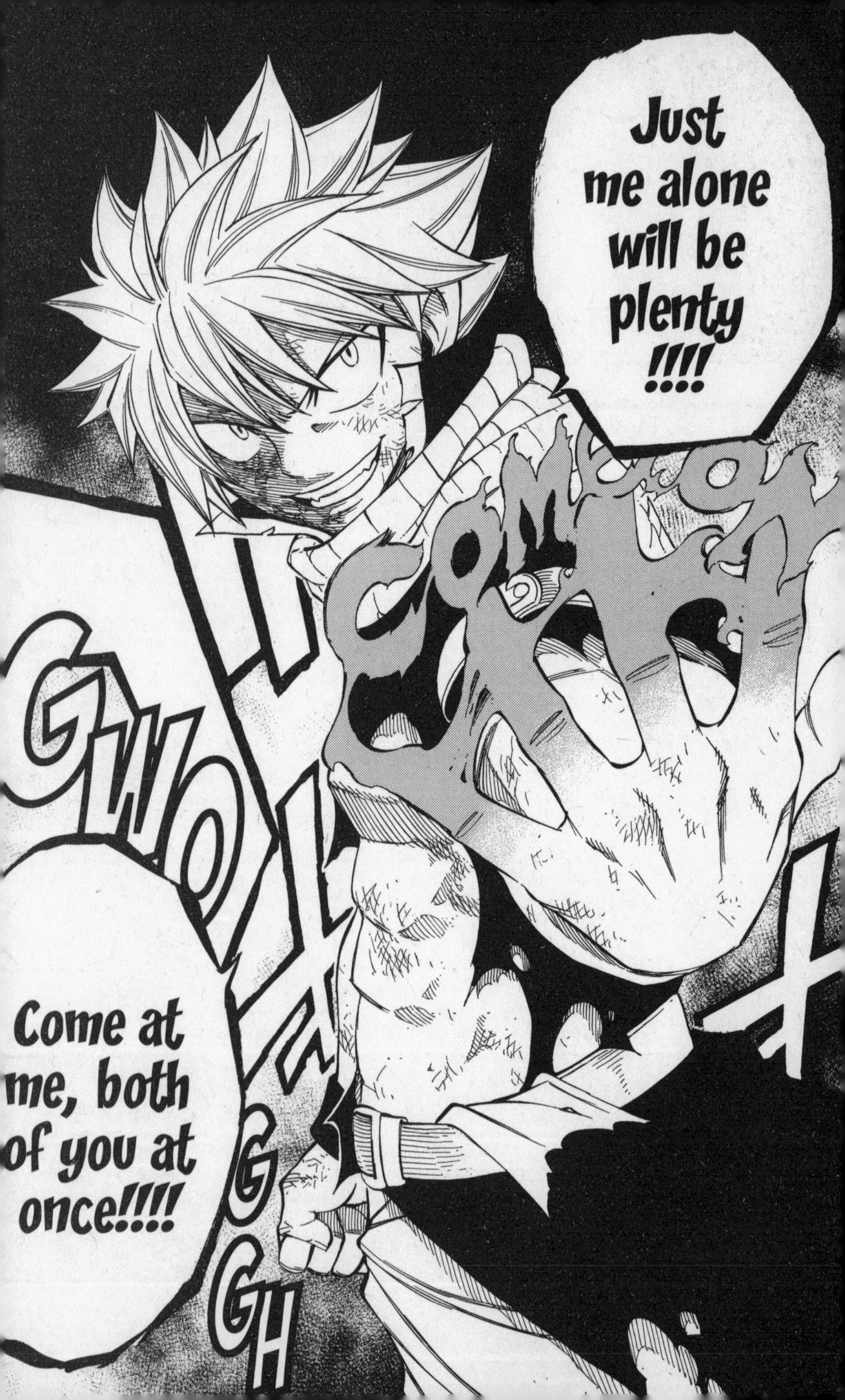
Just me alone will be plenty!!!!
Come at me, both of you at once!!!!

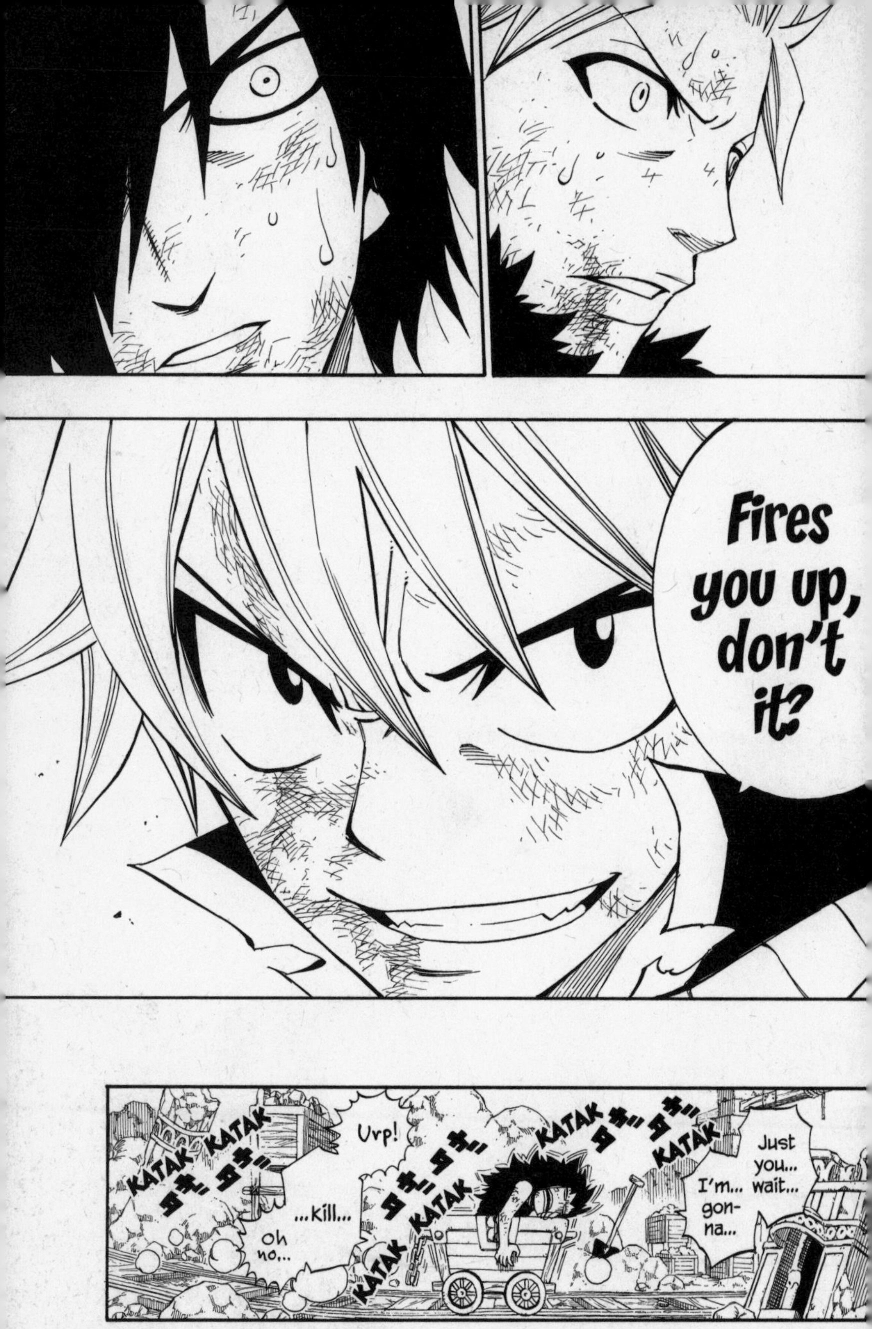
Fires you up, don't it?
Just you... wait...
I'm... gon-na...
KATAK
KATAK
KATAK
KATAK
Urp!
KATAK
KATAK
...kill...
oh no...

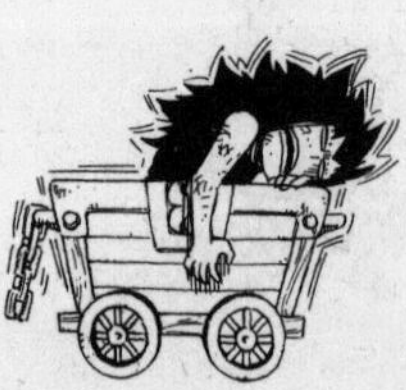

FAIRY TAIL

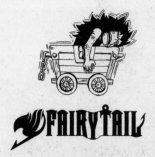

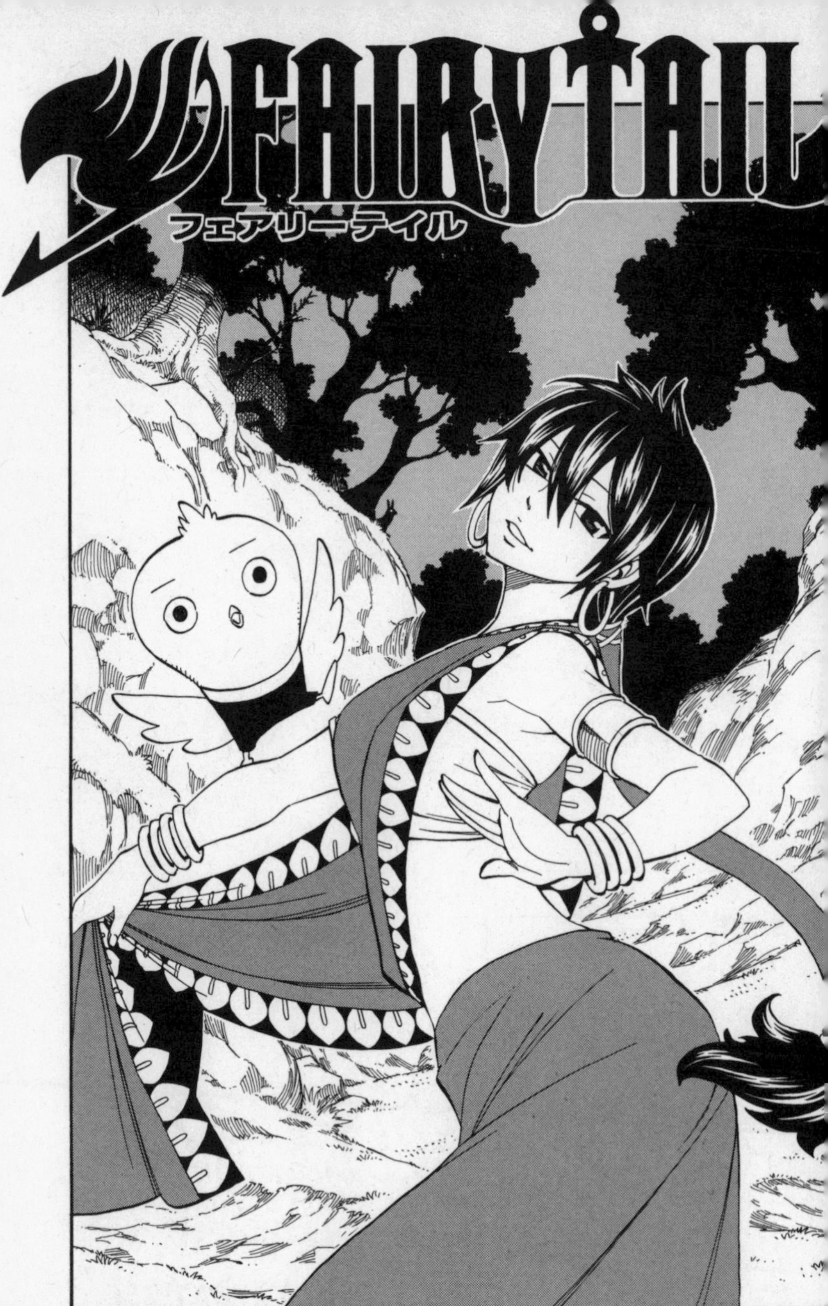
FAIRY TAIL
フェアリーテイル

Chapter 296: Natsu vs. Twin Dragons

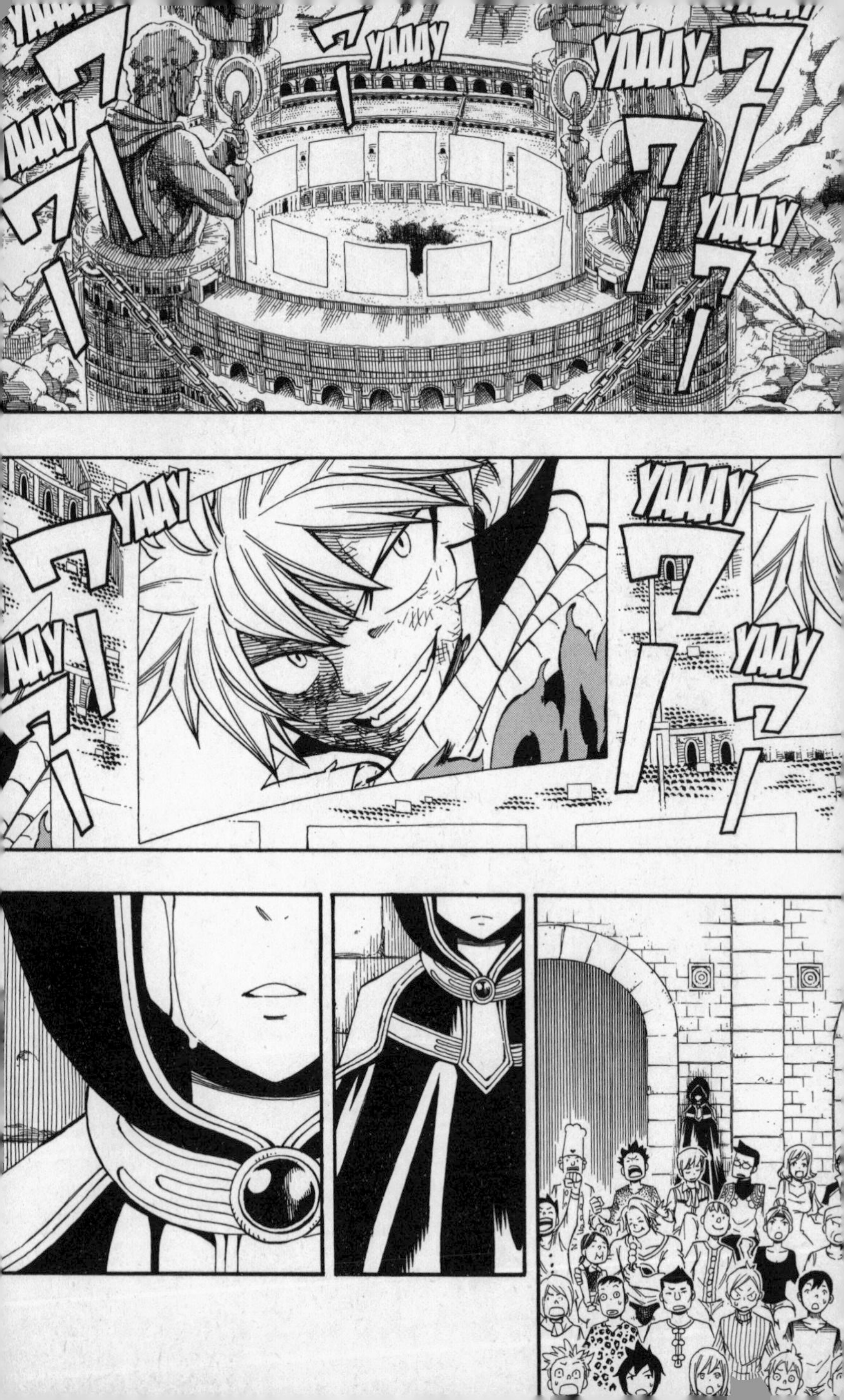
YAAAY
YAAAY
YAAAY
AAAY
YAAAY
YAAY
YAAY
AAY

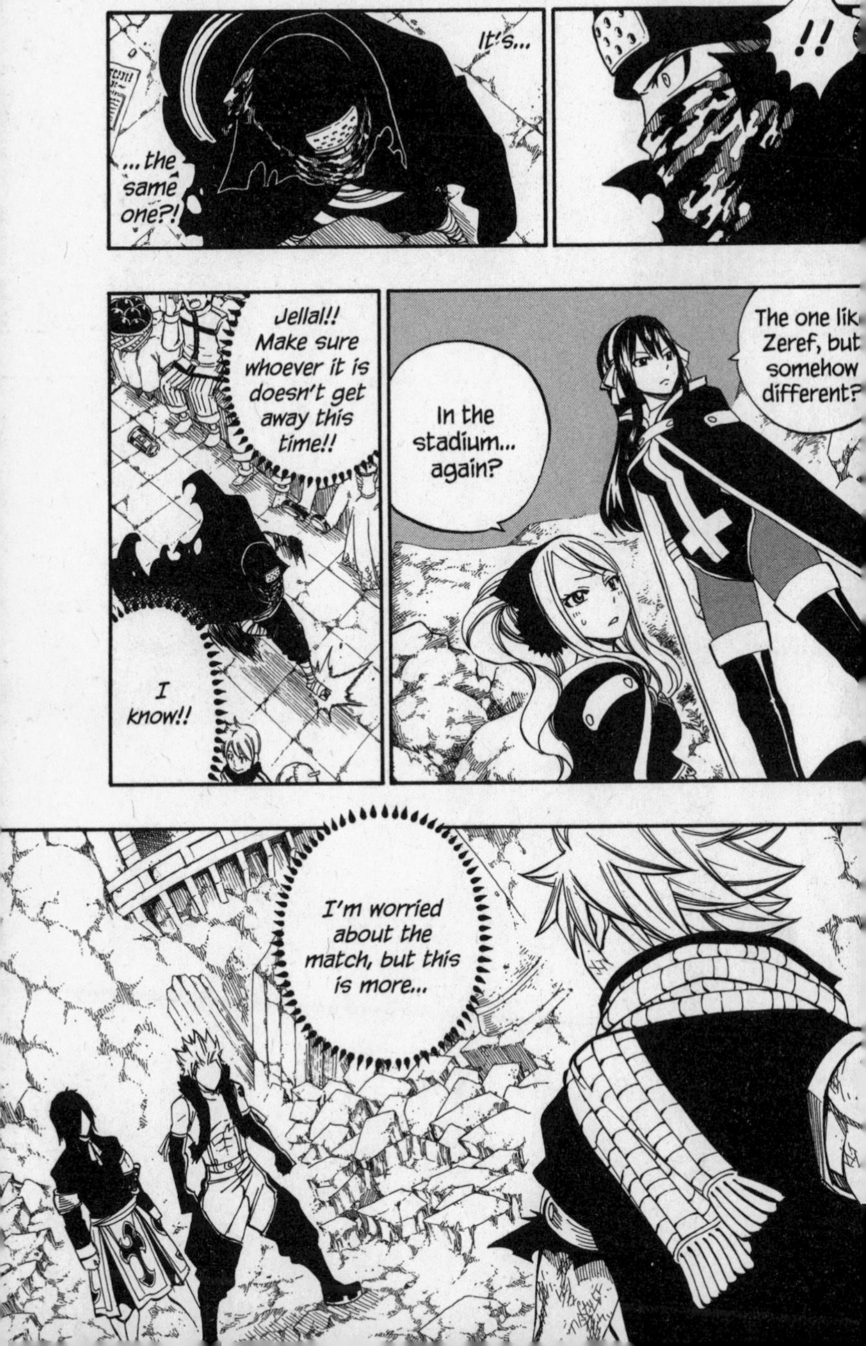
!!
It's...
...the same one?!
The one lik Zeref, but somehow different?
In the stadium... again?
Jellal!! Make sure whoever it is doesn't get away this time!!
I know!!
I'm worried about the match, but this is more...

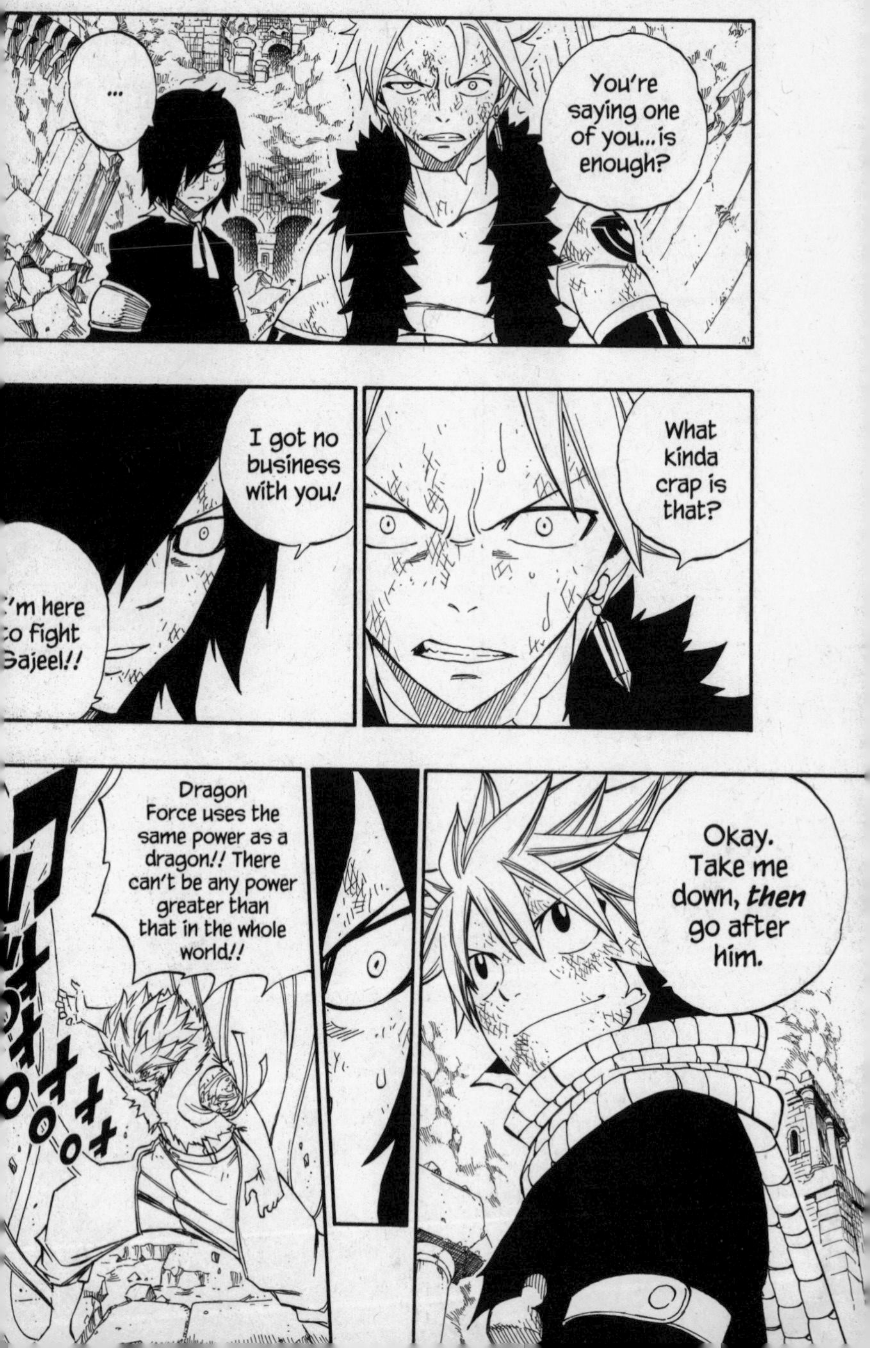

You're saying one of you...is enough?
...
What kinda crap is that?
I got no business with you!
'm here o fight Gajeel!!
Okay. Take me down, *then* go after him.
Dragon Force uses the same power as a dragon!! There can't be any power greater than that in the whole world!!

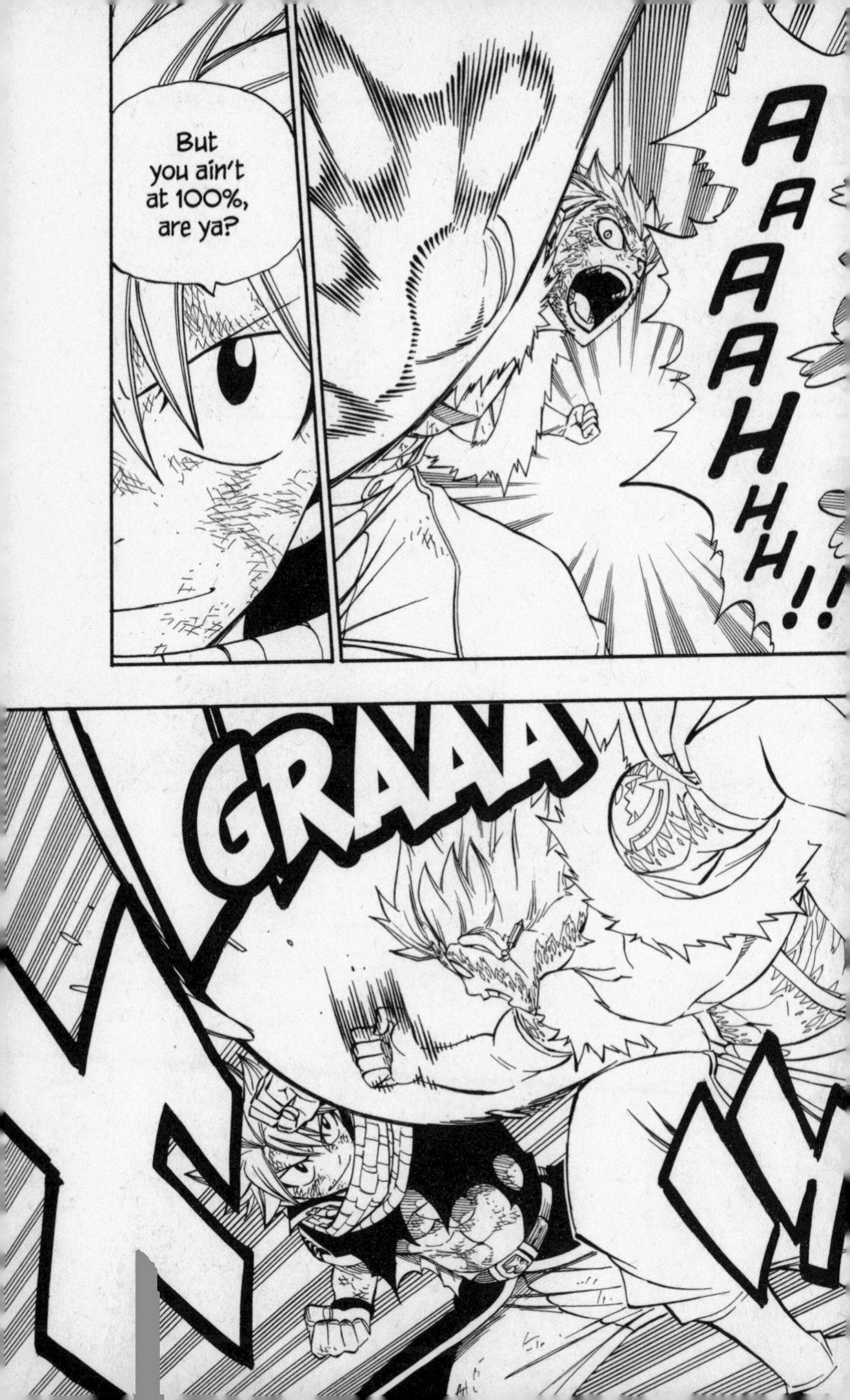
AAAAHHH!!
But you ain't at 100%, are ya?
GRAAA

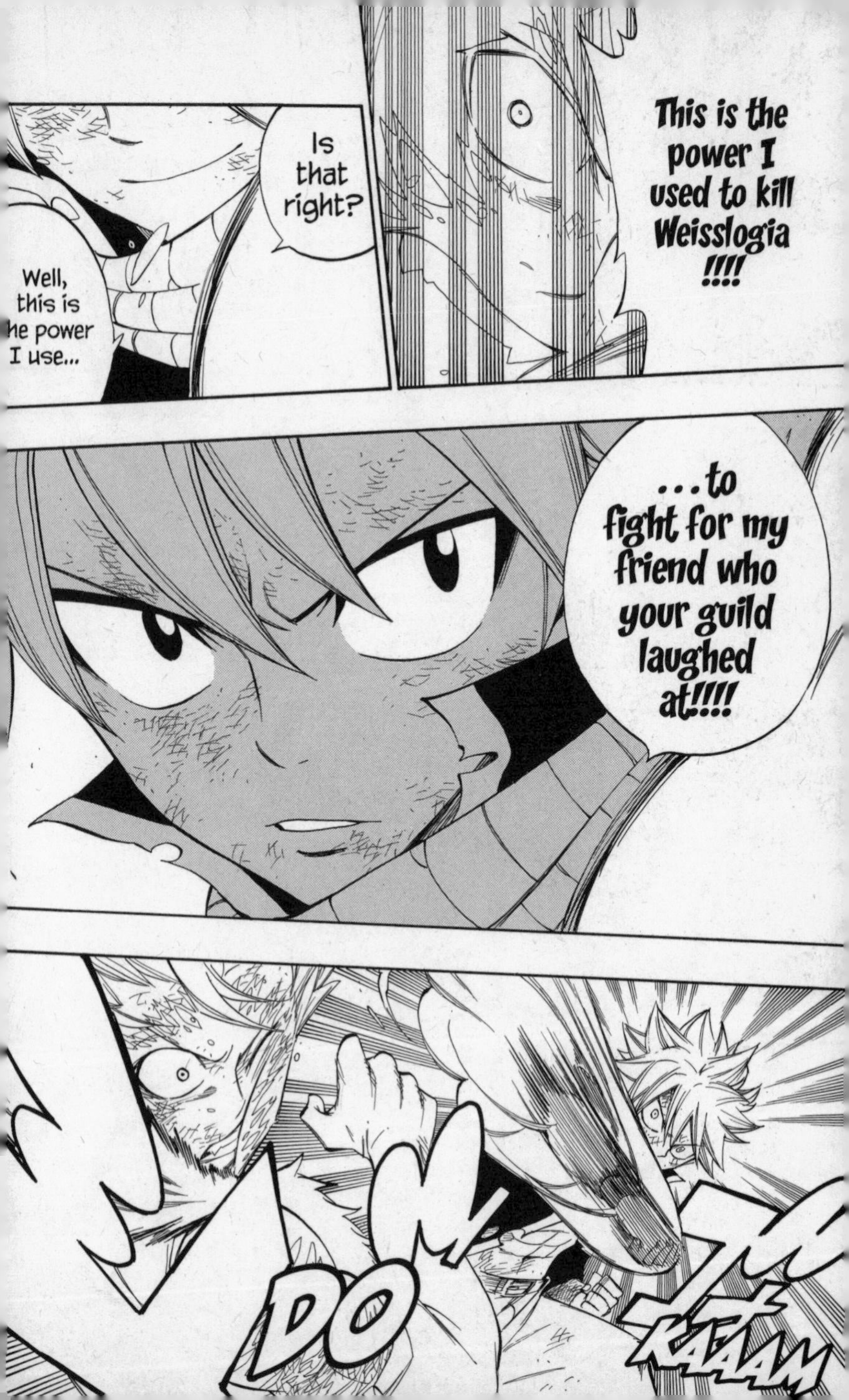
This is the power I used to kill Weisslogia!!!!
Is that right?
Well, this is he power I use...
...to fight for my friend who your guild laughed at!!!!
DOOM
KAAAM

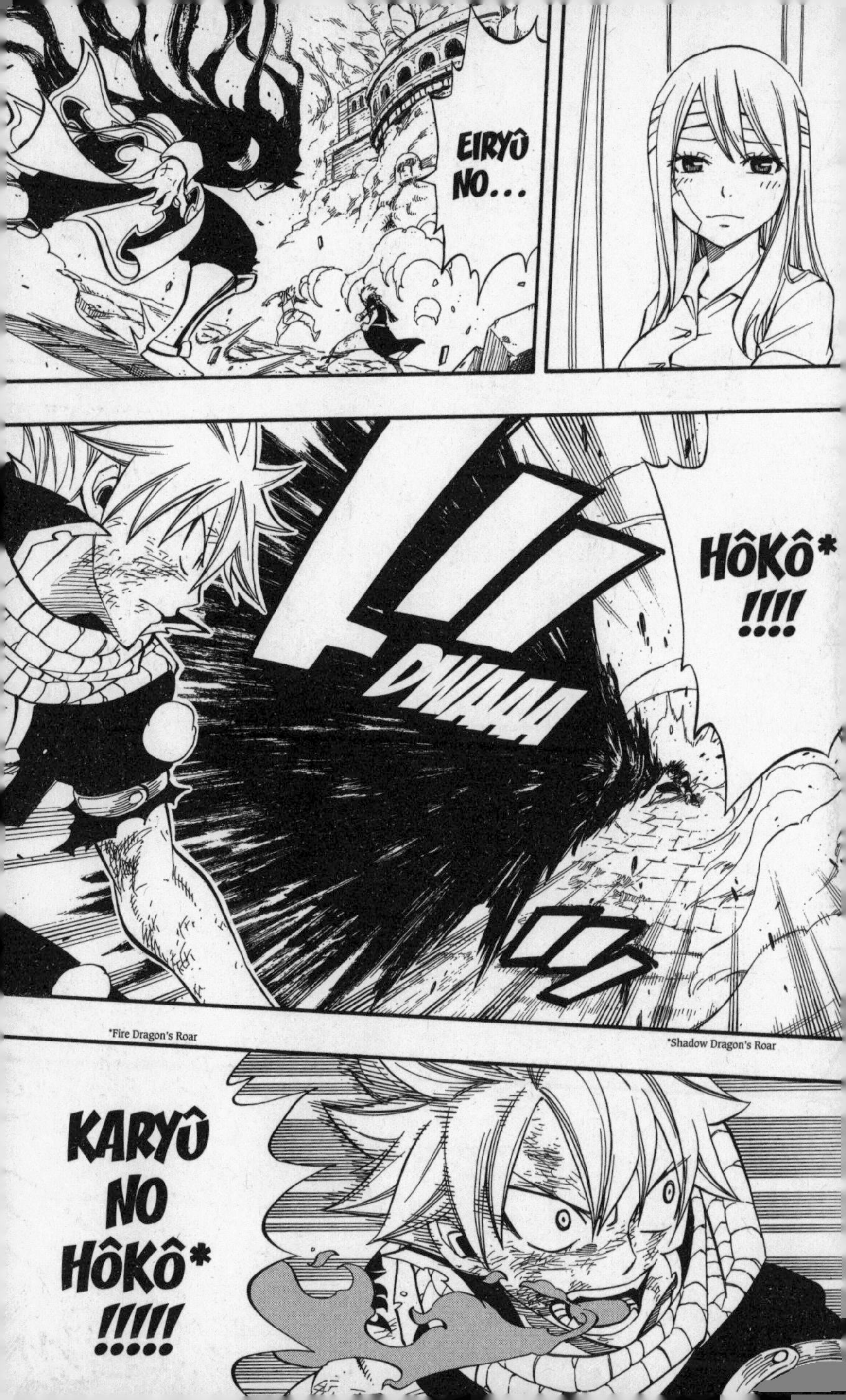
EIRYÛ NO...
HÔKÔ* !!!!
DWAAA
KARYÛ NO HÔKÔ* !!!!!

*Shadow Dragon's Roar

*Fire Dragon's Roar

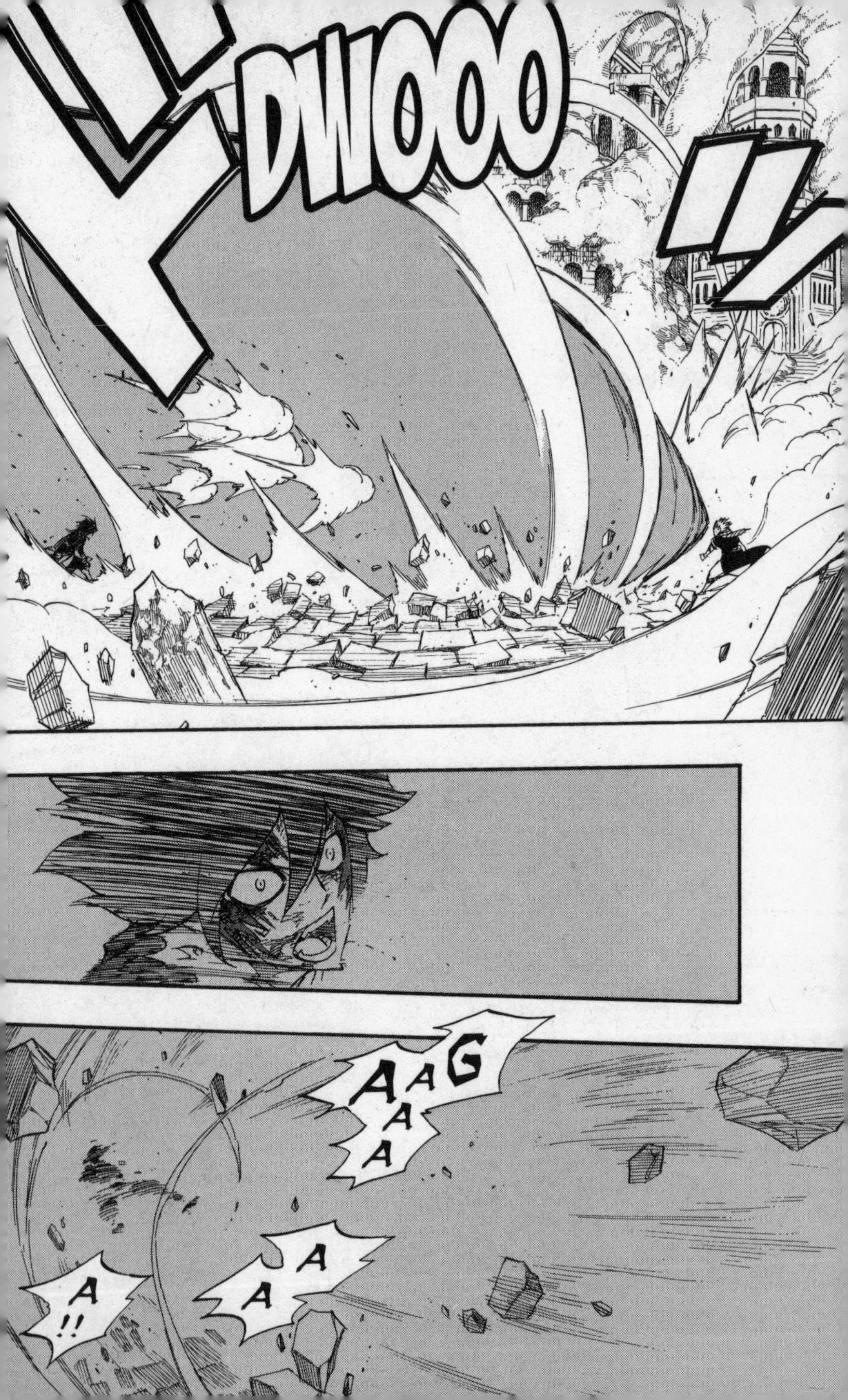
DWOOO
AAGAA
AA
A!!

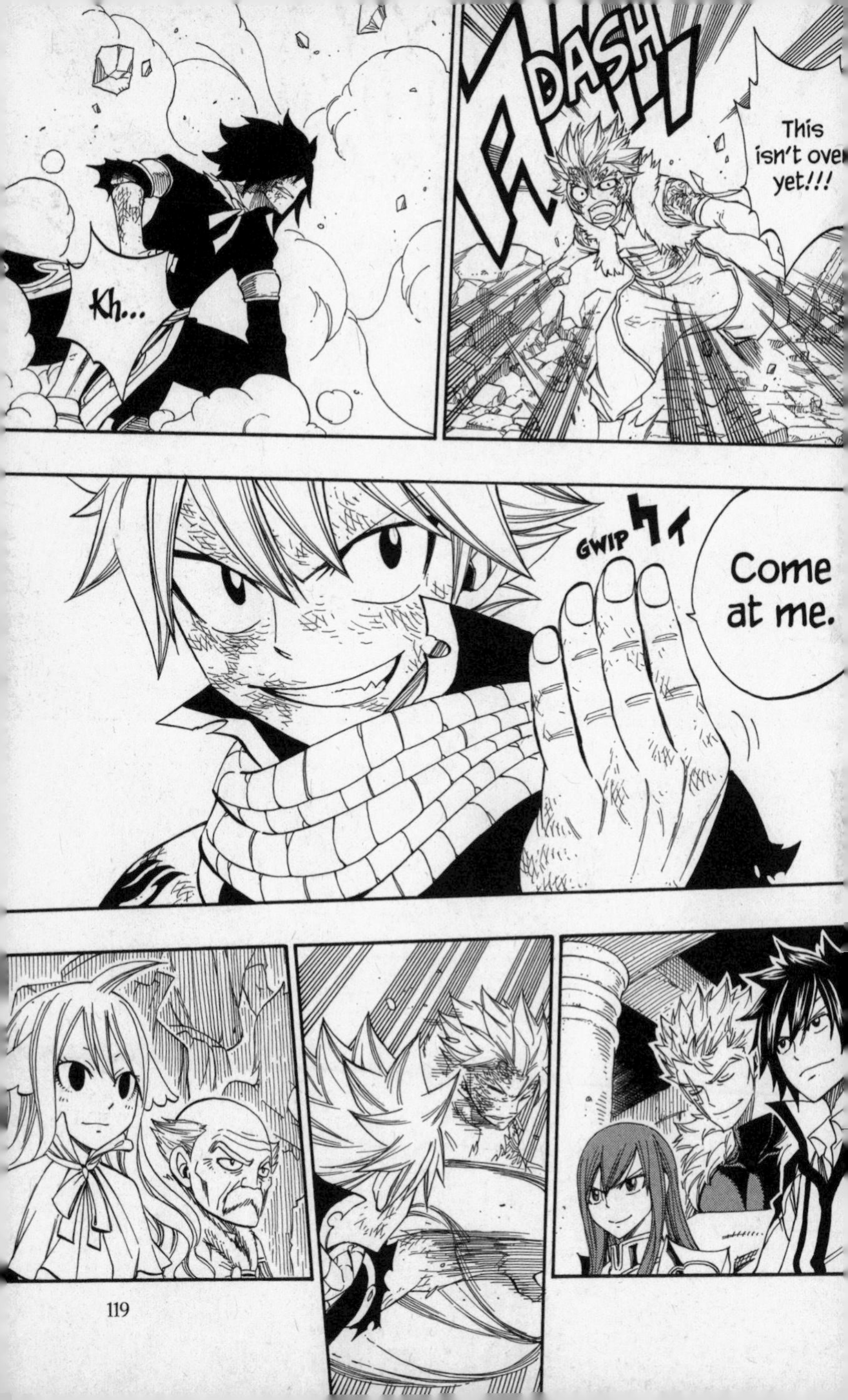
DASH
This isn't over yet!!!
Kh...
Come at me.
GWIP

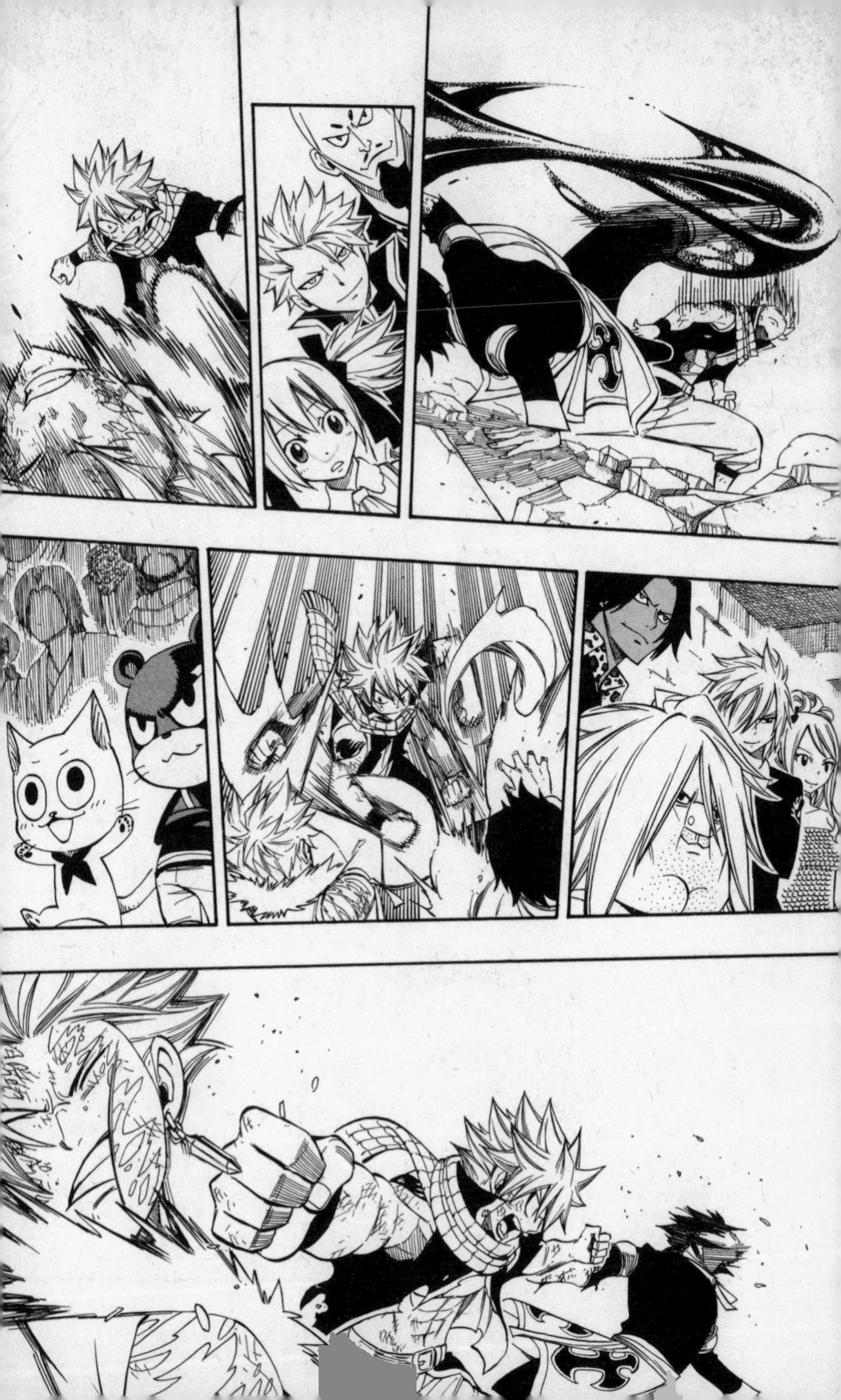

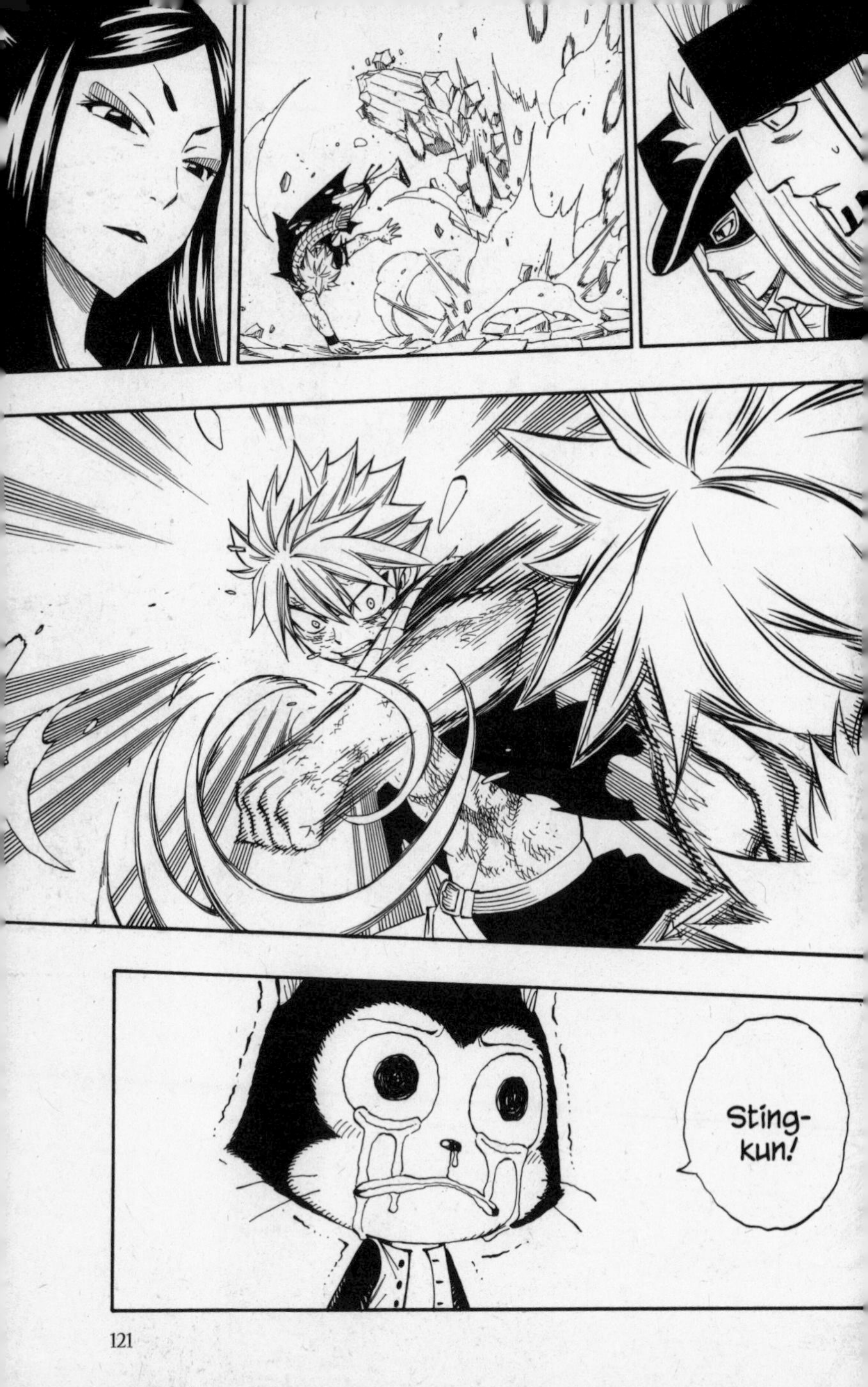
Sting-
kun!

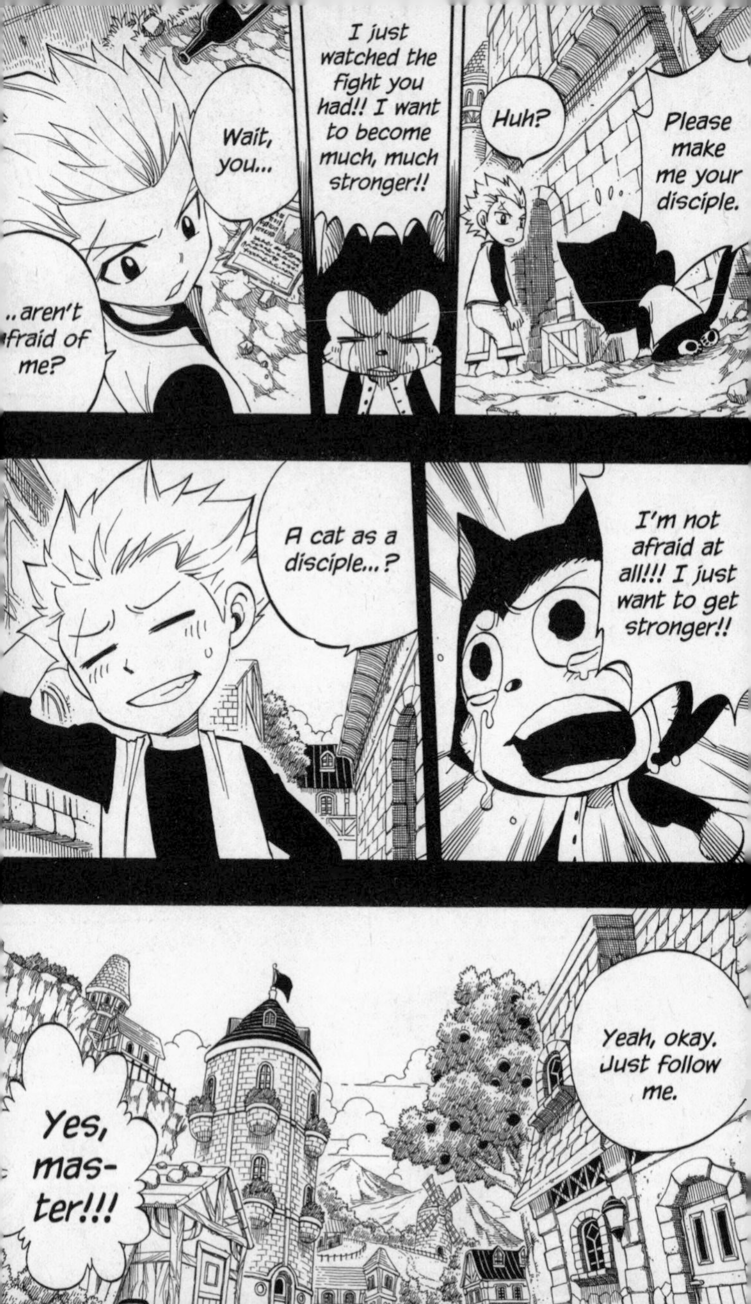
Please make me your disciple.
Huh?
I just watched the fight you had!! I want to become much, much stronger!!
Wait, you...
..aren't afraid of me?
I'm not afraid at all!!! I just want to get stronger!!
A cat as a disciple...?
Yeah, okay. Just follow me.
Yes, mas-ter!!!

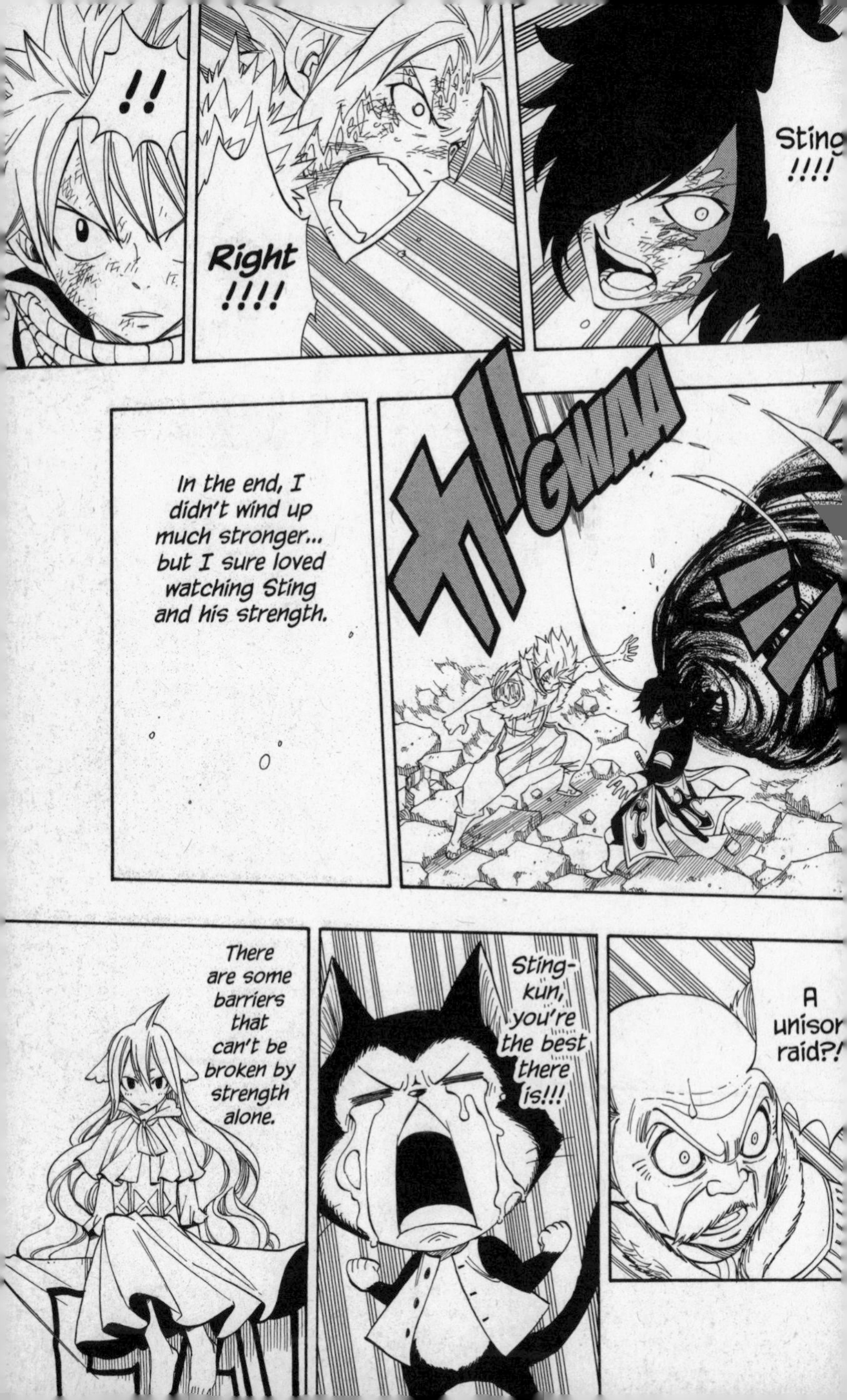

Sting !!!!
Right !!!!
!!
GWAA
In the end, I didn't wind up much stronger... but I sure loved watching Sting and his strength.
A unisor raid?!
Sting-kun, you're the best there is!!!
There are some barriers that can't be broken by strength alone.

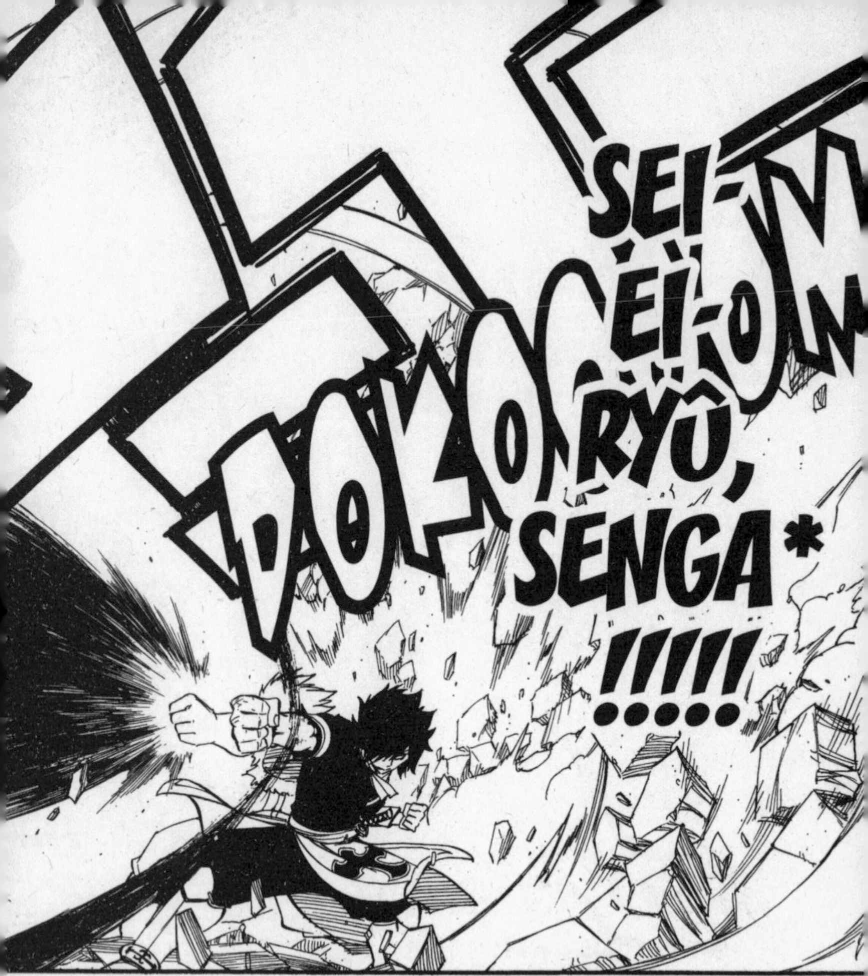
SEI-EI-RYŪ, SENGA*!!!!!

*Divine-Shadow Dragon, Light Fang

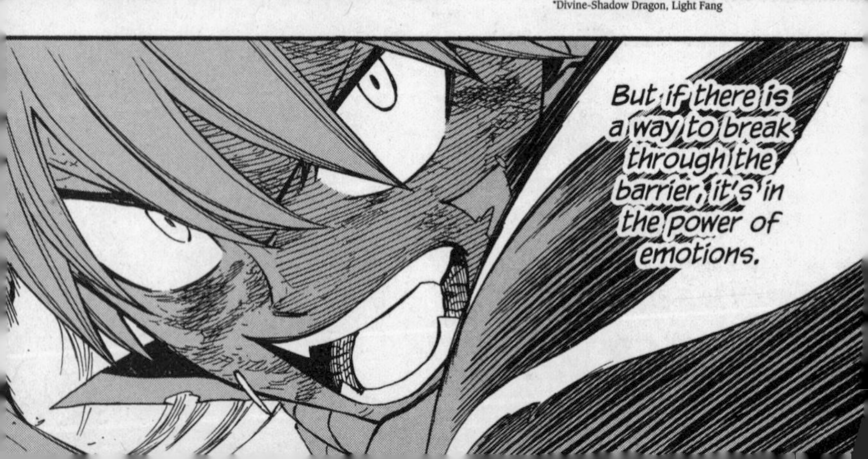
But if there is a way to break through the barrier, it's in the power of emotions.

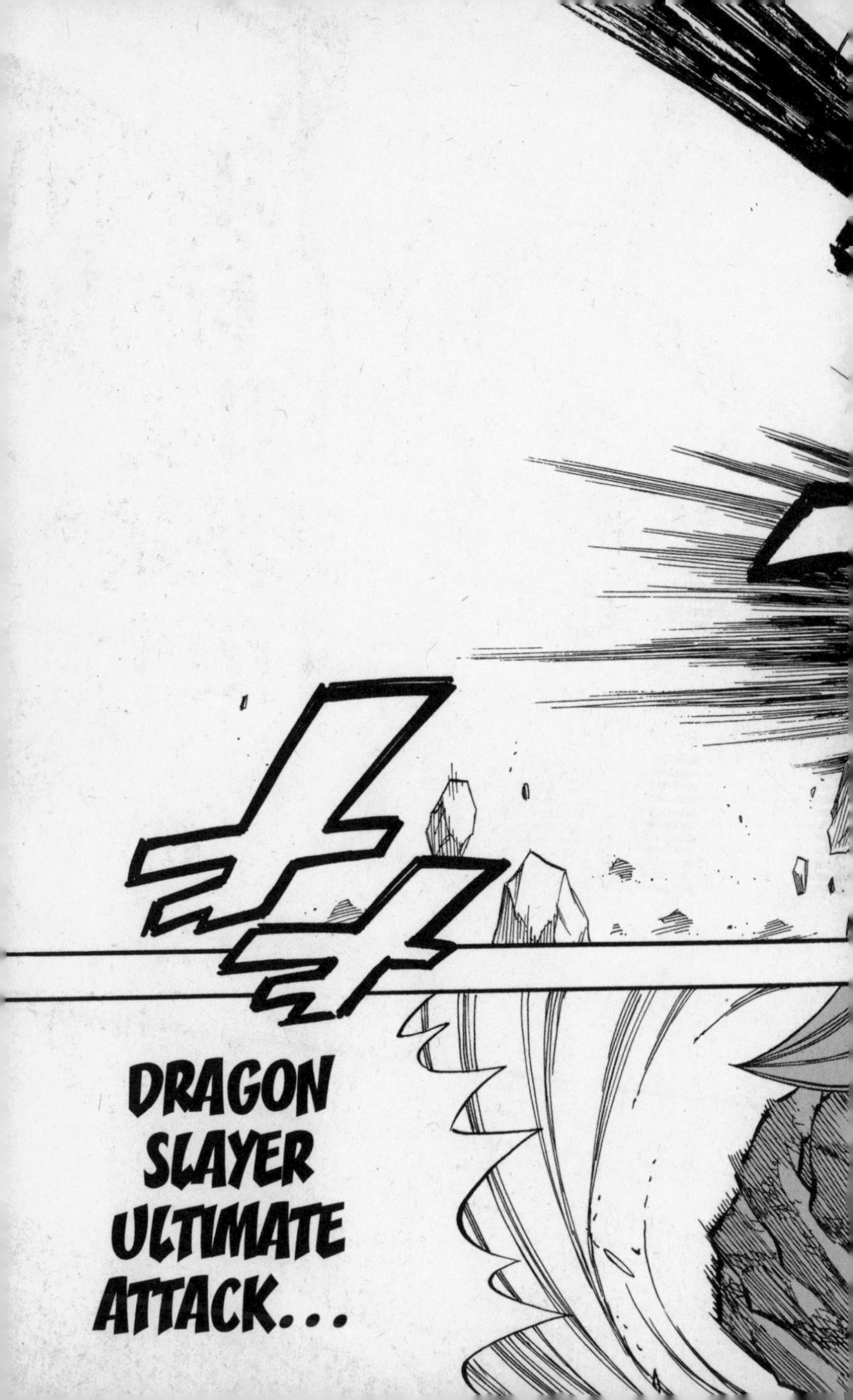
DRAGON SLAYER ULTIMATE ATTACK...

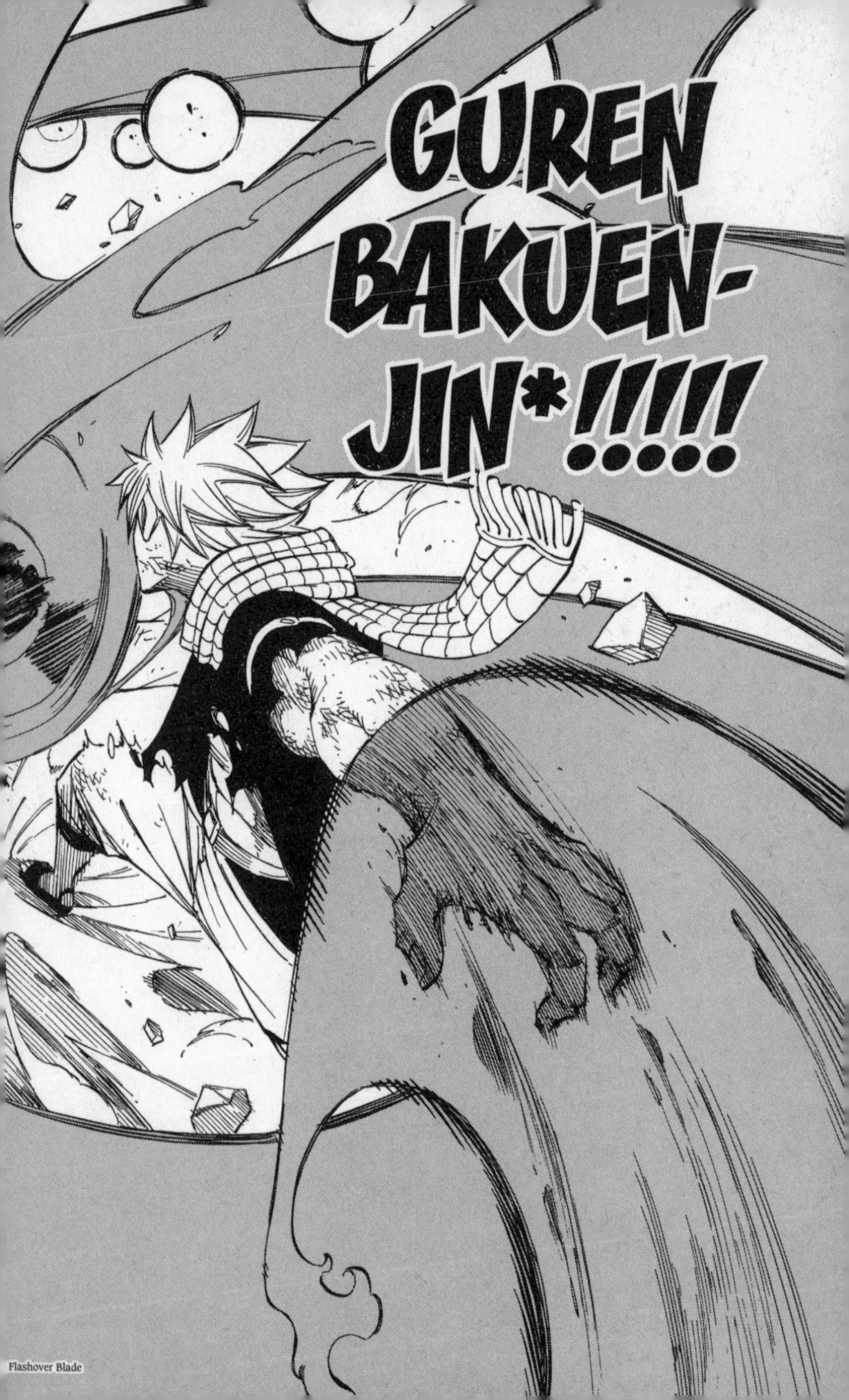
GUREN BAKUEN-JIN*!!!!!
Flashover Blade

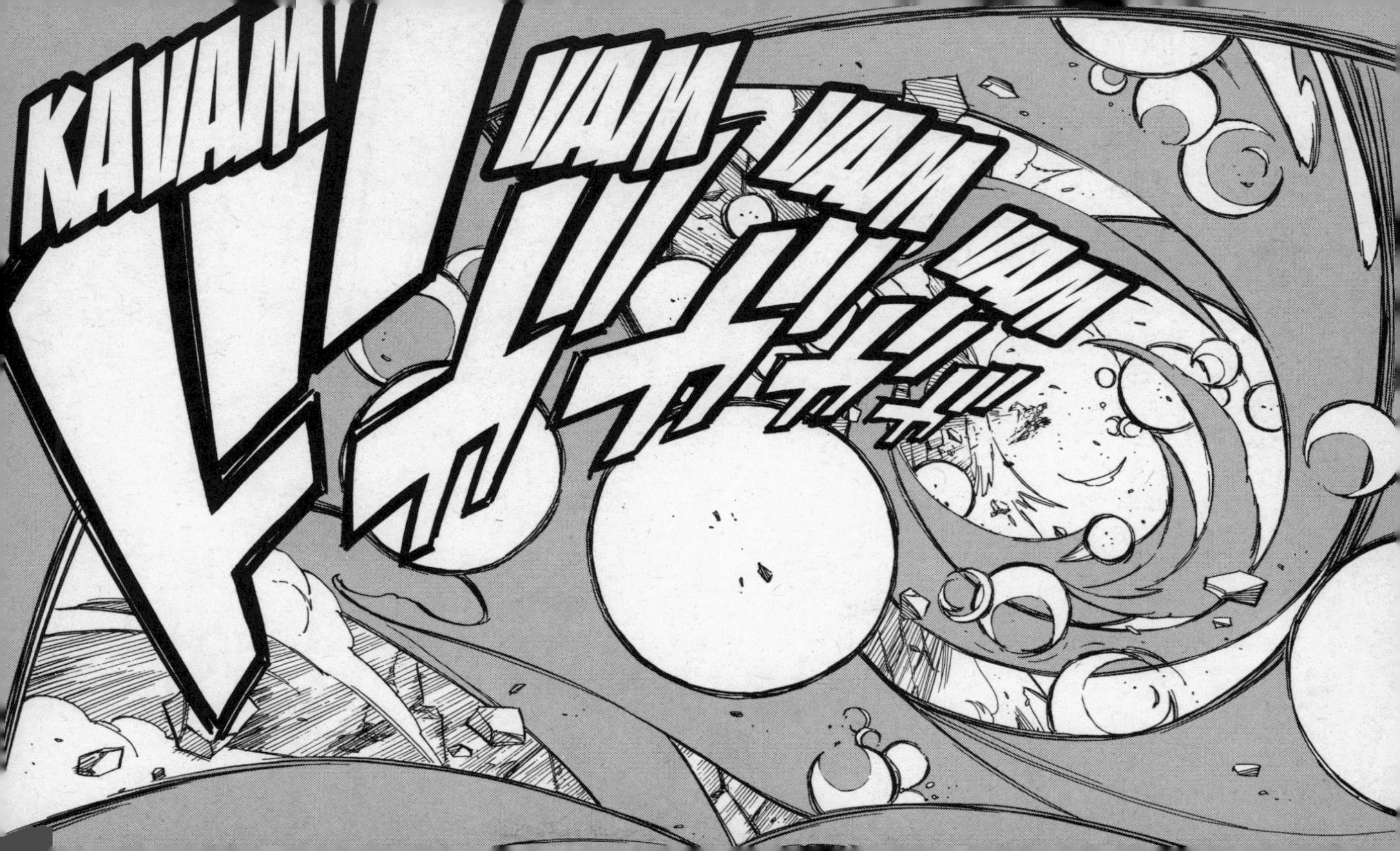
KAVAM VAM VAM VAM

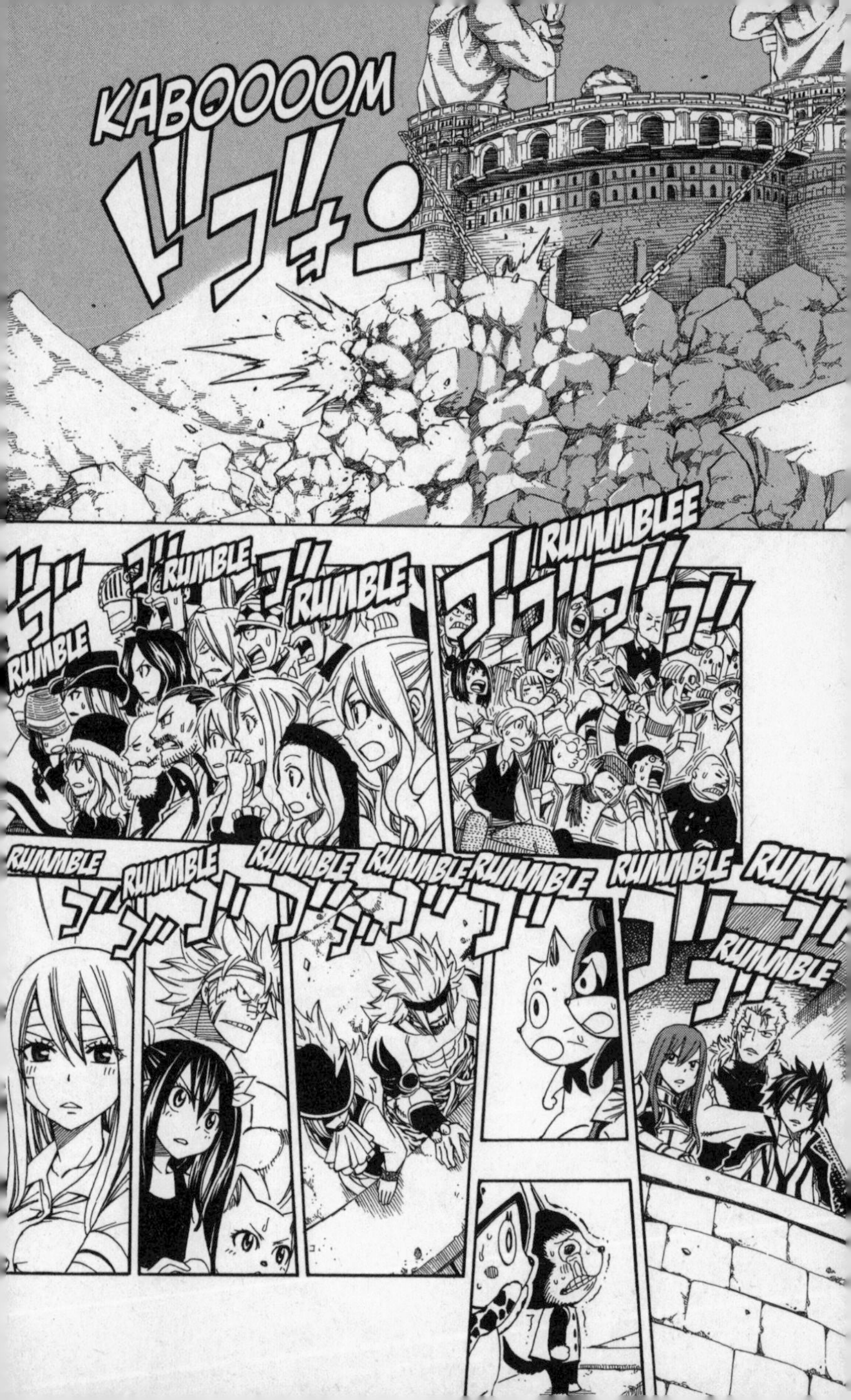
KABOOOOM
RUMMBLEE
RUMBLE
RUMBLE
RUMBLE
RUMM
RUMMBLE
RUMMBLE
RUMMBLE
RUMMBLE
RUMMBLE
RUMMBLE
RUMMBLE

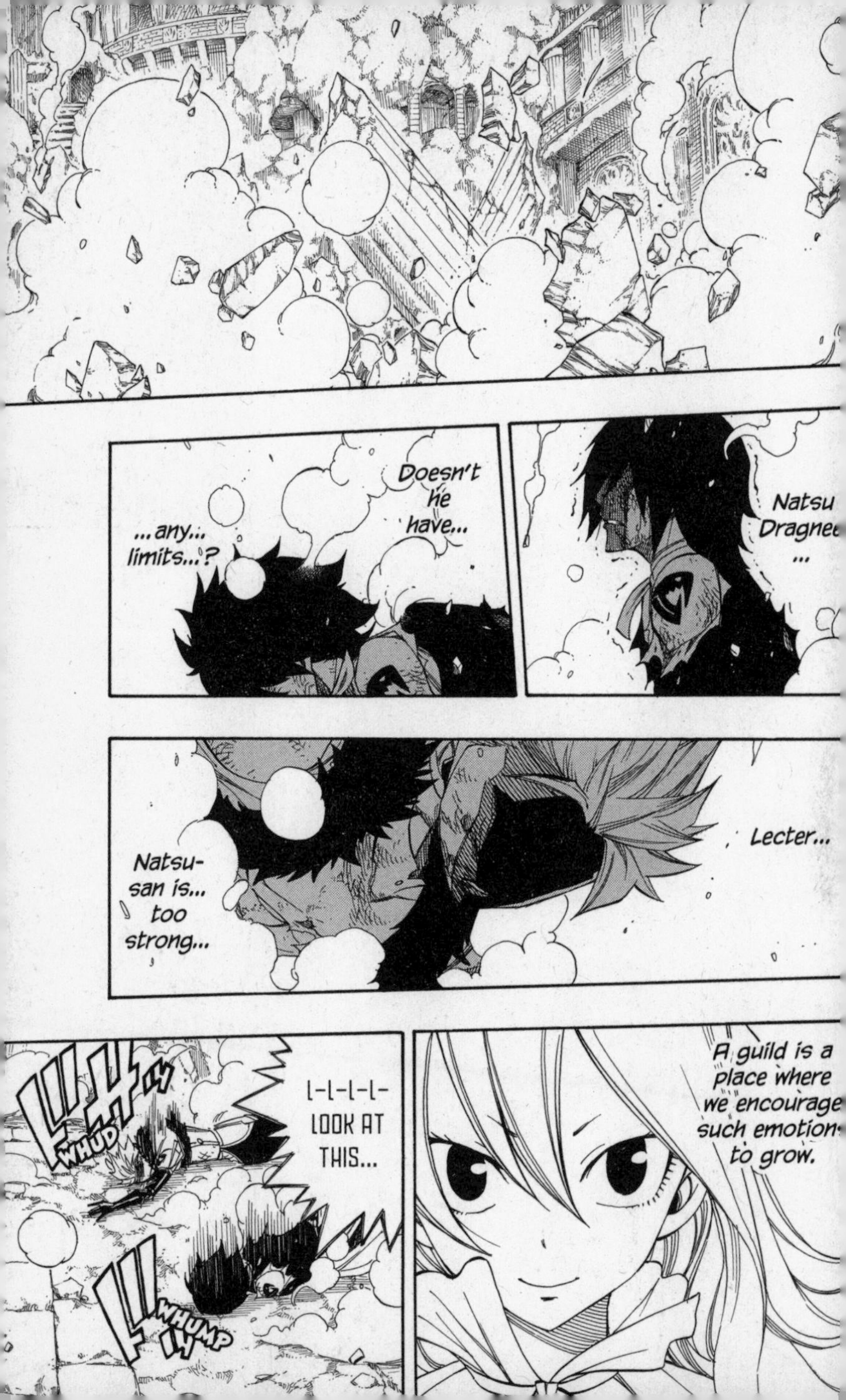
Natsu Dragnee
...
Doesn't he have...
...any... limits...?
Lecter...
Natsu-san is... too strong...
A guild is a place where we encourage such emotion to grow.
L-L-L-L-LOOK AT THIS...
WHUD
WHUMP

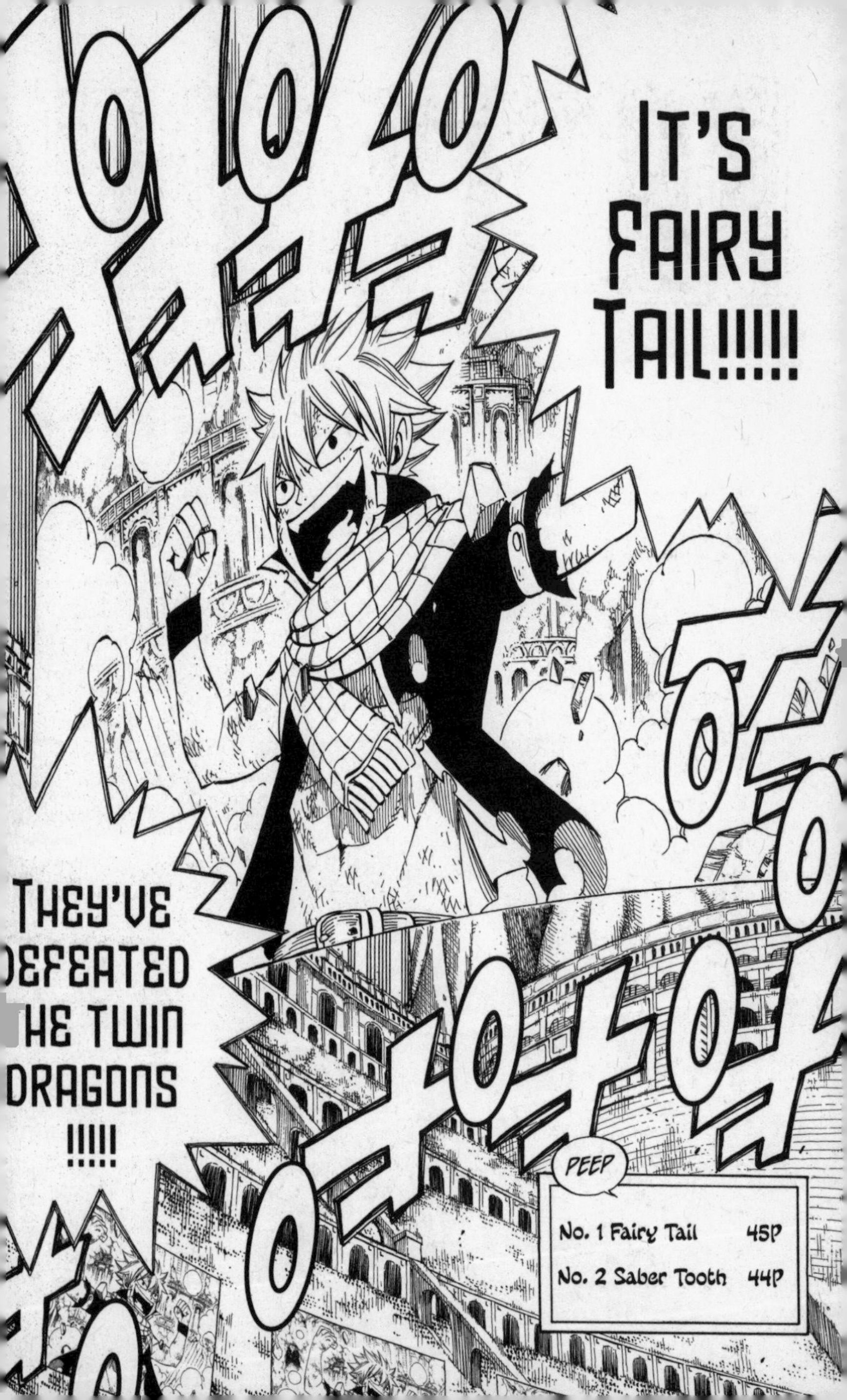
IT'S FAIRY TAIL!!!!!
THEY'VE DEFEATED THE TWIN DRAGONS!!!!!
PEEP
No. 1 Fairy Tail 45P
No. 2 Saber Tooth 44P

FAIRY TAIL

フェアリーテイル

Chapter 297: The Girl's Face He Saw

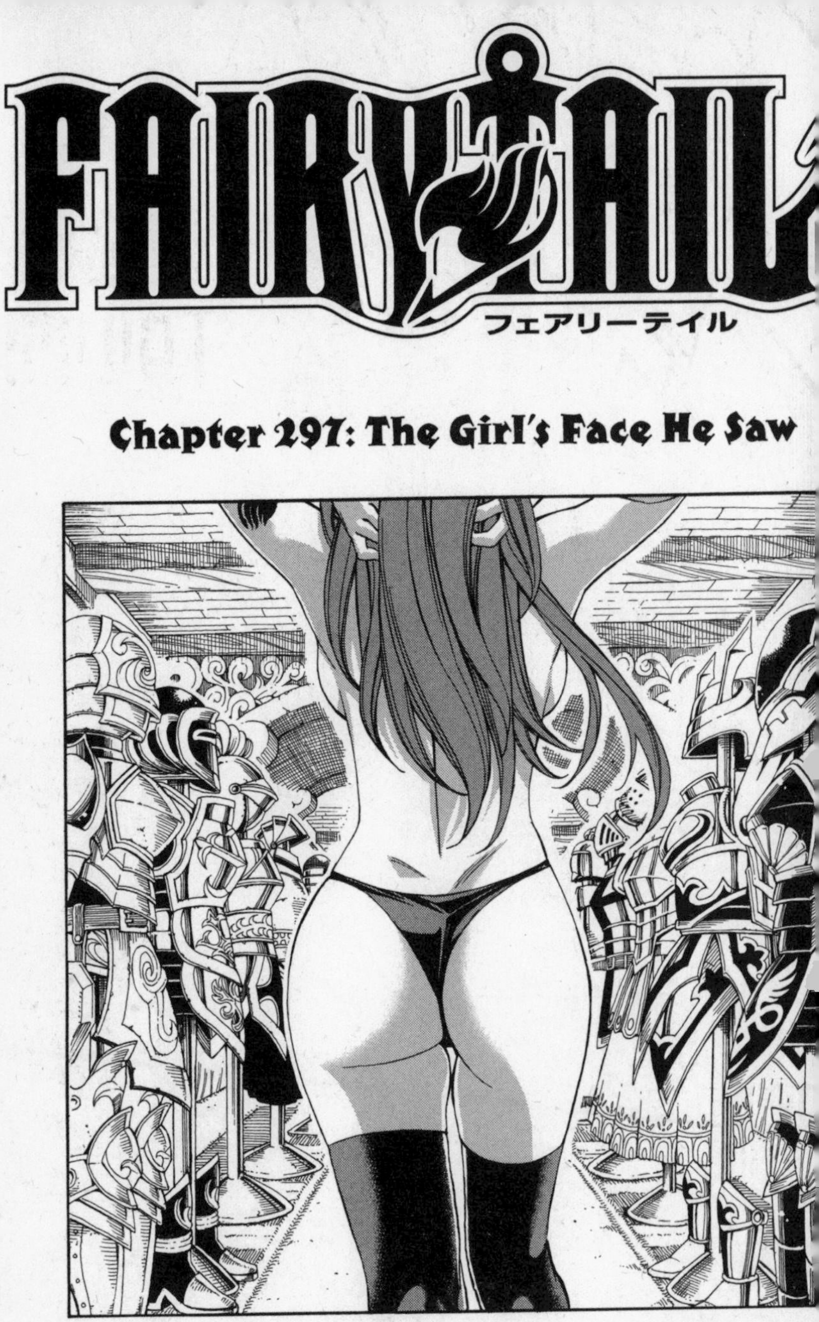

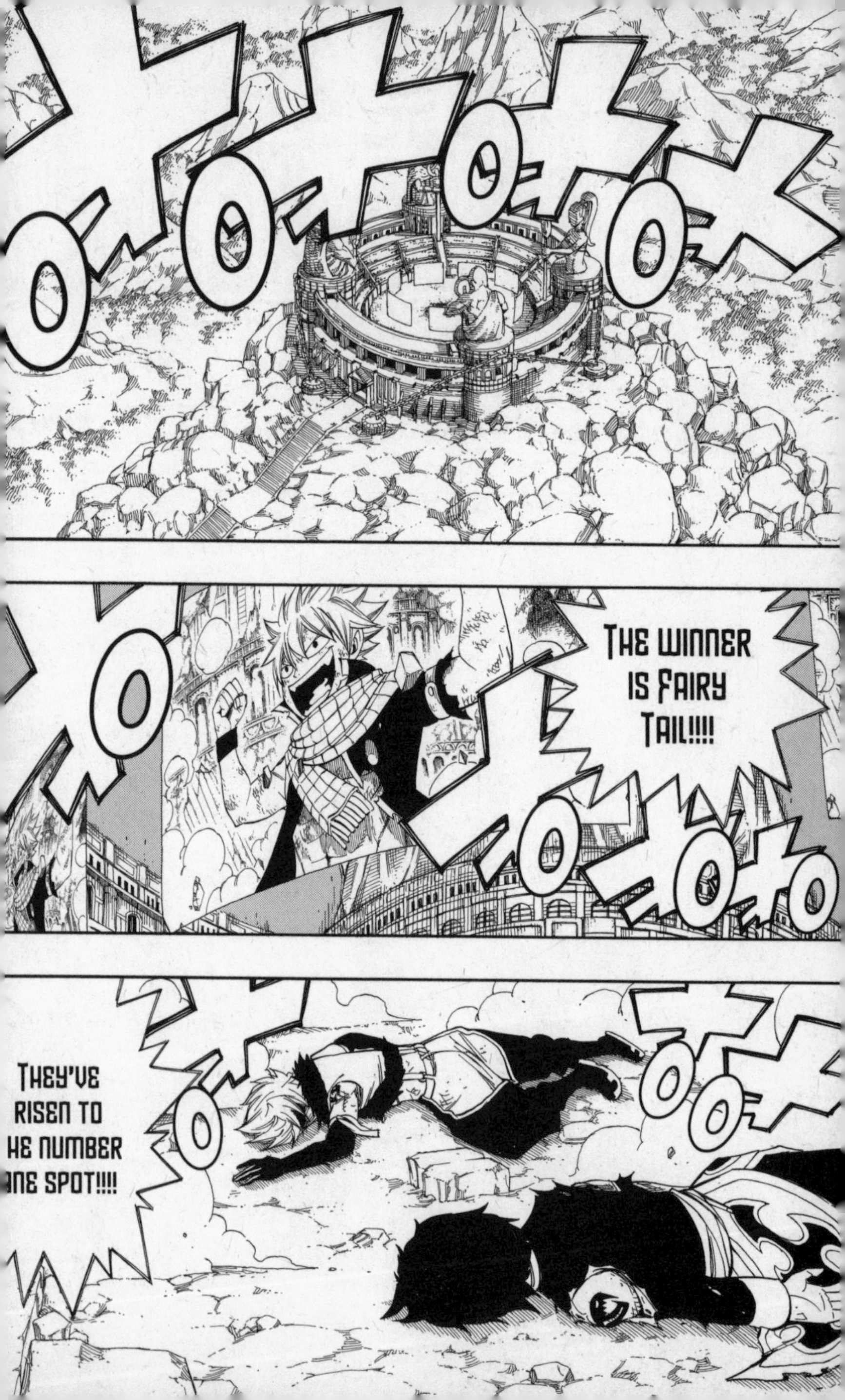
THE WINNER IS FAIRY TAIL!!!!
THEY'VE RISEN TO HE NUMBER NE SPOT!!!!

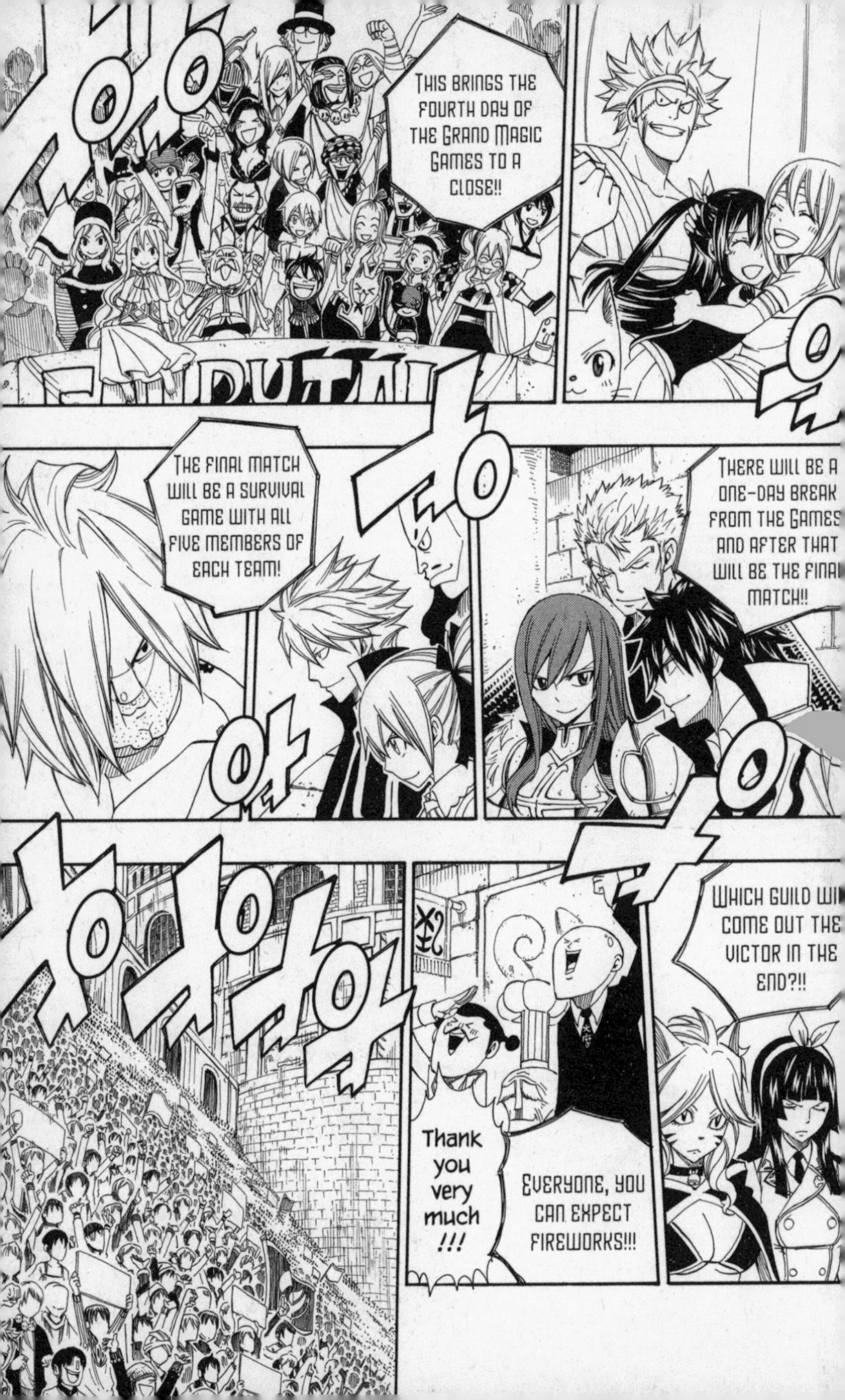
THIS BRINGS THE FOURTH DAY OF THE GRAND MAGIC GAMES TO A CLOSE!!
THERE WILL BE A ONE-DAY BREAK FROM THE GAMES AND AFTER THAT WILL BE THE FINA MATCH!!
THE FINAL MATCH WILL BE A SURVIVAL GAME WITH ALL FIVE MEMBERS OF EACH TEAM!
WHICH GUILD WI COME OUT THE VICTOR IN THE END?!!
EVERYONE, YOU CAN EXPECT FIREWORKS!!!
Thank you very much!!!

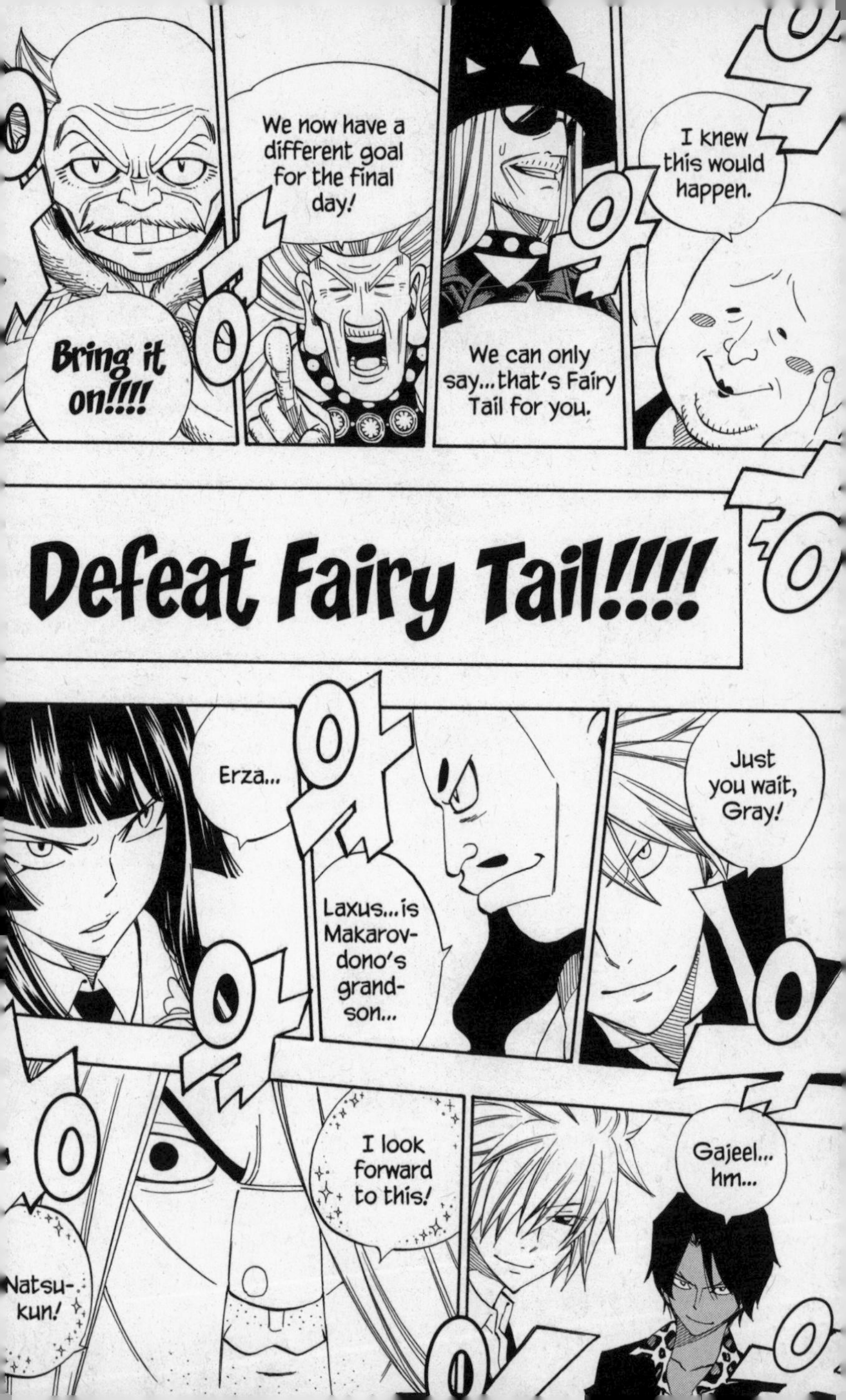
I knew this would happen.
We can only say...that's Fairy Tail for you.
We now have a different goal for the final day!
Bring it on!!!!
Defeat Fairy Tail!!!!
Just you wait, Gray!
Laxus...is Makarov-dono's grandson...
Erza...
Gajeel... hm...
I look forward to this!
Natsu-kun!

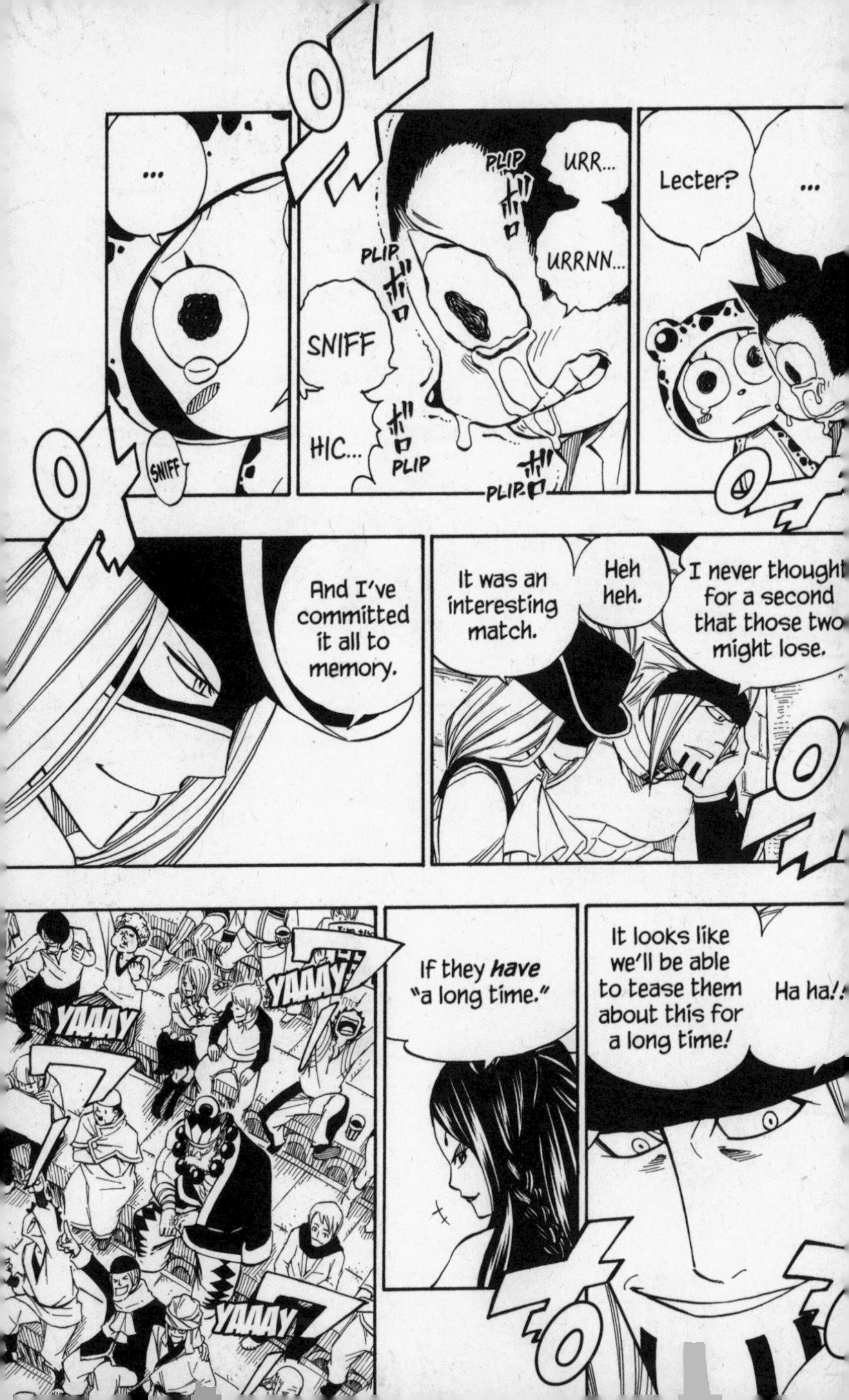
...
Lecter?
URR...
PLIP
URRNN...
PLIP
SNIFF
HIC...
PLIP
PLIP
...
SNIFF
I never thought for a second that those two might lose.
Heh heh.
It was an interesting match.
And I've committed it all to memory.
Ha ha!!
It looks like we'll be able to tease them about this for a long time!
If they *have* "a long time."
YAAAY!
YAAAY
YAAAY

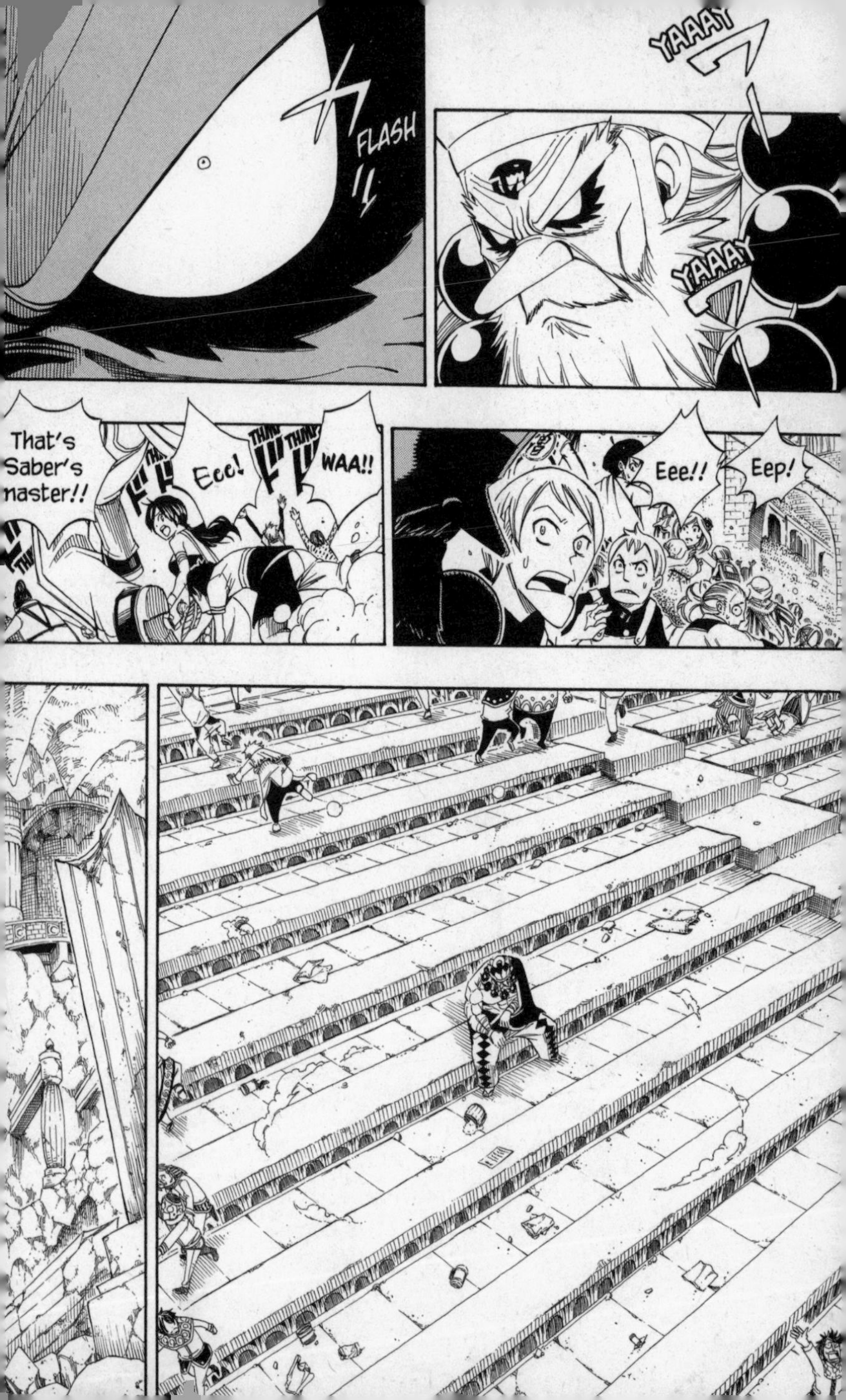

YAAAY
YAAAY
FLASH
Eep!
Eee!!
WAA!!
THUMP
Eee!
That's Saber's master!!

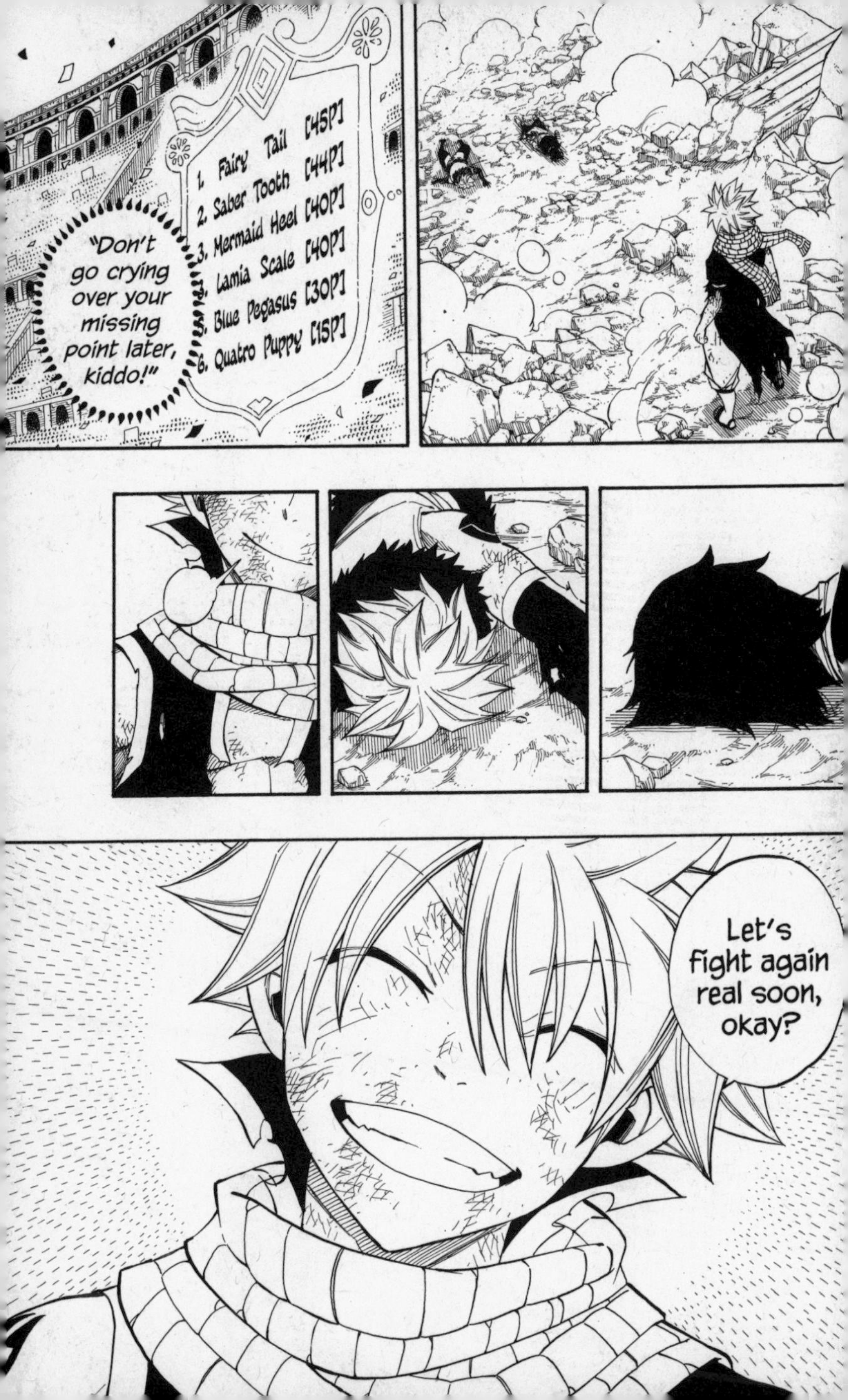
1. Fairy Tail [45P]
2. Saber Tooth [44P]
3. Mermaid Heel [40P]
3. Lamia Scale [40P]
5. Blue Pegasus [30P]
6. Quatro Puppy [15P]
"Don't go crying over your missing point later, kiddo!"
Let's fight again real soon, okay?

*A complete
failure...*

*...has
the same
fighting
strength
as Natsu...*

*And if
Gajeel...*

PANT

WHEEZE

PANT

WHEEZE

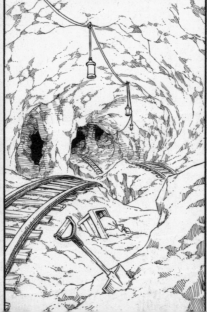

*Just how
overly
cocky was
I this
time?*

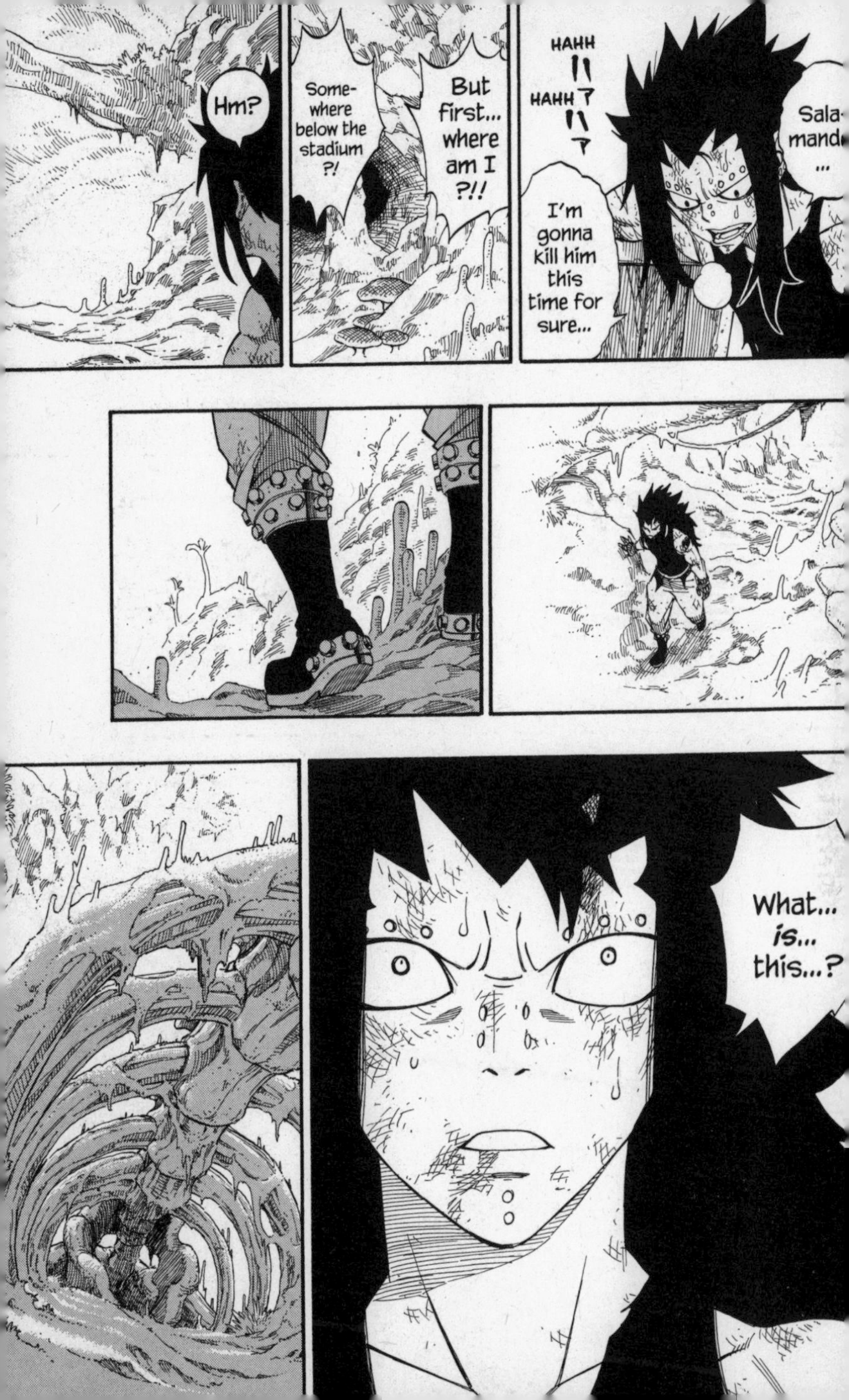
Sala-mander...
HAHH HAHH
I'm gonna kill him this time for sure...
But first... where am I ?!!
Some-where below the stadium ?!
Hm?
What... *is*... this...?

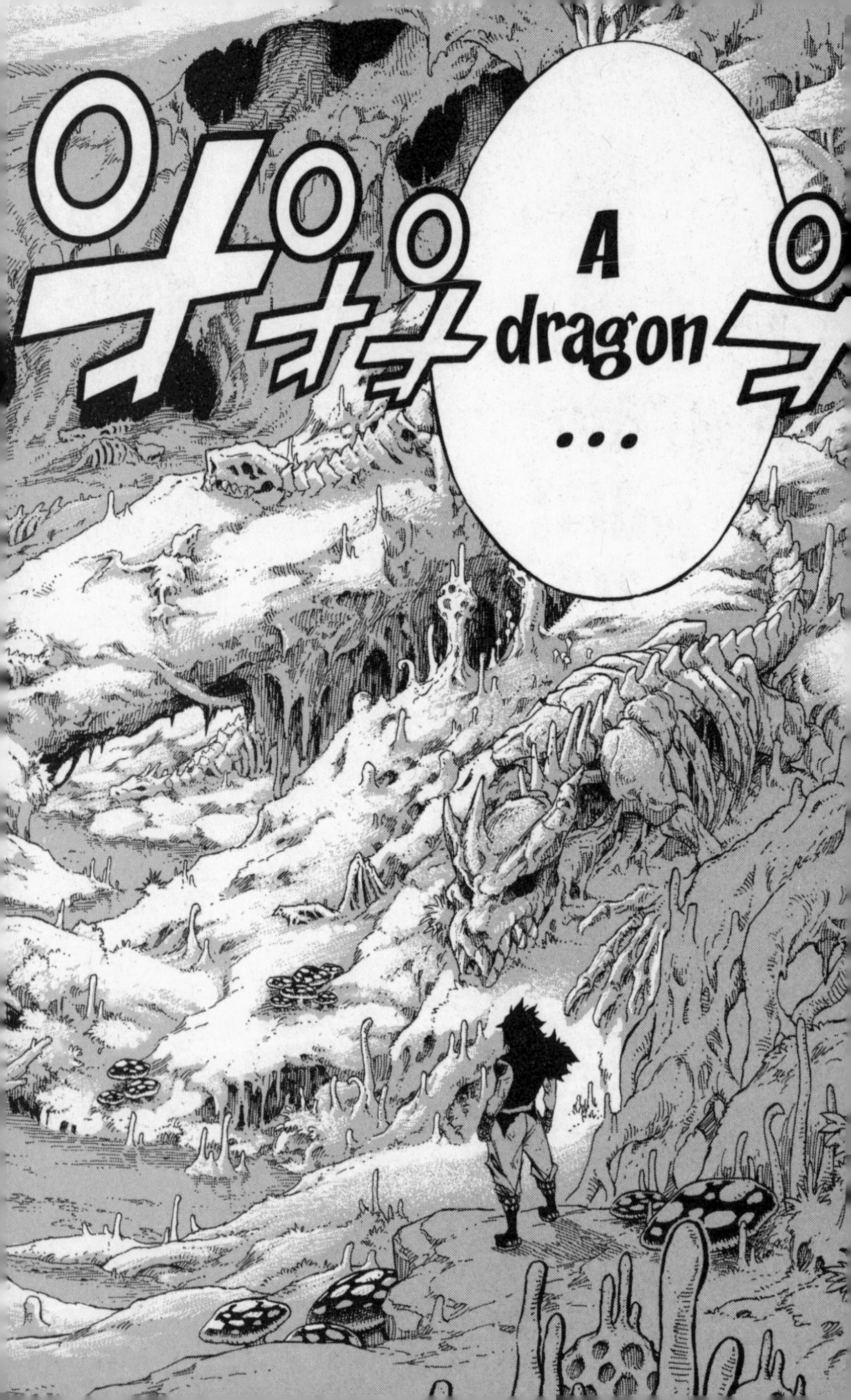
A dragon ...

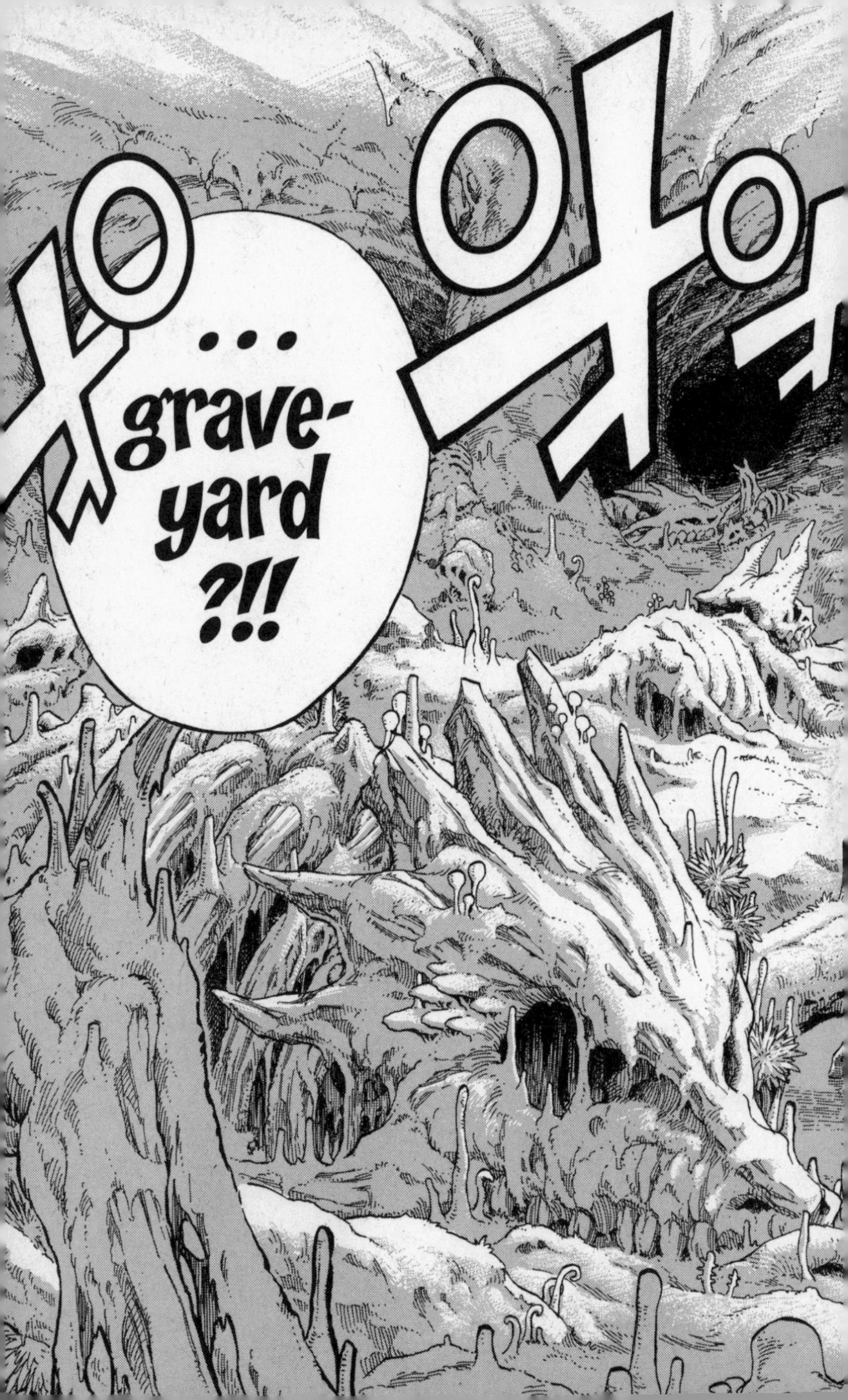
... grave-yard ?!!

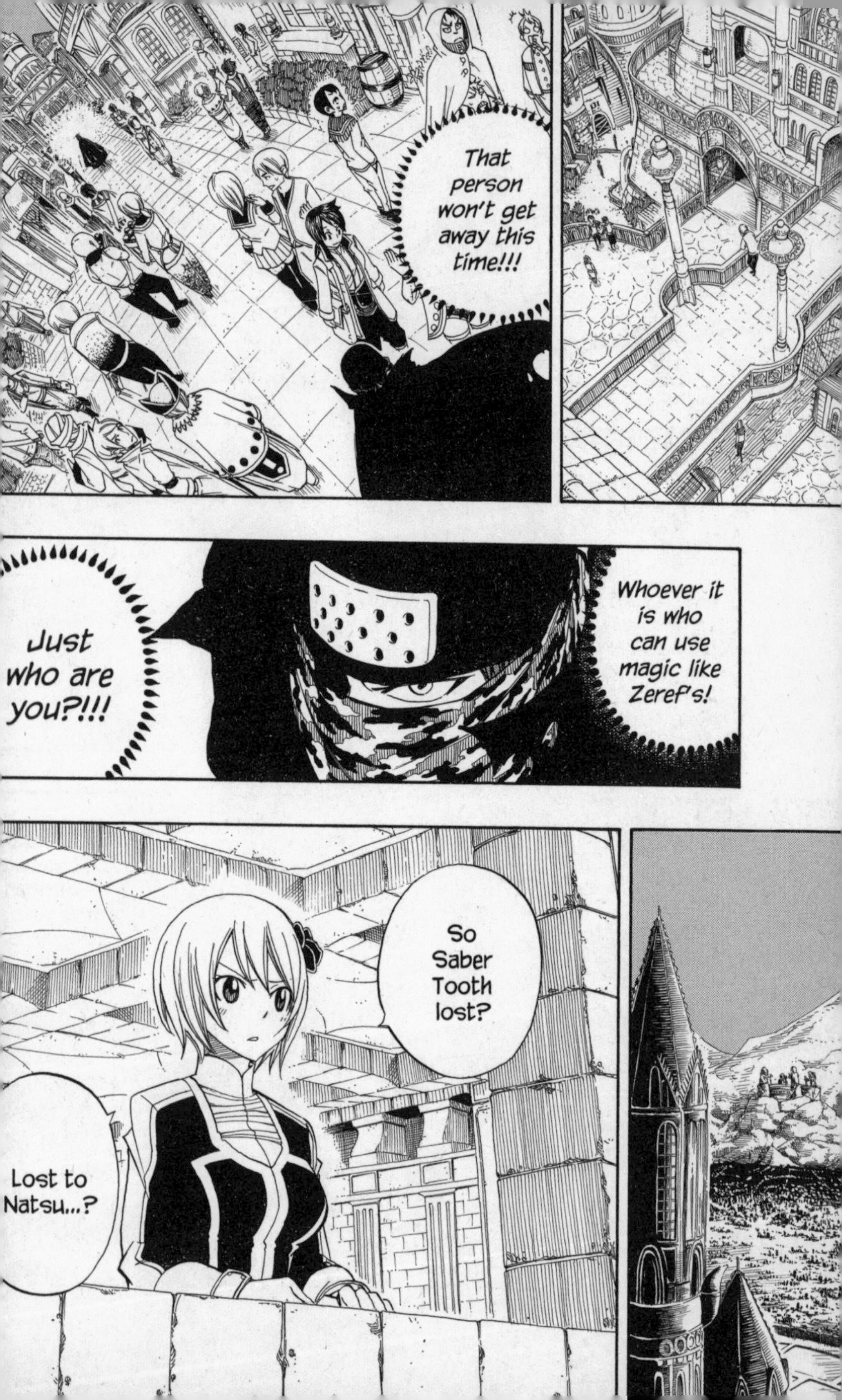
That person won't get away this time!!!
Whoever it is who can use magic like Zeref's!
Just who are you?!!!
So Saber Tooth lost?
Lost to Natsu...?

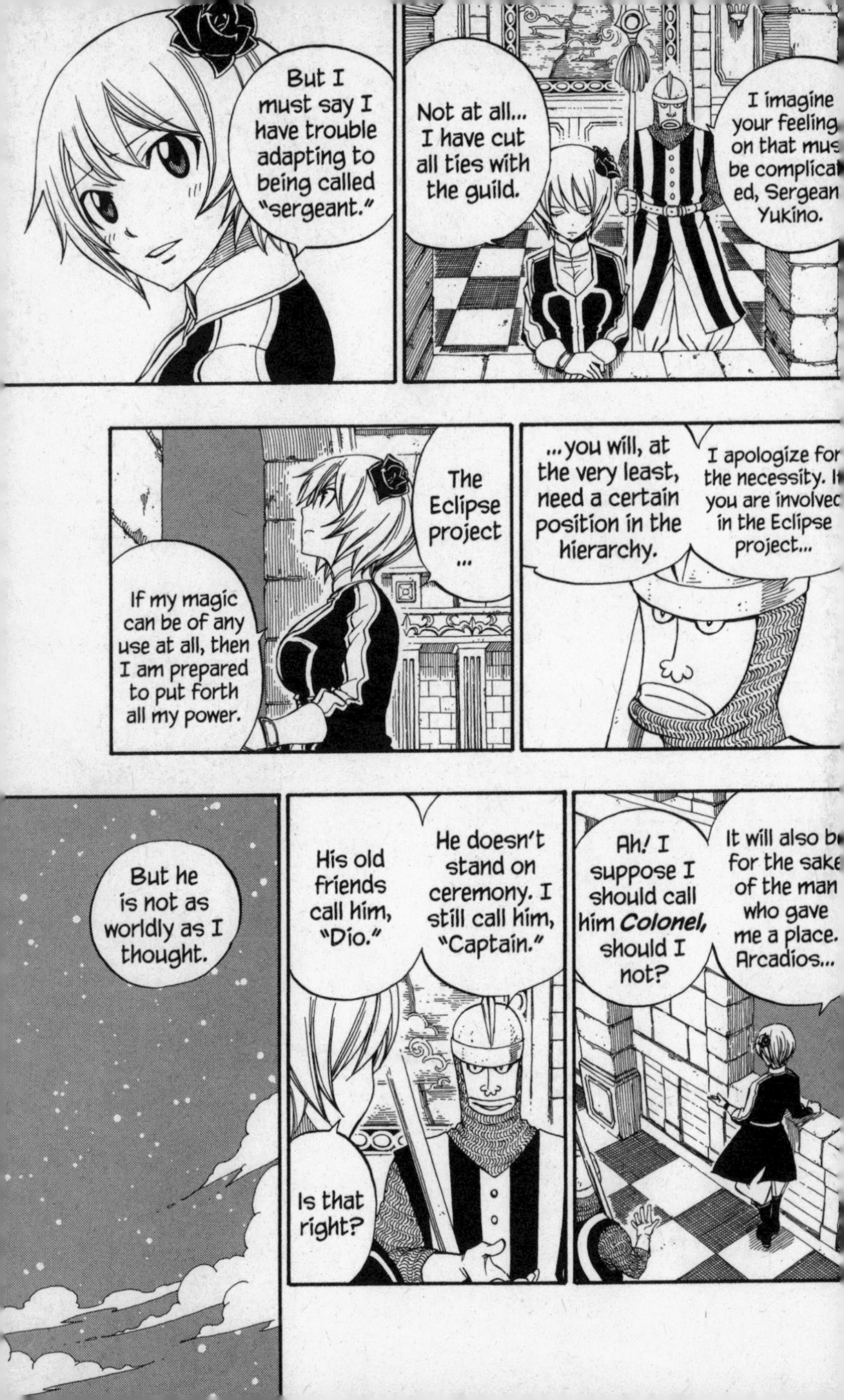
I imagine your feeling on that mus be complica ed, Sergean Yukino.
Not at all... I have cut all ties with the guild.
But I must say I have trouble adapting to being called "sergeant."
I apologize for the necessity. I you are involved in the Eclipse project...
...you will, at the very least, need a certain position in the hierarchy.
The Eclipse project ...
If my magic can be of any use at all, then I am prepared to put forth all my power.
It will also b for the sake of the man who gave me a place. Arcadios...
Ah! I suppose I should call him *Colonel,* should I not?
He doesn't stand on ceremony. I still call him, "Captain."
His old friends call him, "Dio."
Is that right?
But he is not as worldly as I thought.

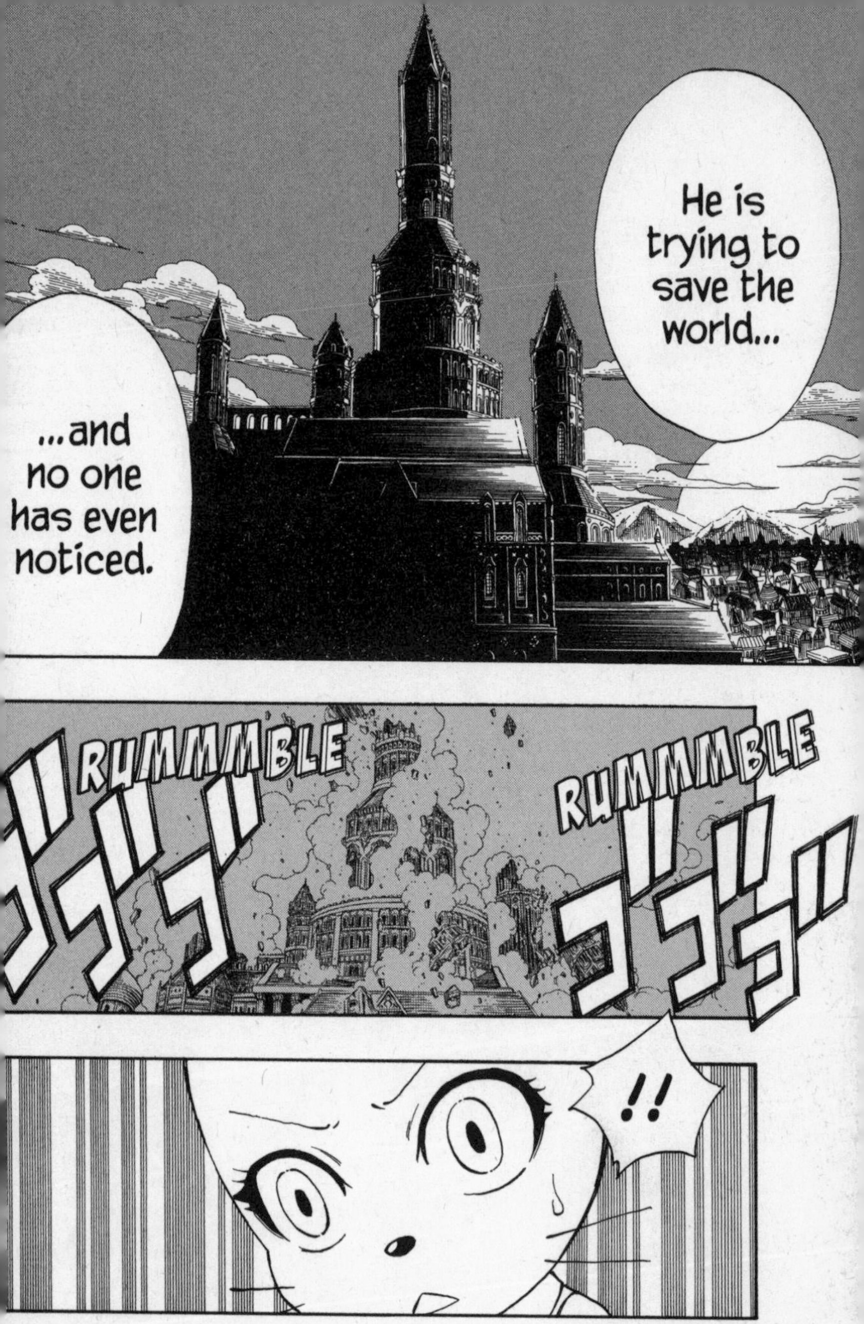
He is trying to save the world...
...and no one has even noticed.
RUMMMMBLE
RUMMMMBLE
!!

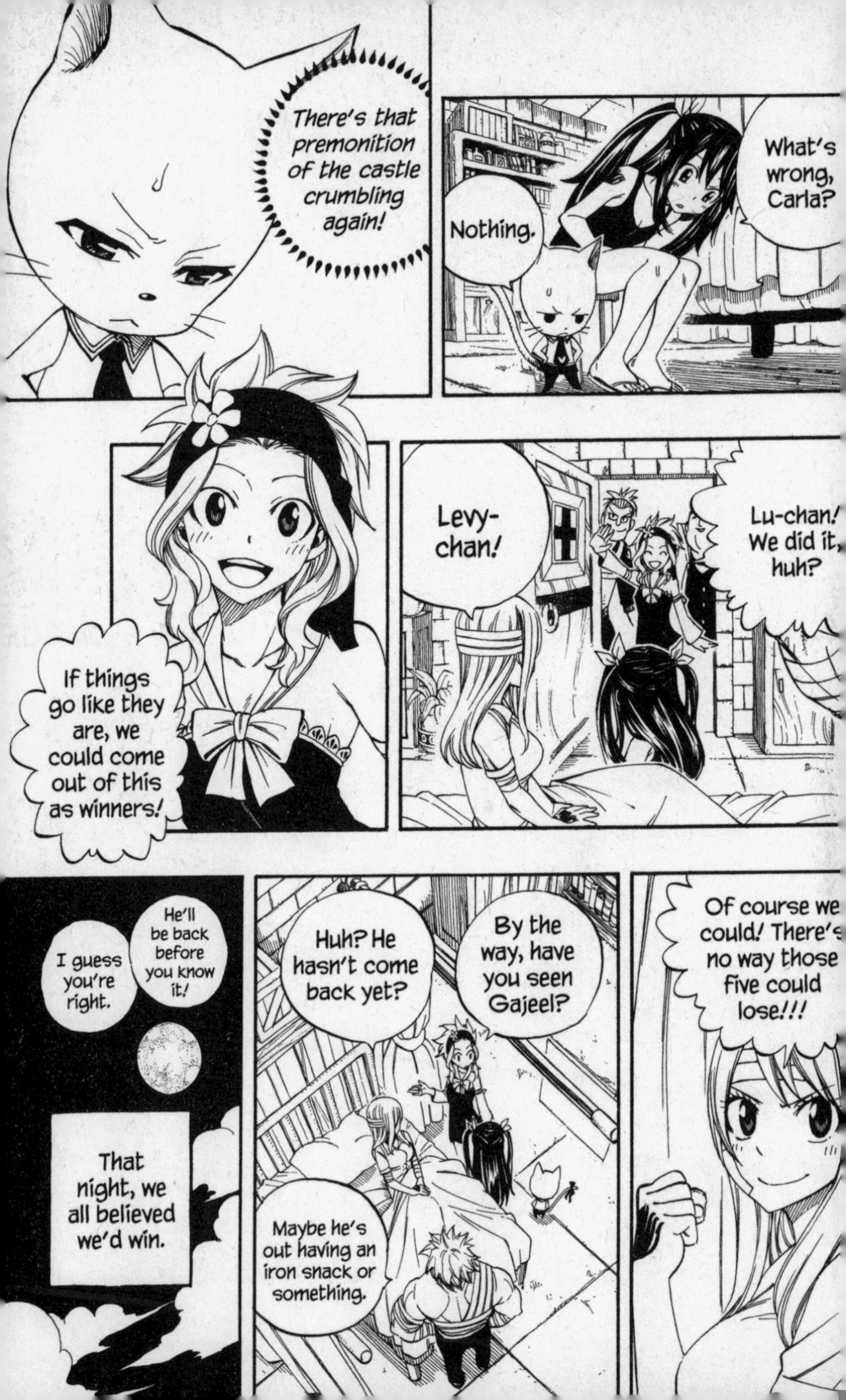
What's wrong, Carla?
Nothing.
There's that premonition of the castle crumbling again!
Lu-chan! We did it, huh?
Levy-chan!
If things go like they are, we could come out of this as winners!
Of course we could! There's no way those five could lose!!!
By the way, have you seen Gajeel?
Huh? He hasn't come back yet?
Maybe he's out having an iron snack or something.
He'll be back before you know it!
I guess you're right.
That night, we all believed we'd win.

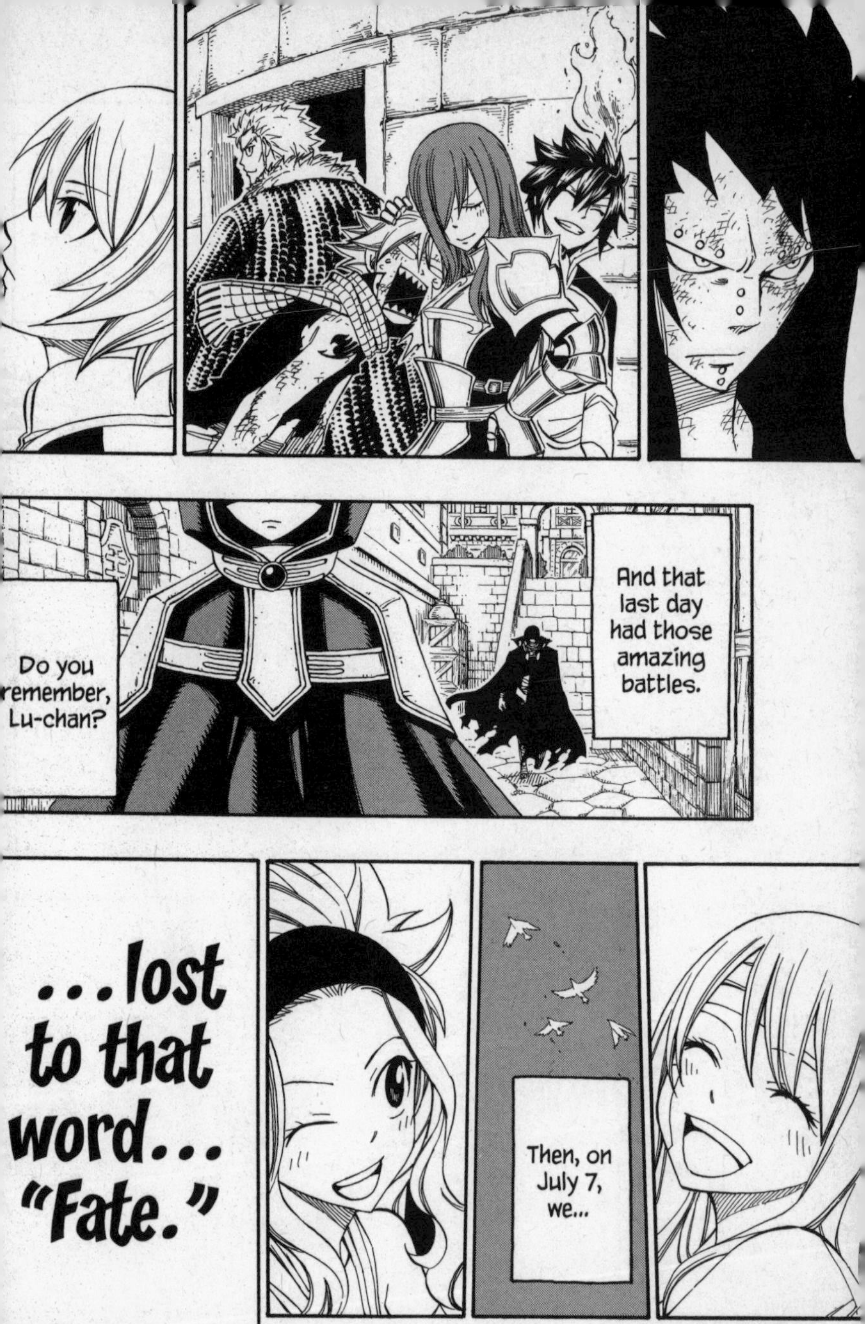
And that last day had those amazing battles.
Do you remember, Lu-chan?
Then, on July 7, we...
...lost to that word... "Fate."

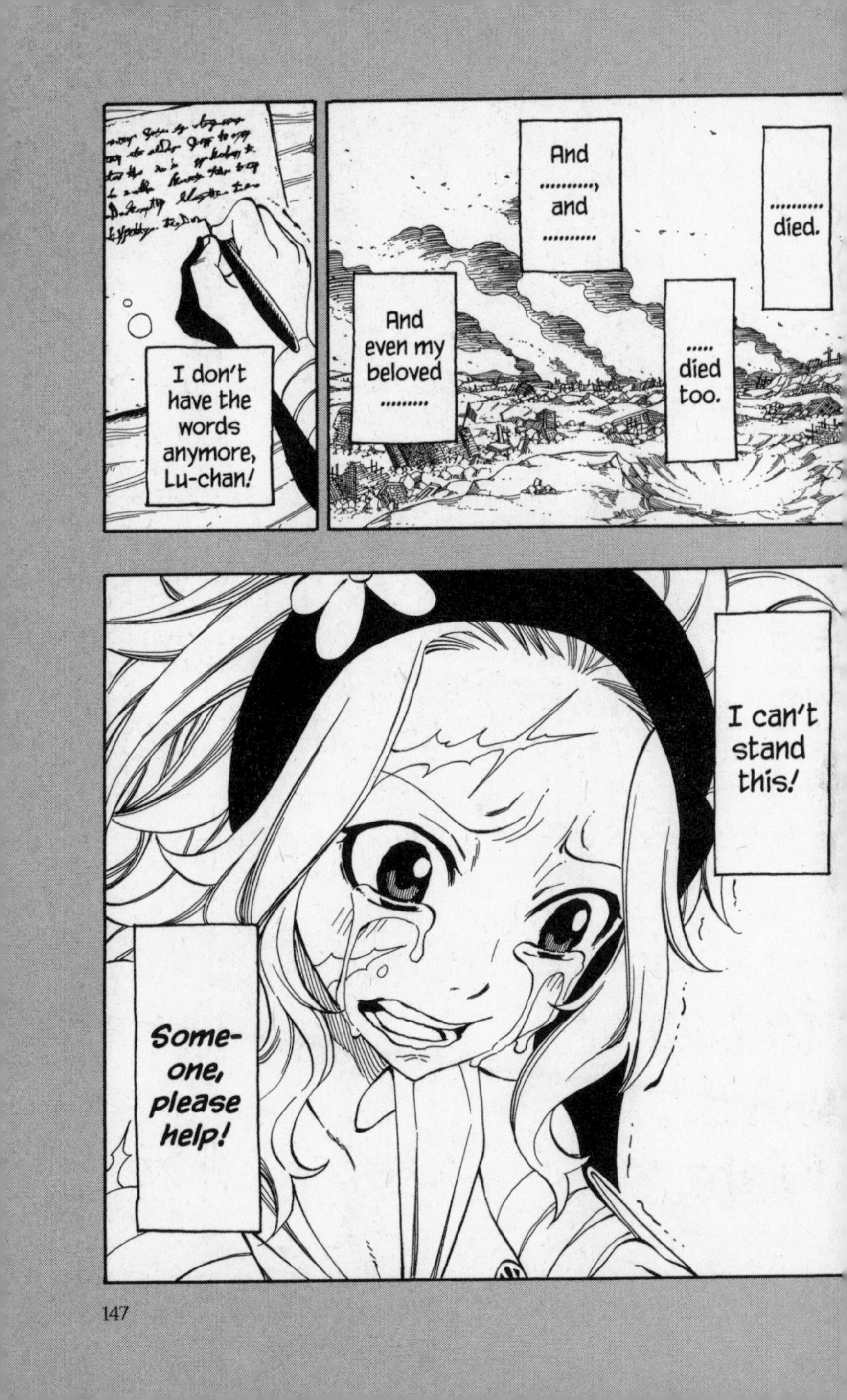
.... died.
And ...., and ....
..... died too.
And even my beloved ....
I don't have the words anymore, Lu-chan!
I can't stand this!
Someone, please help!

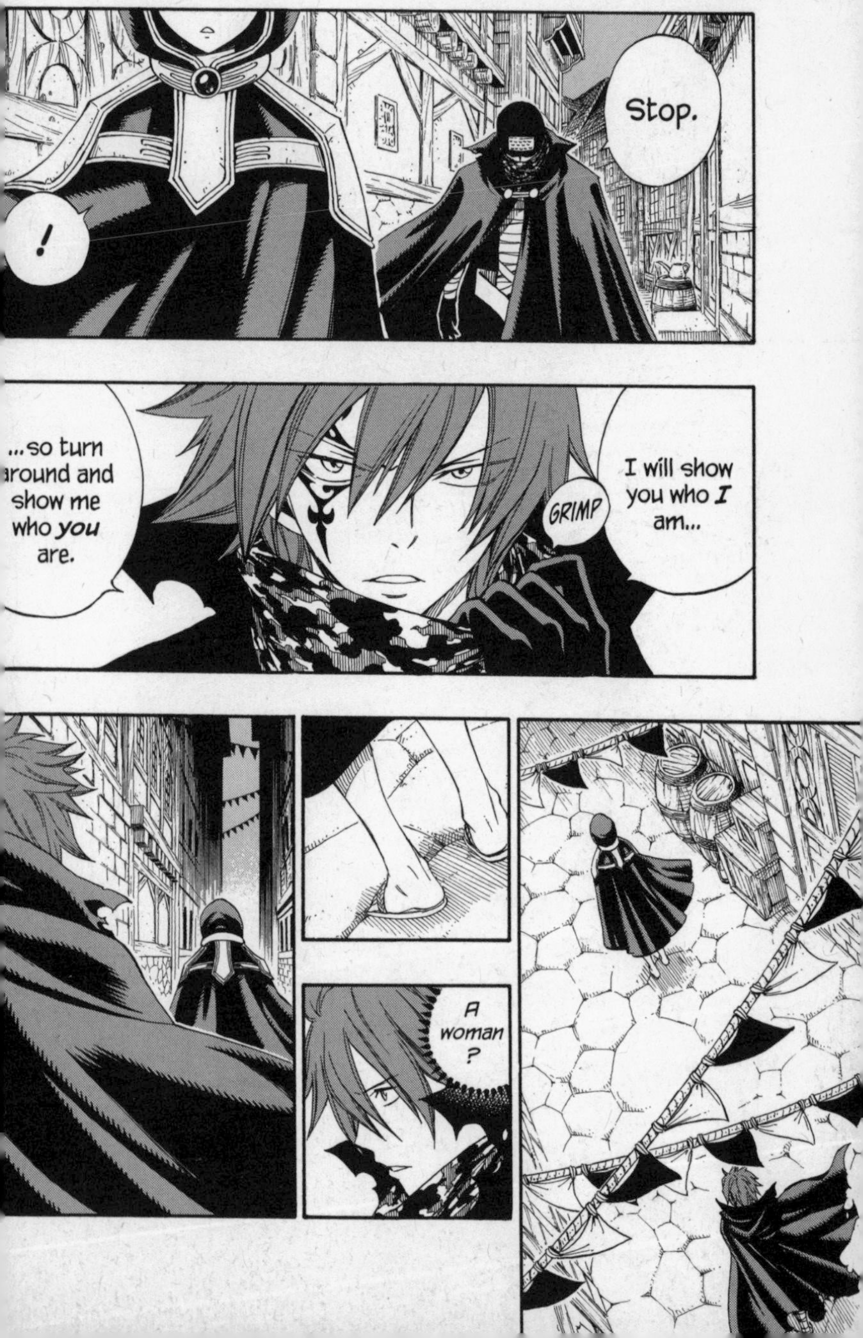
Stop.
!
I will show you who *I* am...
GRIMP
...so turn around and show me who *you* are.
A woman?

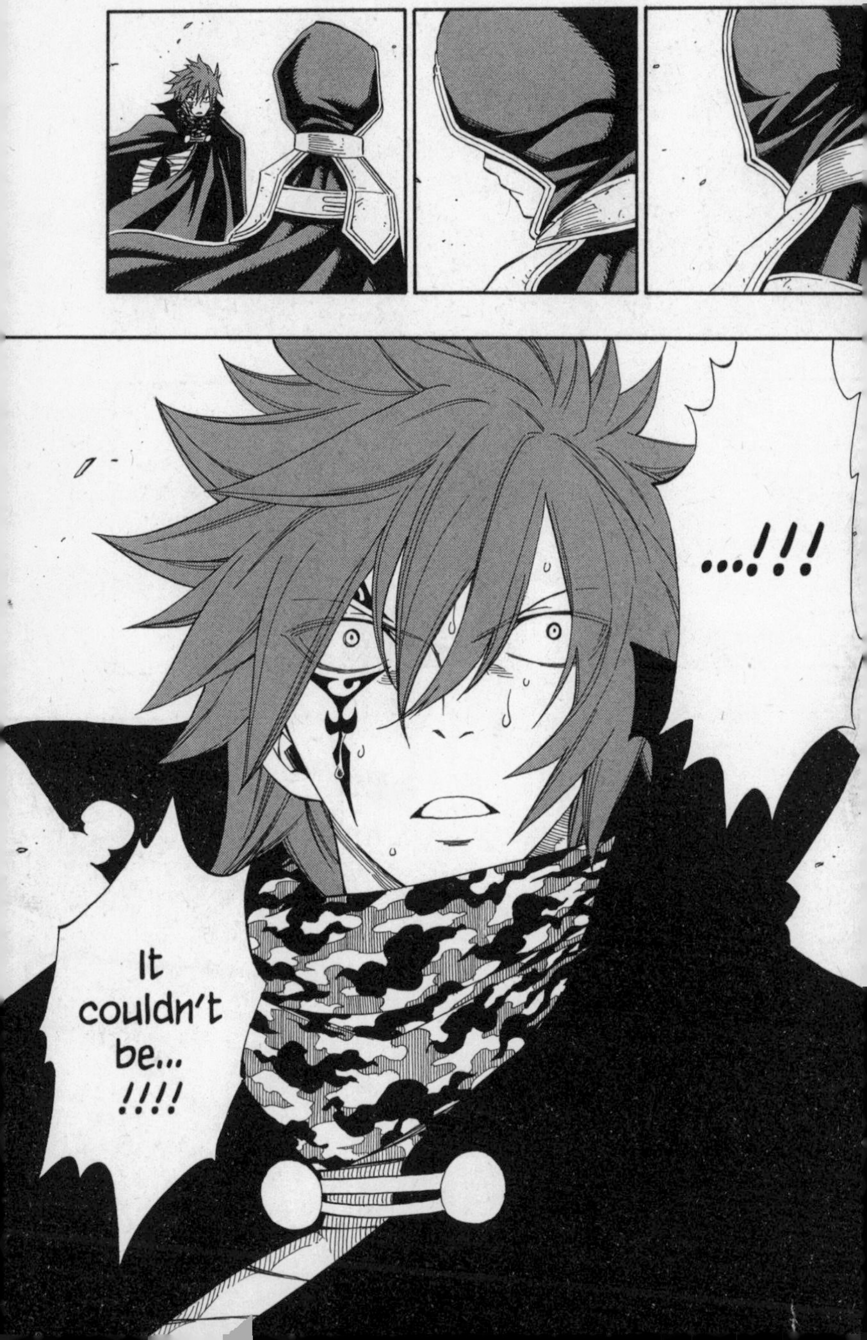
...!!!
It couldn't be... !!!!

TO BE CONTINUED!

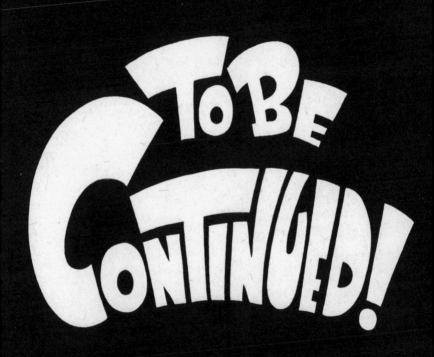

FAIRY TAIL
フェアリーテイル

Chapter 298: Exciting Ryuzetsu Land

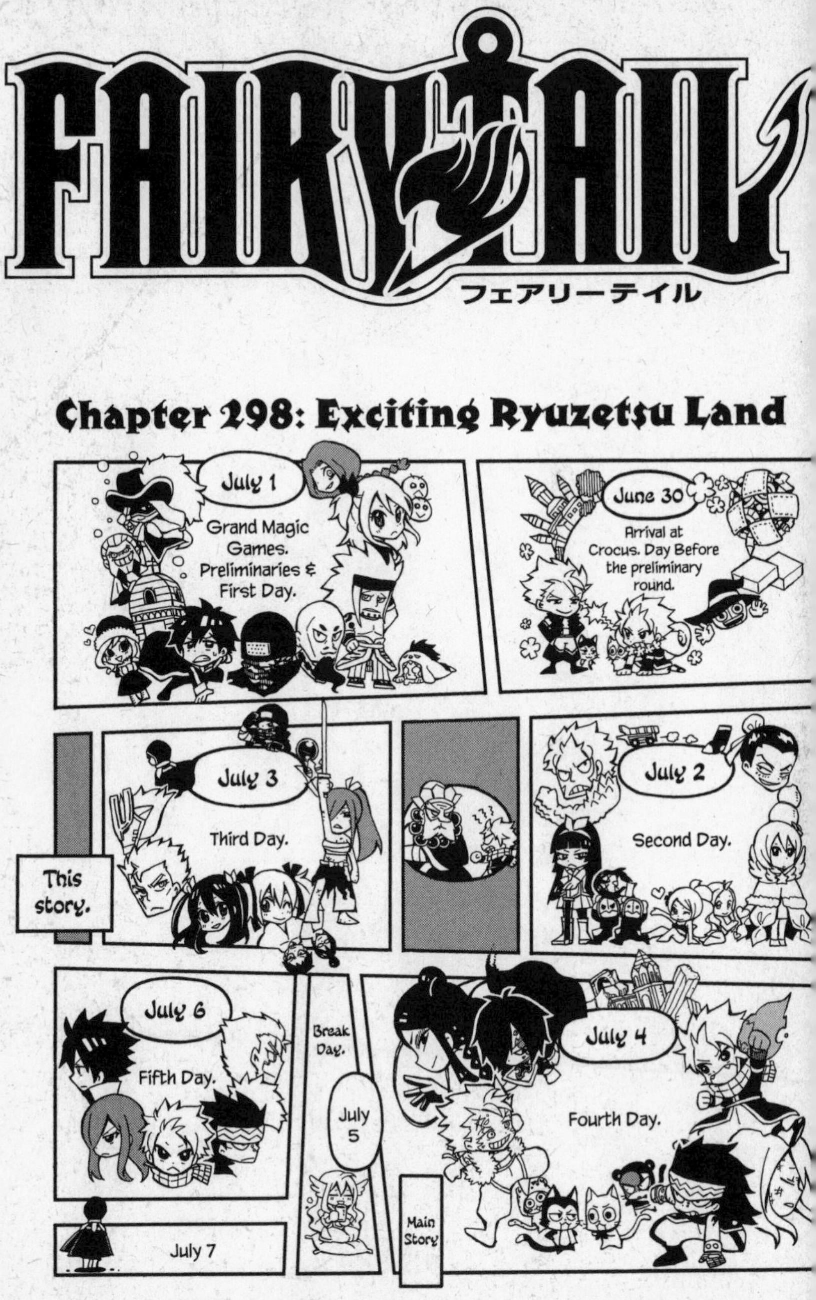
June 30
Arrival at Crocus. Day Before the preliminary round.
July 1
Grand Magic Games. Preliminaries & First Day.
July 2
Second Day.
July 3
Third Day.
This story.
July 4
Fourth Day.
Main Story
July 5
Break Day.
July 6
Fifth Day.
July 7

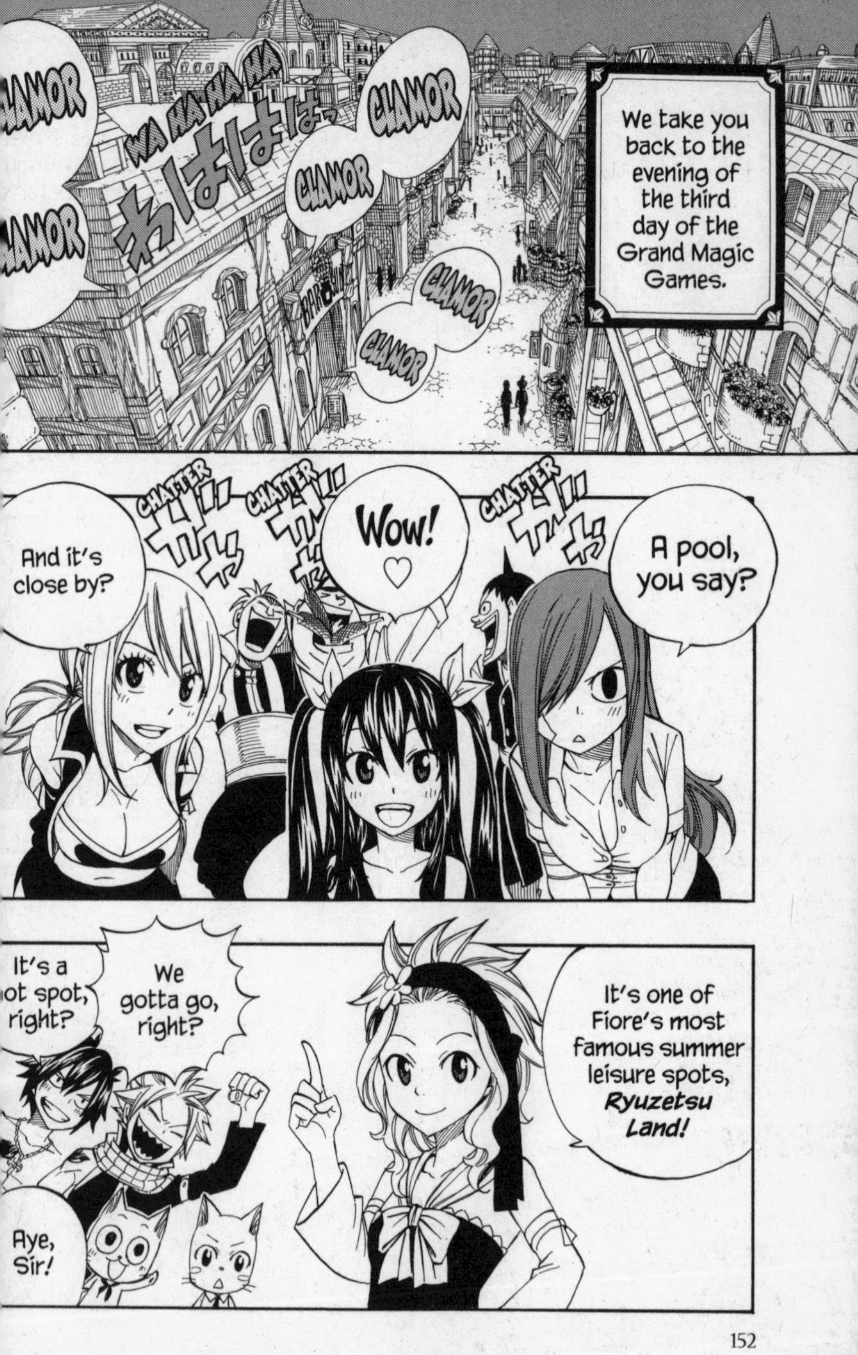
We take you back to the evening of the third day of the Grand Magic Games.
CLAMOR
CLAMOR
CLAMOR
CLAMOR
WA HA HA HA わははは
CLAMOR
CLAMOR
A pool, you say?
CHATTER
Wow! ♡
CHATTER
CHATTER
And it's close by?
It's one of Fiore's most famous summer leisure spots, *Ryuzetsu Land!*
We gotta go, right?
It's a ot spot, right?
Aye, Sir!

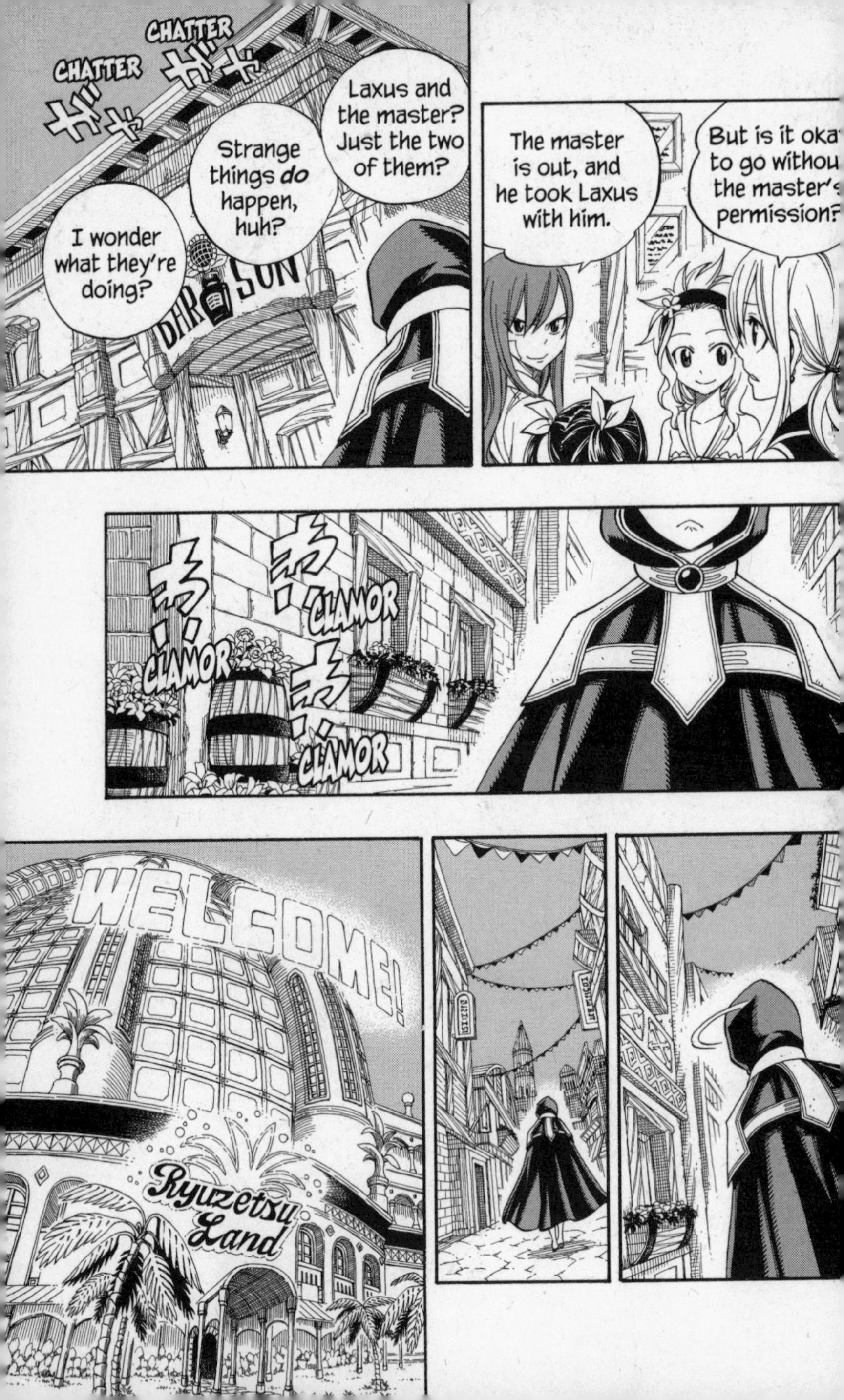

But is it oka
to go withou
the master's
permission?
The master is out, and he took Laxus with him.
Laxus and the master? Just the two of them?
Strange things do happen, huh?
I wonder what they're doing?
CHATTER
CHATTER
CLAMOR
CLAMOR
CLAMOR
WELCOME!
Ryuzetsu Land

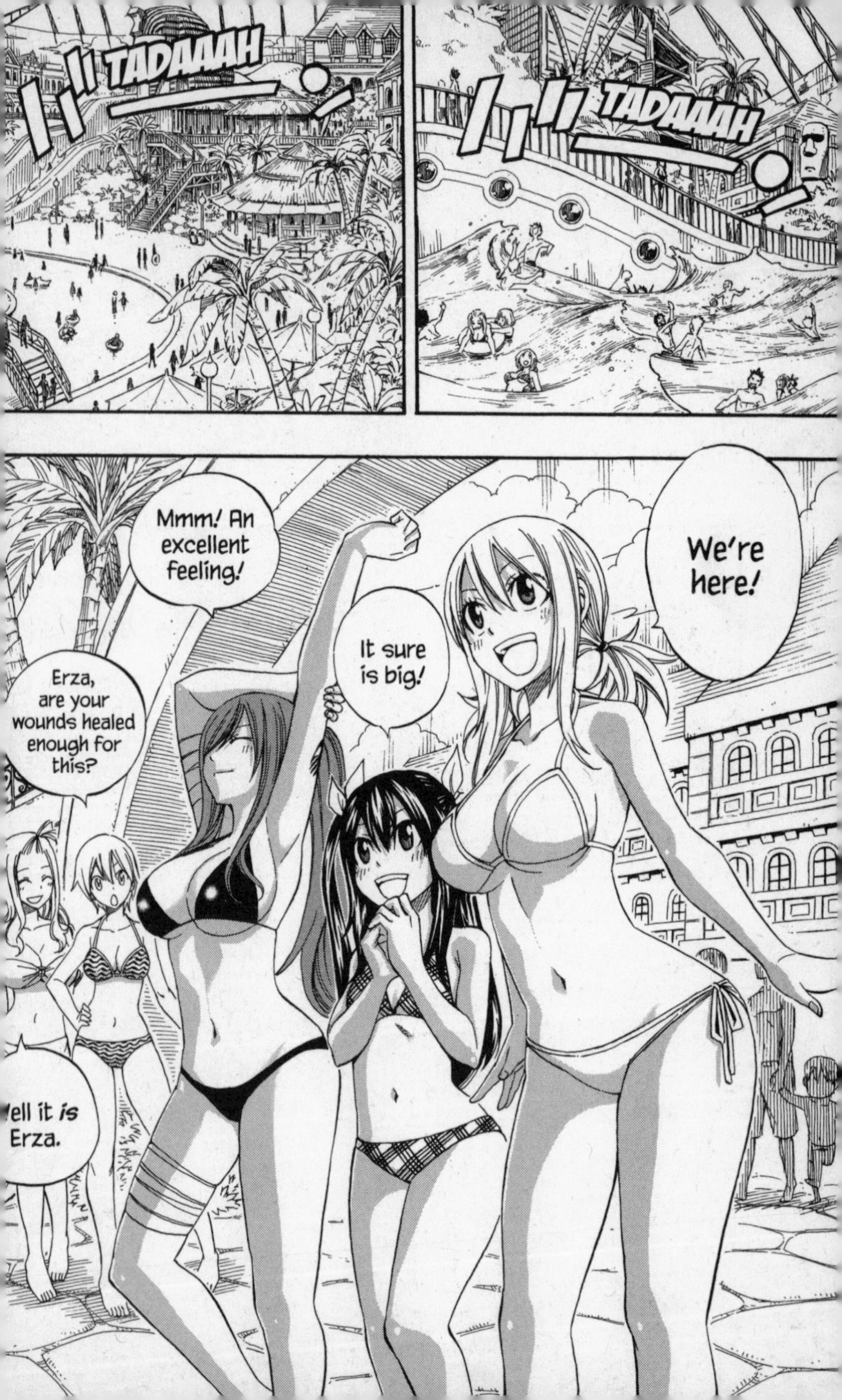
TADAAAH
TADAAAH
We're here!
It sure is big!
Mmm! An excellent feeling!
Erza, are your wounds healed enough for this?
ell it *is* Erza.

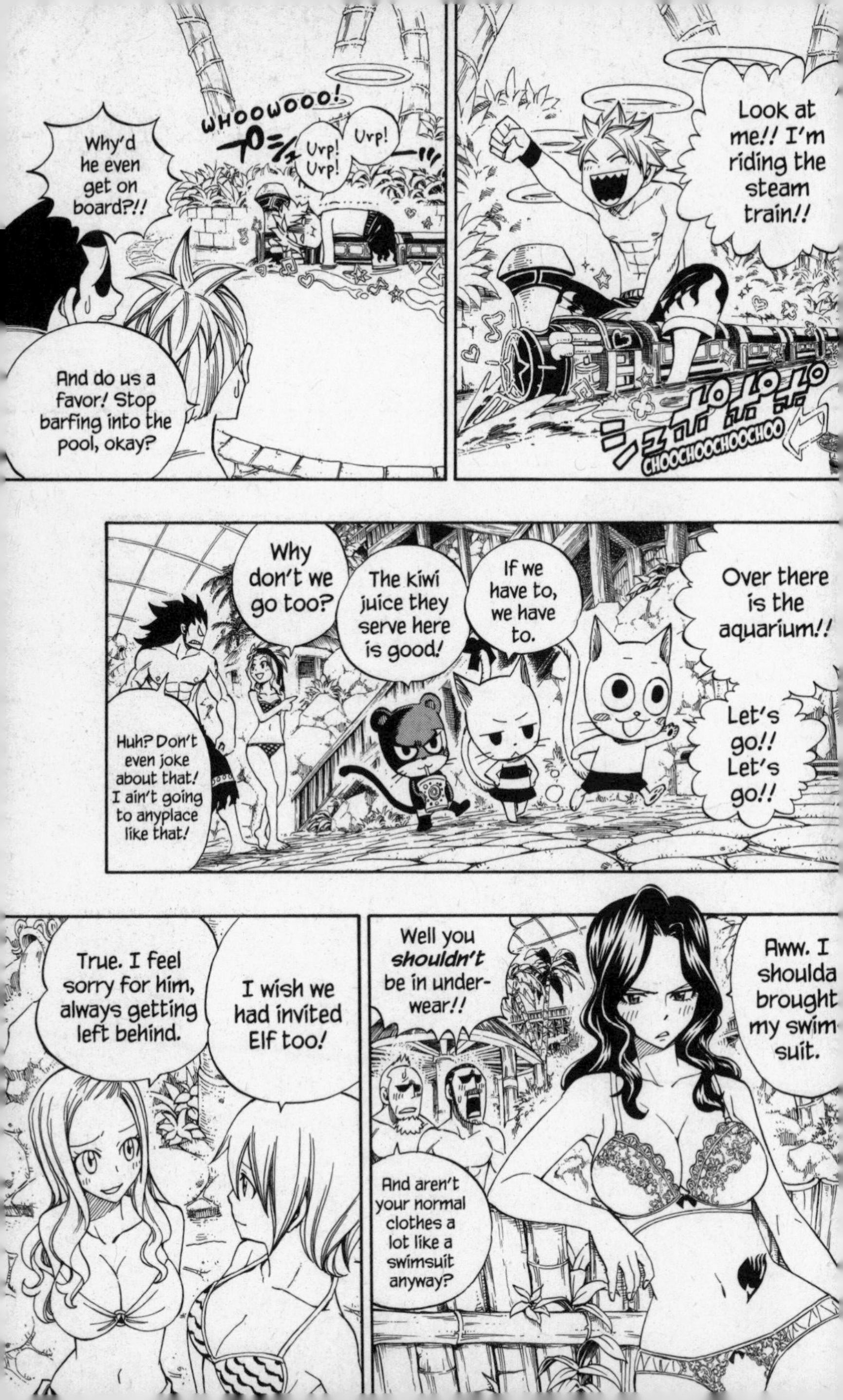
Look at me!! I'm riding the steam train!!
CHOOCHOOCHOOCHOO
WHOOWOOO!
Urp!
Urp! Urp!
Why'd he even get on board?!!
And do us a favor! Stop barfing into the pool, okay?
Over there is the aquarium!!
Let's go!! Let's go!!
If we have to, we have to.
The kiwi juice they serve here is good!
Why don't we go too?
Huh? Don't even joke about that! I ain't going to anyplace like that!
Aww. I shoulda brought my swim suit.
Well you *shouldn't* be in under-wear!!
And aren't your normal clothes a lot like a swimsuit anyway?
I wish we had invited Elf too!
True. I feel sorry for him, always getting left behind.

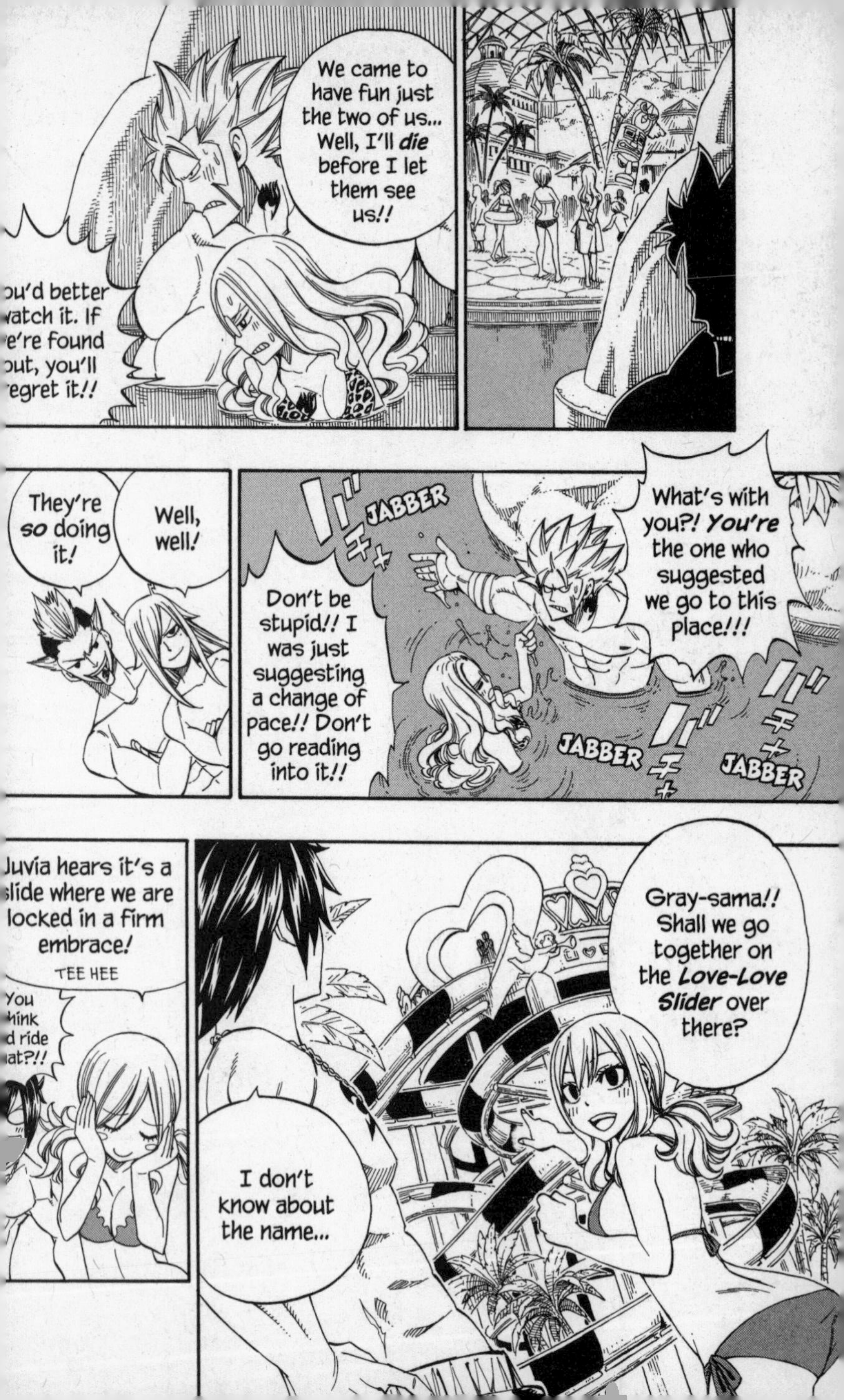

We came to have fun just the two of us... Well, I'll *die* before I let them see us!!
ou'd better watch it. If e're found out, you'll egret it!!
What's with you?! *You're* the one who suggested we go to this place!!!
JABBER
Don't be stupid!! I was just suggesting a change of pace!! Don't go reading into it!!
JABBER
JABBER
Well, well!
They're *so* doing it!
Gray-sama!! Shall we go together on the *Love-Love Slider* over there?
I don't know about the name...
Juvia hears it's a lide where we are locked in a firm embrace!
TEE HEE
You hink d ride at?!!

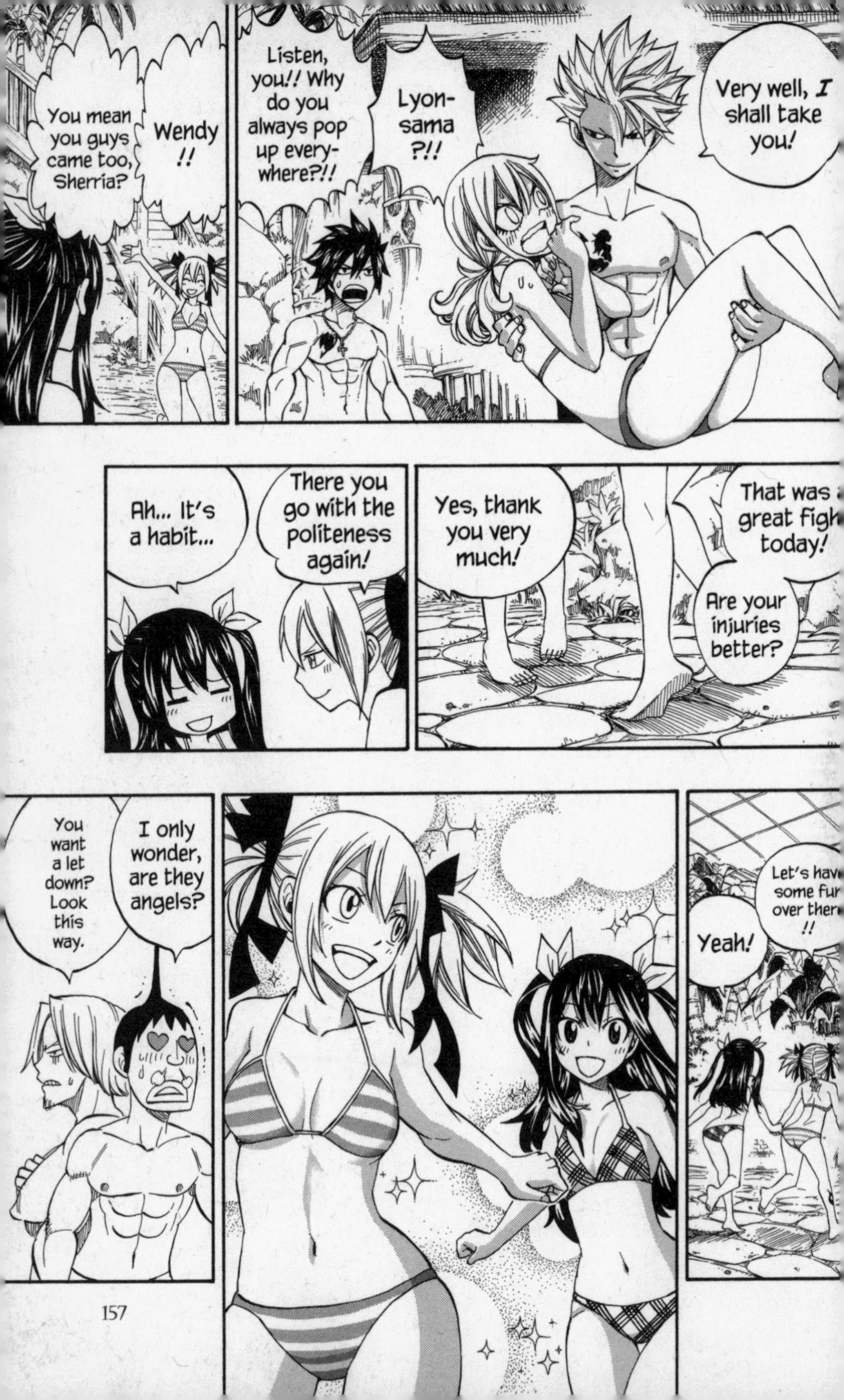
Very well, I shall take you!
Lyon-sama?!!
Listen, you!! Why do you always pop up every-where?!!
Wendy!!
You mean you guys came too, Sherria?
That was great figh today!
Are your injuries better?
Yes, thank you very much!
There you go with the politeness again!
Ah... It's a habit...
Let's hav some fu over ther !!
Yeah!
I only wonder, are they angels?
You want a let down? Look this way.

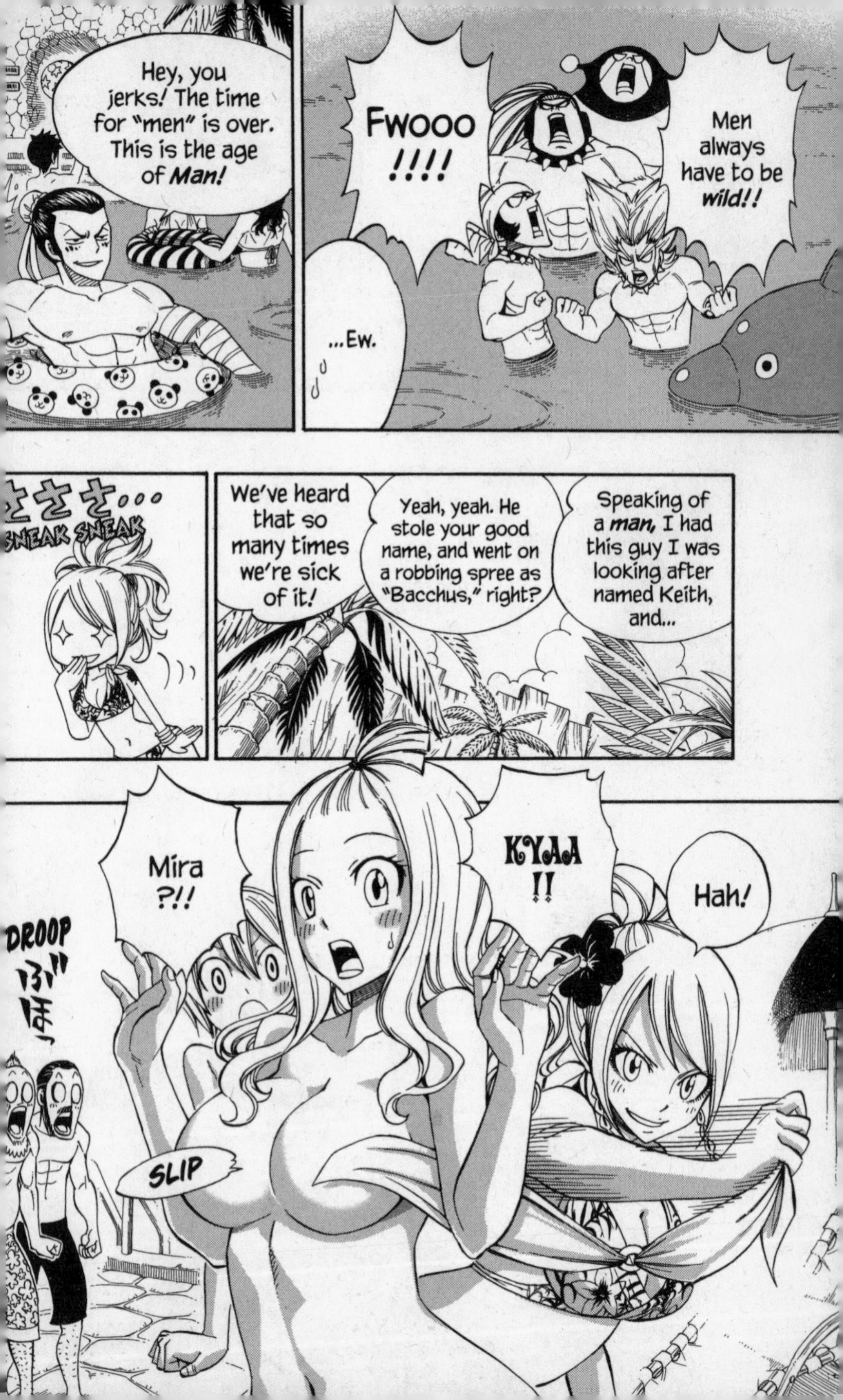
Men always have to be wild!!
Fwooo !!!!
...Ew.
Hey, you jerks! The time for "men" is over. This is the age of Man!
Speaking of a man, I had this guy I was looking after named Keith, and...
Yeah, yeah. He stole your good name, and went on a robbing spree as "Bacchus," right?
We've heard that so many times we're sick of it!
さささ
SNEAK SNEAK
Hah!
KYAA !!
Mira ?!!
DROOP
ぶほ
SLIP

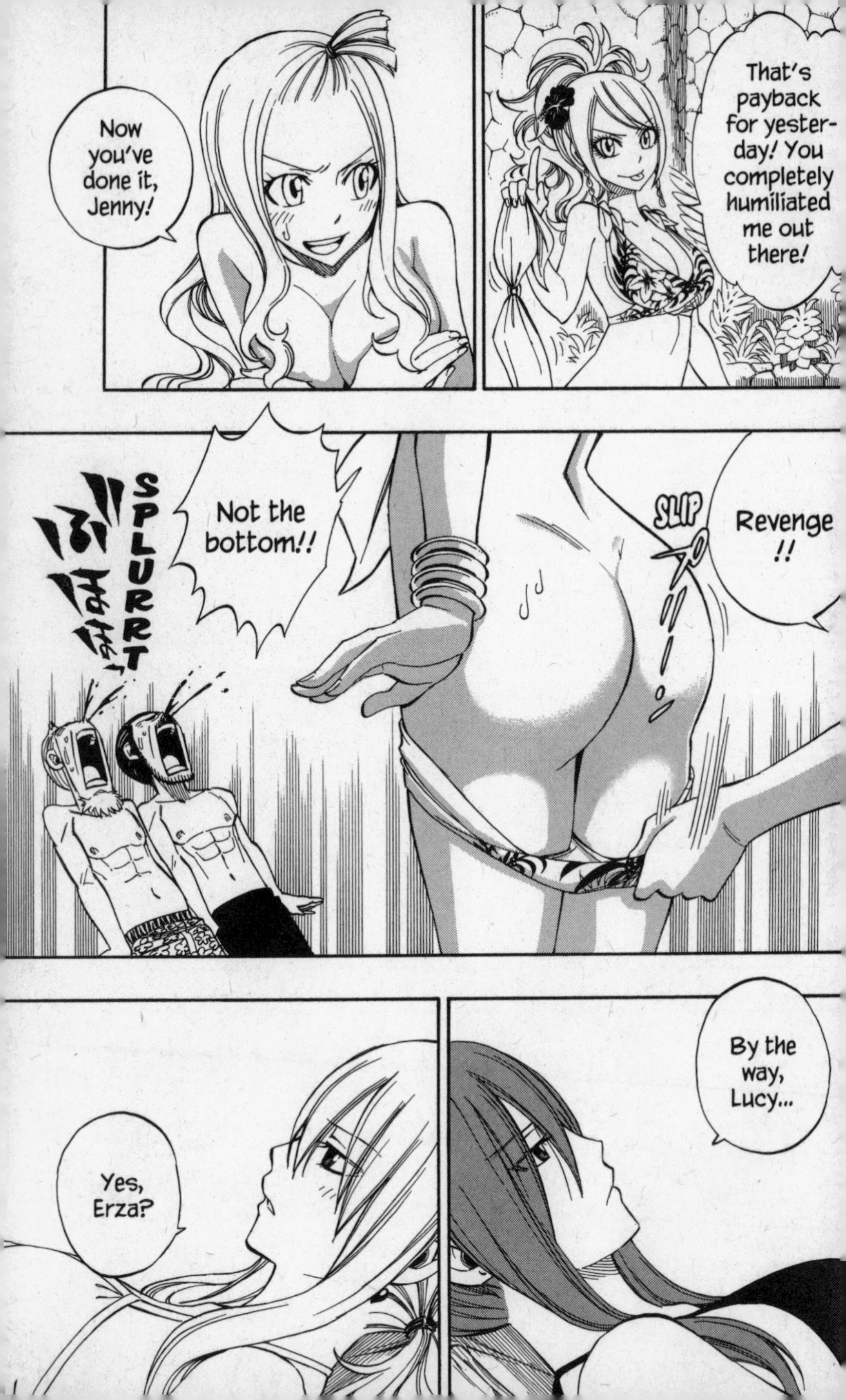
That's payback for yesterday! You completely humiliated me out there!
Now you've done it, Jenny!
Revenge!!
SLIP
Not the bottom!!
SPLURRT
By the way, Lucy...
Yes, Erza?

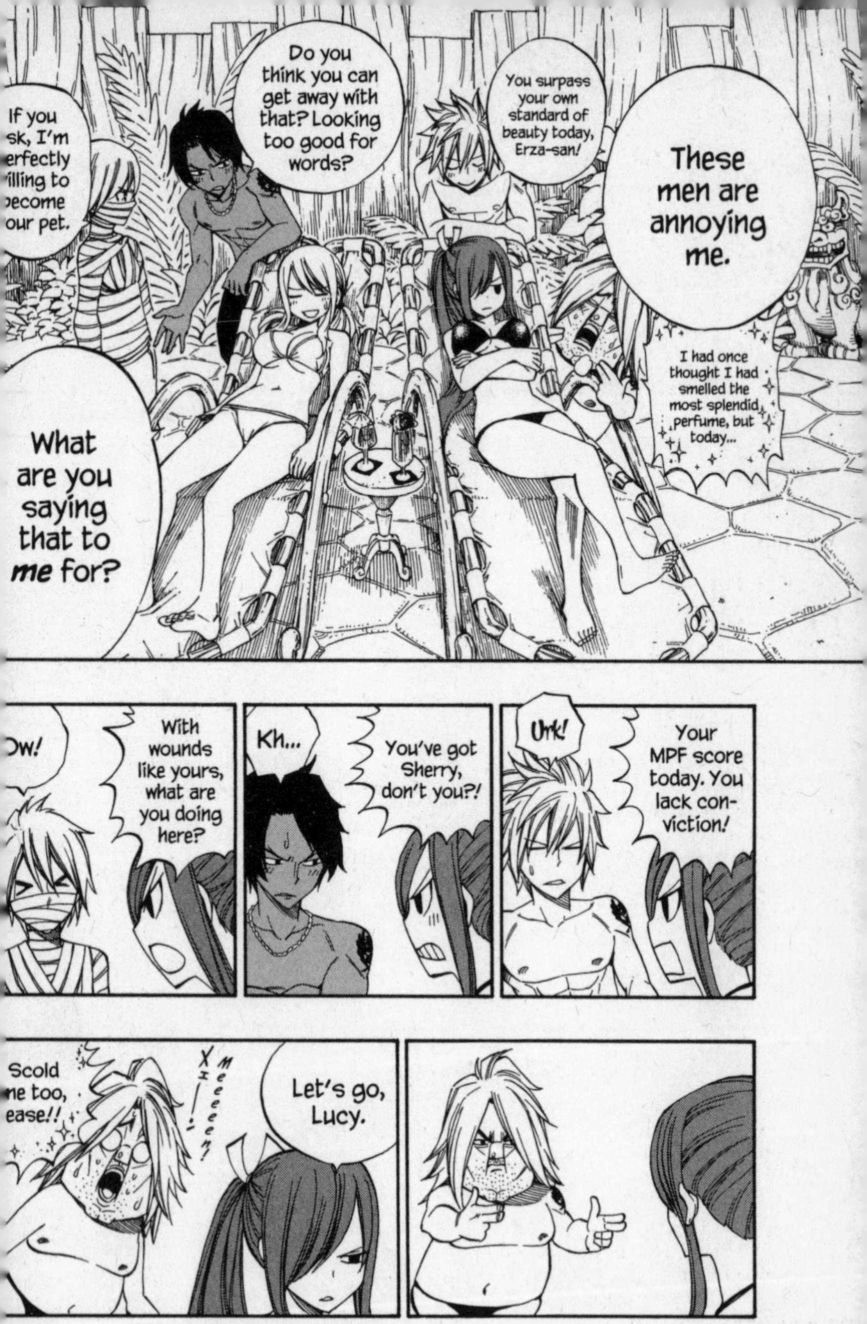
These men are annoying me.
You surpass your own standard of beauty today, Erza-san!
I had once thought I had smelled the most splendid perfume, but today...
Do you think you can get away with that? Looking too good for words?
If you sk, I'm erfectly illing to ecome our pet.
What are you saying that to *me* for?
Your MPF score today. You lack con-viction!
Urk!
You've got Sherry, don't you?!
Kh...
With wounds like yours, what are you doing here?
w!
Let's go, Lucy.
Meeeeen!
Scold ne too, ease!!

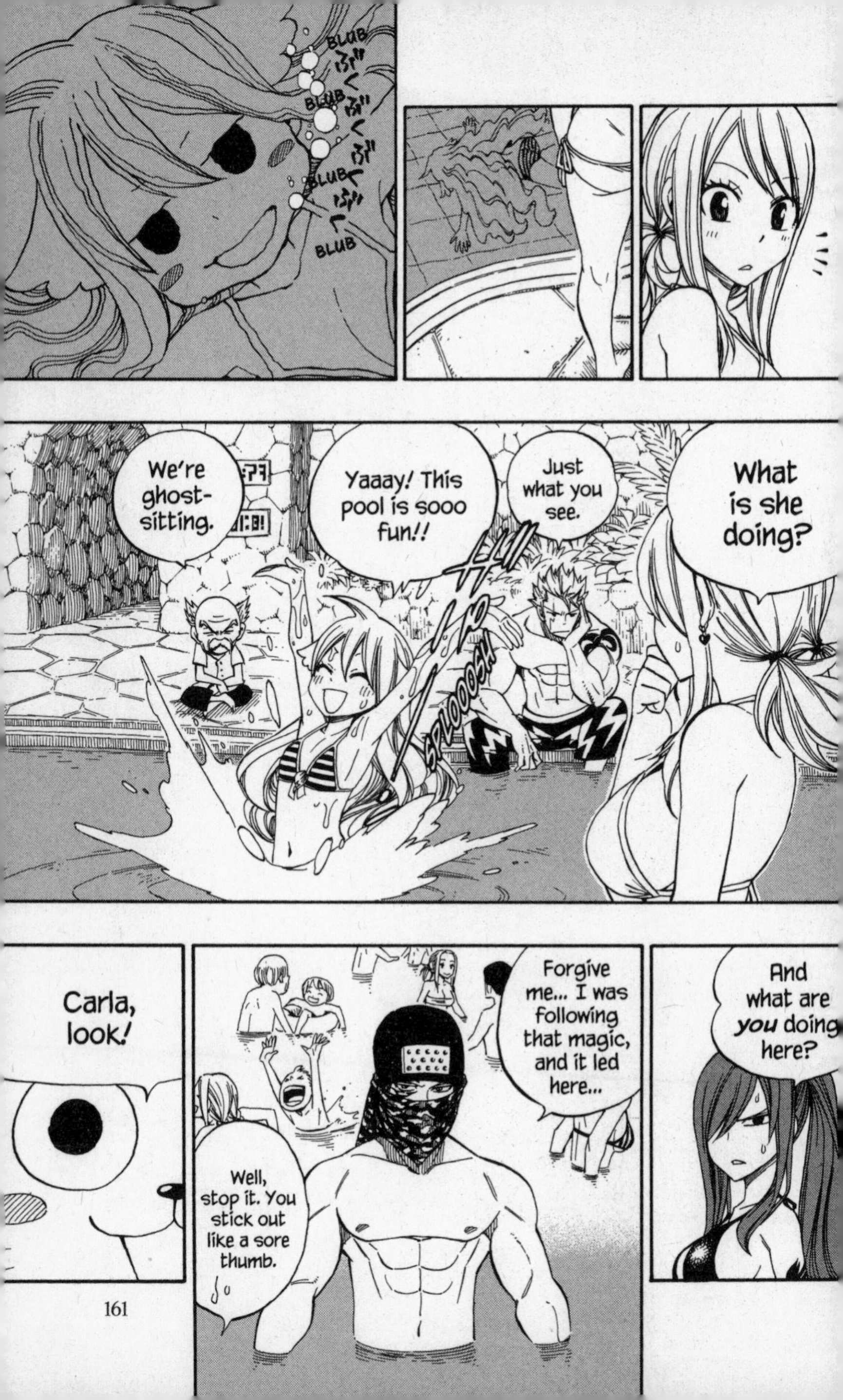
BLUB
BLUB
BLUB
BLUB
What is she doing?
Just what you see.
SPLOOOSH
Yaaay! This pool is sooo fun!!
We're ghost-sitting.
And what are *you* doing here?
Forgive me... I was following that magic, and it led here...
Well, stop it. You stick out like a sore thumb.
Carla, look!

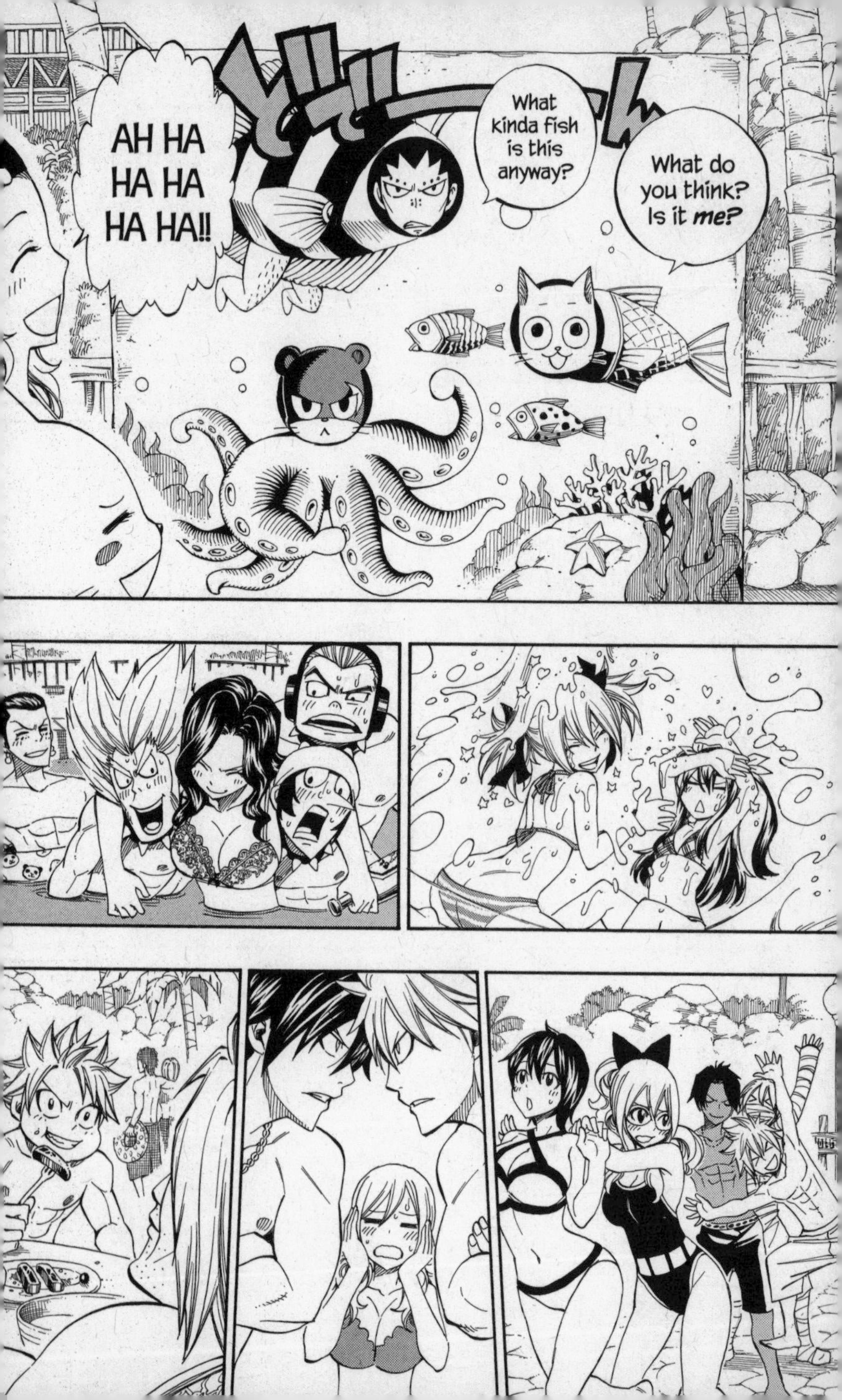
What do you think? Is it *me?*
What kinda fish is this anyway?
AH HA HA HA HA HA!!

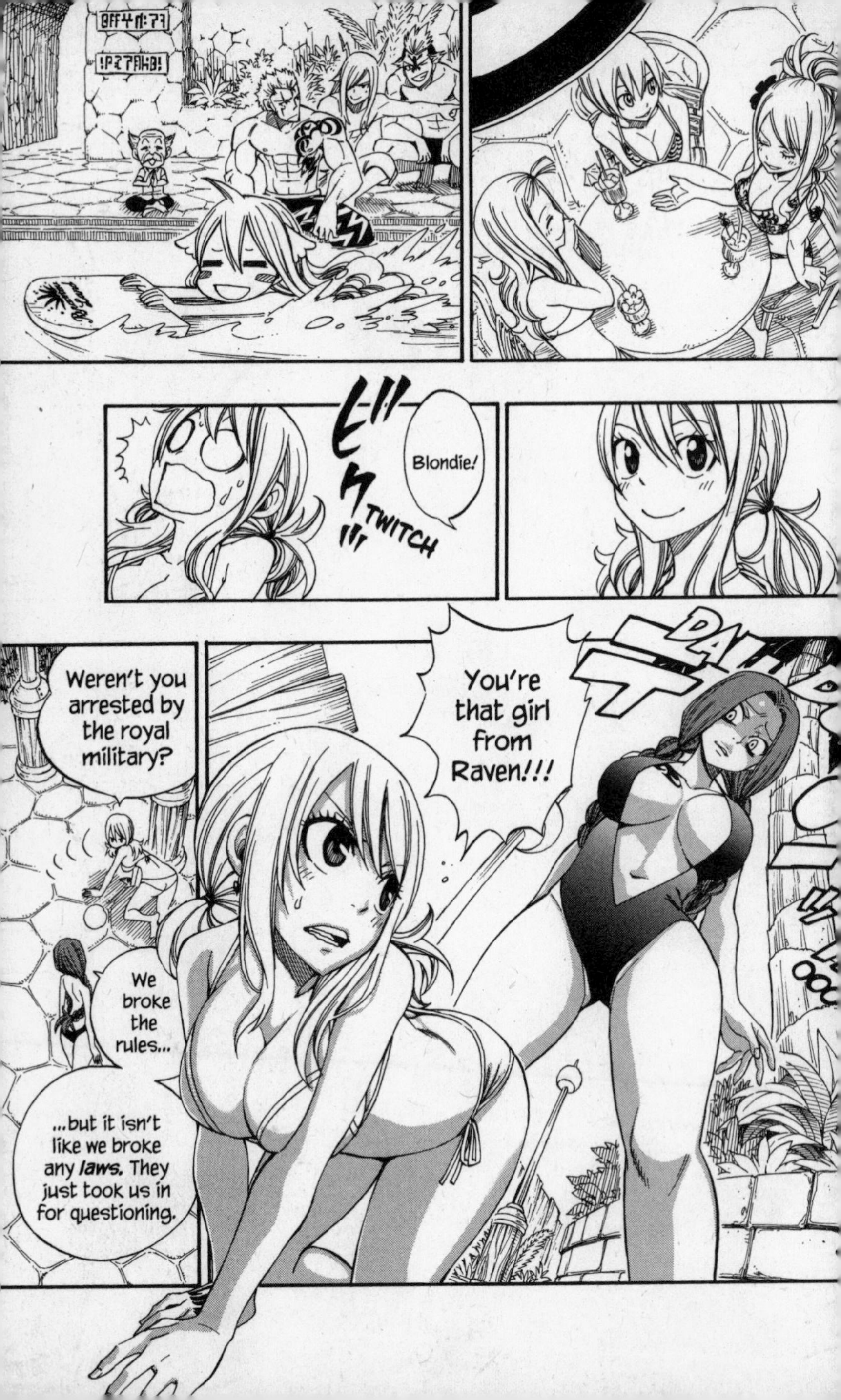

Blondie!
TWITCH
You're that girl from Raven!!!
Weren't you arrested by the royal military?
We broke the rules...
...but it isn't like we broke any *laws.* They just took us in for questioning.

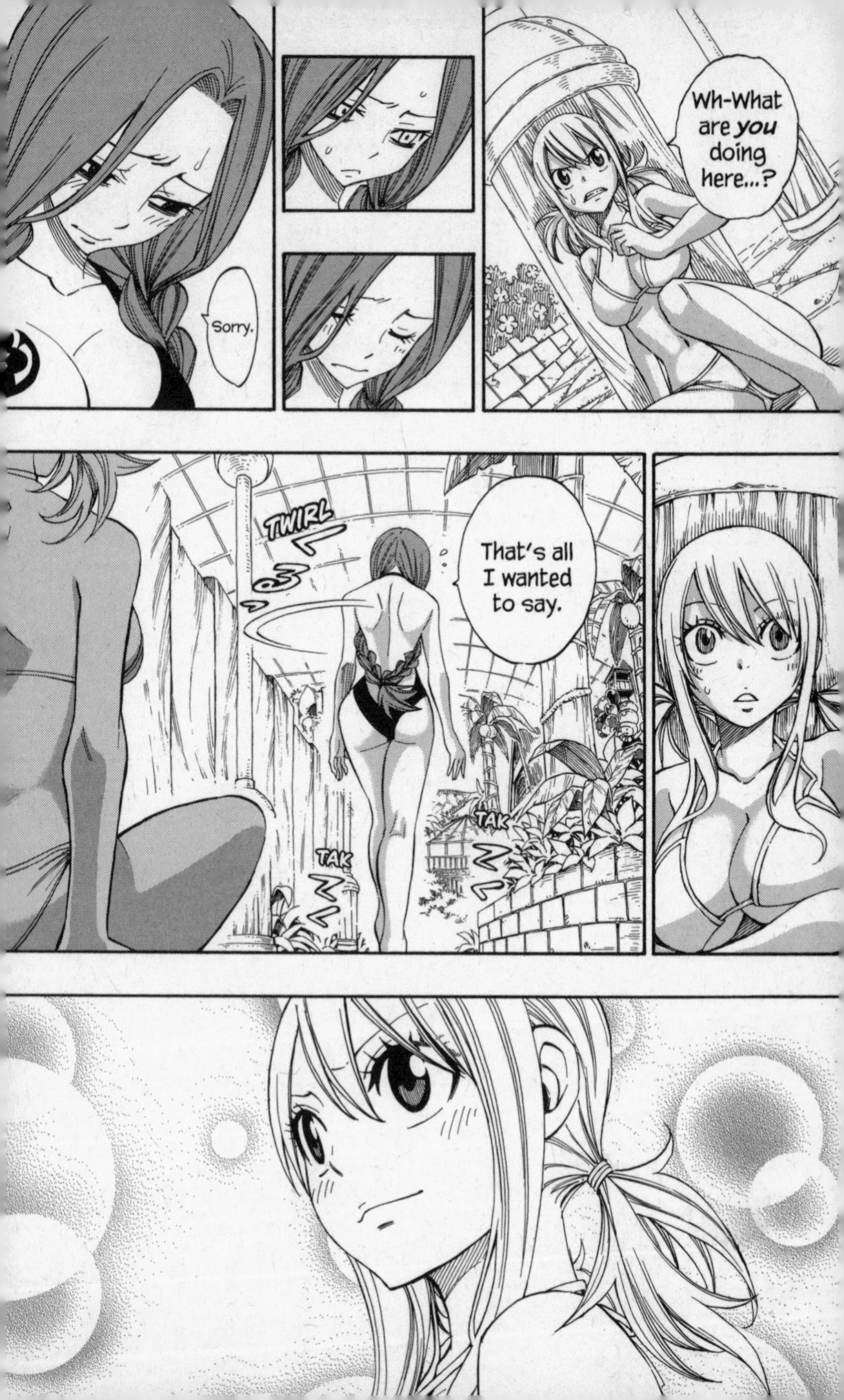
Wh-What are *you* doing here...?
Sorry.
That's all I wanted to say.
TWIRL
TAK
TAK

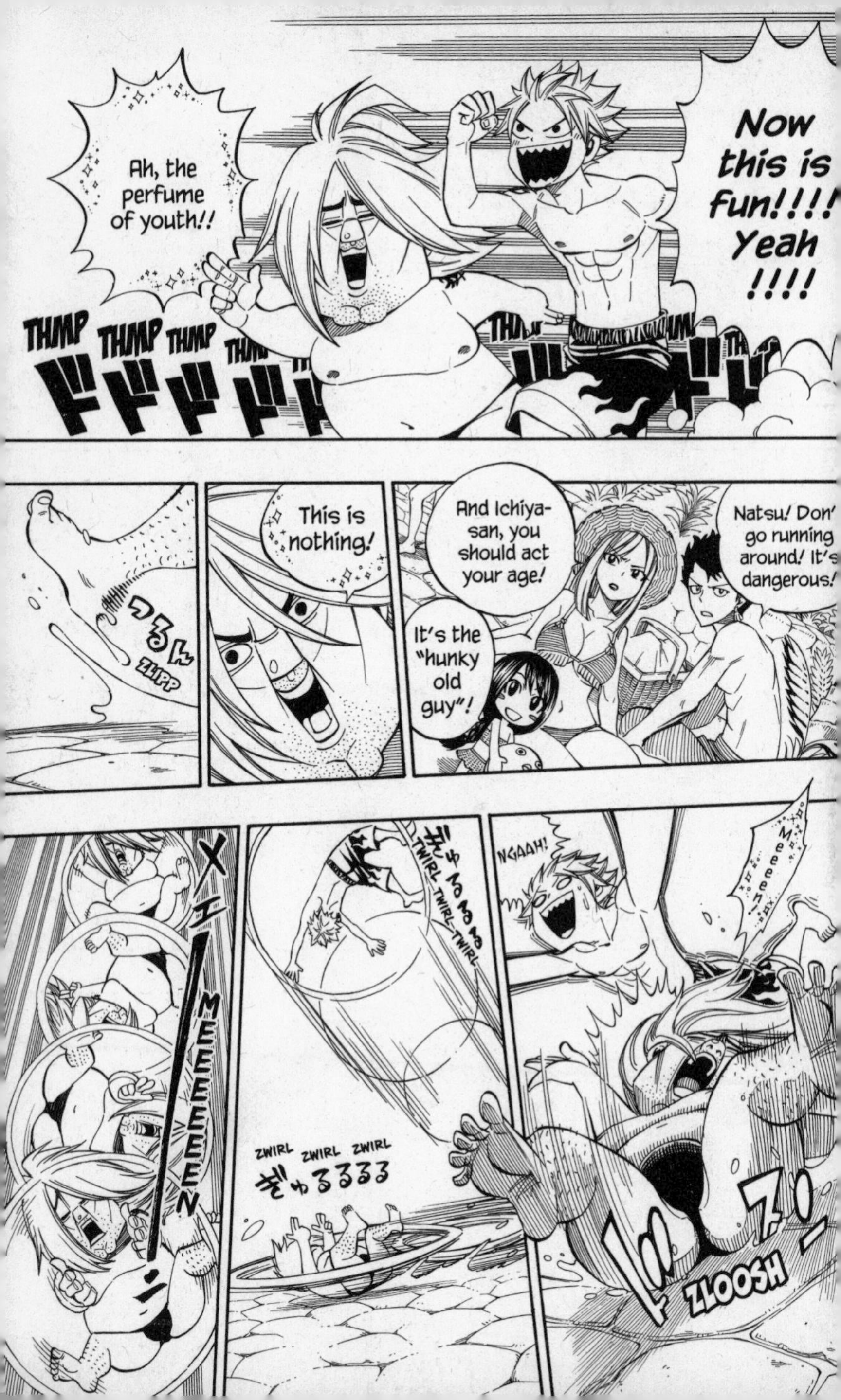
Now this is fun!!!! Yeah!!!!
Ah, the perfume of youth!!
THMP THMP THMP THMP
Natsu! Don't go running around! It's dangerous!
And Ichiya-san, you should act your age!
It's the "hunky old guy"!
This is nothing!
つるん
ZIPP
Meeeen!
NGAAH!
ZLOOSH
TWIRL TWIRL TWIRL
ZWIRL ZWIRL ZWIRL
ぎゅるるるる
MEEEEEEEN

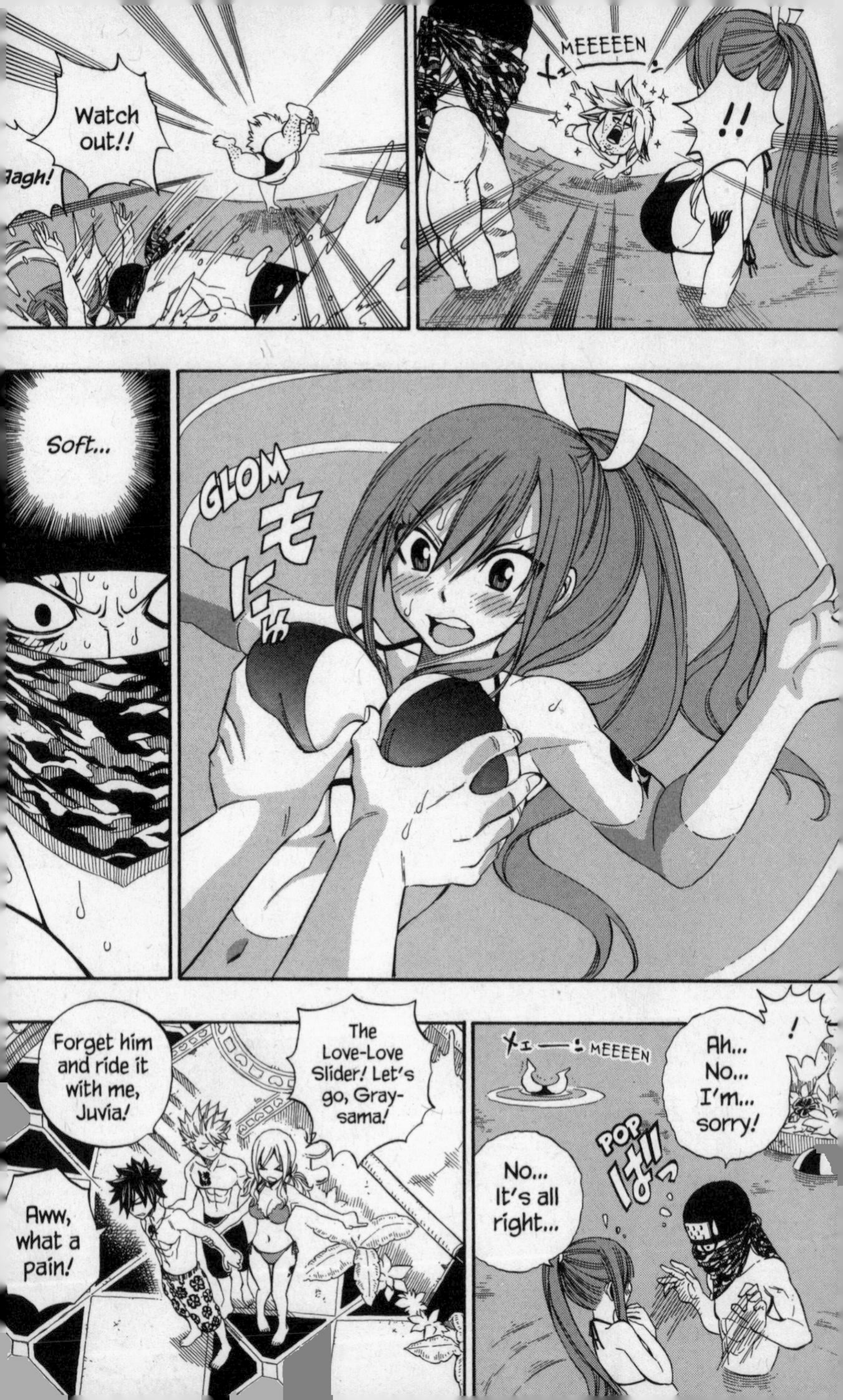

メェ MEEEEEN
!!
Watch out!!
agh!
GLOM
もにゅ
Soft...
メェー MEEEEN
!
Ah... No... I'm... sorry!
POP
ぱっ
No... It's all right...
The Love-Love Slider! Let's go, Gray-sama!
Forget him and ride it with me, Juvia!
Aww, what a pain!

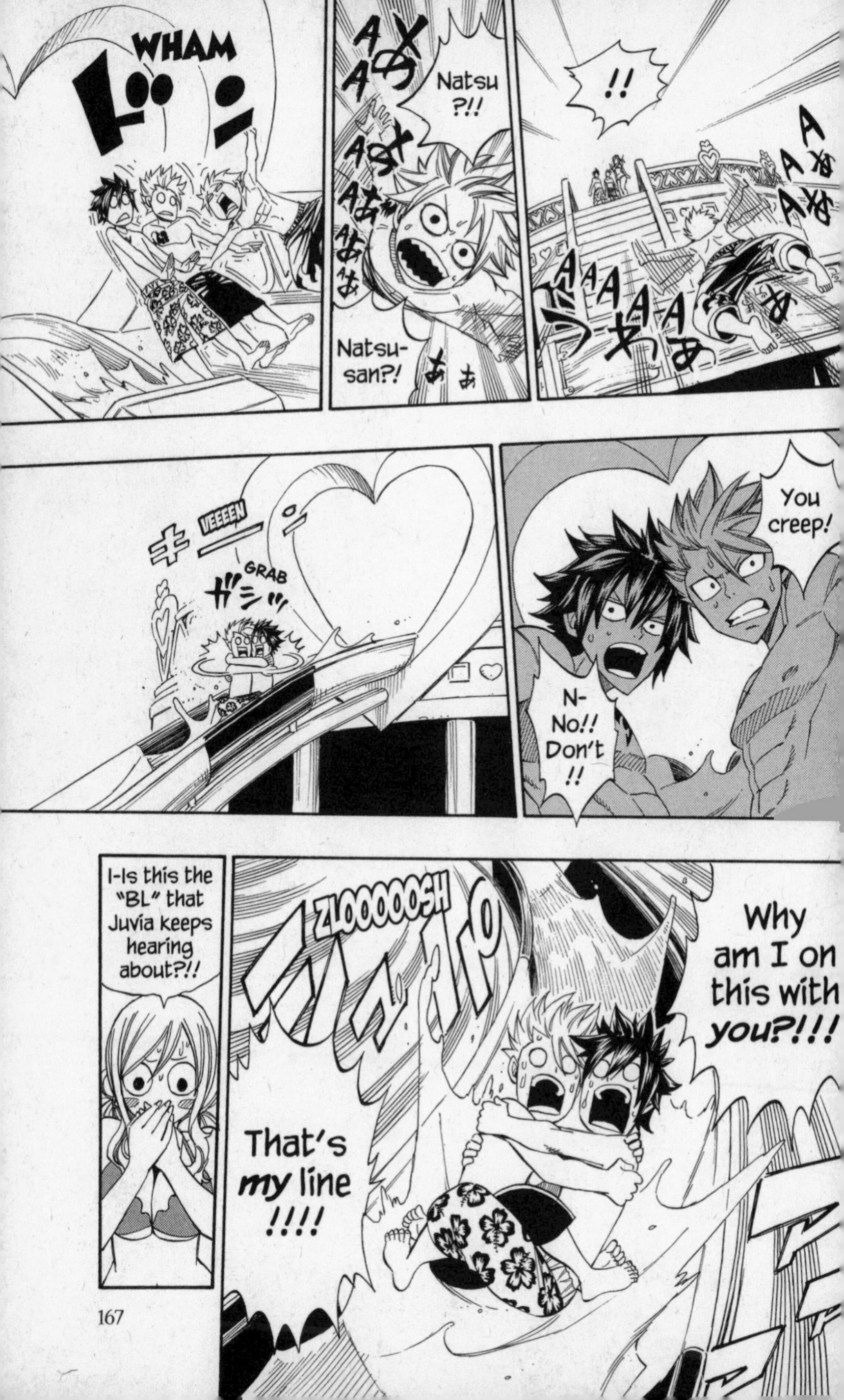
!!
Natsu ?!!
Natsu-san?!
WHAM
You creep!
N-No!! Don't !!
VEEEEN
GRAB
Why am I on this with *you*?!!!
ZLOOOOOSH
That's *my* line !!!!
I-Is this the "BL" that Juvia keeps hearing about?!!

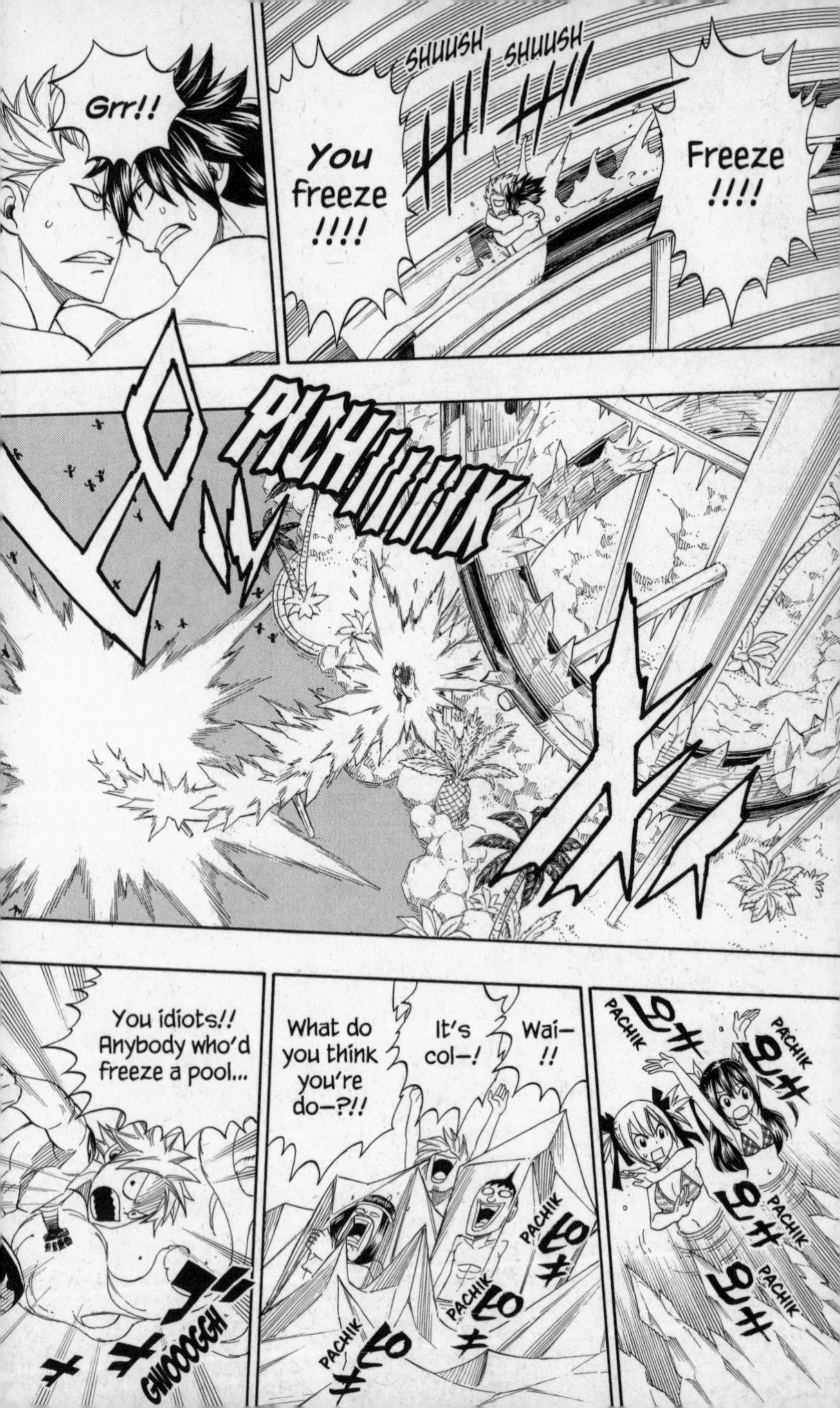
Freeze !!!!
SHUUSH
SHUUSH
You freeze !!!!
Grr!!
PICHIIIIK
PACHIK
PACHIK
PACHIK
PACHIK
Wai— !!
It's col—!
What do you think you're do—?!!
PACHIK
PACHIK
PACHIK
You idiots!! Anybody who'd freeze a pool...
GWOOOGGH

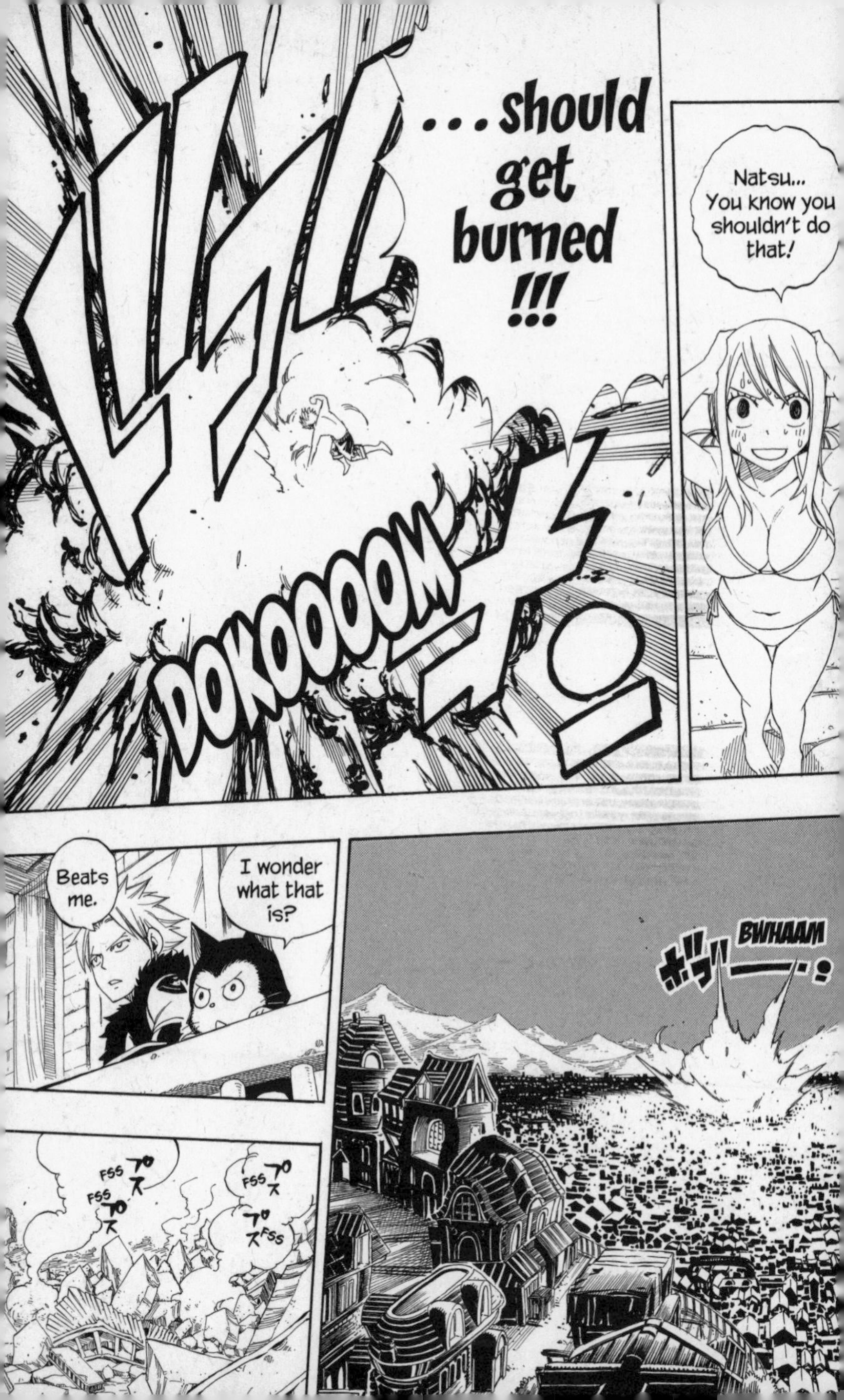
Natsu... You know you shouldn't do that!
...should get burned!!!
DOKOOOOM
BWHAAM
I wonder what that is?
Beats me.
FSS
FSS
FSS
FSS

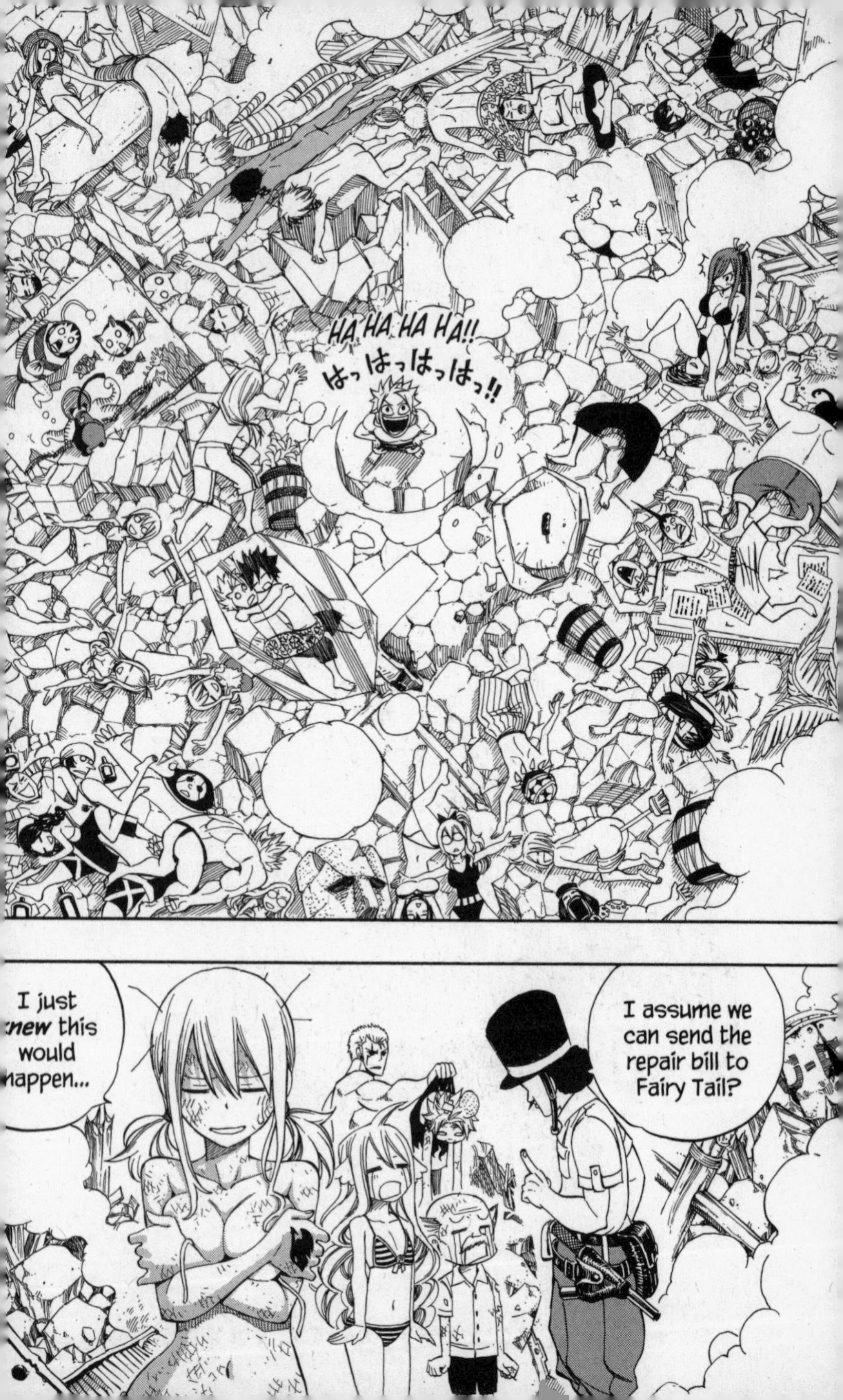

HA HA HA HA!!
はっはっはっはっ!!
I assume we can send the repair bill to Fairy Tail?
I just *new* this would appen...

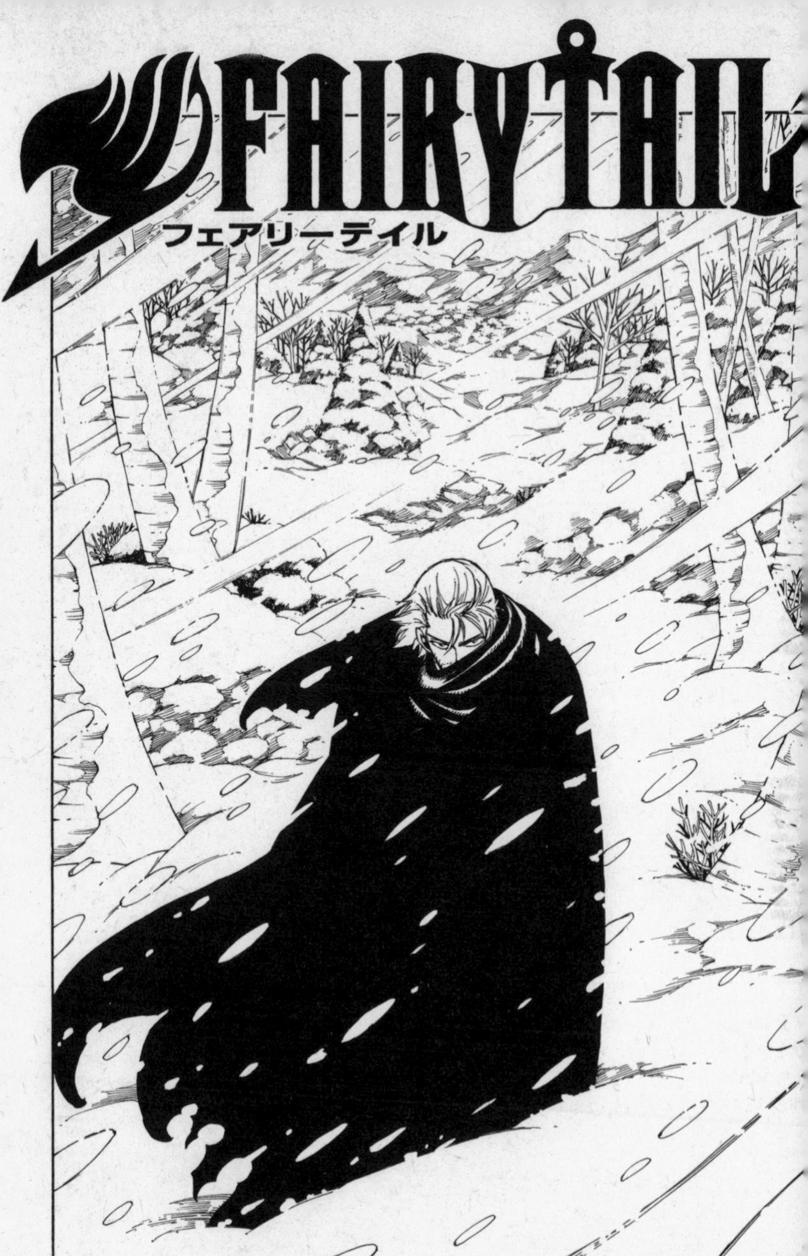
FAIRY TAIL
フェアリーテイル

Chapter 299: Lone Journey

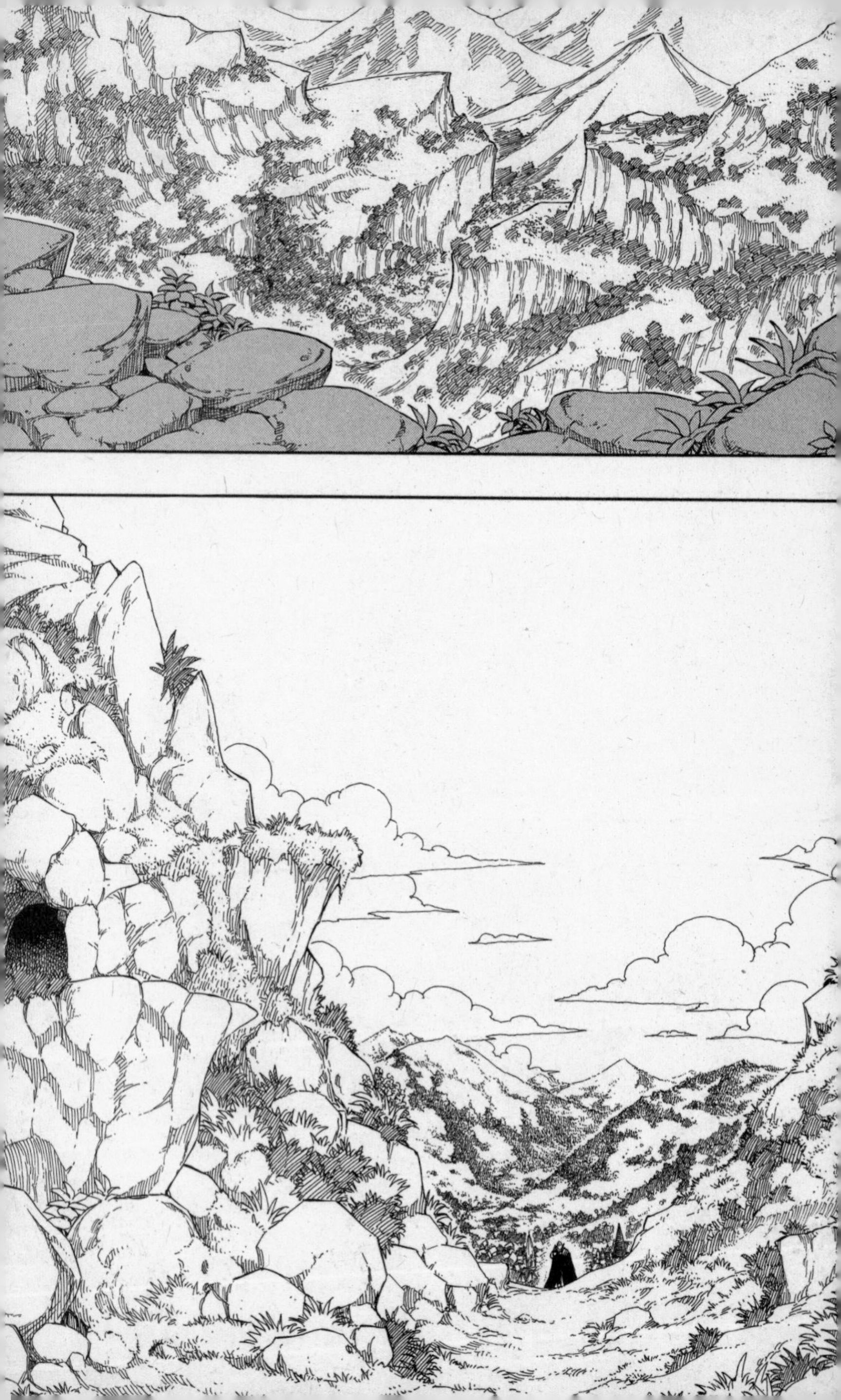

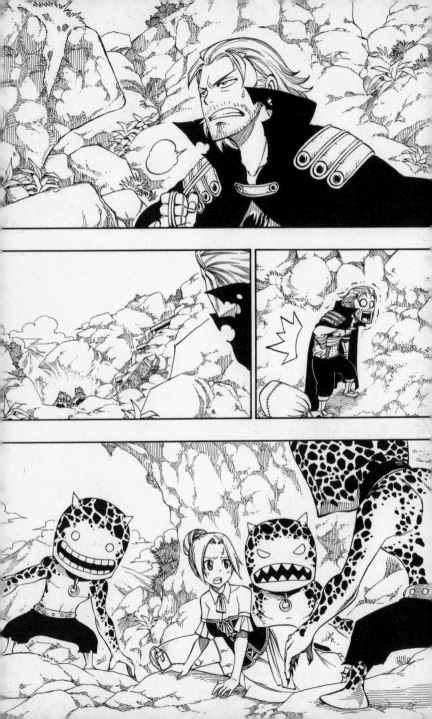

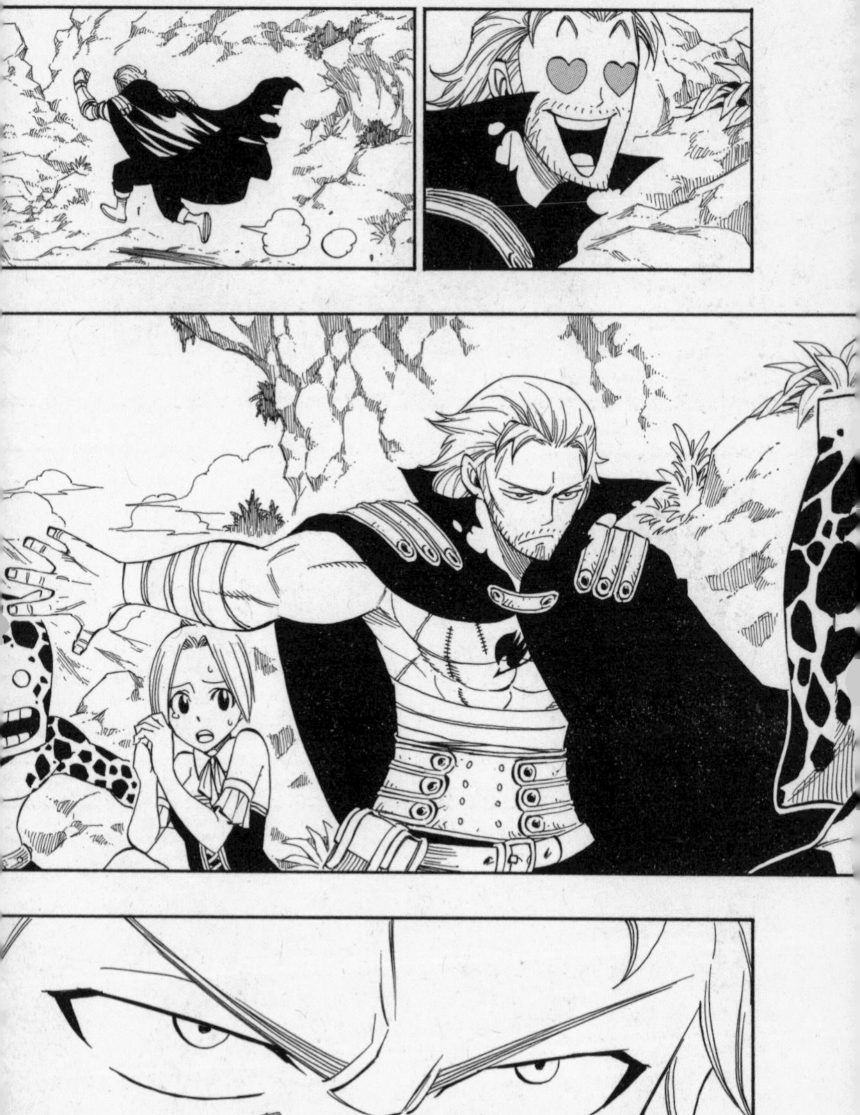

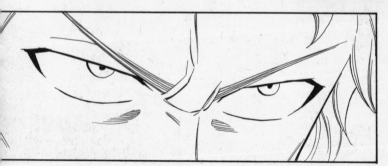

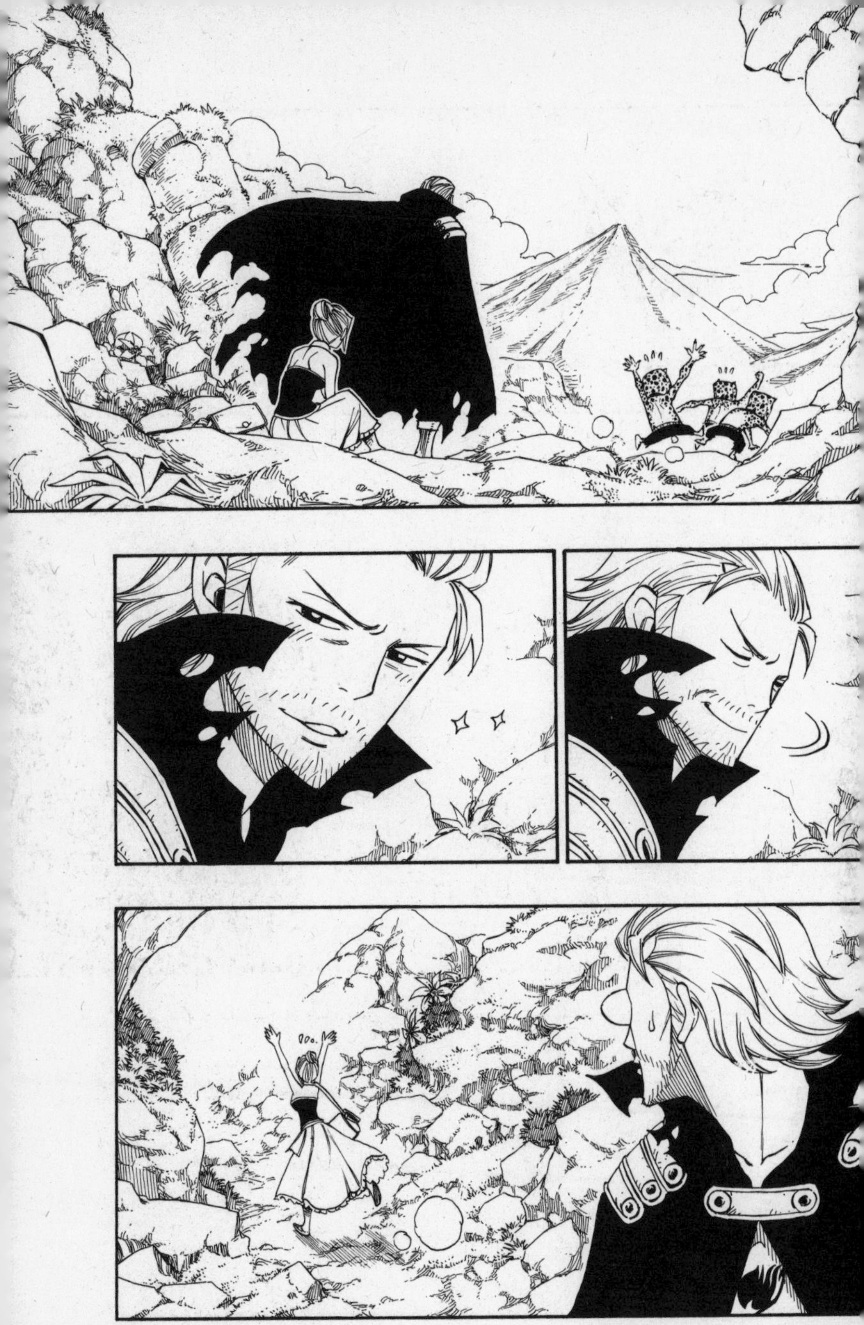

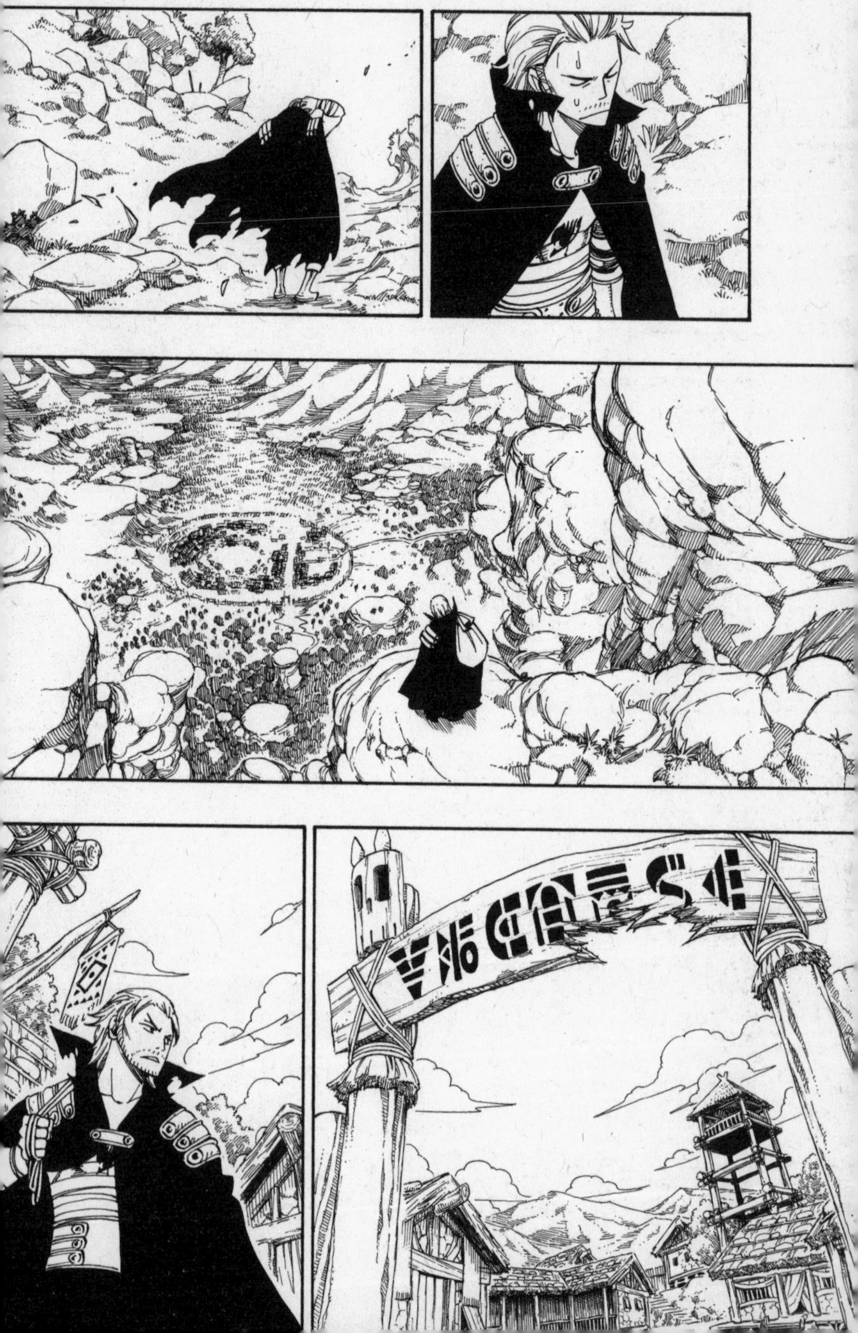

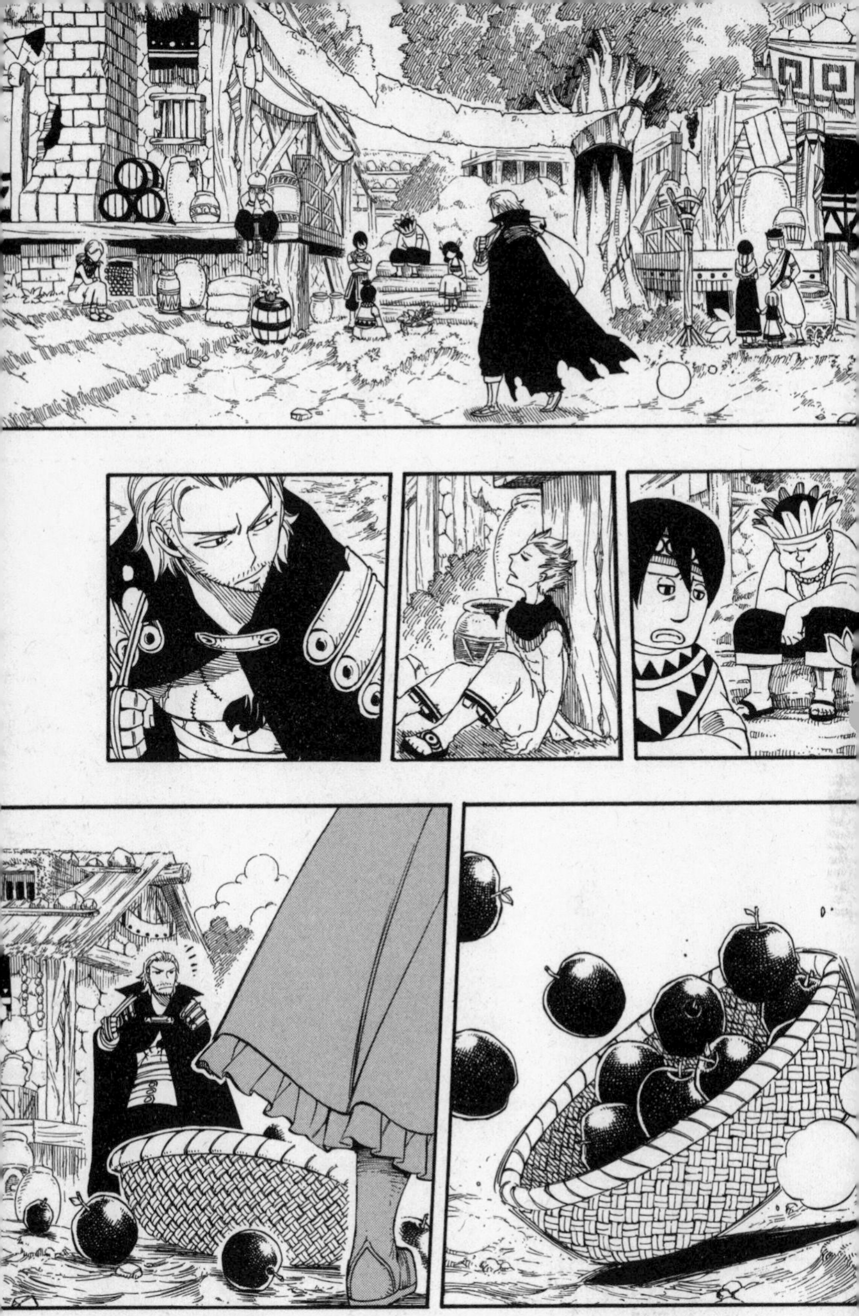

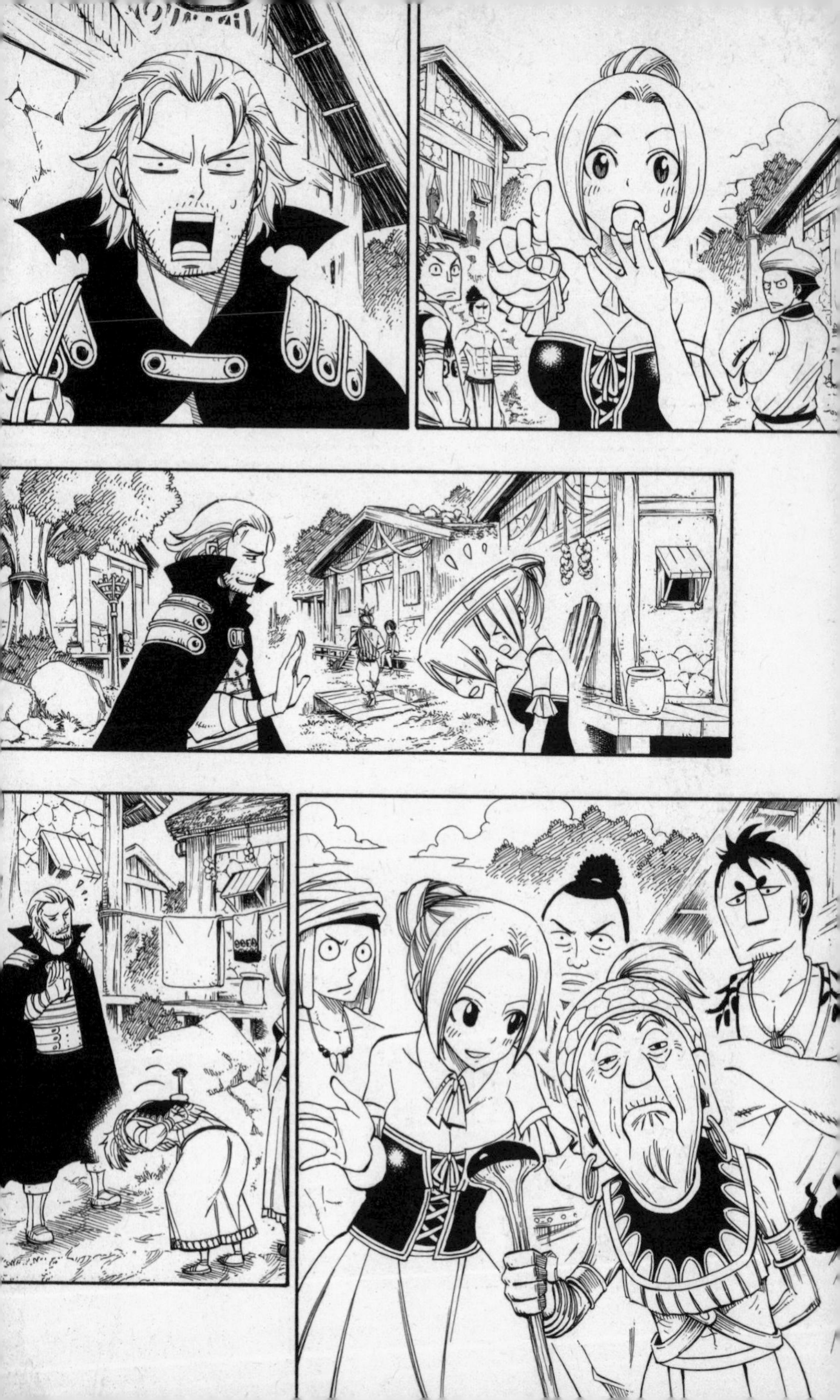

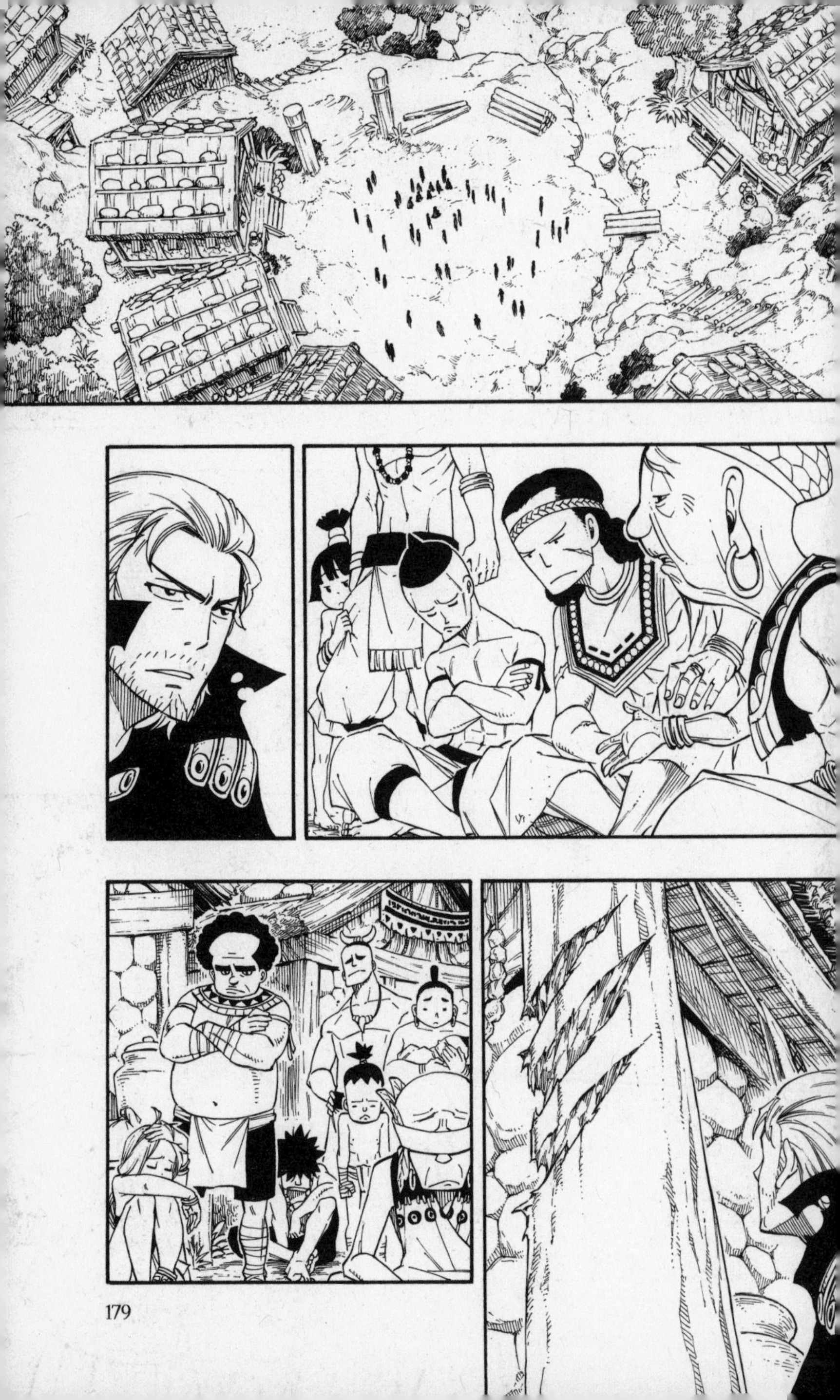

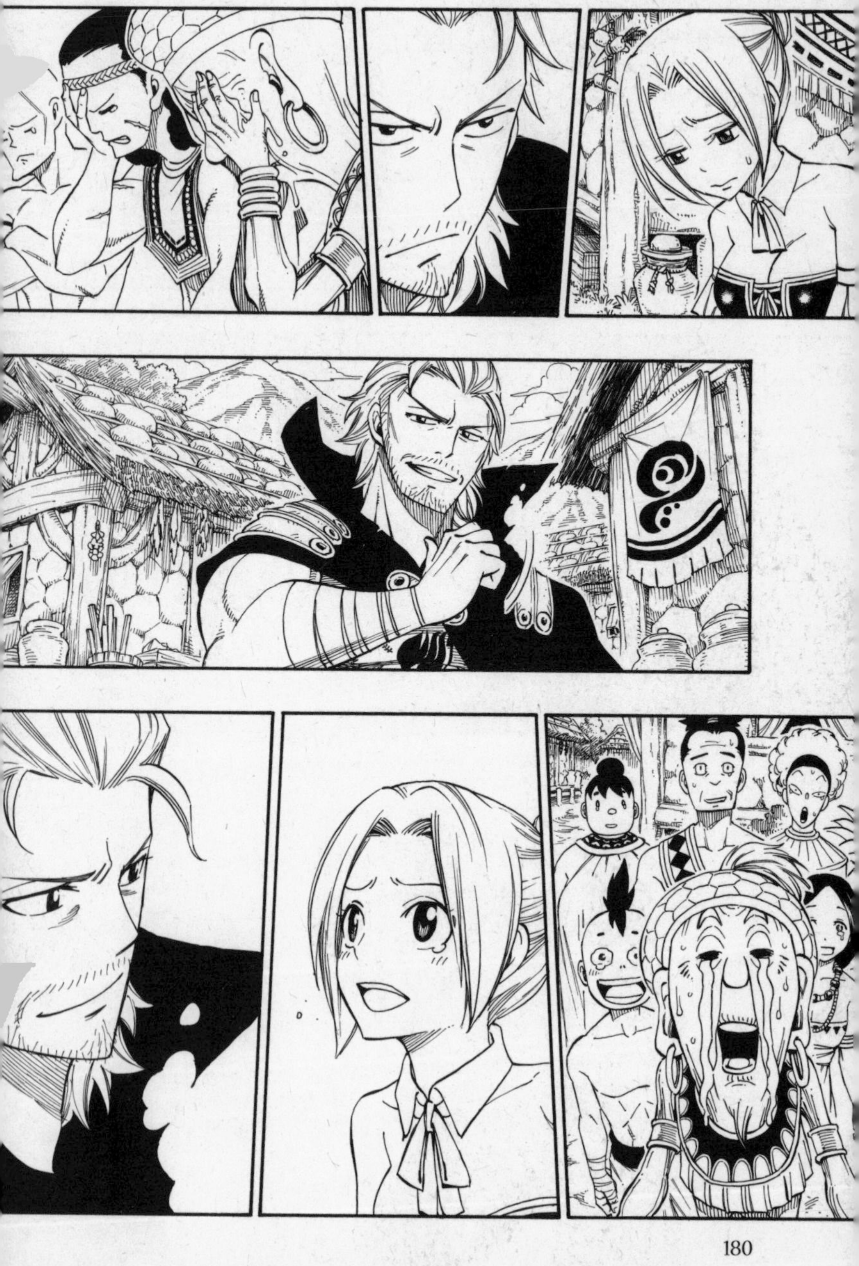

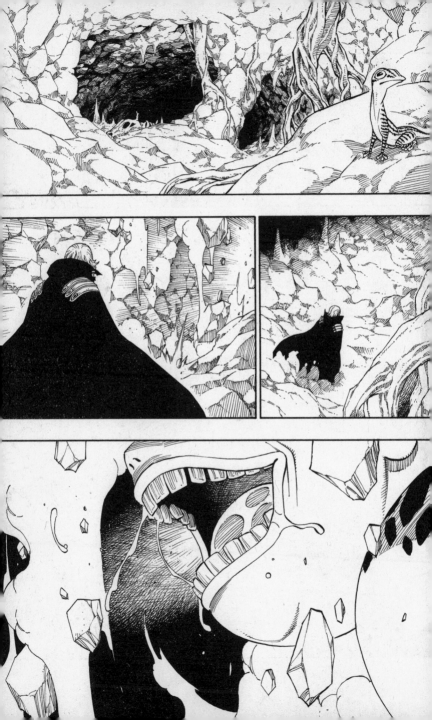

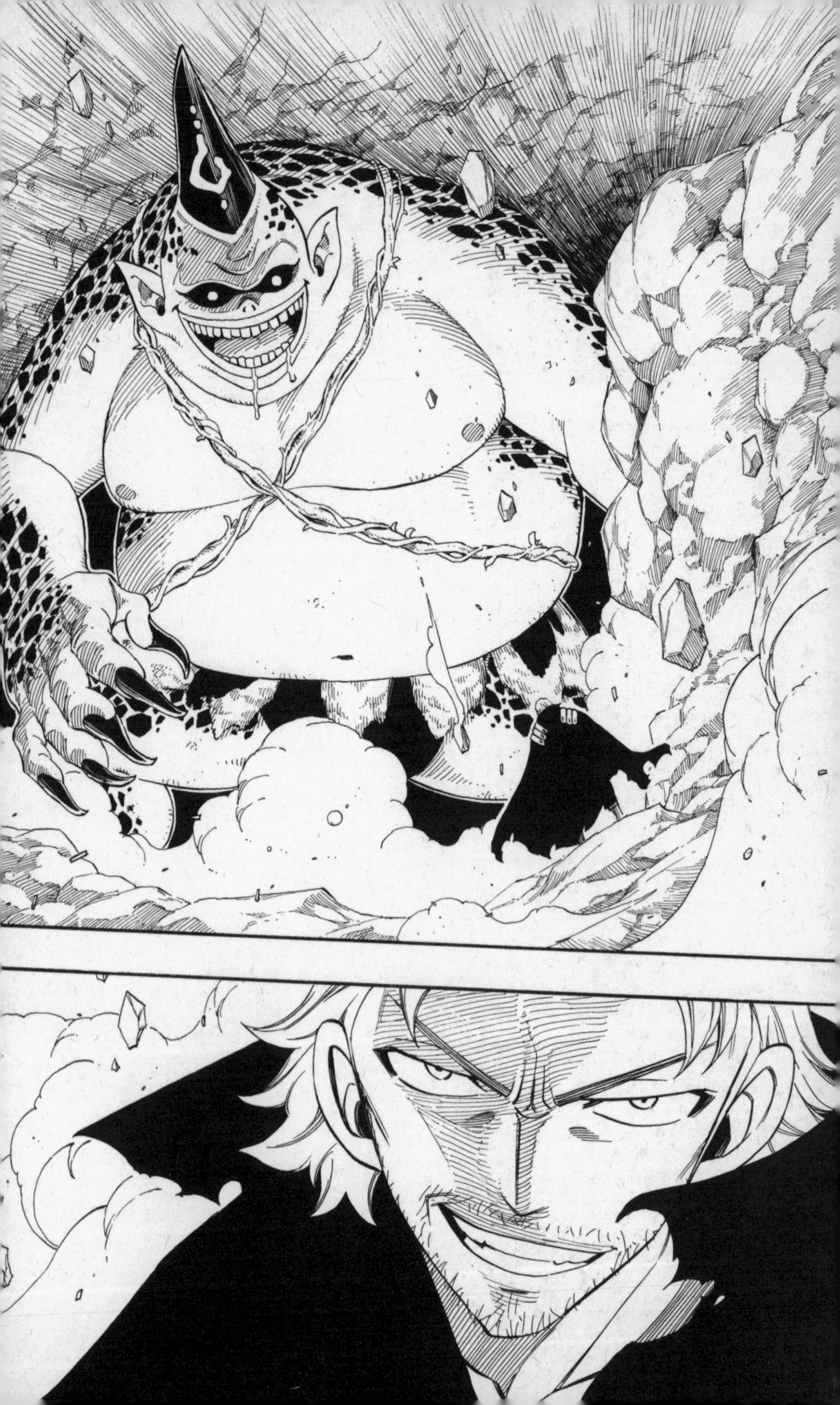

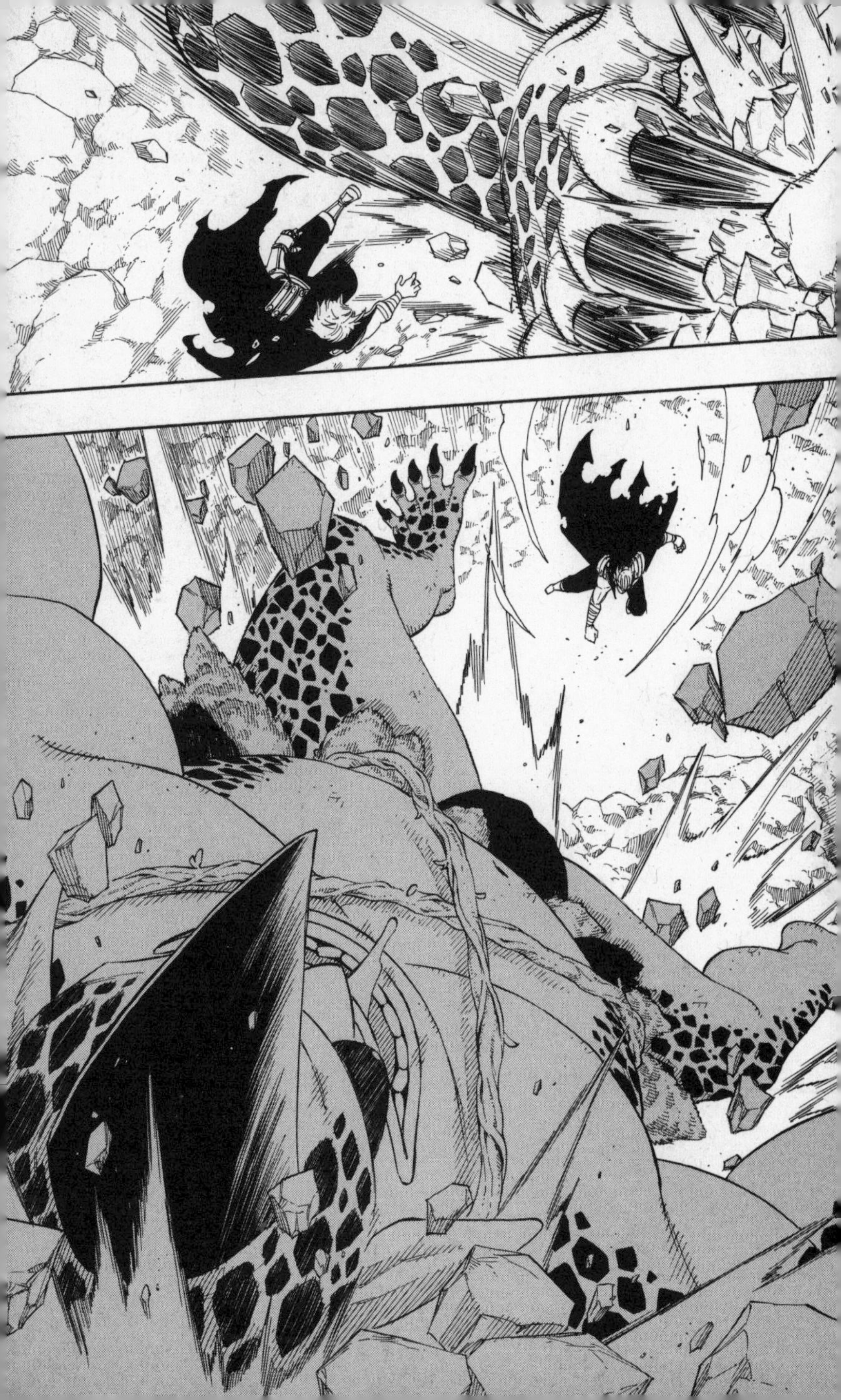

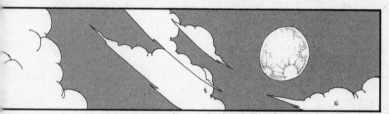

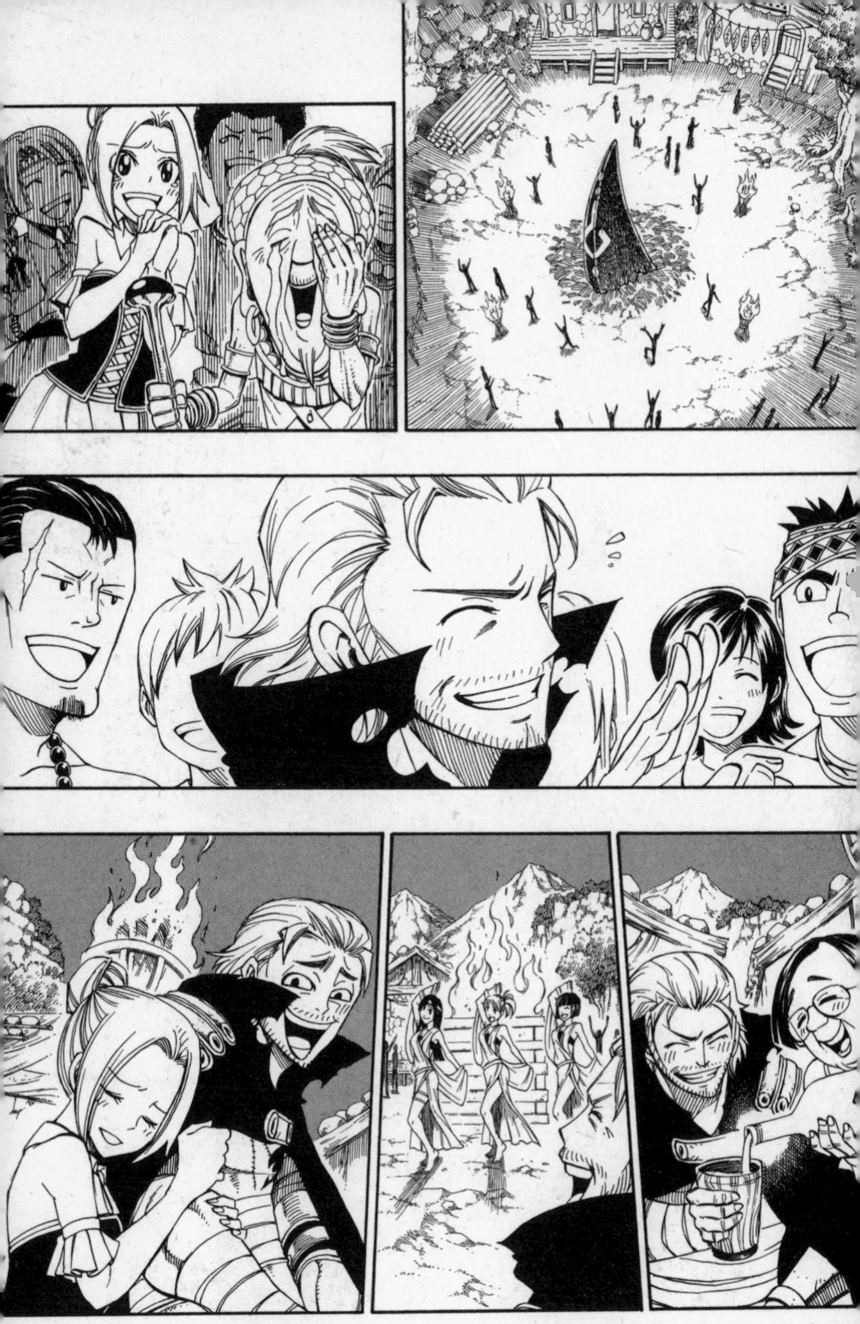

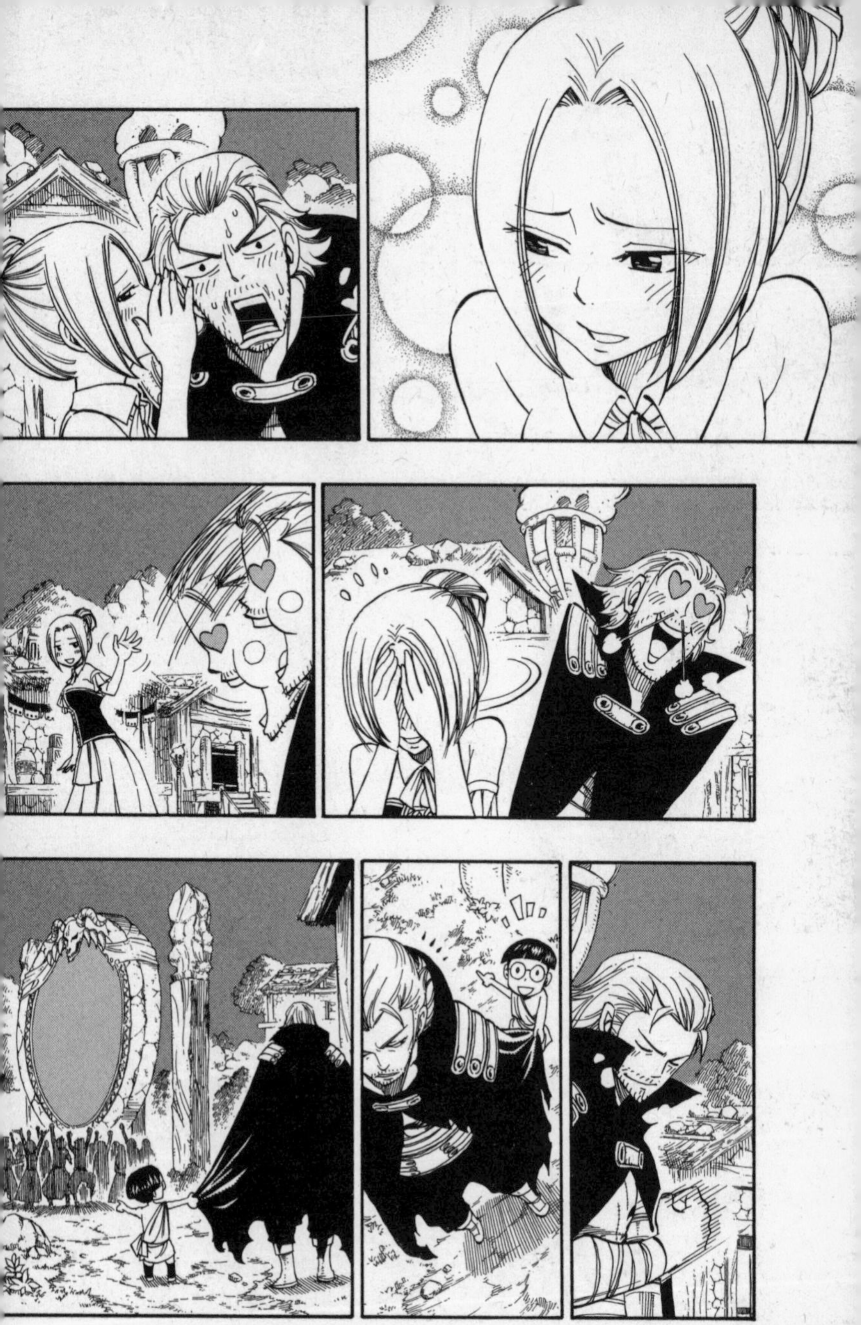

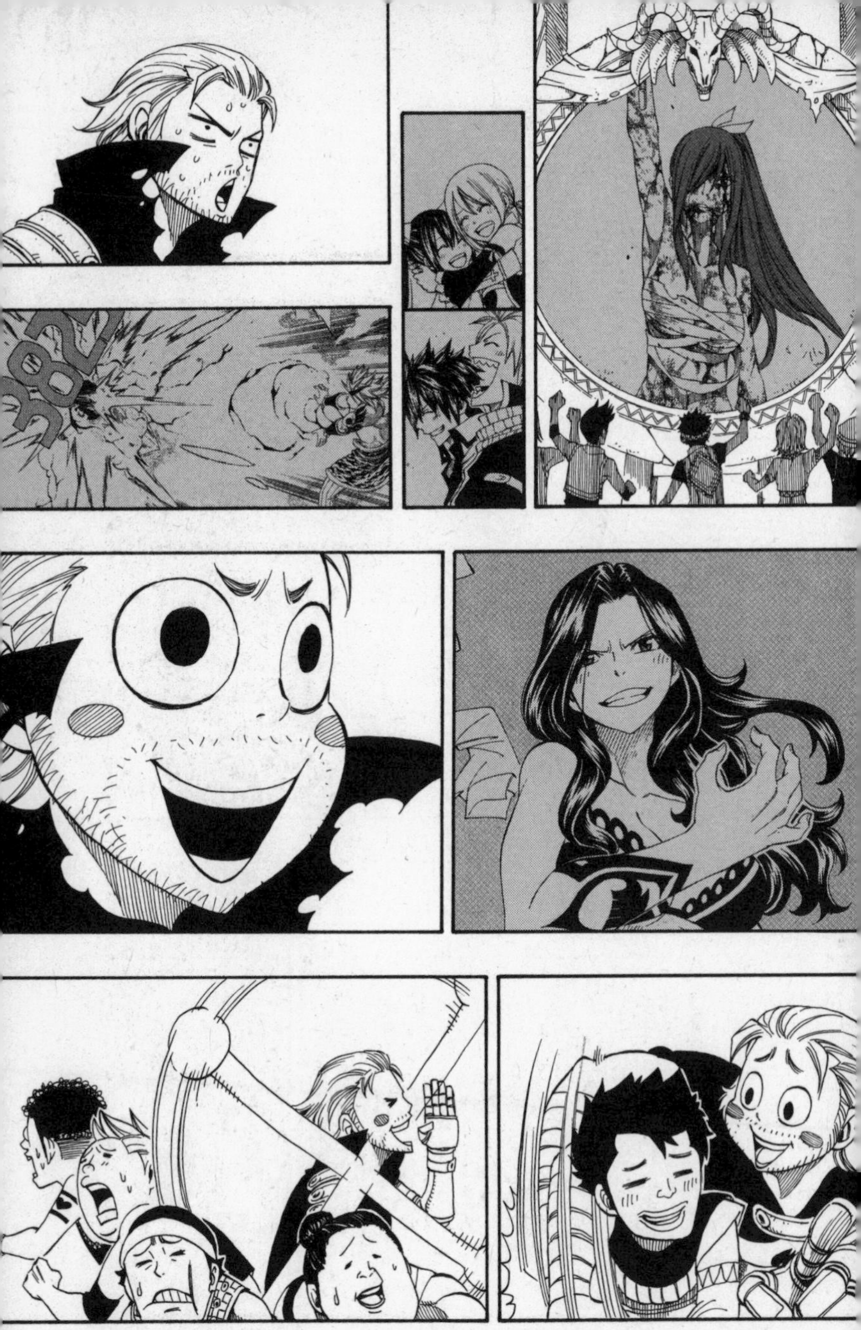

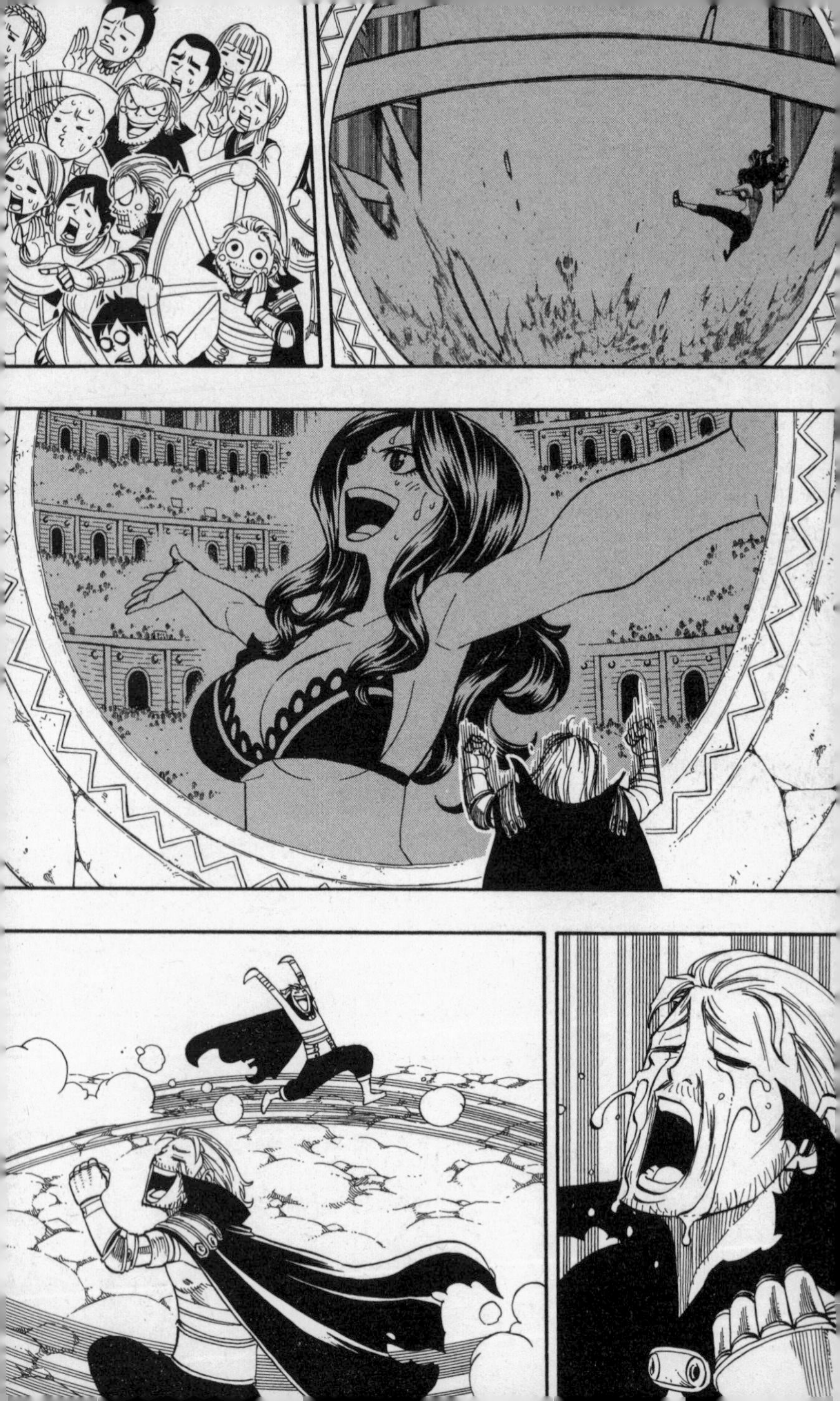

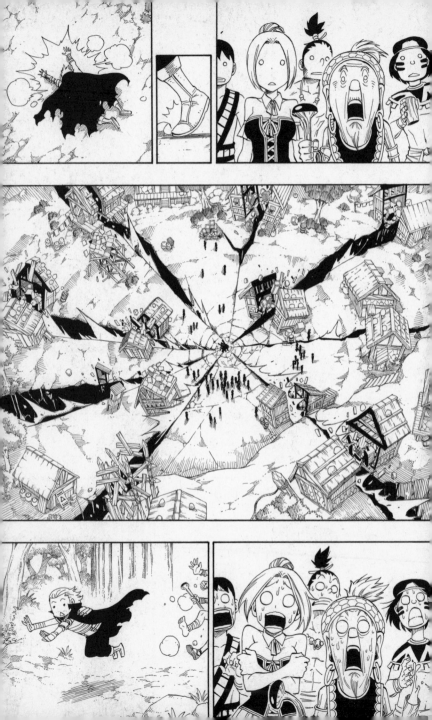

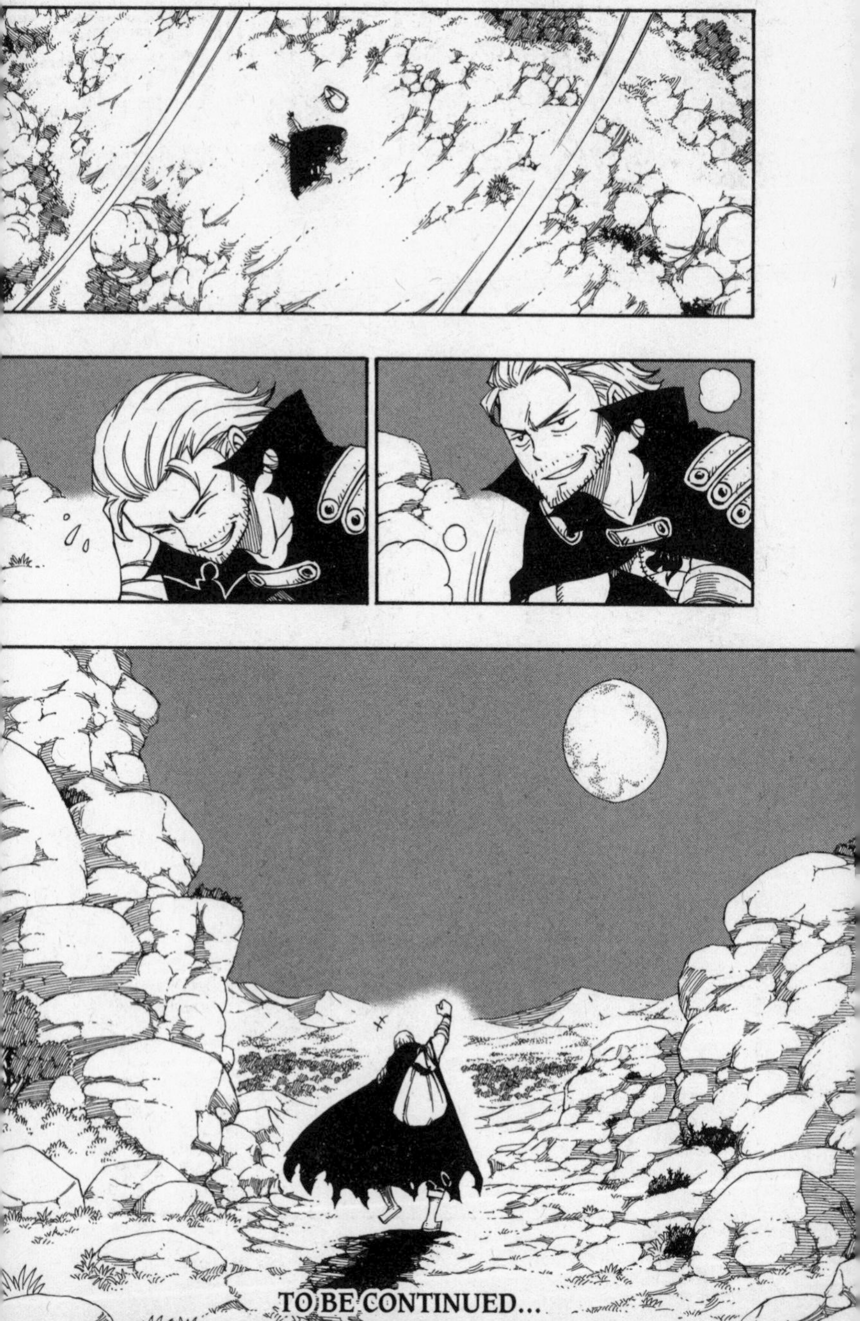

TO BE CONTINUED...

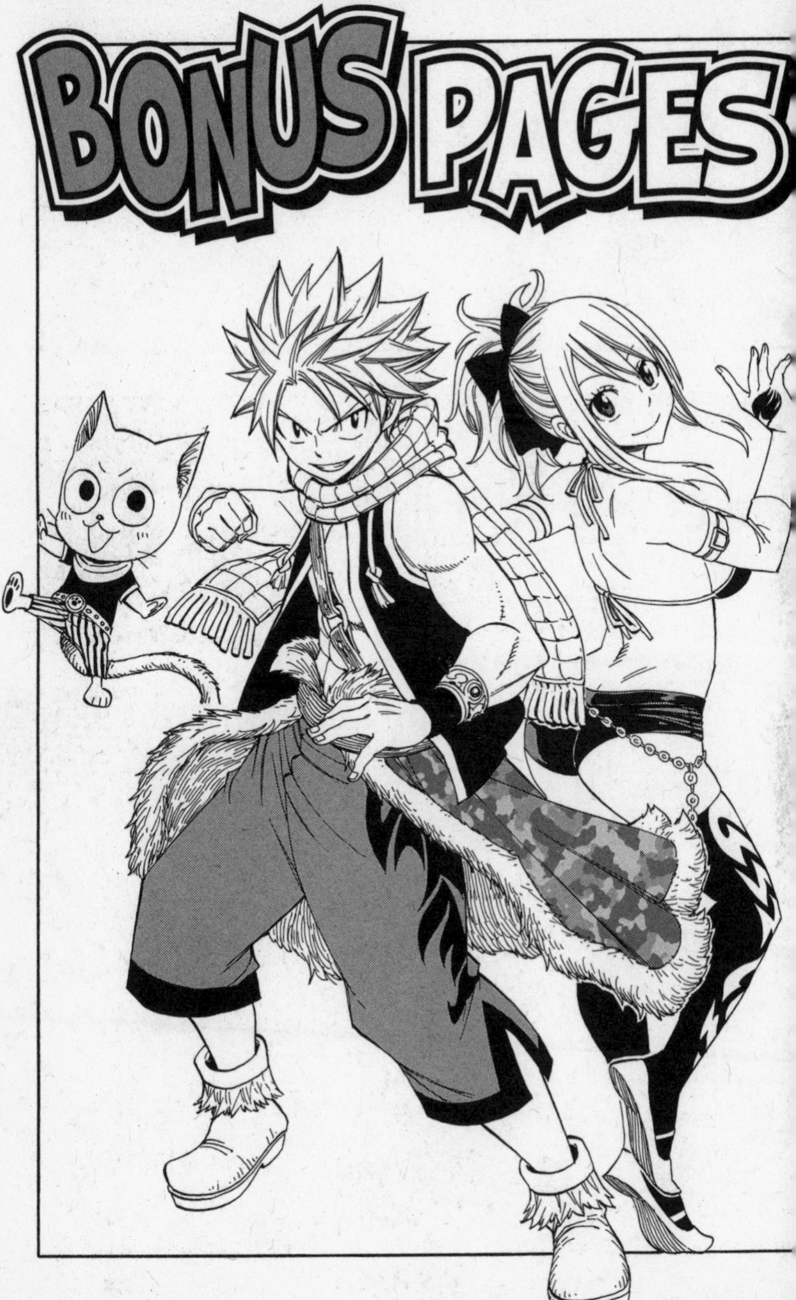
BONUS PAGES

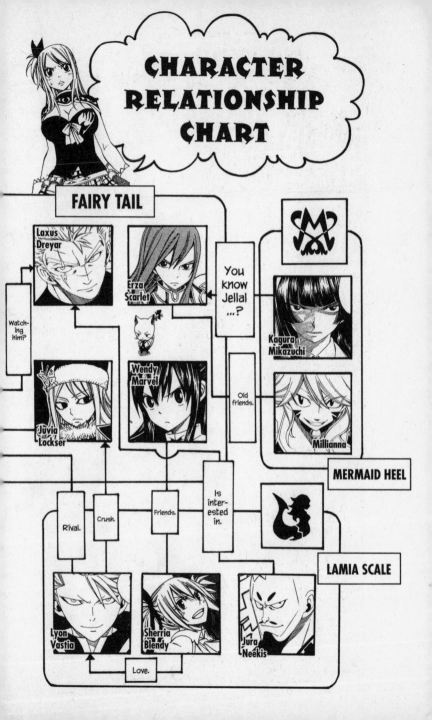

CHARACTER RELATIONSHIP CHART

FAIRY TAIL

Laxus Dreyar

Erza Scarlet

Watching him?

You know Jellal ...?

Kagura Mikazuchi

Juvia Lockser

Wendy Marvel

Old friends.

Millianna

MERMAID HEEL

Is interested in.

Rival.

Crush.

Friends.

LAMIA SCALE

Lyon Vastia

Sherria Blendy

Jura Neekis

Love.

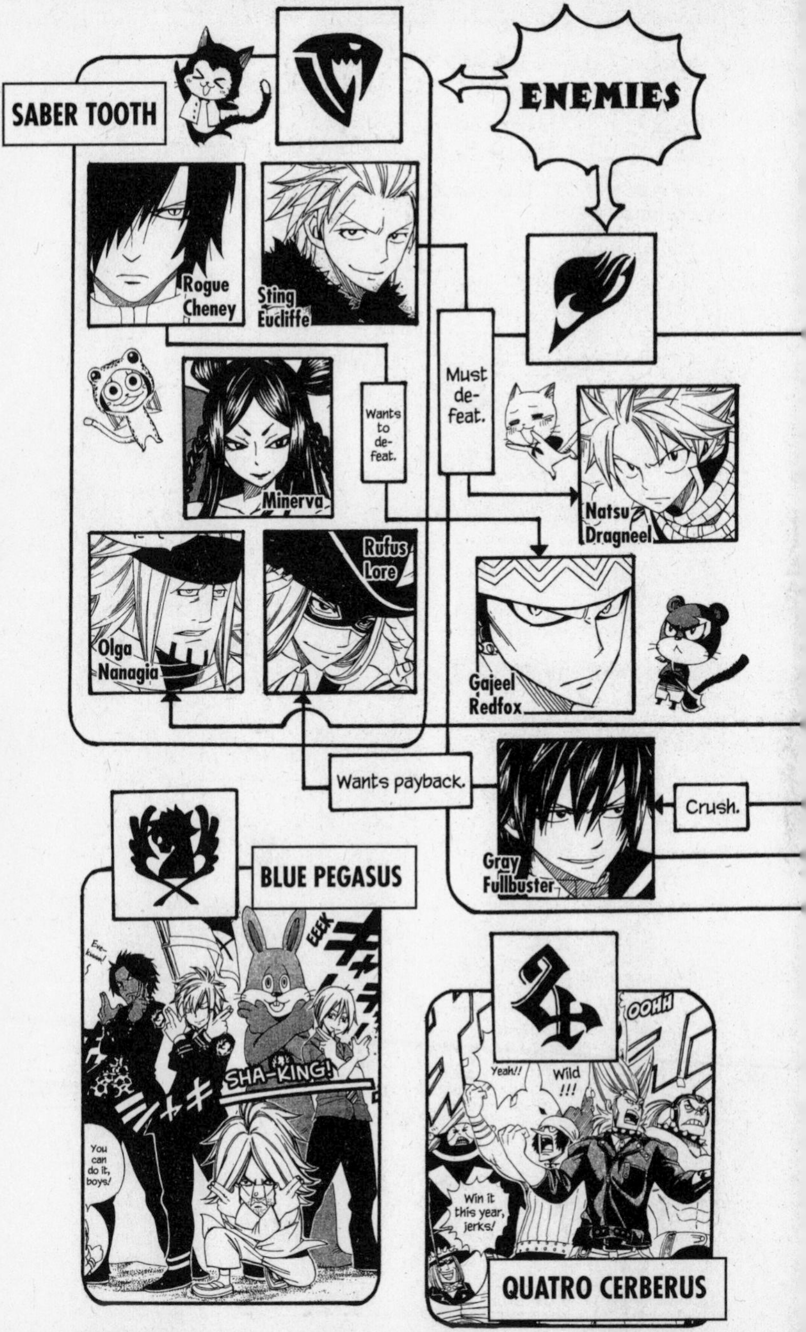

ENEMIES
SABER TOOTH
Rogue Cheney
Sting Eucliffe
Minerva
Wants to de-feat.
Must de-feat.
Natsu Dragneel
Rufus Lore
Olga Nanagia
Gajeel Redfox
Wants payback.
Crush.
Gray Fullbuster
BLUE PEGASUS
EEEK
SHA-KING!
You can do it, boys!
OOHH
Yeah!!
Wild !!!
Win it this year, jerks!
QUATRO CERBERUS

tinued from the
ft-hand page. ⬇

Lucy: If we have to give an answer, it's because he's a dumb guy.

Mira: Let's go to the next question.

Won't the master of Mermaid Heel ever show up?

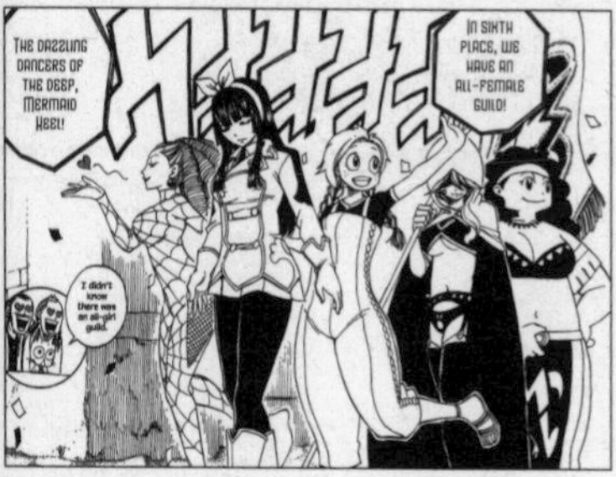
IN SIXTH PLACE, WE HAVE AN ALL-FEMALE GUILD!
THE DAZZLING DANCERS OF THE DEEP, MERMAID HEEL!
I didn't know there was an all-girl guild.

Lucy: No master *has* shown up, huh?

Mira: Actually, there is a big secret surrounding this.

Lucy: What?! Now I want to know!!

Mira: You know that Mermaid Heel has a strict rule that it's an all-female guild, right?

Lucy: Yeah!

Mira: Well the master *looks* like an old lady, but in reality she's a

man!

Lucy: Whaaaaaaa?!!

Mira: The guy goes in drag and is surrounded by girls, so he thinks of them as his harem!

Lucy: You're lying to me, aren't you?!!

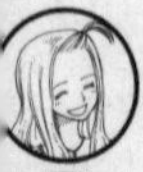:Of course I am! (smile)

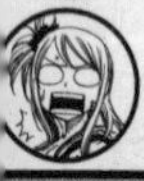:..........

Mira: It's all a lie! But if the story requires it, the master will probably show up sometime.

Lucy: This girl here tells some pretty elaborate lies.

Mira: And the last question of the column.

Just what is Mato anyway?

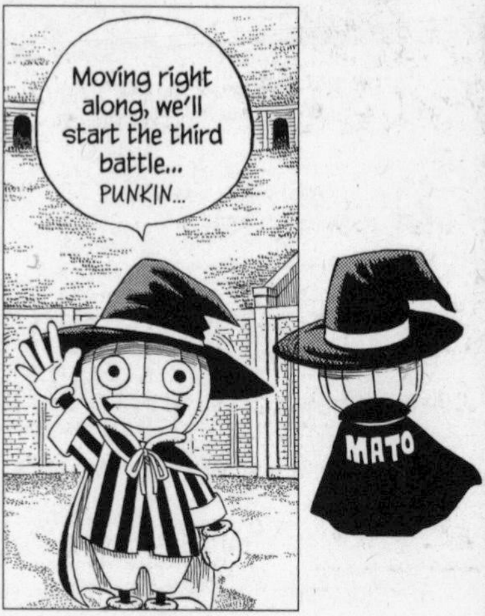
Moving right along, we'll start the third battle... PUNKIN...
MATO

Lucy: He's the official mascot of the Grand Magic Games. That much I know...

Mira: You can buy all sorts of Mato-kun goods all over Crocus!

Lucy: I saw those too! Key holders, notebooks...

Mira: If you're wondering about who is inside, well that's just something you have to look forward to! ♡

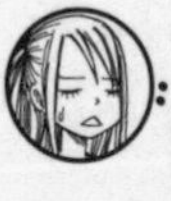: I can't say I'm expecting much out of it. (After all, there was the big reveal of the Blue Pegasus Rabbit, and we know how that turned out...)

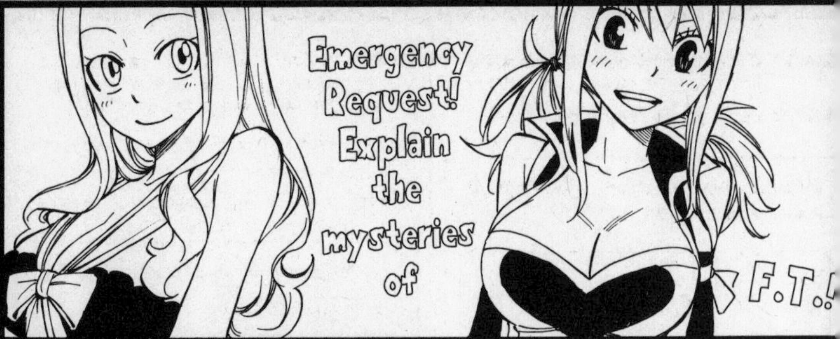
Emergency Request! Explain the mysteries of F.T.!

At a bar in Crocus...

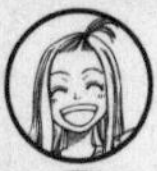
: Let's celebrate!! We're past chapter 299!!

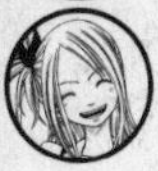
: Yaaay!! Wait... If we're going to celebrate, shouldn't we be celebrating at Chapter 300?

Mira: And we're going to kick off our question corner for this volume!

Lucy: Yaaay!! Ignoring me this time, too!

Mira: The first questivon.

Is Frosch male or female?

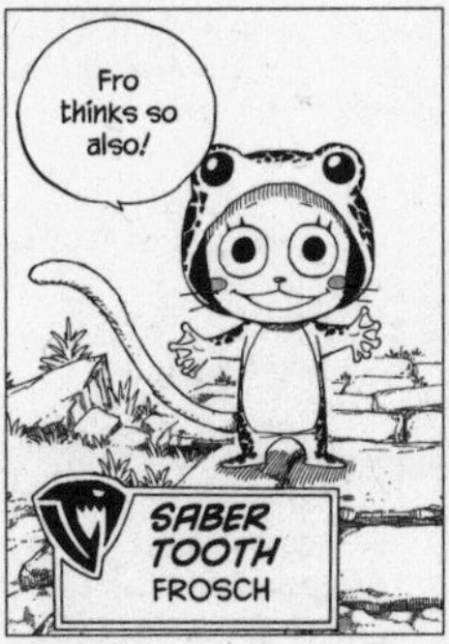
Fro thinks so also!
SABER TOOTH
FROSCH

Lucy: We get this question a lot.

Mira: I think she's a she!

Lucy: Huh? I figure that he's a he.

Mira: Then, let's do rock-paper-scissors to decide it.

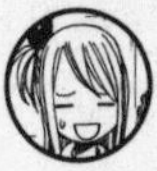
: It isn't something that can be decided that way!

Mira: Actually, I'm less concerned about whether Frosch is male or female, and more about whether Frosch is a frog or a cat.

Lucy: I'd have to side heavily with "cat."

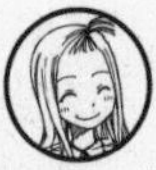
: Well, we have a "questionable" character anyway, so go ahead and have fun forming your own conclusions.

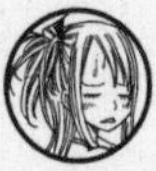
: There doesn't seem to be an answer coming...

Mira: Next question!

Why didn't Toby notice a sock that's been hanging around his neck for three months?

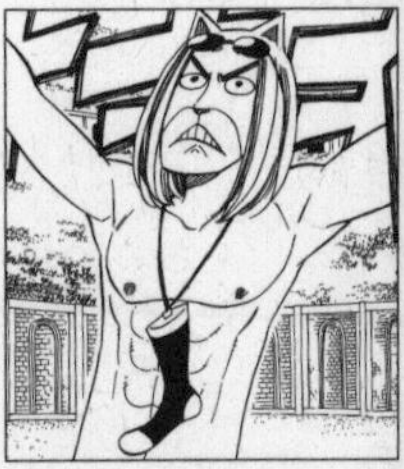

Lucy: I think it should be forbidden to ask this question seriously. (laughter)

Mira: Right. It's just surrealism!

Continued on the right-hand page.

TAIL d'ART

The Fairy Tail Guild is looking for illustrations! Please send in your art on a postcard or at postcard size, and do it in black pen, okay? Those chosen to be published will get a signed mini poster! ♪ Make sure you write your real name and address on the back of your illustration!

Hiroshima Prefecture, Miruky

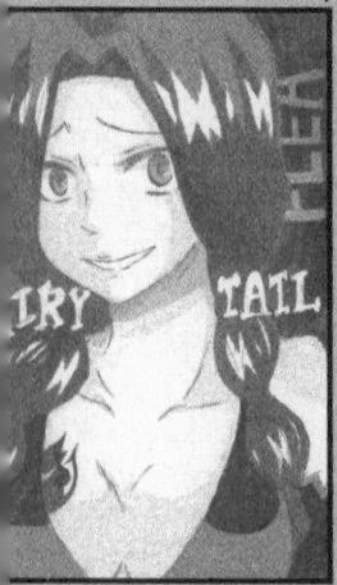

lare is really popular
ong a certain section
Fans. I can't say that
islike her myself.

Osaka, Daiki Yoshimoto

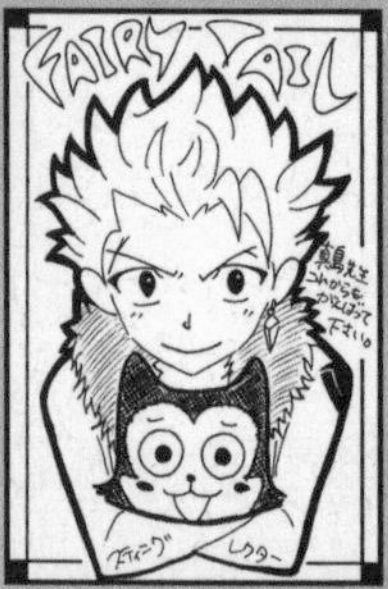
FAIRY TAIL

▲How cute! Looking at this, I like Lecter even better!

Tokyo, Iwaken

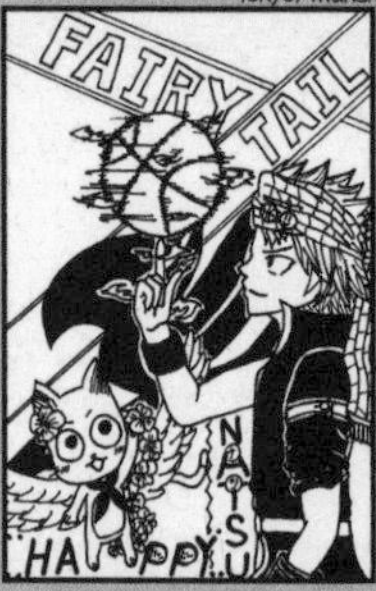
FAIRY TAIL
NATSU
HAPPY

▲Basketball Natsu. What is Happy doing?

Gifu Prefecture, Pokerface

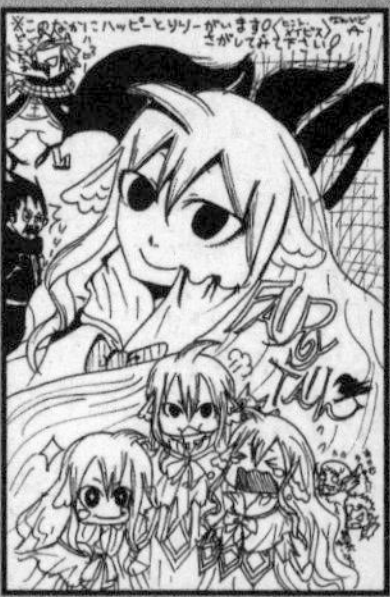

▲All sorts of faces for Mavis! In the next volume, Mavis will...

kuoka Prefecture, Macho-Micho

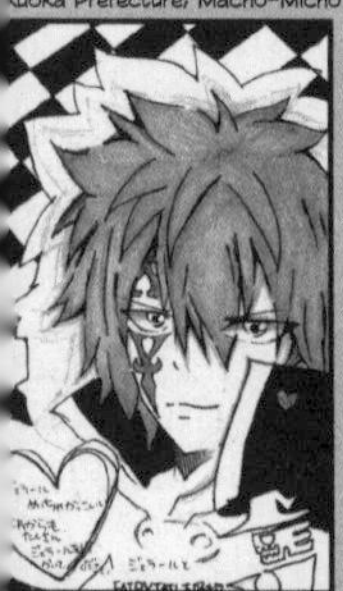

This character has gone
ough a lot of changes,
?

Saga Prefecture, Ryōsuke Morisaki

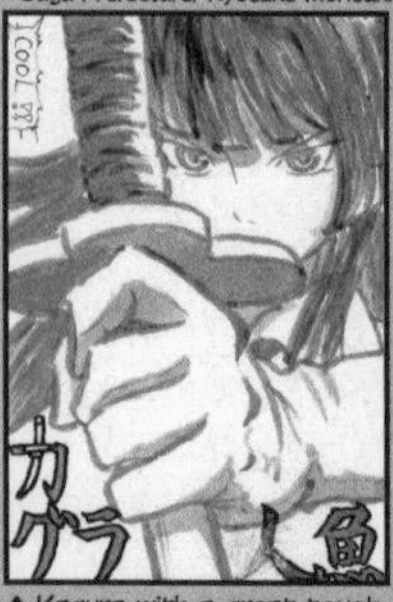
カグラ

▲Kagura with a great touch for drawing! Very cool!

An image of Pisces. Actually, they have a secret that's still hidden. ▶

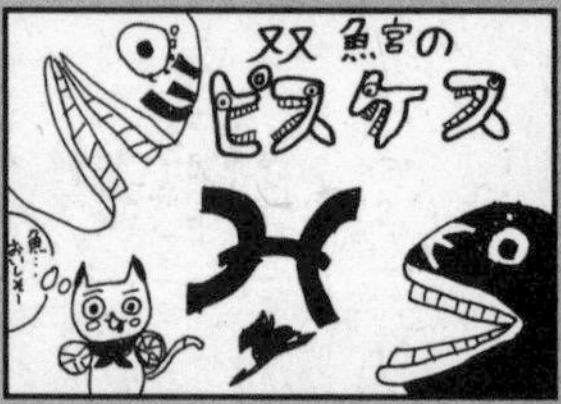
双魚宮の
ピスケス

Kanagawa Prefecture, Tatsuya Yamamoto.

Team assemble!! They're all ready to rumble! ▶

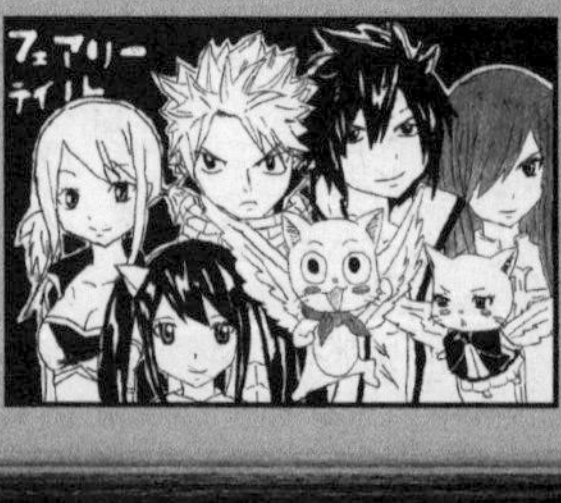
フェアリー
テイル

Niigata Prefecture, Akemi Wakatsuki

Send to Hiro Mashima, Kodansha Comics
451 Park Ave. South, 7th Floor New York, NY 10016

FAIRY
GUILD

Mie Prefecture, The Lady Next Door Is Scary

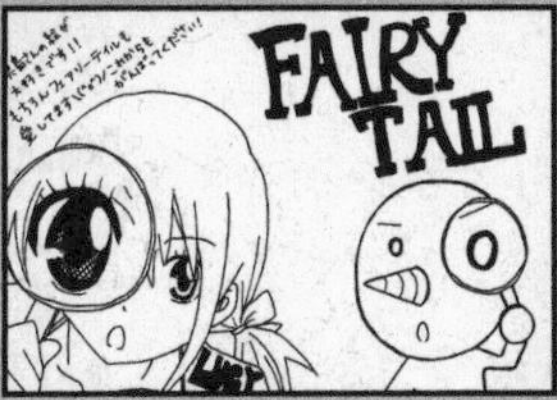
FAIRY TAIL

The great detective... maybe?

Okayama Prefecture, Arashi

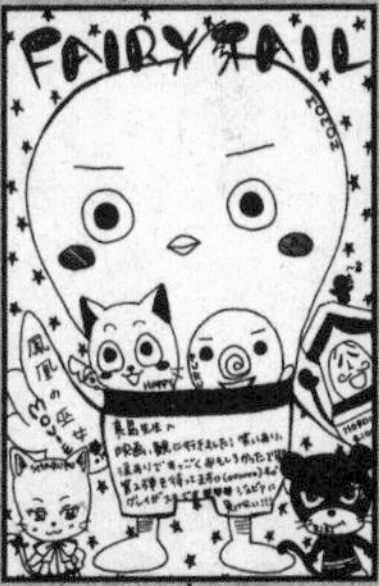
FAIRY TAIL

It's Momon! Thank you to everyone who went to see the movie!

Tokyo, Mayuko W

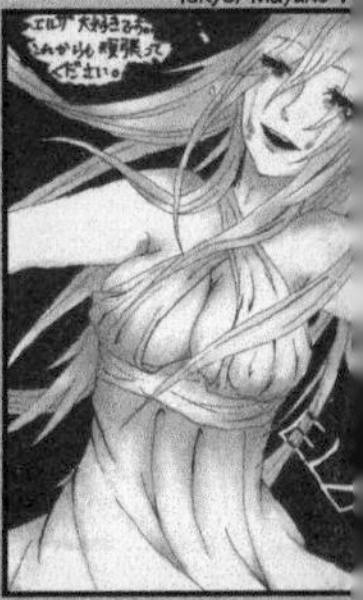

This is so well done! And Erza retains her high level of popularity!

Shizuoka Prefecture, Misora Haraga

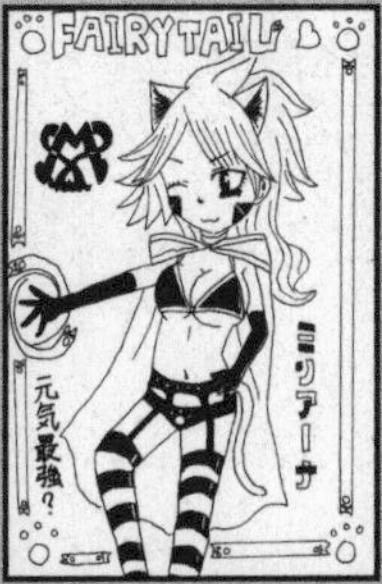
FAIRY TAIL
ミリアーナ
元気最強?

What Millianna always says, "Are you pumped up?"

Any letters and post cards you send means that your personal information such as your name, address, postal code, and other information you include will be handed over, as is, to the author. When you send mail, please keep that in mind.

REJECTION CORNER

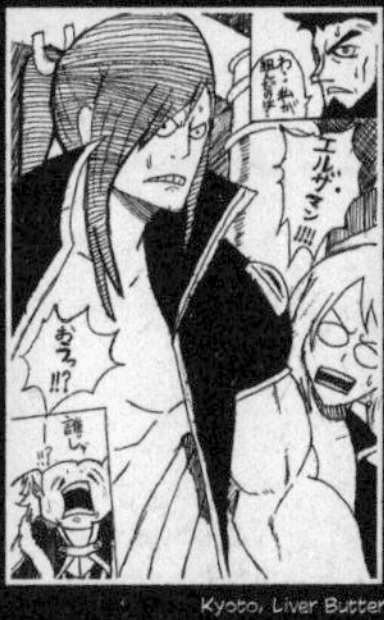

I... I never expected that mash-up!!

Kyoto, Liver Butter

Hokkaido, Fumika @ Now 14 Years Old

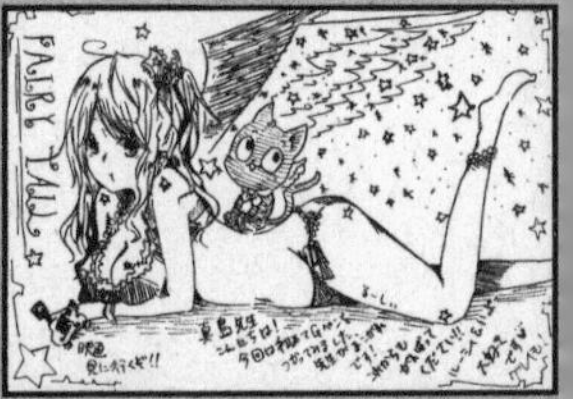
FAIRY TAIL

Wow, sexy! Yes, more of this, please.

Hyogo Prefecture, Daiki Murata

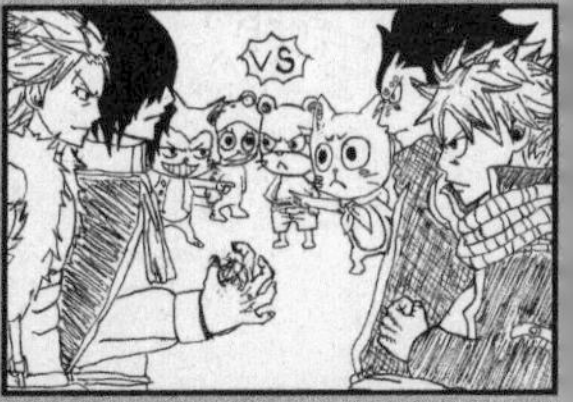
VS

The rivals!! What will the final day bring?

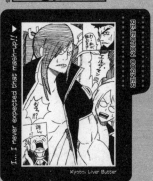

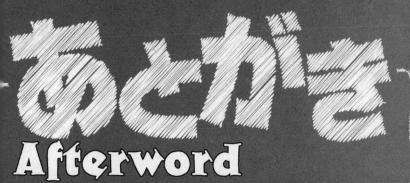

Afterword

This one's long, huh? This series! I can't seem to wrap it up in three volumes like I usually do. I've had this vague idea of a story structure, but recently I've been doing a string of long arcs. I feel the urge to do a short arc once the Grand Magic Games arc is over. This time, without so many characters. And I counted this time, and we've gone over 80 named characters! (cries) That makes it really hard to draw every week, it wears me out! Well, sure, we don't draw all 80 characters in every chapter, but in the next volume, the number of characters will increase again, it seems. What is with this series...?

Actually, this series began with an idea of "a festival!!" sort of feeling. And in trying to take all the best ideas from my previous story-telling experience, it's given this series a very climactic feel. There have been a lot of rumors running around saying, "This will be the end of Fairy Tail." Well, it isn't ending. I know that **someday,** we'll have an ending, but for right now, there are at least three full episodes I'd like to play out. That means somewhere around 15-20 volumes maybe? Of course, it's always possible that it **could** end sooner, but it's also possible that it **could** go on much longer than that. I'm certainly not thinking about doing the final chapter yet.

So here we are at volume 35. I mentioned this before, but my previous work ended at this same number of volumes. So you can think of 36 as a "beginning." I hope you will still support me!

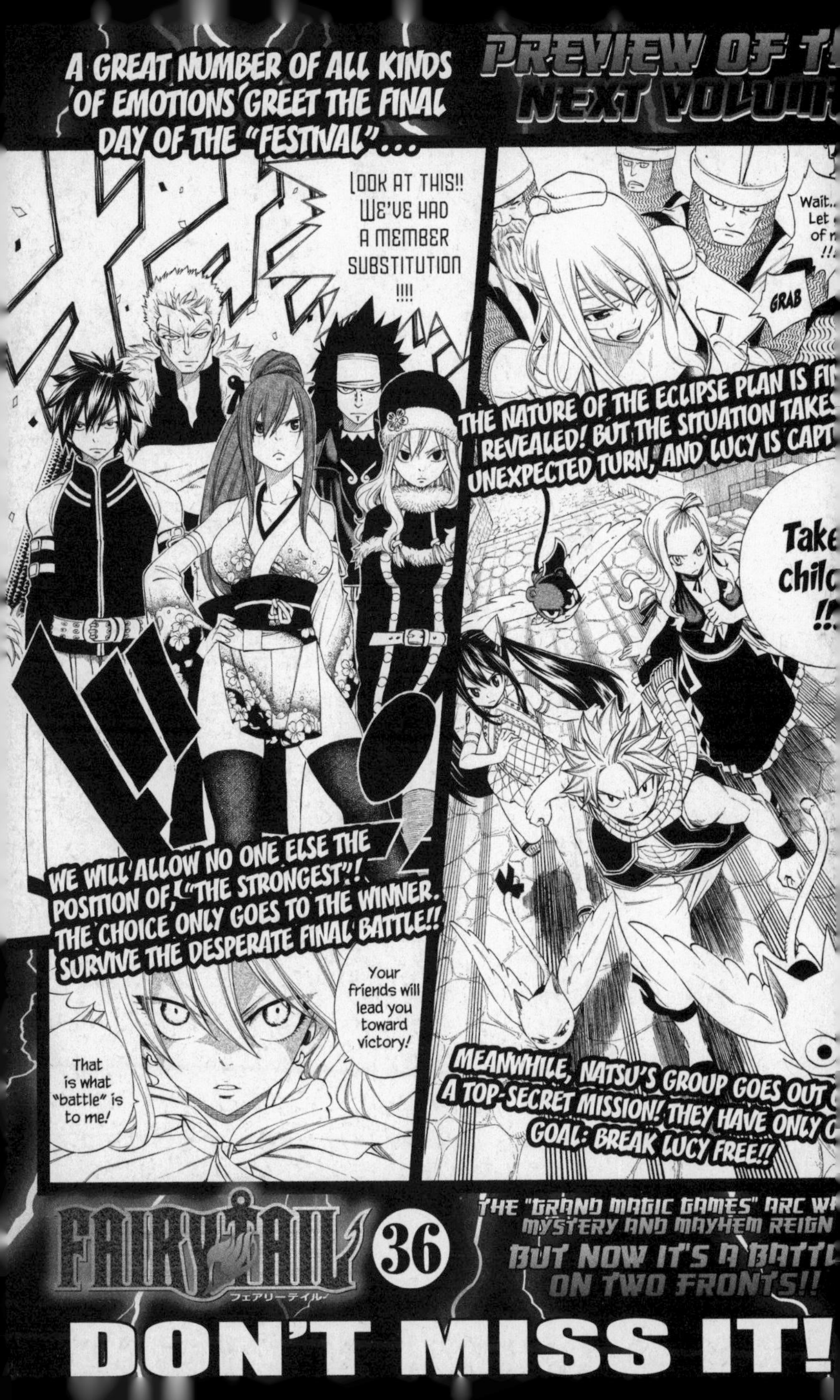

PREVIEW OF T
NEXT VOLUM
Wait... Let of r !!
GRAB
THE NATURE OF THE ECLIPSE PLAN IS FI REVEALED! BUT THE SITUATION TAKES UNEXPECTED TURN, AND LUCY IS CAPT
Take chilc !!
MEANWHILE, NATSU'S GROUP GOES OUT A TOP-SECRET MISSION! THEY HAVE ONLY GOAL: BREAK LUCY FREE!!
A GREAT NUMBER OF ALL KINDS OF EMOTIONS GREET THE FINAL DAY OF THE "FESTIVAL"...
LOOK AT THIS!! WE'VE HAD A MEMBER SUBSTITUTION !!!!
WE WILL ALLOW NO ONE ELSE THE POSITION OF "THE STRONGEST"! THE CHOICE ONLY GOES TO THE WINNER. SURVIVE THE DESPERATE FINAL BATTLE!!
Your friends will lead you toward victory!
That is what "battle" is to me!
FAIRY TAIL
フェアリーテイル
36
THE "GRAND MAGIC GAMES" ARC W MYSTERY AND MAYHEM REIGN
BUT NOW IT'S A BATT ON TWO FRONTS!!
DON'T MISS IT!

January

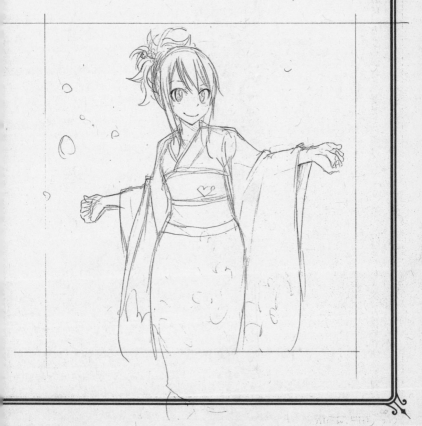

FAIRY TAIL
フェアリーテイル

35

HIRO MASHIMA

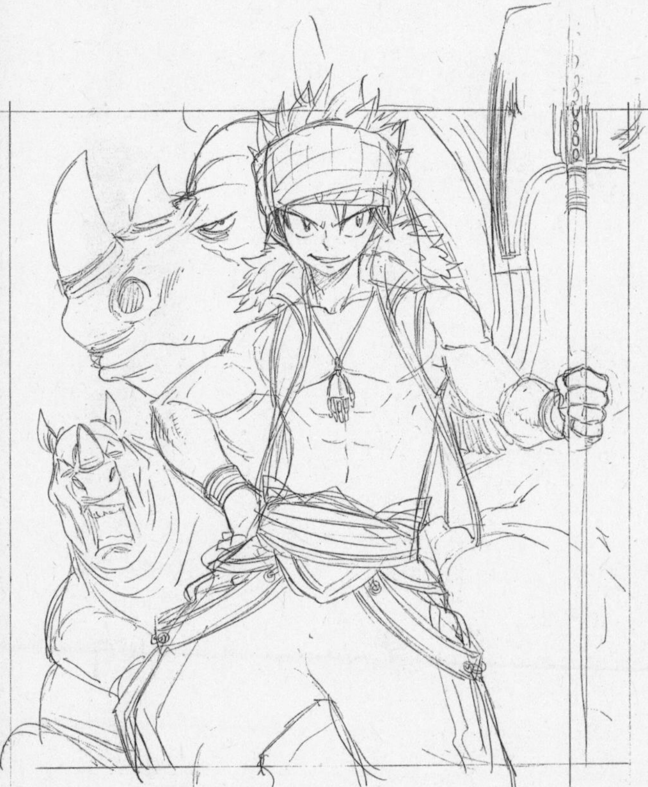

FROM HIRO MASHIMA

In the Japanese version, this volume, Vol. 35, has the normal edition and a special edition released with an OAD (original animation DVD). The two have different covers, but the manga on the inside is exactly the same, so be sure not to buy both by mistake! Also the DVD this time is pretty incredible…

Original Jacket Design: Hisao Ogawa

Translation Notes:

Japanese is a tricky language for most Westerners, and translation is often more art than science. For your edification and reading pleasure, here are notes on some of the places where we could have gone in a different direction with our translation of the work, or where a Japanese cultural reference is used.

Page 19, Lord Zeref

In the Japanese, "Lord Zeref" is "Zeref-*kyô*." As mentioned in the notes of Volume 26, there are a number of honorifics that are known to modern Japanese, but are not in common usage. More often seen is *-dono* (see below), and a less-common, more polite honorific is *-kyô*.

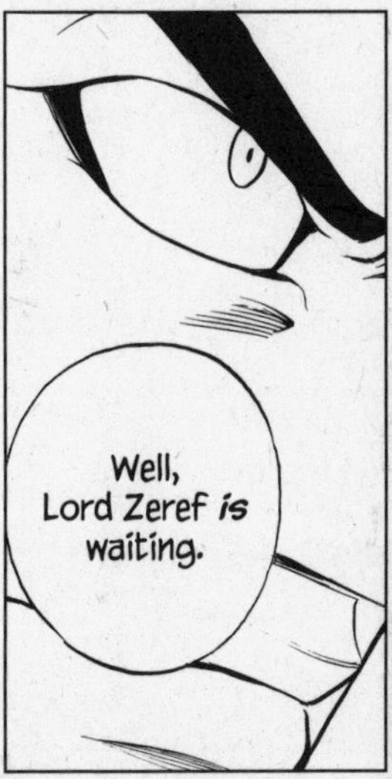
Well, Lord Zeref *is* waiting.

Page 35, Penitent Meeen.

In Japanese, Nichiya uses a rather formal and archaic way of apologizing, *menbokunai* (literally, "I have no honor," but it is a way of expressing shame and guilt for an action). However, being an Ichiya clone, he does it by saying, "meeen-bokunai."

Page 134, Makarov-dono

As mentioned in previous notes, *-dono* is an honorific much like *-sama*, an honorific that indicates a lot of respect. But it is also somewhat archaic and is not used in everyday society. It has a somewhat old-fashioned feel to it. Still, the character of Jura uses this honorific quite often.

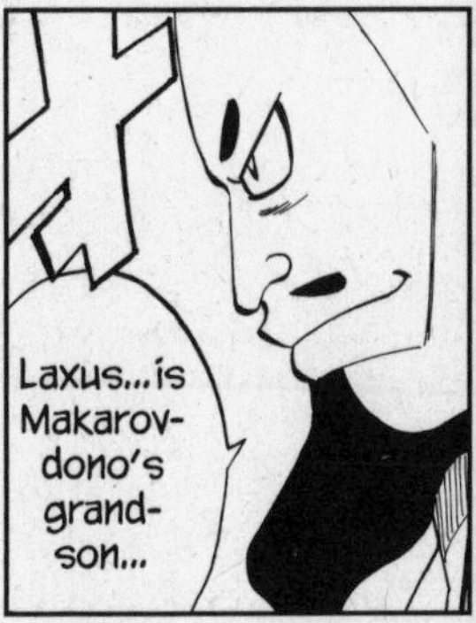
Laxus...is Makarov-dono's grandson...

ATTACK ON TITAN

Humanity
has been decimated!

A century ago, the bizarre creatures known as Titans devoured most of the world's population, driving the remainder into a walled stronghold. Now, the appearance of an immense new Titan threatens the few humans left, and one restless boy decides to seize the chance to fight for his freedom, and the survival of his species!

KC
KODANSHA
COMICS

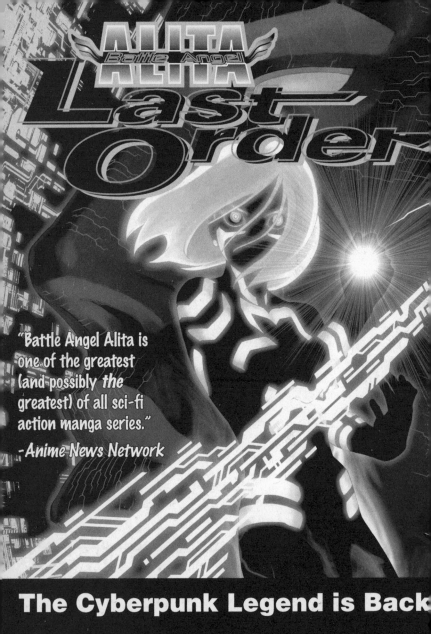

ALITA
Battle Angel
ALITA
Last Order

"Battle Angel Alita is one of the greatest (and possibly *the* greatest) of all sci-fi action manga series."

-Anime News Network

The Cyberpunk Legend is Back

In deluxe omnibus editions of 600+ pages, including ALL-NEW original stories by Alita creator Yukito Kishiro!

KODANSHA
COMI

ANIMAL LAND

MAKOTO RAIKU

WELCOME TO THE JUNGLE

In a world of animals where the strong eat the weak, Monoko the tanuki stumbles across a strange creature the like of which has never been seen before - **a human baby!**

While the newborn has no claws or teeth to protect itself, it does have the rare ability to speak to and understand all the different animal.

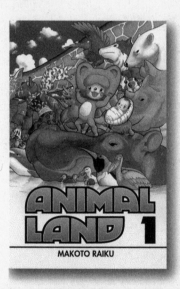

ANIMAL LAND 1

MAKOTO RAIKU

Special extras in each volume! Read them all!

RATING OT AGES 10+

KC
KODANSHA
COMICS

A Kodansha Comics Trade Paperback Original.

Fairy Tail volume 35 copyright © 2012 Hiro Mashima
English translation copyright © 2014 Hiro Mashima

All rights reserved.

Published in the United States by Kodansha Comics, an imprint of Kodansha USA Publishing, LLC, New York.

Publication rights for this English edition arranged through Kodansha Ltd., Tokyo.

First published in Japan in 2012 by Kodansha Ltd., Tokyo
ISBN 978-1-61262-412-9

Printed in the United States of America.

www.kodanshacomics.com

9 8 7 6 5 4 3 2 1

Translation: William Flanagan
Lettering: AndWorld Design
Editing: Ben Applegate

TOMARE!

[STOP!]

You're going the wrong way!

Manga is a completely different type of reading experience.

To start at the *beginning*, go to the *end!*

at's right! Authentic manga is read the traditional Japanese way—m right to left, exactly the *opposite* of how American books are ad. It's easy to follow: Just go to the other end of the book and read ch page—and each panel—from right side to left side, starting at e top right. Now you're experiencing manga as it was meant to be!